HUMAN
FACIAL
EXPRESSION

HUMAN FACIAL EXPRESSION

AN EVOLUTIONARY VIEW

ALAN J. FRIDLUND
University of California, Santa Barbara

Academic Press

San Diego   New York   Boston
London   Sydney   Tokyo   Toronto

This book is printed on acid-free paper. ∞

Academic Press, Inc.
A Division of Harcourt Brace & Company
525 B Street, Suite 1900, San Diego, California 92101-4495

United Kingdom Edition published by
Academic Press Limited
24-28 Oval Road, London NW1 7DX

Library of Congress Cataloging-in-Publication Data

Fridlund, Alan J.
    Human facial expression : an evolutionary view / by Alan J.
Fridlund
        p.   cm.
    Includes bibliographical references (p.   ) and index.
    ISBN 0-12-267630-0
    1. Facial expression.   2. Face--Evolution.   I. title.
QP327.F75   1994
153.6'9--dc20   94-2020
                                                       CIP

PRINTED IN THE UNITED STATES OF AMERICA
94   95   96   97   98   99   BB   9   8   7   6   5   4   3   2   1

To Amy, Jason,
and Goldie

CONTENTS

Preface   xi
Acknowledgments   xiii

1   Pre-Darwinian Views on Facial Expression
The Rise and Fall of Physiognomy   2
Reading Passions into Facial Actions   9

2   Darwin's Anti-Darwinism in *Expression of the Emotions in*
Man and Animals
How and Why Darwin Wrote *Expression*   15
Darwin's Mechanisms of Expression as Grounds to
      Presume the Nonadaptiveness of Expression   20
Summary of Darwin's Views in *Expression* and Their
      Unfortunate Consequence   25
The Transition from Darwinian Reflexology to
      Behavioral Ecology   26

3   Facial Expression and the Methods of Contemporary
Evolutionary Research
What Kinds of Evidence Could Substantiate an
      Evolutionary Account of Facial Display?   33
Why Genetic Control and Learning Are
      Not Dichotomous   52

4   Mechanisms for the Evolution of Facial Expressions
Displays as Hypertrophied Behavior   56
Displays as Formalized Intention Movements   64
Complementarity of Displays and Vigilance for Them   75

5   Facial Hardware: The Nerves and Muscles of the Face
The Facial Mask: Structure and Neural Control   80
Why Is There Dual Neurological Control of the Face?   94

6   Facial Reflexes and the Ontogeny of Facial Displays
The Facial Reflexes   100
Other Facial Reflexive Coordinations   104
Protective Reflexes as Phyletic Preadaptations for
   Displays   107
Reflexes as Constituent Actions in the Ontogenesis of
   Displays: Four Mechanisms   108
Research Strategy for Evaluating Ontogenetic
   Mechanisms   112
Three Ontogenetic Hypotheses   114
Summary of Ontogenetic Accounts and Research
   Strategy   121

7   Emotions versus Behavioral Ecology Views of Facial
Expression: Theory and Concepts
The Emotions View of Faces   124
The Behavioral Ecology View of Faces   128
Summary   139

8   Emotions versus Behavioral Ecology Views of Facial
Expression: The State of the Evidence
Ramifying of Displays in Phylogeny   141
Deception in Phylogeny   143
Facial Display Variation with Sibling Competition   144
The Displays of Social versus Solitary Species   144
Audience Effects and the Context-Dependency
   of Displays   145
Do "Fundamental Emotions" Underlie Facial Displays?   168
The Relations of Facial Displays to Emotion
   and Physiology   169
Is an Emotions Account of Facial Displays Viable?   182

9   Introduction: Cross-Cultural Studies of Facial Expressions
of Emotion   187

10 Is There Universal Recognition of Emotion from Facial
Expression? A Review of the Cross-Cultural Studies, by
James A. Russell
A Partial History   194
The Universality Thesis   198
The Scope of This Chapter   201
Judgment Studies in Literate Cultures   203
Judgment Studies in Isolated Cultures: The Evidence
    from "Those Associated but Little with Europeans"   238
Validity of the Judgment Studies   251
Alternative Interpretations   260
Conclusion   265

11 How Do We Account for Both Universal and Regional
Variations in Facial Expressions of Emotion?
Ekman's Neurocultural Model   271
Alternative Explanations of Commonality Findings   276
Alternative Explanations of Findings of Cultural
    Differences   283
Why Have Classical Emotions Views of Faces Persisted?   293

12 Facial Paralanguage and Gesture
Types of Human Facial Paralanguage   296
Probable Origins of Paralanguage   302
Population Similarities and Differences in Human
    Paralanguage   309
Interpretation of Evidence from Diverse Human
    Populations   310
What Isn't Paralanguage about the Face?   312

13 Epilogue: The Study of Facial Displays—Where Do We Go
from Here?   314

References   317
Author Index   348
Subject Index   359

PREFACE

This book is about the nature of human facial expressions. It provides a scientific account of human faces that squares with modern evolutionary theory.

In *Human Facial Expression*, I discuss contemporary theories of human expressions and emotions, methods and findings in ontogeny–phylogeny relations, interactions of genes and culture, animal signaling, and so forth, all with the intent to discover what they can teach us about the face.

I also survey much of the literature on human faces and try to clarify how facial displays relate to reflexes, motives and intentions, emotion and its phenomenology and psychophysiology, and language and paralanguage. Along the way I touch on relevant topics from zoology, physiology, anthropology, sociology, and linguistics. This survey cannot be exhaustive, but I hope that it is representative.

This is the "review" aspect of the book, which should find it a home as a graduate or advanced undergraduate text. But it is just as much a manifesto for a new—and to some, a heterodox—way to understand human faces; its "behavioral ecology" approach explains how faces function in everyday interaction, and reestablishes their connections with the signals of our extended kin in the animal world.

Human Facial Expression is not and cannot be just about facial expressions. From the theologians who saw our faces as windows on the soul, to the artists and physiognomists who used them to judge character, and to the clinicians and researchers who saw emotions revealed in them, faces were always more than movable bone, muscle, and flesh.

Our faces always meant something transcendental; they have always said something about *us*. The behavioral ecology view found in these pages is no exception. We are, it holds, thoroughly social, so that when we gaze at other's faces, we see not revelations of soul, character, or emotion—but declarations of their intentions toward us, and reflections of ours toward them. Our faces, together with our language, are social tools that help us navigate the social encounters that define our "selves" and fashion our lives. This is transcendentalism of a different sort.

ACKNOWLEDGMENTS

I began this book at the University of Pennsylvania in 1986, where I met several scholars who shook the scales from my eyes and forced me to take a fresh look at the face and what it said about ourselves. They have become good friends and supportive colleagues:

Avery Gilbert taught me what behavioral ecology is all about, and helped me understand how to extend an evolutionary view of displays to human faces;

Paul Rozin shared his knowledge of biology and cultural anthropology, and showed me that scholarship was compatible with humor;

John Sabini kept badgering me to clarify my concepts and would have been guilty of sophistry were he not always right;

and John Smith, who with kindness and a twinkle in his eye, shared his far-reaching vision of contemporary ethology.

Many other colleagues along the way have been kind and generous in sharing their work and their thinking. They include: Bernard Apfelbaum, Janet Beavin Bavelas, Don Brown, Joseph Campos, Nicole Chovil, Leda Cosmides, Robert DeRubeis, Phoebe Ellsworth, Alan Fiske, Stephen Fowler, Gerald Ginsburg, Henry Gleitman, Barbara Ivins, Adam Kendon, Richard Lazarus, Arnold Leiman, George Mandler, Peter Marler, Miles Patterson, David Premack, Gary Schwartz, Robert Seyfarth, Jay Shulkin, Craig Smith, Donald Symons, John Tooby, Philip Walker, and David Williams. I also thank Paul Ekman, Carroll Izard, and Gary Schwartz, who started me thinking about faces and supported and encouraged me early on.

Dick Jennings did me great kindness in publishing a précis of this work in *Biological Psychology*. Marc Boggs was wonderfully gracious in remembering an old acquaintance. Nikki Fine, Steven Martin, and Sharon Hartley at Academic Press were wise and patient editors, who always knew what to do.

Jim Russell generously allowed me to include his masterful chapter on cross-cultural studies of faces, and provided many, many helpful comments. The editorial staff at *InfoWorld*, especially Carla Mathews, Jeff Senna, and Anne Kaliczak, were immensely supportive in providing me the software to do the illustrations.

Finally, my deepest thanks to my wife, partner, and colleague, Amy Jaffey, who endured my author's monomania and returned love, support, canny intellectual criticism, and the best son a father could have—and to Jason, who napped just enough to let me finish.

To all these people, thanks.

Alan J. Fridlund

PRE-DARWINIAN VIEWS ON FACIAL EXPRESSION

The current practice of reading "emotion in the human face" is only the most recent of many. Preoccupation with facial morphology came first, in the practice of face-reading known as *physiognomy*.

THE RISE AND FALL OF PHYSIOGNOMY

"Face-reading" goes back to classical antiquity. It existed in ancient Egypt and Arabia, and was a profession in China before Confucius. In Chinese face-reading, for example, a high forehead portended good fortune, the eyes indicated energy and intelligence, the nose symbolized wealth and achievement, and the mouth conveyed the personality. The Chinese also studied facial asymmetry. The left side of the face was Yang, masculine and paternal, whereas the right side was Yin, feminine and maternal. A symmetrical face implied psychological balance (Landau, 1989).

Pythagoras probably began the scientific study of physiognomy, and reportedly selected his pupils based on their facial features. Hippocrates and Galen both incorporated physiognomy in their medical diagnoses (Tytler, 1982). Socrates was charged by a physiognomist with having a face that indicated brutality and an excessive love for women (Wilson & Herrnstein, 1985; Tytler, 1982).

The first treatises on physiognomy (e.g., the *Physiognomonica* and the *Historia animalium*) are usually attributed to Aristotle. They were written approximately 340 B.C., but even by then physiognomic systems were common. Aristotle noted attempts by predecessors to compare the physical characteristics of several peoples (Egyptians, Thracians, Scythians) with the intent to understand them psychologically, but was cautious about the conclusions. Ever the empiricist and biologist (he, like Darwin, was an insatiable specimen collector), he believed that physiognomic traits were best discerned by comparing people with animals. He thus anticipated Darwin by 2200 years by recommending the "comparative method" for understanding the meanings of faces (more on this in Chapter 3).

Aristotle provided several cross-species interpretations. Fat ears like an ox's indicated laziness. Men with prominent upper lips were, he contended, stupid like apes and donkeys. Noses called for special interpretation: fat noses like the pig's signified stupidity, pointed noses like the dog's implied a choleric temperament. People with flat noses like the lion's were generous, whereas those with "hawk" noses like the eagle's were magnanimous. The hair on one's head was also meaningful. Fine hair (like that of stags, rabbits, and sheep) meant timidity, but rough hair (like that of lions and boars) implied courage.

In propounding his physiognomy, Aristotle downplayed the reading of sentiments from facial expressions. Although the "passions" certainly showed in the face, he considered them so variable and short lived that they were scarcely informative and gave no clue to the lasting, important character traits discernible through physiognomy (Piderit, 1886).

During the Middle Ages, Europe's turn away from naturalism toward the occult had its effect on physiognomy. Facial morphology now provided clues not to temperament but to fate, and face-reading joined the astrologer's armamentarium along with numerology, soothsaying, and palmistry. This physiognomy was cosmological: for example, the lines on the forehead were named for planets (Figure 1.1).

The Renaissance figure Giambattista Della Porta resurrected Aristotle's comparative method and melded it with the Hippocratic typology of temperament. In his 1586 *De humana physiognomonia*, Della Porta interpreted faces and heads based on their likenesses to animals (Figure 1.2), and detailed how specific facial features could diagnose whether one was sanguine, phlegmatic, melancholy, or choleric. On the basis of his theory, Della Porta found Plato to be most similar to a canny hunting dog. Della Porta attained wide prominence as a physiognomist, and *De*

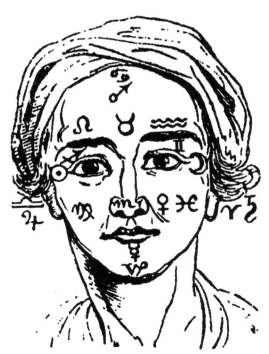

FIGURE 1.1.   The physiognomy of the Middle Ages diverged from its basis in Aristotle's comparative anatomy and became an astrological technique. Lines in the forehead, for example, were named for the five known planets. From Landau (1989).

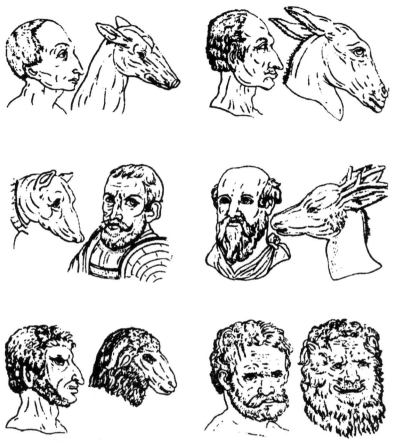

FIGURE 1.2. Renaissance physiognomist Giambattista Della Porta resurrected Aristotle's methods of deducing traits from physiognomic similarities to animals (as depicted by Lavater).

humana physiognomonia eventually reached 20 editions and numerous translations.

But the greatest expositor of physiognomy was also the most responsible for its disrepute: Johann Caspar Lavater. Lavater was an eighteenth-century Swiss Protestant pastor and poet who believed that he was imbued with special expertise at recognizing the God in humans through the divination of traits from the shapes and lines in the face. His frequent public talks were spiced with oracular physiognomic readings, and he pleaded with Elmer Gantry-like messianic fervor for the widespread use of physiognomy to improve the lot of humanity. This was the message throughout his four-volume exegesis, *Fragments of physiognomy for the increase of knowledge and love of mankind*, published from 1775 to

1778. These volumes became best sellers, and his public persona and personal charisma gained him many illustrious adherents. Among the many who made pilgrimages to Zurich for special audiences was Goethe, who became his friend and traveling companion.

Lavater opposed any scientific physiognomy, and he constantly invoked the physiognomist's (i.e., his) expertise as against scientific objectivity. Piderit (1886) cites from the *Essays*:

> What folly it is to make physiognomy into a science so that one can speak on it or write about it, hold seminars or listen to them! (p. 72)

> What is science in which everything can be determined, nothing is left to taste, feelings, genius. Woe to science, if it were such! (p. 71)

Lavater's methods of interpretation were inscrutable, and his own descriptions of his methods are vague and condescending ("anyone with any physiognomic talent will agree that . . .").

For better or worse, physiognomy became identified with Lavater, and though not without its critics, Lavaterian physiognomy swept Europe through the late eighteenth century, when it was overshadowed by the newest morphological enterprise, the phrenology of Franz Joseph Gall. Despite Gall's antipathy for Lavaterian physiognomy and his desire to keep phrenology separate, the two were often practiced together. Face-reading revealed one's character, while phrenological bump-reading elucidated one's reason, memory, and imagination (Tytler, 1982). Face-reading became part of "having one's head examined" (Figure 1.3).

Not content to cede to the phrenologists the "hard data" provided by cranial landmarks, a few physiognomists began to construct equally analytical systems. In some cases, these new analytical physiognomies used both bony and muscular landmarks to discern character traits. These landmarks were numerous, and their correlated traits were broad. This lent an air of exactitude but still allowed ample opportunity for the usual physiognomic proclamations (Figure 1.4).

Compared to the phrenologists, early nineteenth-century physiognomists were less concerned with clinical practice than with assembling woodcuts, lithographs, and daguerreotypes of historical figures and then providing characterological commentaries. These commentaries foreshadowed today's psychobiographies. Physiognomy affected descriptions of character in nineteenth-century novels (Tytler, 1982), and so that artists could create accurate renderings of character, physiognomy also became part of formal training in aesthetics.

By the mid-nineteenth century, physiognomists extended their talents beyond the reputed to the ill reputed, to criminals and the mentally ill. Under the sway of high Victorian culture and pre-Darwinian recapitulationism, both were considered *atavisms* (evolutionary reversions),

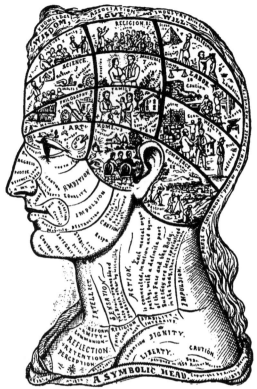

FIGURE 1.3.   The rise of phrenology saw the incorporation of physiognomy, with mental faculties read from the head and character interpreted from the face. From Rosensweig and Leiman (1982).

whose constitutions did not complete the climb up the evolutionary scale. Criminals were brutish animals incapable of maintaining a Social Contract, and the mentally ill were too morally weak to resist succumbing to baser urges. At the time, this belief was not considered Neanderthal but progressive, leading to custodial care no worse than society provided its domesticated herd animals.

One well-known case of this supposed evolutionary reversion was first observed by the English physician John L. H. Down. Down described several cases of mental retardation in children whose facial features and skin color, he contended, had not evolved to attain Anglo-Saxon pristineness. These children were, like their mental abilities, developmentally arrested at the level of the inferior Mongolian race. In his paper "Observations on an ethnic classification of idiots" (Down, 1886), he called these children "Mongolian idiots," and the terms "Mongolism" and "Mongoloid child" stuck until their recent supplanting by

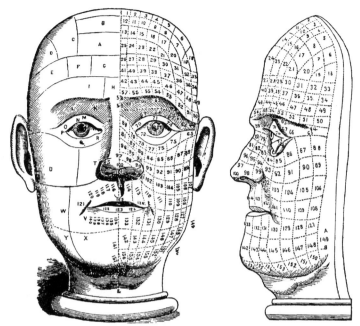

FIGURE 1.4.   Physiognomy was eventually extended to include both the bony landmarks and the muscular contours of the face (anatomical left and right sides, respectively). This system by Redfield probably constituted the apotheosis of physiognomic complexity. From Wells (1871).

two terms, "Down's syndrome" and the name of the actual genetic defect, "Trisomy-21 syndrome." Needless to say, Trisomy-21 is a nondisjunction defect having nothing do to with the Mongolian peoples, whose intelligence is no longer in question (see Gould, 1981, for discussion).

That criminals might be atavisms was nowhere more clearly stated than by the Italian physician Cesare Lombroso, who founded "criminal anthropology":

> The atavism of the criminal, when he lacks absolutely every trace of shame and pity, may go back far beyond the savage, even to the brutes themselves . . . the most horrible crimes have their origin in those animal instincts of which childhood gives us a pale reflection. (1968, p. 368)

Lombroso provided an ever-larger litany of traits that signified criminal atavism, and physiognomic ones figured largely. Criminals, for example, had large jaws, low foreheads, masculine faces in females, and craniofacial asymmetry.

Traditional physiognomy, with its concentration on morphology, never quite died, but ramified to several other disciplines. It found applica-

FIGURE 1.5.   The British psychiatrist Hugh Diamond founded "psychiatric photography," which used face-reading to describe psychopathology. This photograph by Diamond of a manic patient was interpreted by the leading psychiatric physiognomist John Connolly: "Activity, and a certain strength of character seem depicted in the general form of the face; in the well-formed forehead, wide and high; in the broad and pronounced chin; in the development of the superciliary region of the brow, and perhaps, even in the nose" (cited in Gilman, 1977, p. 49). From Gilman (1977).

tion in mid-nineteenth century psychiatry. The British psychiatrist Hugh Welch Diamond founded "psychiatric photography," taking photographs of his Surrey Asylum patients; these were intended in part to provide physiognomists with better materials for interpreting mental illness (Gilman, 1977; see Figure 1.5). Efforts to associate morphology with criminality—stripped of the atavistic connotations—were led by the German psychiatrist Ernst Kretschmer (e.g., 1925), the American physical anthropologist E. A. Hooten (1939a,b), and in the "somato-type" theory of William H. Sheldon (e.g., 1940, 1942; Sheldon worked closely with his graduate student S. S. Stevens, who proceeded to link the mind and body in a slightly different way; e.g., Stevens, 1956, 1975). Oddly enough, many of the old physiognomic hypotheses about crimi-nality and personality may turn out to be valid, but they are now ex-pressed with a new behavior–genetic sophistication (Wilson & Herrn-stein, 1985).

READING PASSIONS INTO FACIAL ACTIONS

Even during periods when physiognomy was especially in vogue, the belief was pervasive that the face was the window to the soul. Socrates often said to his new students, "Speak, so that I may see you." He believed that although words deceived, faces did not. Leibniz agreed:

> Were men to observe and study more carefully which external move-ments accompany the passions, it would be difficult to dissemble.

The "passions" were, since Descartes, seen as the turbulence of bodi-ly humors, which Descartes himself had sorted into six classes: ad-miration and contempt, love and hatred, and joy and sadness. The artist Charles LeBrun, who dictated nearly all the artistic mores of seventeenth-century France, applied the Cartesian system to the move-ments of the face (Browne, 1985). For LeBrun, the face "read out" the passions, as a clock face reads out the time, and the gamut of passions in the face reflected mixtures of Descartes's six "simple" ones.[1] This was intuitive for an artist like LeBrun, who was used to mixing colors from a palette of primary pigments. LeBrun's concepts were reinvented by the "basic emotions" and "differential emotions" theorists of the 1950s through the 1980s.

LeBrun's interest in the "passions" made him the exception. Until the nineteenth century, interest in the face was primarily morphological and physiognomic, and most observers abided by Aristotle's skepticism about whether fleeting facial movements were at all worth studying. A number of forces may have led to a turn toward interest in facial move-ments: the new fascination with electricity and its contractile effect on animal muscles (known as "galvanism," after Luigi Galvani), the advent of early neurophysiology and faradic stimulation studies, and improve-ments in photography that enabled the "freezing" of facial actions too evanescent for Aristotle to interpret or for painters to record.

But facial muscular actions were nothing if not a puzzle to the early

---

[1] LeBrun placed the readout of the passions mostly in the eyebrows, whose proximity to the pineal gland made them closest to the soul (Piderit, 1886).

nineteenth-century scientist. Why did certain facial movements occur in certain circumstances? Johannes Müller, who formulated the Law of Specific Nerve Energies, confessed that he found facial movements inexplicable:

> Regarding specific changes in facial expressions in the cases of joy, sadness, and other feelings we can state neither purpose nor reason. (1833–1834, Vol. 2, p. 92)

Pre-Darwinian evolutionists attempted explanations. One of the early nineteenth century's most prominent comparative anatomists and pre-Darwinian evolutionists, Lorenz Oken, believed that the bones and muscles of the head were but transformed extremities. In his *Naturgeschichte* ("Natural History," and circa 1810), Oken stated:

> The movement of facial expressions is nothing but a repetition of the movement of the limbs, caused by a momentary psychological state. (cited in Piderit, 1886, p. 6)

One of Oken's illustrations was of social greetings: arms opened wide in friendship are accompanied by wide mouth opening (a smile). Oken's student Huschke extended his reasoning in an 1821 doctoral dissertation. Huschke also believed that the head was a metamorphosed torso, and that the facial muscles each mapped onto a different limb or trunk muscle. For example, humans who are threatened will crouch and simultaneously furrow their brows and pull them down. Using this inductive mapping method, Huscke deduced that the *orbicularis oris*, the sphincter muscle surrounding the mouth, was analogous to the anus (Piderit, 1886, p. 6). One wonders if the mouth's actual relation to the anus was not analogy but proximity, at least for both Huschke and Oken.

Charles Bell (*Essays on the anatomy of expression in painting*, 1806) attempted to explain facial actions simply as indicating pleasant versus unpleasant sentiments. Pleasant sentiments relaxed the facial muscles, whereas unpleasant ones tensed them. The actions of specific muscles were of little concern to Bell, since they were placed by God so as to make the human countenance in His image. (Bell's assumption that the facial muscles were God given to express the passions was Darwin's chief target in the *Expression of the emotions in man and animals*, 1872, as the next chapter details.)

Under the sway of the exploratory and therapeutic fad of the day, electrical stimulation, G. B. Duchenne de Boulogne (1859) studied the muscular anatomy of the face just as Luigi Galvani, Emil duBois-Reymond, and Hermann von Helmholtz had with frogs and other animals (Basmajian & DeLuca, 1985). He selectively "galvanized" the facial muscles. Although his methods were physiological, he sidestepped a psychological explanation of facial expressions and resorted to the same theology as Bell:

> Once the language of physiognomy had been created, the Creator, in order to make it general and permanent, was satisfied to provide each human being with the instinctive ability to express his feelings by the contraction of the same muscles. (cited in Piderit, 1886, p. 7)

Apart from Oken's and Huschke's crypto-evolutionary treatises, Charles Darwin was probably the first to attempt to explain why certain facial actions occurred when they did. His *Expression of the emotions in man and animals* provided the first natural-history account of human facial behavior, and it struck a well-intentioned coup de grace to previous theological treatments. I detail Darwin's account and the politics behind *Expression* in the next chapter.

Darwin was eventually to reroute interest in the human face from its morphology to its behavior, but there was one final attempt to devise a physiognomy that combined the two. This was the neo-physiognomy of the German physician Theodur Piderit, who disclaimed Lavaterian physiognomy and the Gall–Spurzheim phrenology, and placed himself squarely on the side of orthodox science. His thesis was simple: facial muscular movements indicate sentiments, and sufficient exercise of those muscles yielded permanent changes in the face (mostly through habitual looks and wrinkles). Piderit (1886) stated:

> Facial expressions provide not only insight into a person's momentary psychic state; his individual peculiarity, up to a certain point, can likewise be guessed from them. In young faces, in which characteristic physiognomic traits have not yet been developed, one is solely dependent upon the careful observation of such signs. When during lively conversation certain mimetic facial movements are repeated very often, with little provocation, one may be sure that these mimetic traits will, over time, develop into physiognomic ones, and in judging such a person one will rarely be wrong to attribute physiognomic significance to such mimetic indicators . . . Physiognomic traits may be assumed to be mimetic movements that have become permanent. (pp. 139–140)

Like Lavaterian physiognomists, Piderit's seven editions of his *Expression and physiognomy* (1886) provided line drawings of both the illustrious and the notorious, along with physiognomic interpretations that were far less oracular than his predecessors'. Although part of common lore (e.g., "worry lines," "crow's feet," etc.), the relations posed by Piderit's neo-physiognomy between habitual facial actions and facial appearance are, to my knowledge, completely ripe for investigation.

I now turn to Darwin's account of facial expression, which launched the research tradition, popular in the 1960s through the 1980s, that attempted to link iconlike faces with discrete "basic emotions." This tradition was ironically similar to that of classical physiognomy. The physiognomist divined character traits from the conformation of the face despite the range of factors that may have produced it (e.g., nutritional variation, specific inheritance, general somatotype, and even craniofacial dysplasia). Likewise, the "emotions" researcher divined emotional state from the face apart from the context in which the facial behavior was emitted and observed. This iconic view of faces was Darwin's legacy. It was finally to prove inadequate to reconcile facial behavior with contemporary knowledge about human and animal communication. But it may have been a necessary step, because the long-standing theological hold on facial expressions had to be defeated before scientific research could begin. Darwin's attack took the form of a volume on the face and emotion, the *Expression of the emotions in man and animals*, which I discuss next.

2

DARWIN'S ANTI-DARWINISM IN *EXPRESSION OF THE EMOTIONS IN MAN AND ANIMALS*

I want, anyhow, to upset Sir C. Bell's view . . . that certain muscles have been given to man solely that he may reveal to other men his feelings.

—Charles Darwin to Alfred Russel Wallace, 1867

The formal evolutionary[1] treatment of facial display began with Charles Darwin's *Expression of the emotions in man and animals* (1872). Darwin sought evidence for continuity of humans with nonhuman primates and nonprimates. Although perplexed by the apparent uniqueness of language, he found evidence for continuity in bodily movements and gestures that humans shared with, for example, dogs, cats, monkeys, and apes (see Premack, 1985, for discussion of implications of human language for the continuity view). Much of the *Expressions* volume consists of a cataloging of display movements that show resemblances across species.

Darwin also sent questionnaires to various observers around the world. He wanted to ascertain whether peoples of different cultures made the same expressive movements in similar circumstances. For Darwin, cross-cultural communalities in displays would suggest—but not prove—shared phylogeny, thereby corroborating an evolutionary account of display behavior. These anecdotal data indeed suggested communalities in several expressions, although a century passed before these observations were tested with any rigor. I discuss the cross-cultural evidence on facial expressions later.

Because Darwin triumphed in explaining evolution via natural selection, his writing about human facial expression certified the field and rescued it from its prior association with a discredited physiognomy (e.g., that of Lavater). In fact, Darwin's continuity views on facial expressions were accepted by most of his contemporaries, including the psychologist Romanes (1883, 1888) and the neurologist Sigmund Freud (see Sulloway, 1979). In America, they were promulgated by the evolutionist James Mark Baldwin (1895, 1896) and psychologists William James (1890) and G. Stanley Hall (1914).

Although the emotion field benefited by invoking Darwin, it nonetheless misinterpreted his emotional account of expression. I now discuss the reasons for, and the ramifications of, this misinterpretation. I present three points:

1. *Expression* was not a dispassionate evolutionary work, but a tactical blow against creationist accounts of facial expression.

---

[1] In fact, with the exception of certain actions that resulted from sexual selection, Darwin's view of expressions was not "evolutionary" at all, because—as we shall discover—he did not consider them adaptations but accidents or vestiges.

2. Darwin is typically thought to have proposed that expressions evolved for the communication of emotion.[2] In fact, his conclusion was precisely the opposite. Darwin's mechanisms of expression furthered his anticreationist program by demonstrating that most displays were not evolutionary adaptations, but vestiges or accidents.

3. Darwin's nonadaptationist stance on expressions precluded him from maintaining that expressions had been selected for communication. Thus, Darwin's account in *Expression* has been largely abandoned in modern conceptions of the evolution and function of animal signals, covered in this volume. Theories of faces and emotions that derived from *Expression* became atavisms that neglected the social nature of human faces and their place in everyday interaction.

HOW AND WHY DARWIN WROTE *EXPRESSION*

The Writing of *Expression*

Darwin's *Expression* is typically considered apart from its unique relationship to his other work, specifically *Origin of Species* and *Descent of Man* (hereafter, *Origin* and *Descent*). This renders the intent of *Expression* "largely unintelligible" (Ghiselin, 1969). And "intent" is apt. Darwin hagiography depicts him as the quintessentially dispassionate observer who, with British reserve, came to develop his theories after years and even decades of collecting facts (e.g., De Beer, 1963). To the contrary, he formulated his mechanisms of expression *before* collecting data on expressions (Gruber, 1974). As La Vergata (1985) stated, "Darwin students today generally agree that Darwin's theory was constructed, not discovered" (p. 934).[3] The key to understanding *Expression*, then, lay (naturally) in its origins.

[2] The claims are ubiquitous that Darwin viewed facial expressions as evolved, selected, or adapted for communication (e.g., Buck, 1984; Chevalier-Skolnikoff, 1973; Ekman, 1973; Plutchik, 1980). Exceptions include Izard (1971), who described Darwin's mechanisms of expression but did not invoke adaptation, and Arnold (1960), whose frank skepticism about Darwin's three mechanisms departs strikingly from their usual reverential treatment. Craig (1921–1922), Allport (1924), and Honkavaara (1961) correctly observed that Darwin's mechanisms were nonadaptationist, but mistakenly attributed this to Darwin's neglect of the communicative functions of faces (see review by Izard, 1971).

I use the term "expression" here for consistency. I use it advisedly, because I do not assume that facial displays necessarily "express" (i.e., read out or reflect) anything. Darwin also discovered the difficulty with terminology: "Even such words as that 'certain movements serve as a means of expression' are apt to mislead, as they imply that this was their primary purpose or object" (*Expression*, p. 357). In the second portion of this chapter I begin to refer to the comparable facial movements as "displays."

[3] Darwin would certainly agree with this conclusion, because he believed that theory enabled the organization of facts. As he stated in his autobiography, "What I believe was strictly true is that innumerable well-observed facts were stored in the minds of naturalists ready to take their proper places as soon as any theory which would receive them was sufficiently explained" (F. Darwin, 1887, Vol. 1, p. 71).

Darwin's interest in expressions was always minor, and he referred to it as a "hobby-horse." His thinking on the subject was first aroused in 1826, when as a medical student at Edinburgh, he heard fellow student W. A. Browne present a materialist attack on Sir Charles Bell's *Essays on the Anatomy of Expression in Painting* (Bell, 1806; hereafter, *Anatomy*; see Bowlby, 1990; and Gruber, 1974).[4] Bell's views, it turned out, became Darwin's eventual focus of attack in *Expression*. Darwin began observing expressions in 1838, when he watched a cousin's newborn. He also started making regular trips to the London Zoo, conducting informal experiments on each trip, such as holding up a mirror to a monkey, or offering it a nut and withdrawing it; making a face to an orangutan (*M* notebook, p. 107; in Barrett, Gautrey, Herbert, Kohn, & Smith, 1987, p. 545; and Gruber, 1974, p. 321). He soon began a longitudinal project, assiduously recording the expressions of his firstborn, William; his notes were eventually condensed and published (Darwin, 1877). As he reminisced in 1876:

> My first child was born on December 27th, 1839, and I at once commenced to make notes on the first dawn of the various expressions which he exhibited, for I felt convinced, even at this early period, that the most complex and fine shades of expression must all have had a gradual and natural origin. During the summer of the following year, 1840,[5] I read Sir C. Bell's admirable work on expression, and this greatly increased my interest in the subject, though I could not at all agree with his belief that the various muscles had been specially created for the sake of expression. From this time forward I occasionally attended to the subject, both with respect to man and our domesticated animals. (Darwin, 1887, Vol. 1, pp. 76–77)[6]

Although Darwin began taking notes on expression in 1838, he did not begin to assemble them until 1867. Even then the topic was a minor

---

[4] Bell was an early nineteenth-century Renaissance man: a natural theologian, artist, physiologist, and physician. He achieved prominence for his independent discovery with François Magendie of the principle that sensory and motor nerves were distinct and emanated from separate branches of the spinal cord, a principle now known as the Bell–Magendie Law. Bell's *Anatomy* is at once a credo on the importance of art, a paean to human divinity, and an enjoinder to painters that they must know anatomy in order to capture that divinity. In *Anatomy*, animals are ugly, instinctive "brutes," and thus the humans that look minimally "brutish" are the most "beautiful." Bell's ascriptions of beauty (and therefore divinity) favored Greeks and Anglo-Saxons, and blacks were relegated to the status of "a degraded race" (*Anatomy*, p. 79).

[5] Apparently 14 years elapsed between Darwin's first acquaintance with Bell's volume at Edinburgh and his own reading of it. By then, Bell's book was in its third edition, published two years posthumously (Bell, 1844), and renamed *Anatomy and Philosophy of Expression as Connected with the Fine Arts*. Except as noted by date, all citations are to this edition.

[6] Darwin's observation of his children was anything but dispassionate, as his son Francis (1887) indicates: "The 'Expression of the Emotions' shows how closely he watched his children; it was characteristic of him that (as I have heard him tell), although he was so anxious to observe accurately the expression of a crying child, his sympathy with the grief spoiled his observation. . . . He seemed to retain a sort of regretful memory of the childhoods which had faded away" (Vol. 1, p. 111). Indeed, his

concern. He was vexed by another problem, the operation of sexual selection and its relations to natural selection. This issue was central to the book he was planning on human evolution.

Darwin's comparatively small investment in expressions can be gathered from an 1867 letter to the codiscoverer of natural selection, Alfred Russel Wallace:

> The subject is in no way an important one; it is simply a 'hobby-horse' with me, about twenty-seven years old; and after thinking that I would write an essay on man, it flashed on me that I could work in some 'supplemental remarks on expression.' (Darwin, 1887, Vol. 2, p. 278)

Darwin's treatment of sexual selection was published in 1871 as the iconoclastically titled *The Descent of Man* (1871). It carried *Origin* to its logical (but not *theo*logical) conclusion that humans, like other animals, were products of evolution by natural selection; races of humans, in turn, derived from sexual selection. He intended his notes on expression to comprise a single chapter in *Descent*, but they proved too numerous. Moreover, he began to believe that his accumulated observations on expressive similarities across human cultures, and spanning humans and nonhumans, could independently corroborate the thrust of *Descent*. He therefore placed only a few mentions of expression in *Descent*, reserving the bulk for a separate volume, which became *Expression*.[7] As Desmond and Moore (1991) described it, "the book was the amputated head of the *Descent* that had assumed a life of its own" (p. 593). By the time that Darwin finally wrote *Expression* in 1871,[8] it appears that he well knew his mission and his opponents. If *Descent* promoted a biological account of reason, then *Expression* would do so for emotion. The hobbyhorse became a passion. It was to be "the concluding shot in his fight for evolution" (Browne, 1985, p 322).

---

writing just after the death of his 10-year-old daughter recounts the movements and gestures that endeared her to him; it reads like a passage from *Expression*.

Many of Darwin's insights about nonhuman displays stemmed from his beloved dogs, his retriever Bob and his fox terrier Polly. These insights pepper *Expression* and are extended considerably in *Descent*. Darwin's keen interest in the interactions of humans with their domesticated companions has with few exceptions (e.g., Fridlund, MacDonald, & Laverty, 1992; Mitchell & Thompson, 1991) been neglected.

[7] This spontaneous generation of a new volume was not Darwin's first; *Descent* itself was originally intended to be part of his *Variation of Animals and Plants under Domestication* (1868; see F. Darwin, 1887, Vol. 2, p. 292).

[8] Darwin wrote *Expression* hurriedly in the four months (precisely, January–April, 1871; F. Darwin, 1887, Vol. 2, p. 313) between his completing *Descent* and beginning revisions to *Origin* for a sixth and final edition. Scholars who find *Expression* tedious or meandering can thus find ready explanation in the pressures under which Darwin wrote it. The published volume had a mixed reception. Perhaps the most interesting review was by a theologian who wrote that *Expression* was the most "powerful and insidious" of the corpus of Darwin's writings. Given common belief that the passions are close to the soul, Darwin certainly knew the subversiveness of a natural-history account of emotion via expression. As he wrote in the M notebook after a visit to the zoo, "He who understands baboon would do more toward metaphysics than Locke" (M 84, in Gruber, 1974, p. 317).

Where did he aim that shot? Darwin put it succinctly when he testified in a letter to A. R. Wallace:

> "I want, anyhow, to upset Sir C. Bell's view . . . that certain muscles have been given to man solely that he may reveal to other men his feelings." (F. Darwin, 1887, Vol. 2, p. 278)

I now summarize Bell's thinking and the logic of Darwin's arguments against it. As I illustrate, Darwin's *Expression* was intended to strike a fatal blow specifically to Bell's view, as well as the more general argument it represented, the argument from design.

Expression as an Attack on the Argument from Design

Charles Bell proposed that certain facial muscles are found uniquely among humans, with human faces God given to express character and emotion. Bell simply deduced the divine nature of the face from his natural theology, with its premise that "the design of man's being was, that he might praise and honor his Maker" (*Anatomy*, p. 105). Bell's view had two implications. First, it made humans discontinuous with other animals:

> It is obvious thus to observe how the muscles, by producing distinct impressions, afford a new occasion of distinguishing the tribes of animals; and, as signs of superior intelligence, become proofs of the higher endowments of man, and a demonstration of the peculiar frame and excellence of his nature. (*Anatomy*, 1806, p. 141)

Second, expressions for Bell served to convey feelings and impressions:

> In man there seems to be a special apparatus, for the purpose of enabling him to communicate with his fellow creatures, by that natural language which is read off the changes of his countenance. There exist in his face, not only all those parts which by their action produce expression in the several classes of quadrupeds, but there is added a peculiar set of muscles to which no other office can be assigned than to serve for expression. (*Anatomy*, p. 121)

Bell's teleological views were instances of two of Darwin's major targets: human discontinuity and divine creation. First, by showing communalities among the expressive movements of humans and nonhumans, Darwin could vitiate Bell's position on humans' "peculiar frame and excellence" and reassert a place for humans in normal phylogeny. This was why Darwin undertook personal experiments with the apes at the London Zoo and with his dogs at home, and asked contacts worldwide to complete questionnaires about the expressions of diverse cultures.

Darwin's strategy for rebutting Bell's second point (divine creation) was far smarter and subtler, and is often misunderstood. From the outset of his evolutionary theorizing, Darwin knew that arguments for evolution via natural selection could not be based upon observations that creatures were well suited (in common parlance, "adapted") to their niches. Functional behavior is certainly consistent with adaptation via natural selection. However, evidence for adaptation *also* supports creationists who use the beauty and "perfection" of biological structure and process as evidence of the existence of God and His design for the world, the so-called "argument from design." Its major nineteenth-century proponent, William Paley, noted that when we find a watch, we necessarily infer a watchmaker (Gruber, 1974, p. 52). As Paley himself put it, "the examination of the eye was a cure for atheism" (Paley, 1816, p. 26). By the mid-nineteenth century, the argument from design took two forms:

1. *Special Creation.* God designed all creatures *ex nihilo* with the forms appropriate to their places in the world, with humans uniquely close to God and having dominion over other creatures. As a promulgator of special creation, Charles Bell not only considered the human face divine, but matched Paley's admiration for the eye with his own for the tool-making human hand, in *The hand, its mechanism and vital endowments as evincing design* (Bell, 1833).

2. *Directed Evolution.* God set the world in motion and directed the evolutionary process toward perfection, with humans the culmination of this evolution. As the biologist Lorenz Oken (1847) stated, "Man is the summit, the crown of nature's development" (p. 202). With regard to the place of humans compared to that of nonhumans, Oken added, "What are the lower animals but a series of human abortions?" (cited in Gould, 1977, p. 36).

Had Darwin pursued an "argument from adaptation" for expression, it would have left him a foil for the creationists. Demonstrating adaptation would merely affirm Bell. Consequently, the way to deny Bell's second claim (that certain muscles were "designed" for expression) was to show that expressions had *no* function, that they were *non*adaptive movements that were unrelated to natural selection. This tactic was a familiar one to Darwin. He had previously used it with regard to morphology in *Origin*, wherein he paradoxically offered the existence of "rudimentary, atrophied, or aborted organs" (*Origin*, p. 255) as evidence *for* evolution by natural selection over either special creation or directed evolution.

Thus webbed feet on land birds, male breasts, five phalanges in the seal flipper, and the human appendix (all from *Origin*) would provide better evidence for natural selection than, say, the oft-mentioned "perfection" of the eye. Darwin, in fact, discussed the eye extensively in *Origin*; in *Descent* (p. 441) he cited Helmholtz's enumeration of its *imperfections* as further evidence for natural selection, and against the argument from design.

In *Expression* Darwin disclosed his strategy of countering the argument from design by demonstration of the nonutility of expression:

> No doubt as long as man and all other animals are viewed as independent creations, an effectual stop is put to our natural desire to investigate as far as possible the causes of Expressions. By this doctrine, anything and everything can be explained; and it has proved as pernicious with respect to Expressions as to every other branch of natural history. With mankind some expressions, such as the bristling of the hair under the influence of extreme terror, or the uncovering of the teeth under that of furious rage, can hardly be understood, except under the belief that man once existed in a much lower and animal-like condition. (*Expression*, p. 12)[9]

Darwin was especially primed to make nonadaptationist arguments in *Expression*. He had already recoiled from criticism that he had overplayed the roles of adaptation and natural selection in early editions of *Origin*. He addressed this criticism directly in *Descent*, the volume that spawned *Expression*:

> I had not formerly sufficiently considered the existence of many structures which appear to be, as far as we can judge, neither beneficial nor injurious; and this I believe to be one of the greatest oversights as yet detected in my work. (*Descent*, p. 152)

Simply put, then, Darwin was apparently in a can't-lose situation. By presenting nonadaptationist accounts of expression, Darwin could depose Bell's view while redressing his own error. Darwin's mechanisms of expression were, in fact, merely continuations of his plan to develop a general reflexive psychology and psychophysiology (Ghiselin, 1969). Moreover, he had already conceived them in their basic form by 1838, in the *M* notebook (Barrett et al., 1987; Gruber, 1974). I now summarize these mechanisms.

DARWIN'S MECHANISMS OF EXPRESSION AS GROUNDS TO PRESUME THE NONADAPTIVENESS OF EXPRESSION

Darwin proposed three mechanisms for the development of expressions. The simplest was the *Principle of Direct Action of the Nervous System*, which he derived from Herbert Spencer (e.g., 1863) and Johannes Müller

[9] Darwin was also prepared for the creationist fall-back argument that vestiges were placed there by God to fool man (a strategy employed today with regard to the fossil record): "Thus we can understand

(1838–1842). With it Darwin explained certain expressions as signifying an overflow of nerve force from an overstimulated sensorium. These often accompanied other, habitual expressive movements, but were themselves "independent of the will, and to a large extent, of habit" (*Expression*, p. 66). They included loss of hair color in terror or grief; trembling of the lips or limbs; writhing; clenching and gnashing of teeth; and autonomic signs such as glandular secretions, tachycardia, defecation, urination,[10] and perspiration. Their form was due almost entirely to accidents of nervous system organization. For example, facial irritation produced tears because the eyes and face are supplied by the same nerves (Ghiselin, 1969, pp. 205–206).

Darwin's direct-action principle was enigmatic at best; it prematurely forced many disparate phenomena to fit one mechanism. Darwin, too, was unhappy with it, as he revealed in a letter to the physiologist Alexander Bain:

> "What you say about the vagueness of what I have called the direct action of the autonomic nervous system, is perfectly just. I felt so at the time, and even more of late." (F. Darwin, 1887, Vol. 2, p. 350)

Darwin did not explore whether the neural organization that produced a particular expression was itself an adaptation resulting from natural selection (more on this below). Rather, he presented those expressions that resulted from direct action as merely the overt manifestations of internal upheaval. This was sufficient to claim that the expressions were "of no service, often of much disservice" (*Expression*, p. 67) or "purposeless" (*Expression*, p. 76). Considering them useless or even disadvantageous constituted another refutation of Bell's argument that the muscles producing them existed *in order to* reveal character or emotion.

Darwin called his most important expressive mechanism the *Principle of Serviceable Associated Habits*. As he stated it, "Certain complex actions are of direct or indirect service under certain states of the mind . . . and whenever the same state of mind is induced, however feebly, there is a tendency through the force of habit and association for the same movements to be performed, *though they may not then be of the least use*" (*Expression*, p. 28, italics mine). This principle, like the principle of direct action, owed much to Spencer, who earlier discussed the "nascent excitation of psychical state" (Spencer, 1855).

---

how it has come to pass that man and all other vertebrate animals have been constructed on the same general model . . . and why they retain certain rudiments in common. Consequently we ought frankly to admit their common descent; to take any other view, is to admit that our own structure, and that of all animals around us, is a mere snare laid to entrap our judgment" (*Descent*, p. 25).

[10] For example, "Hyena pisses from fear so does man.—and so dog" (*M* notebook, p. 153; Gruber, 1974, p. 296). Darwin borrowed many of these "autonomic" signs of emotion from the *Zoonomia* volume by his grandfather, Erasmus Darwin (E. Darwin, 1794; see discussion by Montgomery, 1985).

Darwin's final principle, the *Principle of Antithesis*, was merely a corollary of the second. It held that once "a state of mind" was accompanied by an associated habit, a contrary state of mind would tend to evoke an opposite habit. Thus a depressed dog lowers its tail by virtue of its raising the tail when euphoric. Darwin's presentation of the principle is confusing; Lloyd Morgan conveyed his inability to understand it (Ghiselin, 1969, p. 206), and the neo-physiognomist Theodur Piderit stated, "This principle seems to me to be only an arbitrary one, an axiom not proved in any way, a filler to explain what cannot be adapted to the first and third principles" (1886, p. 17). James said with his typical acerbity, "whether it expresses a *causal* principle is more than doubtful" (1890, p. 1096). The Principle is also dubious ontologically because it fails to specify which movements of the antithetical pairs are the antitheses, and it presupposes that the ostensible antithetical habit was not also originally serviceable (Fridlund, 1991a).

Whether the expressions were original or antithetical, Darwin believed that they were simply habits, formed by the contiguity learning propounded by Hume, Locke, Spencer, Bain, and other British associationists. This was the same thorough-going associationist psychology that Darwin espoused in *Descent* (Ghiselin, 1969). Darwin described how serviceable (functional) actions became reflexive, that is, associated *habits*:

> Some actions, which were at first performed consciously, have become through habit and association converted into reflex actions . . . In such cases the sensory-nerve cells excite the motor cells, without first communicating with those cells on which our consciousness and volition depend. (*Expression*, p. 40)

Darwin went further. Given that expressive habits seemed to show panspecies and pancultural communalities, yet now seemed not to be "of the least use," he could conclude that they must have been serviceable only in ancestry and then transmitted by descent.

The expressions governed by the Principle of Serviceable Associated Habits were readily explained. Emotions formerly accompanied by functional acts would tend to elicit those acts, even in offspring for whom the acts were useless. For instance, humans sneer simply because ancestors exposed their canine teeth repeatedly during the course of attack, and sneering became associated with the emotions of attack (e.g., anger or contempt).

Darwin believed that many common expressions were associated habits derived from serviceable acts, including: (1) startle (from jumping away); (2) head-scratching during problem solving (the problem is an "irritant"); (3) wincing upon attack, or (4) tearing in sadness (both from ocular irritation); (5) laughter (from tickling; see Chapter 6).

Proposing the inheritance of acquired *expressive* habits was an easy step for Darwin. Having no knowledge of genetic modes of transmission (Mendel's writings were not rediscovered until circa 1900), his inheritance mechanism was the widely accepted "use-inheritance" of Jean-Baptiste Lamarck (1809),[11] which held that habits, once sufficiently exercised, were transmitted to offspring. In *Descent*, Darwin had invoked use-inheritance to explain a litany of human morphological traits. For example:

> Different occupations, habitually followed, lead to changed proportions in various parts of the body. . . . It is asserted that the hands of English laborers are at birth larger than those of the gentry. From the correlation which exists . . . between the development of the extremities and the jaws, it is possible that in those classes which do not labor much with their hands and feet, the jaws would be reduced in size from this cause. That [the hands] are generally smaller in refined or civilized men than in hard-working men or savages, is certain. (*Descent*, pp. 32–33)

Darwin, then, applied the same mechanism he used for morphological traits in *Descent* to the expressions in *Expression*. The sufficient exercise of an expressive movement, like the exercise of a structure, would "stamp it in" and preserve it in progeny (see Figure 2.1).[12]

Because the expressive habits were not "of the least use," Darwin could then directly compare many expressions to the "rudimentary, atrophied, or aborted organs" described in *Origin*. His act had breathtaking ramifications: many of the expressions held to reveal the "passions" that lay so close to the soul were simply biological vestiges like male breasts and the human appendix. He could again refute arguments based on special creation, directed evolution, and adaptation, and thereby use "imperfection" to bolster his mechanism of evolution via natural selection.

Darwin's inherited expressive habits, like habits in general, were independent of the will. He mocked his opponents and forced the point when he quipped:

> He who rejects with scorn the belief that the shape of his own canines, and their occasional great development in other men, are due to our early

---

[11] Darwin was a lifelong Lamarckian in his regarding use-inheritance as the mode of hereditary transmission by which natural selection could create evolutionary trends. His Lamarckism was nonetheless selective. Only briefly, when he first entertained alternative mechanisms of evolution (circa 1837), did he share Lamarck's view that evolution had an intrinsic momentum in which organisms evolved to fill the gaps created as others became extinct (Gruber, 1974). Darwin's natural selection was, of course, random and undirected.

[12] In *Origin*, Darwin reasoned about vestigial *structures*: "Changed structures, which are in no way beneficial, cannot be kept uniform through natural selection, though the injurious will be thus eliminated" (p. 62). Thus vestigial expressive movements would persist because they were benign and would not be selected against. Curiously, Darwin never dealt with a possible contradiction in his logic: he claimed simultaneously that rudimentary movements should be highly variable in form, but he banked on their communalities to claim phylogenetic continuity.

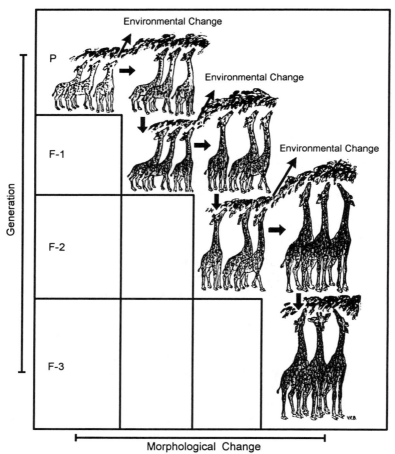

FIGURE 2.1.   The inheritance of acquired characteristics as formulated by Jean-Baptiste Lamarck (1809). According to Lamarck, the use of a structure preserved or enhanced it in progeny, so that giraffes who strain to reach tall leaves will have offspring with long necks. Darwin used Lamarck's use-inheritance as his mode of hereditary transmission throughout *Expression of the emotions in man and animals*. It has, of course, been supplanted by Mendelian genetics. From Kraus (1964).

forefathers having been provided with these formidable weapons, will probably reveal, by sneering, the line of his descent. (*Descent*, p. 41)

If the expressive habits themselves were not willful, one could none-theless mimic them deliberately. These imitations, unlike the acts they imitated, could be useful; *they* could be issued as signals to others:

Every true or inherited movement of expression seems to have had some natural and independent origin. But when once acquired, such movements may be voluntarily and consciously employed as a means of communication. (*Expression*, p. 356)

Darwin also allowed that these voluntary communicative acts themselves might, with sufficient practice, become habitual and transmitted to progeny (*Expression*, pp. 356–357).

Darwin never explored this possibility. It would permit the formation of a serviceable, *communicative* habit by the repeated, willful exercise of a voluntary act—even though the original, mimicked act was not "of the least use." It would also controvert his own Principle, because any expressive movement could then be claimed to have arisen not directly from a serviceable act, but by the instinctualization of a previous movement mimicked willfully for communication! It is thus remarkable that Darwin did not at this point construct a fourth principle (cf. Burkhardt, 1985), whereby communicative acts could evolve by natural selection *because* their communicative functions were advantageous. I submit that his reason was tactical, and should by now be obvious.

SUMMARY OF DARWIN'S VIEWS IN *EXPRESSION* AND THEIR UNFORTUNATE CONSEQUENCE

In *Expression* Darwin extended to facial expressions the Lamarckian, reflexive psychology of *Descent*. Expressions resulted from mechanisms that had no current function. Except for a few movements that may have resulted from sexual selection,[13] Darwin showed that expressions were either accidents of nervous system wiring ("direct actions") or vestiges of old habits. The vestigial habits were the behavioral equivalents of the "rudimentary, atrophied, or aborted organs" that he had cited so effectively as evidence for natural selection, and against arguments from special creation or directed evolution.

Expression was a direct attack upon the natural theology of Charles Bell and its twin tenets about expressions. First, Darwin's documenting of communalities in expressions across species and human cultures countered the dogma of special human creation and placed humans within normal phylogenesis. Second, that "expressions" of emotion were rudiments or accidents mitigated the belief that the structures embodying them were there for that purpose. Thus facial expressions did not "express" emotion; this would have implied a communicative function. They simply accompanied emotion by force of habit. Communicative function was restricted to those faces deployed willfully, including those that intentionally resembled the habitual ones.

---

[13] Darwin granted that a few expressive movements might be the results of intraspecific competition and subsequent sexual selection (typically, male–male competition for access to females). Examples from *Expression* include two "threat" expressions: (1) *erectores pilorum* (piloerection, or goosebumps), which makes a feathered or furry body appear larger; and (2) the rattle of the rattlesnake.

Darwin's views, *mutadis mutandis*, persisted in several popular emotion-based theories of facial expression. They retained Darwin's distinction between those faces that are evolved, involuntary, reflexive, and intimately associated with emotion, and those that are willful and employed to social ends. These distinctions form the basis for the so-called "two-factor" (Fridlund, 1991a) emotions views of facial expressions. I detail these later in this volume (see Chapter 7).

Darwin's strategy of demonstrating nonadaptiveness of expressions was successful. It extended to the passions the victory over natural theology he had achieved in morphology.[14] However, his victory was Pyrrhic. He achieved it at the cost of forsaking an intrinsic communicative role for facial expressions *qua* expressions. Burkhardt (1985) stated the predicament precisely:

> In constructing his argument against the idea that special structures in man had been designed by the Creator for the purpose of non-verbal communication, Darwin appears to have over-reacted, thereby leaving him ill-disposed to develop an idea that would later be advanced by the ethologists of the twentieth century—the idea that certain expressive actions, whatever their primary origin, had been developed over time by natural selection. (p. 360)

THE TRANSITION FROM DARWINIAN REFLEXOLOGY TO BEHAVIORAL ECOLOGY

Two developments in the first half of the twentieth century served to undermine Darwin's views on facial expressions. First, the rediscovery (circa 1900) of Mendelian particulate inheritance forced the abandonment of Lamarckian use-inheritance as the mechanism for hereditary transmission.[15] This had a major implication for Darwin's views. His Principle of Serviceable Associated Habits was gutted of its inheritance mechanism, and thus became untenable. Second, Darwin's need to depose dogmas of special creation or directed evolution led him, as I demonstrated, to promulgate nonadaptationist accounts of displays. Ironically, his triumph in demonstrating natural selection as the guiding mechanism of evolution enabled later biologists to develop accounts of signaling that were distinctly adaptationist. Expressive (hereafter, "display" behavior) could then be conceived as an adaptation like any other.

---

[14] Darwin was less successful in *Descent*, when he extended it to human cognition. Despite the biological determinism of psychoanalysis (see Sulloway, 1979), the mental evolution of Romanes (1883, 1888), and the brief reign of American functionalism (esp., Angell, 1904; Carr, 1925), the notion of cognition as biological adaptation had to wait until the late twentieth century to take hold (e.g., Brothers, 1990; Tooby & Cosmides, 1990; Rozin & Schull, 1988).

[15] There may be some inheritance of acquired traits, but the paths are pseudo-Lamarckian (e.g., retroviruses that insert themselves in nuclear genetic material and thereby form new genomes whose genes are transmitted via normal mechanisms). Such inheritance pathways are not useful in this context.

If signaling behavior was adaptation, then a new selection mechanism, operating via Mendelian inheritance, was required to account for signal evolution. This change from Darwin's Lamarckian reflexology to modern views of signaling was via Oskar Heinroth's conception of "intention movements" (cf. Heinroth, 1911), fragmentary movements (e.g., beak-snapping) that statistically predicted complete acts (e.g., attack). Huxley (1923, 1966) finally conceived the process by which natural selection might create displays by "ritualizing" (i.e., "schematizing" or simplifying) elements of complete acts for use as signals.[16] The ritualization concept led to the informational, "behavioral ecology" model of signaling that dominates modern ethology. It supplants Darwin's but is more "Darwinian." Later, I will extend the behavioral ecology model to human facial expressions.

[16] A transitional period was marked by work in the 1920s and 1930s by Heinroth's student Konrad Lorenz (Lorenz, 1970). Lorenz suggested that intention movements were "inherited coordinations" (*Erbkoordination*, now translated "fixed action patterns") that indicated accumulation of excitation prior to the complete "release" of an instinct. His friend Niko Tinbergen (1939, 1952) regarded many displays as "displacement activities" resulting from the blockade of drive energy from release along the usual channels. The Lorenz–Tinbergen ethology was thoroughly hydraulic, and reminiscent of Darwin's premise that expressions signified either internal upheaval or the presence of emotion. Like Darwin's views in *Expression*, it too has been abandoned.

3

Facial Expression and the Methods of Contemporary Evolutionary Research

Research on human facial displays never abated after Darwin published *Expression* in 1872. In the 1920s and 1930s, it became a cottage industry. The focus was upon whether judges who were shown still photos of faces could agree when asked to match them to emotion words or other labels. Cross-cultural data were sparse, and the *Zeitgeist* in cultural anthropology was the linguistic analysis of gestures and expressions with the emphasis on their cultural variation. (I treat the impact of this *Zeitgeist* more extensively when I discuss cross-cultural studies of "facial expressions of emotion.") Despite the relativistic mood the common assumption, repeated by Darwin, was that human faces were in some way "universally" understood.

The 1940s and 1950s saw the emergence of two trends that furthered the study of facial behavior. First, Woodworth (1938) and Schlosberg (1941, 1954) revived Wundt's (1896) thinking about the dimensionality of emotion and attempted to investigate it through factor-analytic studies of photographed faces, and such investigations of "affective space" continue today (e.g., Russell, 1980; Watson & Tellegen, 1985).

Second, under the sway of Helmholtzian physicalism, ethologists such as Lorenz and Tinbergen emphasized the innateness and almost comical stereotypy of some nonhuman consumatory and social behavior. In this mechanistic view, organisms were substantially preattuned to respond to "sign stimuli" or "releasers" that triggered the emission of appropriate behavior patterns known as "fixed action patterns" (FAPs), and even complex organisms were considered just reflex conglomerates. One technical offshoot of ethology's early influence was the development of the "ethogram," a diagrammatic view of nonverbal behavior as a hierarchy or sequence of discrete acts (see Figure 3.1). Ethogrammatic methods allowed the inductive derivation of taxa for acts such as postures, gestures, and facial displays without preconceptions of the meanings or relations among them (Colgan, 1978; Fridlund, Ekman, & Oster, 1987).

Early ethology's documenting of instinctual, reflexlike behavior gave new impetus to evolutionary views of human behavior, and some ethologists ambitiously extended their findings to human societies (e.g., Lorenz, 1952, 1966, 1970). Releaser theory dovetailed with instinctivist conceptions of the face and emotion (e.g., Plutchik, 1962; Tomkins, 1962, 1963), and resurrected the Darwinian position that human faces were "iconic" readouts of eruptile affects. One derivative view of facial expression, Ekman's "neurocultural" model (e.g., Ekman, 1971, 1977), had at its center the selectively triggered "facial affect program," acronymously *also* an FAP (I summarize Ekman's model in Chapter 11). The quasi-reflexive view of facial expressions had several positive consequences, including the development of quantitative facial coding sys-

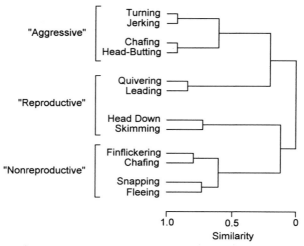

FIGURE 3.1.   Ethogram showing the pattern of reproductive behavior of the male bitterling, *Rhodius amarus*. The ethogram here is presented as a dendrogram and was derived from hierarchical cluster analysis. Clusters (branches off a common trunk) indicate related types of behavior. The ethogram is one of ethology's classic "atheoretical" inductive methods—but of course, the behavioral measures are selected according to some theory about their salience. Illustration adapted from Colgan (1978), after data by Wiepkema (1961); copyright © 1978 by John Wiley & Sons, Inc.

tems, and a reconsideration of the issues of innateness, phylogenetic continuity, and human cross-cultural communalities.

In the interim, the discovery that many "simple" reflexes like the patellar-tendon reflex were actually servo-loops forced a wholesale revision of the Sherringtonian concept of the nervous system (Miller, Galanter, & Pribram, 1960), and animals became motivated, open-loop systems rather than automatons (Gallistel, 1980). Nonhuman postures, squawks, and grunts were observed to be context dependent in their emission and perception (e.g., Smith, 1969, 1977). "Fixed action patterns" were even renamed "modal action patterns" to emphasize their variability (Barlow, 1977). Contemporary ethologists sound more like communications theorists than reflexologists, and the ethological *Weltanschauung* is now one of signals, semantics, kin selection and social learning.

Quasi-reflexive theories of human faces, because their models were predicated upon early ethology, were left stranded by the new understanding of the complexity of *non*human signals. Moreover, evolutionary theory and methods have also advanced beyond those known by Darwin and early ethology, and they both offer new possibilities and undermine old assumptions about the nature of human faces.

As I discussed earlier, Darwin's evolution via use-inheritance was vitiated by the rediscovery of Mendelian genetics, and the fact that genetic inheritance was particulate meant that the mathematics of gene pools, meiosis, assortment, and recombination had to be pressed into service to explain the inheritance and selection of whole traits. The integration was via the population genetics work by R. A. Fisher (1930), Sewall Wright (1931), and J. B. S. Haldane (1932), culminating in the now-predominant "synthetic view" of evolution by natural selection first articulated by Theodosius Dobzhansky in the landmark *Genetics and the Origin of Species* (Dobzhansky, 1937). The synthetic theory has promoted the development of advanced techniques for answering questions of genetic control, inheritance, and phylogenesis, and an increased sophistication about the possible twists and turns that can occur during evolution. For a detailed review and appraisal of modern synthetic evolutionary theory, see Grant (1985).

From this synthetic view, I will try to articulate criteria for determining whether and how facial displays evolved. Before presenting these criteria, it might be helpful to define the key evolutionary terminology.

"Evolution" of behavior denotes a diachronic process, that is, a trend over time. Behavior can evolve because the genes producing or contributing to it have proliferated through natural selection, or via cultural transmission with no specific genetic basis. Thus one can justifiably speak both of the "evolution of sexual behavior" and the "evolution of violent themes in cinema," but imply the evolution of genotypes in the first and strictly cultural evolution in the second.

"Genetic control" implies that a trait is determined substantially by the genotype. Common parlance about whether a trait "is genetic" forces an improper dichotomy, because any phenotypic trait—even one that is obviously acquired culturally—must at least have a genotype that permits its acquisition. It is nonetheless valuable to consider the extent and specificity of a trait's genetic control. In the case of facial displays, *many* features of facial expressivity could be under genetic control: (1) whether or not particular displays are deployed; (2) the frequency, amplitude, and temporal dynamics of the displays; (3) the relative contributions of specific muscular actions to the displays; and (4) the contexts in which an individual makes the displays. Genetic control of any of these features may be either weak (dispositional) or substantial (determinative), general (resulting from a superordinate trait such as "striate muscle contractility") or specific ("facial expressivity"). And the control may be mono- or polygenic.

Genetic control of a trait implies that its origins are in natural selection. It does *not* imply current evolution through natural selection. This is so for two reasons. First, variability in a trait is required for any selection pressures to exert change. This variability requisite for natural selection is now thought to result only minimally from mutation, with any selection based substantially on the existing composition of the gene pool.

In some cases, however, genetic control of a trait may have become so complete—and the costs of an alternative form so high—that the trait is, except through rare and often lethal mutation, invariant throughout phylogeny. One clear example is the development of two eyes, for which the propensity did evolve and variability is nil (cyclopean humans nearly always die *in utero* or soon after birth). Genetic control of development that is so fixed that further evolution is impossible is called "canalization" (Waddington, 1957). If traits are not fixed but are variable in a population (e.g., temperament; see Tellegen, Lykken, Bouchard, Wilcox, Segal, & Rich, 1988), and their development is under both genetic and epigenetic (i.e., environmental) control, then it is proper to speak of their "heritability" (that proportion of phenotypic variance due to the genotype). Thus, heritability requires genetic inheritance, but complete genetic inheritance can occur with *zero* heritability. Each of the four features of facial displays I delineated could result from differing genetic versus epigenetic contributions. Each feature could have evolved under separate selection pressures.

There is a second reason why genetic control does not imply ongoing evolution. Even when a trait is variable and at least partially under genetic control (i.e., the trait is heritable), there may be no selection pressures for one genotype over another. As I discussed earlier regarding Darwin's treatment of facial expressions, the stable persistence of heritable traits is seen clearly in the case of vestigial, periodically recurrent structures whose costs are so minimal that there are no pressures for their deselection (e.g., the supernumerary breasts that appear on some human females, often seen as multiple birthmarks on the abdomen).

The term most congruent with the casual use of the word "evolution" is "evolution via natural selection." This refers to descent with modification, a change in a trait because gene frequencies, and thus genotypes, are altered due to selection pressures in the environment. Evolution through natural selection thus requires: (1) genetic control over traits, (2) variability in traits (hence, their heritability), and (3) selection pressures that override the conservative forces of canalization (Grant, 1985). Increasing knowledge of natural selection suggests that selection pressures do not direct new directions for adaptation so much as they form inhibitory contours that constrain genotypes against endogenous, spontaneous molecular variation. This is the evolutionary "neutralism" proposed by Kimura (1982, 1983).

As I will discuss later, cross-cultural studies of human "facial expressions of emotion" were originally (but wrongly) interpreted as implying their genetic control, which would be requisite for shared phylogeny and evolution by natural selection. In formal terms, researchers in human facial displays have not been interested in the evolution of the displays, but rather in the *products* of their evolution. Whether there is ongoing evolution of human displays is completely indeterminate.

With these terms and distinctions explicit, it will be easier to discuss how we might discover the extent to which human facial displays may be products of evolution by natural selection.

WHAT KINDS OF EVIDENCE COULD SUBSTANTIATE AN EVOLUTIONARY ACCOUNT OF FACIAL DISPLAY?

Whether the focus is on a behavior or a morph (i.e., the form of any biological entity), an array of investigative strategies can be brought into play to help determine the extent of a trait's genetic control or the extent and trend of its evolution.

Comparison of Morphology

In studying morphology, taxonomies based on fossil data have traditionally been the gold standard. They chart the historical development of structures over evolutionary time. For the paleontologist or comparative anatomist, fossils from different time periods that show changes in target traits (e.g., the jaw shapes and sizes of an evolutionary line of anthropoid apes) are like the detective's chain of evidence. They suggest the trait's origin and the direction(s) of its evolution. Traditionally, fossil evidence has constituted the prime method of constructing species taxonomies.

In tracking the evolution of forms of behavior, the fossil record is rarely useful. There are notable counterexamples. For instance, feeding habits can be deduced from the conformation of jaw, limbs, and dentition (Martin, 1990; Walker & Murray, 1975; Wolpoff, 1980), and the position of the face in locomotion can be deduced from the conformation of the occiput of the skull (Le Gros Clark, 1950; Ashton & Zuckerman, 1951; Davis & Napier, 1963). Attachments of facial muscles to craniofacial bone could be informative about the evolution of primate and human facial muscles used in display, but this strategy is limited by the fact that most of these mimetic muscles attach to fascia rather than bone (Dzubow, 1986; Moldaver, 1980). The exceptions that do have bony attachments are the so-called "deep muscles" of the face; these are the muscles critical to mastication but only minimally involved in display (I discuss these muscles further in Chapter 5). A comparison of some of the deep facial muscles is depicted in Figure 3.2.

One of the major advances in twentieth-century evolutionary biology is the development of "molecular evolutionary" techniques for establish-

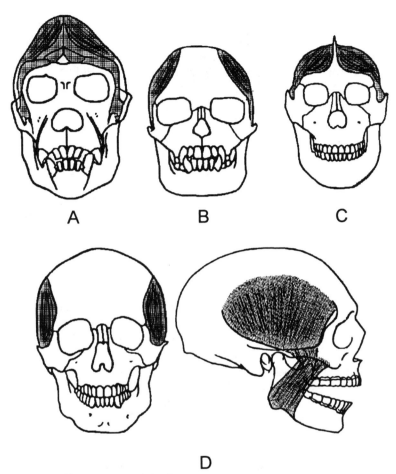

FIGURE 3.2. Comparison of skulls and points of attachment of temporal muscles on either temporal line or sagittal crest for four primate species: (A) *Gorilla gorilla*; (B) *Procosul*; (C) *Australopithecus*; and (D) humans. Cross-species comparisons of fossil skulls can be informative about common origins of facial muscles, but they are limited to those muscles that have bony attachments, such as the "deep" muscles of mastication (see Chapter 5). Reprinted with permission from: Campbell, Bernard. *Human Evolution: An Introduction to Man's Adaptations*. 3rd Edition. (New York: Aldine de Gruyter) copyright © 1985 Bernard Campbell.

ing a chain of evidence for an evolutionary trend based not on fossil but on biochemical data. Species can now be related, and taxonomies constructed, based on the concordances of any number of their genetic and chemical constituents. These include the

1. number of base-pair mismatches in nuclear or mitochondrial DNA (the latter is transmitted strictly via maternity). These are used to construct so-called DNA-hybridization taxonomies.

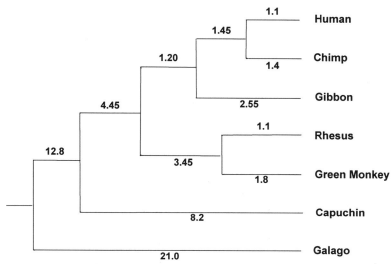

FIGURE 3.3.   The place of humans in primate phylogeny based on DNA similarities, as determined by the molecular evolutionary technique of DNA hybridization. Such reconstructions of primate phylogeny can be used to construct muscular homologies and map the origins of facial displays. Data from Kohne, Chiscon, and Hoyer (1972). From *Evolution*, by Dobzhansky, Ayala, Stebbins, and Valentine. Copyright © 1977. Reprinted by permission of W. H. Freeman and Company.

2. genetic distances among selected, well-known gene loci.
3. distances among selected immune-related antigens as they appear using electrophoresis.
4. distributions of blood types derived from serological tests.
5. number of amino acid substitutions in blood hemoglobin.

Taxonomies or clads[1] derived using these biochemical techniques produce results that coincide overall with those derived inductively from the fossil record, but they may be more precise (e.g., Goodman & Lasker, 1975; Kimura, 1983). This precision allows the comparison of very close species and has already provided some surprising data about the place of humans in primate phylogeny (see Figure 3.3).

These molecular evolutionary techniques have not yet been applied to the development of display behavior (or, so far as I know, any behavior). How might they be useful? First, any phylogenetic account of a facial display, or feature of a display, should map onto the derived phylogenies, such that the target behavior is most concordant among the most closely related species. Second, these techniques can establish pat-

---

[1] "Cladistics" is a less inductive analytic method based solely on individual characteristics, and which omits the chronological data provided by a fossil record. Clads are the classifications that result (Campbell, 1985).

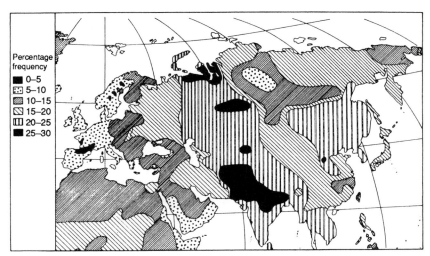

FIGURE 3.4.   Frequency of the form of the hemoglobin gene for Type B blood in Europe, Asia, and Northern Africa, showing repeated migrations of Mongolians and other Central Asians into western Asia and Europe. Such migration data can be used to ascertain the extent to which geographic variations in facial displays are genotypic. From Grant (1985), using data of Mourant, Kopec, and Domainiewska-Sobczak (1976). © Columbia University Press; reprinted with permission of the publisher.

terns of migration (see Figure 3.4), which may be useful in understanding cultural differences in displays.

In the absence of "hard" fossil or molecular evidence for evolution of facial display, three alternatives remain: the neural localization, selective breeding, and comparative approaches. I now discuss each.

Neural Localization

Substantial genetic control of a display is implicated if the display has a definable, isolable neural substrate, and is relatively immutable despite environmental changes. A "model system" for this strategy is, for example, the localization of control of thirst to the preoptic area of the hypothalamus (cf. Rolls, Wood, & Rolls, 1980).

Attempting to establishing genetic control for a facial display using neural localization is much more difficult than even for control of a homeostatic drive such as thirst. I will attempt to illustrate the difficulties, using the human smile as an example. Among human facial displays, the smile is a comparatively easy case, because the muscles comprising it (largely the *zygomatic major* on each side) are well known, as are the distal neural pathways controlling the muscles (Fridlund, 1988; and see Figure 3.5).

At first, it would seem that genetic control of the smile might be

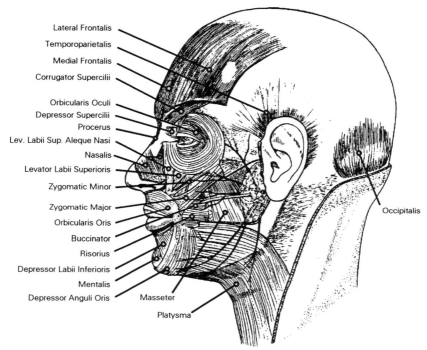

Lateral Frontalis
Temporoparietalis
Medial Frontalis
Corrugator Supercilii

Orbicularis Oculi
Depressor Supercilii
Procerus
Lev. Labii Sup. Aleque Nasi
Nasalis
Levator Labii Superioris
Zygomatic Minor

Zygomatic Major
Orbicularis Oris
Buccinator
Risorius
Depressor Labii Inferioris
Mentalis
Depressor Anguli Oris

Occipitalis

Masseter

Platysma

FIGURE 3.5.   The superficial muscles of the human face in sagittal view. I discuss these in detail in Chapter 4. Adapted from Hiatt and Gartner (1982).

established if one isolated a neural circuit that elicited a natural smile when stimulated, and abolished it when lesioned. This is the classic "turn on and then burn out" (i.e., stimulate and lesion) strategy so established in physiological psychology. But—and here are where the difficulties intrude—genetic control of the natural smile is implied only *if* three other conditions are met.

First, the stimulation or lesioning must be performed in a neonate. Performed on an older animal [human], it could otherwise be evoking or obliterating an acquired habit. I know of no data that satisfactorily localize neural circuits for natural displays in neonates of any species.

Second, any lesion must impair only the natural smile; it must spare muscular contractions generally. It would be of no use if a lesion simply caused muscular paralysis. Purely to make the point, I might mention several lesions that would *not* confirm a fixed, inherited neural basis for the smile. They include (refer to Figure 3.5): (1) bilaterally lesioning the facial nerve branch innervating *zygomatic major*, or (2) any known motor pathway up to the precentral gyrus ("motor" cortex), or, to take the extreme case, (3) denervating the muscles. And lesioning neonates of any species close enough to humans to be informative is questionable ethically.

Third, a neural locus for generating a natural smile must meet one other condition. Damage to the locus, although impairing the smile, must spare general social responding. For example, prefrontal cerebral abnormalities often result in reduced smiling. The reduced smiling, however, is readily explained in terms of general social disengagement resulting from prefrontal damage (see Kolb & Milner, 1981). It is not due to circuits specialized for smiles. Similarly, basal forebrain stimulation can produce smiling—but only because it may be eliciting sexual arousal or other responses which, in the laboratory context, can be embarrassing. This phenomenon would be equally inadequate for demonstrating neural localization for smiling. The hypothetical clinical syndrome that would uniquely corroborate a locus for a natural smile would be *amimia* (lack of spontaneous facial expressiveness), occurring without *apraxia* (loss of skilled movement) or *anhedonia* (loss of emotion or motivation).

Electroencephalographic (EEG) or magnetoencephalographic (MEG) techniques are often used in attempt to localize neuronal activity. The localization they permit is minimal, however, with inferences typically limited to lobe and hemisphere. Moreover, EEG and MEG techniques sample activity of only the neocortical surface, and instigation of natural smiles is probably predominantly subcortical and extrapyramidal (e.g., Fridlund, 1988). Current techniques that sample regions of neuronal physiology are either restricted as well to the neocortical surface (e.g., regional cerebral blood flow studies; Larsen, Skinhoj, & Lassen, 1978), or are too slow to track the amplitude-time envelopes of natural smiles (e.g., positron emission tomography; Phelps & Mazziotta, 1985). Eventually, magnetic resonance imaging (MRI) devices now under development will perform detailed regional scans of neuronal metabolism. These physiological MRI scans should have the spatial and temporal resolution to allow noninvasive assessment of the neural substrates of natural displays (e.g., Holder, 1987).

Note that I do not mean to imply that any natural facial displays are, or must be, localized. One might hope for a facial analogy to the Central Pattern Generators (CPGs) of the spinal cord that govern the antithetical limb movements requisite for walking. These CPGs appear innate and quite modular (their operations survive brainstem transections that spare only spinal motor control of the limbs). There probably are such modular circuits controlling faciorespiratory reflexes like yawning (Provine, 1986) or faciogustatory reflexes like gagging (more on the facial reflexes later). But they are unlikely to account for the instigation of facial displays like frowns or smiles, because the displays do not show the stereotypy in intensity or time course typical of CPGs. Moreover, our displays are attuned precisely to ongoing interaction, exhibiting little of the "physiological inertia" characteristic of reflexive instigation (e.g., we can stop a smile dead in its tracks far more easily than a yawn).

There is the possibility that facial displays may be "localized" in the same sense as speech. Facial displays in humans (e.g., Fridlund, 1988) and now rhesus monkeys (Hauser, 1993) tend to be "lateralized" left, that is, the left side of the display leads the right, and at full intensity the left side predominates (both may indicate greater right-hemisphere involvement in the displays). Conceivably, there may be a "nonverbal facial display motor area" in the right hemisphere corresponding to the Broca's area that generates speech-related movements in the left. This left–right, verbal–nonverbal homology is especially appealing given the probable paravocal origins of many displays (also covered later).

The very limited stimulation data in nonhumans are considered in my discussion of facial reflexes in Chapter 6.

Selective Breeding

This classic behavior-genetic approach is sometimes called "artificial selection" (cf. Dobzhansky, 1951). It involves breeding for or against a target behavior over several generations, by interbreeding individuals with outlying values on the behavior. Controlling for environmental effects, any alteration of the behavior in progeny implies genetic contribution to the behavior. Exemplary is recent experimental selective breeding research showing genetic control of cricket calling: inbreeding of callers selected for either relatively high or relatively low amounts of calling generates progeny that cluster at each extreme (Cade, 1981).

The heritability of facial displays in humans can be tested using selective breeding experiments of nature. These would involve identical twins separated at birth. Recent applications of these experiments of nature have yielded valuable information on heritability of intelligence and temperament (Tellegen et al., 1988). I know of no comparable studies of facial displays.

Showing a predictable inheritance pattern (e.g., sex-linking) would also suffice to establish heritability of expressivity. Human pedigree studies have been quite informative about diatheses for psychopathology (e.g., Nurnberger & Gershon, 1989; Gottesman & Shields, 1982). They have not been used to study human displays, but nonhuman studies suggest that the approach shows great promise. Exemplary of the state of the art in correlating genetics with expressivity is an insect study by Hoikkala and Lumme (1987), who used repeated crossings of strains of *Drosophila virilis* to isolate X-linked genes controlling the signal duration and frequency of the courting male's wing-flapping call. Genome mapping efforts now under way will eventually permit extending this kind of experiment to displays such as mammalian alarm or mating calls, in animals whose life spans are sufficiently short to allow repeated crossings.

The Comparative Approach

General Strategy

In this approach, widely dispersed members of a species, or members of different species, are compared with respect to a specific morph or behavior. In the logic of the comparative approach, traits that evolved early in phylogeny should occur in many species, whereas recently evolved traits should occur in just a few. Implicit in this logic is the assumption— usually satisfied—that phylogenesis is a "tree" on which new species are branches off a common ancestral "trunk." Displays shared among species, then, would be consistent with inheritance and thus genetic control of the displays. The same inference would hold if displays are shared by members of a species whose groups are too dispersed for acquisition by contact. That is, horizontal cultural transmission, or *cross-lineage borrowing*, would be excluded.

Darwin relied extensively upon the comparative approach in *Expression* and *Descent*, but he knew it was not foolproof. Regrettably, many contemporary researchers have not been so circumspect, and misuse of the approach and misinterpretation of the resulting data are rife in studies that compare facial displays across cultures. The problems stem from three assumptions, namely that: (1) similar facial actions must be homologues; (2) communalities necessarily imply genetic control; and (3) phylogenesis can be inferred from comparing phenotypes of extant species. These assumptions are all fallacious, as I now discuss.

Like Actions Do Not Imply Homology Expressive communalities across species are not always clear, and they are often in the eye of the observer (Klopfer & Klopfer, 1982). For example, is the submissive grin of the monkey the "same" as the human smile? Their similarity may conceivably reflect a common origin (i.e., they might be *homologues*), but an alternative explanation must be excluded. Although similar in appearance, the two displays may derive from fundamentally different neuromuscular bases, with their similarity reflecting only convergent evolution (i.e., they are *analogies*; see Lockard, Fahrenbruch, Smith, & Morgan, 1977).

Distinguishing homology from analogy is crucial to the comparative approach. In *Origin of Species* (1859), Darwin established that homology derives from genealogy, and warned against common classification by appearance (Mayr, 1982). Were this principle not abided, then bats would be classified closer to birds than to mice (a clear error given that bats are simply rodents, with "wings" concocted from hypertrophied phalanges and interdigital webbing). Thus, homology in facial display cannot be intuited from visible facial action unless the skeletal and neuromuscular substrates of the displays are also homologous. And even

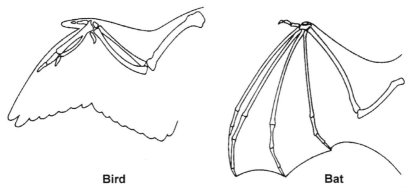

Bird   **Bat**

FIGURE 3.6.   Wings of bird and bat, demonstrating that striking similarities need not imply a common origin. Each wing is an independent product of selection pressures toward flight, fashioned from different raw material—respectively, from the proto-avian arm, and mammalian fingers. A similar principle applies to facial displays: similar appearances need not imply relatedness. From *Evolution*, by Dobzhansky, Ayala, Stebbins, and Valentine. Copyright © 1977. Reprinted by permission of W. H. Freeman and Company.

assuming homologous substrates, the displays could be analogies by convergence (see Figure 3.6 for a morphological example).

Differences in craniofacial structure can vex cross-species comparisons by rendering probable homologues very heteromorphic (for example of homologues that diverged morphologically, see Figure 3.7). One example from the repertoire of human facial displays may be brow-knitting. Humans deploy a knit brow as a social display, for example, when disturbed or concerned. The evolutionary origins are uncertain, and two adaptationist interpretations have been proposed. Herbert Spencer (1855) believed that brow-knitting arose because a knit brow acted as a sunshade, and it became a display by use-inheritance. Andrew (1964) suggested that brow-knitting eased close-up ocular convergence and thus sharpened vision (also see Ekman, 1979, and Redican, 1982, for related adaptationist interpretations).[2]

I believe that human brow-*knitting* is homologous with nonhuman earflap (pinna) *protraction* (i.e., raising and bringing forward). How could such seemingly different behaviors be homologous? The explanation lies in the fact that the shape of the human head, and thus the relations of the skull bones, changed considerably—and, in evolutionary terms—rapidly, during the development of bipedalism and speech.

[2] In adaptationism, any behavior must have some current adaptive function, or its origins should be discernible from its current function. Ekman (1979) discussed adaptationist accounts of brow actions. Adaptationism is often confused with selectionism; it is *not* a tenet of modern evolutionary theory. In fact, adaptations are often difficult to discern, and any aspect of an organism may simply be a vestige or a correlated trait.

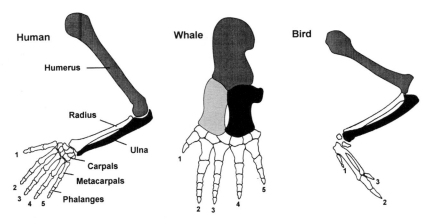

FIGURE 3.7.   The counterpoint of Figure 3.6, showing the upper limb of humans, whales, and birds. This figure demonstrates that, under appropriate selection pressures, structures with common origins can diverge and result in marked differences in appearance. Likewise, facial displays, such as ear protraction in cats and dogs—and brow-knitting in humans (see text). From *Evolution*, by Dobzhansky, Ayala, Stebbins, and Valentine. Copyright © 1977. Reprinted by permission of W. H. Freeman and Company.

The coordinations of morphological changes that occur in adaptation are known as *allometries*. The allometries necessary for bipedalism and speech seem to have been accomplished by a simple retardation in growth rates with delayed maturation (*neoteny*). The effect was to "freeze" juvenile features into the adult human morph (*paedomorphosis*). Figure 3.8 shows, by comparison with the chimpanzee, the paedomorphic characteristics of the human skull that characterize human neoteny.

The effects of the rapid neotenous enlargement of the human neurocranium are well known. They include a reduction in jaw size, orthognathia (literally "straight bite," or the absence of protruding maxilla and mandible), the recession of the brow ridges, and a temporolateral repositioning of the ears (see Alberch, Gould, Oster, & Wake, 1979; Gould, 1977). I believe that these neotenous changes shifted the actions of the pinna protractor muscles. The points of attachment of frontotemporal facial muscles then shifted temporally (Campbell, 1985). As a result, the muscles that formerly flexed the pinnae may now control the brows. Morphological neoteny thereby altered display topography, and the adventitious operation of the brow then took hold (i.e., it was coopted) as a display. Figure 3.9, from Huber (1930) and Hiatt and Gartner (1982), shows how brow-furrowing in *Homo sapiens* may represent an alteration of the muscles that protract the ears in several other primates.

Andrew (1964) speculated that brow-*raising* in the human is homo-

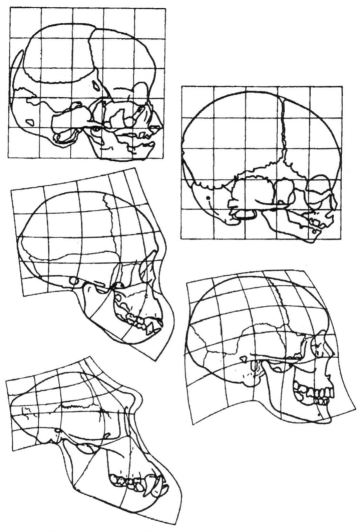

FIGURE 3.8.   The morphology of the chimpanzee and human skulls (left and right panels, respectively), showing remarkable similarity in infancy but divergence throughout development. Compared to the chimp, the adult human's skull more closely resembles its infant counterpart, a characteristic known as *paedomorphism*. The profoundly paedomorphic human adult seems to result from a simple slow-down in growth rates with delay of maturity known as *neoteny*. Human neoteny has altered extensively the shape of the head, and with it the shapes and functions of its mimetic muscles (see text and Figure 3.9). From Gould (1977).

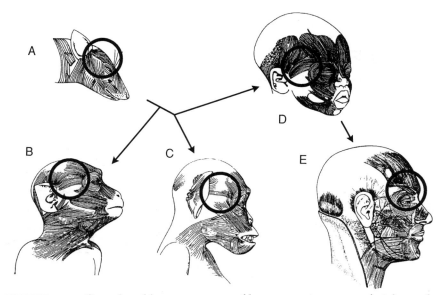

FIGURE 3.9.   One plausible consequence of human neoteny upon facial muscle function. Because of the gradual enlargement of the human neurocranium, the muscles controlling the earflaps in the (hypothetical) proto-mammal (A), the rhesus macaque (B), and the chimpanzee (C) may have become those which in the human (infant and adult, (D,E) knit or retract the brows (the *corrugator supercilii* and *frontalis* muscles, respectively). Illustrations: A–D, Huber (1931); E, Hiatt and Gartner (1982).

logous with protective earflap retraction (flattening) in nonprimates, an explanation that runs counter to the frequent adaptationist interpretation that brow-raising enhances vision (cf. Redican, 1982). In fact, Andrew's speculation on brow-raising is consistent with mine on brow-knitting. Brow-raising and brow-knitting are probable vestiges of protective reflex and auditory orientation, respectively. Any effects of brow actions on vision—the explanatory mechanism for the adaptationist— are probably serendipitous. Corroborating evidence is provided by findings that the innervation of the anterior and superior auricular muscles proceeds from the same subnucleus of the facial nerve (cranial nerve VII) as the upper face muscles that control the forehead and brow (van Boxtel, personal communication, November, 1989; Courville, 1966; Jenny & Saper, 1987; Rinn, 1984; Satoda, Takahashi, Tashiro, Matsushima, Uemura-Sumi, & Mizuno, 1987; Vraa-Jensen, 1942). Additionally, the conjoint operation of brow-raising and ear movements in some monkey species has been noted by Seiler (1973).

Consequently, human brow-raising and -knitting, despite their surface similarity, are probably not homologous with nonhuman primate brow movements, for example, lifting the eyelids to expose colorful folds.

Indeed, brow-knitting is, to my knowledge, undocumented among non-human primates. Brow actions are instead more appropriately analyzed in the same terms as the protraction and retraction of nonhuman pinnae.

Communalities Do Not Imply Genetic Control   It is often assumed that behavioral communality among species or cultures implies genetic evolution via natural selection, whereas variability within species (or for humans across cultures) reflects learning. This assumption simply does not hold when the shared traits are adaptive to individuals in each species or culture. Under this condition, communalities among species or cultures may reflect not genetic control, but learning common to all. Such learning may be transmitted vertically (i.e., from parents) and/or horizontally (i.e., from peers); alternatively, it may be accomplished via indirect pedagogy or imitation (see modes of cultural evolution, and interactions with genetic evolution, described by Boyd & Richerson, 1985).

For example, tongue protrusion is found in disgust across human cultures (see Rozin & Fallon, 1987; Smith, Chase, & Lieblich, 1974). The prevalence of protrusion is often taken to indicate a basis in phylogeny, but the display might develop ontogenetically through aversive conditioning and observational learning.

By analogous reasoning, Lewontin (1976) challenged forcefully the tenet that communality reflects heredity in human intelligence. He argued that cultural differences or communalities in intelligence reflect learning, whereas individual differences reflect heritability (see Figure 3.10). Applying Lewontin's critique reverses the usual assumptions about human facial displays. Plausibly, then, cross-cultural communalities such as tongue protrusion might reflect common learning, and what is heritable would be variations in protrusion among members of the culture, for example, how much one protrudes the tongue, and to what or to whom. This alternative reasoning is crucial in evaluating the cross-cultural studies of human "emotional" displays, as I emphasize later.

The Phenotypes of Extant Species Do Not Necessarily Inform about Phylogenesis   Comparing "higher" with "lower" organisms is often assumed to allow estimation of the genetic control of a display. Under this assumption, if a more "primitive" organism shows a display similar to that of a more "advanced" one, then the display of the "advanced" species is held to be genetically determined, even in the absence of intermediate species. Thus if prosimians grimace when threatened, and humans do as well, the "phylogenetic scale" argument is that the prosimian grimace is the evolutionary progenitor of the human's.

This argument typifies an outdated Spencerian evolution, which was

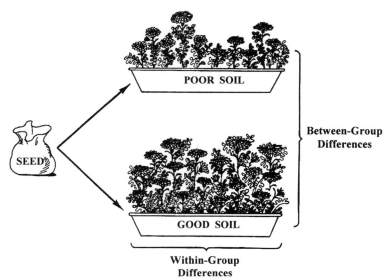

FIGURE 3.10.   Demonstration that within-group effects can result from genetic control, but those between populations can result from immediate environment. This illustration counters the common logic of cross-cultural facial-expression research, that facial "universals" must be "genetic." In fact, as the figure shows, facial universals may result from common learning, and any departures from such universals, whether between or within cultures, may be genotypic. After Lewontin (1976). Reprinted from *Psychology*, Third Edition by Henry Gleitman with the permission of W. W. Norton & Company, Inc. Copyright © 1991, 1986, 1981 by W. W. Norton & Company, Inc.

inexorably progressive and had humans (and specifically, native British males) as its apotheosis (Spencer, 1855).[3] This argument is flawed on several counts.

First, no evolutionary progenitors are alive today, only descendants of progenitors. In other words, all extant species are equally evolved, and none are transitional forms for any others. It might be objected that certain extant species appear to resemble hypothetical common stock more than do others. For example, prosimians seem to resemble our best guess about the "generic" original arboreal primate more than, say, humans or gorillas. Despite the closer resemblance, prosimians have had to adapt morphologically and behaviorally to their current niches, as have hominids to theirs. Consequently, there is no reason to consider

---

[3] Progressivist models of evolution all exemplify *orthogenesis*, the doctrine that there is some internal guiding force to evolution. Grant (1985) notes that the nature of the force has varied historically, from a tendency to greater complexity (Lamarck, 1809), to an impulse to reach God (Bergson, 1911; Teilhard de Chardin, 1959). As I mentioned earlier, modern natural selection is random and undirected (except, of course, by impermanent selection pressures).

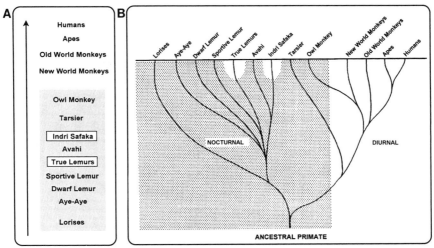

FIGURE 3.11.   Two views of evolution and their implications for humans. (A) Outdated (nineteenth-century) phylogenetic "scale" with humans as the apotheosis of natural selection; (B) contemporary phylogenetic "tree" with humans as one ramification of primate radiation. View B undercuts the progressivist ideology that nonhuman displays—or their brains, or emotions or motivations —are "primitive," whereas those of humans are "advanced," "more evolved," or "better adapted." Actually, all extant species are equally evolved. Primate radiation reprinted with permission from: Campbell, Bernard. *Evolution: An Introduction to Man's Adaptations*. 3rd Edition. (New York: Aldine de Gruyter) copyright © 1985 Bernard Campbell.

the social structure and display behavior of one to be a priori more "primitive," with one representing the "origin" for the other (see Figure 3.11). We will later extend the tree model in our discussion of the supposedly "primitive" human limbic system and its role in human interaction.

Second, comparing extant species to indicate phylogeny ignores the fact that similar displays among species may only be analogies (i.e., products of convergent evolution). Thus, ancestors may have had less similar displays than extant species.

Third, learning more than natural selection may have produced similar displays in both prosimians and humans. Such learning may have occurred through common shaping by the vicissitudes of survival, or via direct cultural transmission.

Note that this section discusses limits on inferring phylogenies from the *phenotypes* of extant species. As I discussed earlier, the genotypes of extant species can be compared to infer phylogeny, but the relatedness of any extant species to a progenitor does not imply that the species is more *primitive*.

When Is the Comparative Approach Useful?

It might seem that the comparative approach is too loose and inductive. Indeed, the molecular evolutionist would argue that amassing comparative data on bones (fresh or petrified) or behavior is just wild guessing, with its imprecision rendering it more art than science. But there is one way in which comparative data can be definitive. Phylogenesis is confirmed using the comparative approach when there is shared possession of a trait across or within species despite no obvious individual adaptive advantage. The existence of *vestiges*, then, provides an open-and-shut phylogenetic case. As I detailed earlier, discovering evolutionary vestiges was the tack Darwin took in *Expression*; he used his finding of "rudimentary, atrophied, or aborted organs" (Darwin, 1859, p. 255) to refute "argument from design" and substantiate the entire theory of natural selection (Ghiselin, 1969; Gould, 1980; Naylor, 1982).

In the case of displays, a behavior that exhibited no biological or communicative function would certainly not represent either learning or convergent evolution. It would, in effect, be a behavioral vestige. Like other vestiges (e.g., the degenerated stomach known as the human appendix; the temporary "gill slits" of mammalian embryos; male breasts; and, debatably, the female orgasm), such a behavior would imply common origins and paths of descent. The principle is simply stated: If two species show similar displays that are demonstrably advantageous to individuals in the first species but not in the second, then the display can be presumed vestigial in the second species and under genetic control in both.

Applying the comparative approach to behavior while mindful of this axiom is an uneviable task. The labyrinthine complexity of the situation might be illustrated best by proposing hypothetical experiments to evaluate genetic control of a simple facial display, the grimace.

Humans and a variety of apes and monkeys grimace, typically when they are in pain, or when they submit under threat. One might thus conclude that grimacing must be under genetic control. But is it? Not necessarily, because the communality might be explained as

1. common learning, wherein members of each species acquire the grimace through social shaping of reflexive teeth-baring, and/or
2. horizontal (cultural) transmission, in which members of each species learn the grimace anew each generation by imitating others.

Note that both explanations presume visual contact. Consequently, if grimacing were also seen in *nocturnal* primates, then genetic control and thus shared phylogeny would be supported. In other words, some primates would grimace without learning how. One would then have to survey nocturnal primates (e.g., prosimians like the Madagascar lemur,

FIGURE 3.12.   A sampling of contemporary primates, including a(n): (B) lemur; (C) tarsier; (D) Old World monkey; (E) chimpanzee; (F) Australian human. (A) is a tree shrew, an extant animal close in form to the probable progenitors of the primates. Reprinted with permission from Campbell, Bernard. *Human Evolution: An Introduction to Man's Adaptations*. 3rd Edition. (New York: Aldine de Gruyter) copyright © 1985 Bernard Campbell.

a few species of New World monkeys), and possibly arboreal primates (e.g., many Old World monkeys) whose visual displays are oftentimes obscured by dense foliage (see Figure 3.12).

But the shared phylogeny conclusion is still premature. One complication concerns whether grimacing found in arboreal or nocturnal monkeys is homologous with that observed in humans. As I noted concerning brow-knitting, homology properly derives from genealogy, and homomorphic behaviors are not necessarily homologous. Only comparisons of homologues allow estimates of genetic control. Analogous but not homologous grimacing would exist if the progenitors of humans and the stipulated species of monkey evolved grimacing by convergence *after* branching from a diurnal common progenitor, but before the extant monkey species became nocturnal. The obverse case of homologous but dissimilar actions would exist if, as in my account of brow-knitting, evolutionary trends in craniofacial anatomy displaced muscles and thereby altered facial action in one or both of the species.

Even if we found a grimacing nocturnal monkey, we are still not out of the woods (or savannah). Grimacing has thus far been cast as a *visual* display. A crucial complexity is that the grimace's function may be fundamentally *auditory* (see discussion of the smile and the grimace in Chapter 12). In most nonhumans, it accompanies high-pitched vocalization. I believe that it coevolved to optimize the conformation of the vocal tract (also see Chapter 12). If so, the grimace's occurrence in nocturnal or arboreal species (which depend heavily on auditory communications) would not itself imply genetic control. Rather, the definitive test would then require discovery of nocturnal or arboreal species that grimaced without vocalization. If no such species were found, then comparative study could not resolve the issue.

There is a final—and fatal—glitch in our attempt to rescue a shared phylogeny argument. If no displays homologous to the human grimace were found among nonhumans whose craniofacial anatomies permitted, then genetic control of human grimacing would still be indeterminate, because nonhuman species may have evolved such that they *lost* the grimace (this would be *divergent evolution*). And the obverse holds as well: even if one manages directly to show genetic control of a display, this does not imply that the display is shared with any other extant species. This must be verified separately. Propositional speech is such a case; it is probably under substantial genetic control, yet so far it seems uniquely human (Premack, 1985).

Although cross-species comparisons of displays are vexed by differences in craniofacial anatomy, shared displays with no conceivable adaptive advantage can sometimes be found *within* a species. For example, one can study congenitally blind human infants, who are for practical purposes absolutely "nocturnal," at least insofar as they react to others. The presence of social grimacing in the congenitally blind infant would be consistent with the genetic control of grimacing. This strategy is the experiment-of-nature analog of acoustic isolation studies of birdsong acquisition. These elegant studies, pioneered by the zoologist Peter Marler (Marler, 1970, 1991), showed that sparrows could produce their species-typical song even with no exposure to it.

I know of only one primate experiment that approximated Marler's isolation studies. Sackett (1966) studied four male and four female rhesus monkeys (*Macaca mulatta*) from 14 days to 9 months of age. The monkeys had been housed from birth in special cages that were covered except for their front wire panels, and thus during rearing they never saw another monkey. The cages were special in one other way: their back walls were actually frosted rear-projection screens. When the monkeys were 14 days old, Sackett began supplying the monkeys, and on other trials allowed them to supply themselves, with brief exposures of a series of color slides of adult and other infant monkeys engaged in various activities, including a threatening adult.

The monkeys responded much more to slides of "threatening" adult and infant monkeys than to slides either of monkeys exploring, playing, sexing, or of humans or nonsense patterns. Slides of the threatening and the playing adult elicited both greater exploration and heightened activity (measured by wall-climbing) throughout the study. When the monkeys were 2–3 months of age, however, vocalizations and "disturbance" (e.g., rocking, huddling, self-clasping, "fear," and withdrawal) increased dramatically to the depicted threat. For our purposes, the question is whether the depicted "threat display" (in this study, the slide showed an adult standing erect with a wide mouth and bared teeth) *was* innately threatening. This would suggest a genetic basis for receptivity to the display, and possibly (assuming coevolution) the display itself. Sackett answered affirmatively:

> At least two kinds of meaningful visual stimuli, pictures of monkeys threatening and pictures of infants, appear to have unlearned, prepotent, activating properties for socially naive infant monkeys . . . Second, the visual stimulation involved in threat behavior appears to function as an "innate releasing stimulus" for fearful behavior. (Sackett, 1966, p. 1473)

Unfortunately, the details of the experiment and the results leave me less enthusiastic about Sackett's conclusion. The main problem with Sackett's interpretation is that it is unclear whether the threat slide *was* interpreted correctly. True, exposure to it produced more "disturbance," but it also produced more exploration and play, even more than the slide of the infant. If the monkey innately understood a threat display, responding in this way would be unexpected. The second issue concerns the isolation. The monkeys were hand-fed by humans for the first 5–9 days of life, affording ample opportunity for neonatal imitation of their presumably smiling caretakers (cf. Meltzoff & Moore, 1977), and the association of bared teeth with caretaking and nutrition. More crucially, although the monkeys had no visual contact with other monkeys, no soundproofing was employed and thus they could readily hear the sounds of other monkeys in the colony. It seems exceedingly "visuocentric" to label as isolates monkeys who were in relatively complete auditory contact and who naturally communicate via auditory displays. Bared-teeth screams, and the commotion that accompanies them, can run rampant throughout a housed colony with just a little provocation, and it is difficult to imagine that the visual isolates refrained from getting in on the action. It is worth considering, then, whether the isolates could identify the stance and face of the threatening adult with the movements *they* make during a teeth-baring scream. This shouldn't be hard for a creature so adept at mimicry—a possibility that could have been excluded with both visual *and* auditory isolation.

The importance of audition leads to an obvious complication in the human analog of Marler's isolation studies, the study of congenitally blind human infants. They typically have sighted caretakers, who may reinforce the child for socially appropriate displays. Differential reinforcement of the displays in question would have to be excluded; blind children of blind caretakers are a better (albeit improbable) test. And even blind caretakers might shape some displays in blind children using *auditory* cues. For example, smiles in social play would probably be elicited adventitiously through the shaping of high-pitched "play" utterances (a smile shortens and flattens the vocal tract and makes it more suited to shrieks and screams). The astuteness of congenitally blind children given auditory training should not be underestimated; they learn spoken language as well and as quickly as sighted children, even words relating to vision like *look* and *see* (cf. Landau & Gleitman, 1985). I discuss evidence from studies of congenitally blind infants in a later section.

Because shared behavior can easily be explained by adaptive learning within species, and by convergence across them, the comparative approach is better suited to the study of morphological than behavioral traits. This is a lesson which could have been heeded better when the major cross-cultural studies of "facial expressions of emotion" were conducted in the 1960's. The interpretive quagmire presented by these data was predictable, as will become clear later in this volume.

WHY GENETIC CONTROL AND LEARNING
ARE NOT DICHOTOMOUS

Asking whether a facial display is innate ("genetic") or learned is woefully oversimplified. It is true that some animals may indeed enter the world with the natural competence to enact their species-typical displays. This natural competence may extend to the apperception and reaction to displays of both their own species and other ecologically relevant species. This is the purely nativist position. On the expressive end, it accords with the early Lorenz-Tinbergen ethology; it is Gibsonian on the receiving side. It may apply to the display repertoires of many animals such as invertebrates, insects, and some reptiles and birds.

But the mistake is to believe that the nativist position exhausts the role of genetics. Any learning or mimicry must rely on a genetic complement that either facilitates or mitigates it, or dictates its contours. This kind of interactive role was demonstrated most persuasively in Marler's studies of song acquisition in acoustically isolated sparrows.

Earlier I mentioned that Marler's isolated sparrows eventually produced their species-typical song. This fact certainly attests to a natural competence for the production of birdsong. However, there was more to the story, as Marler (1991) details. The songs which the isolates produced were simpler and devoid of the embellishments that define a normal adult "dialect." Producing a honed adult song required just a brief exposure to a live tutor. And the best tutelage was provided by an adult of the individuals' own species. When given the choice, the birds preferred learning the adult songs of conspecifics rather than those of other, closely related species. These findings imply yet another natural competence, a "vocal template" that recognizes the preferred songs to mimic, those of conspecifics. Even stronger evidence for such a receptive template came from studies of deafened sparrows—those isolated from even their *own* songs. These sparrows produced only the rudiments of song, indicating that the receptive template is a target which they try to match in their self-guided singing lessons.

These kinds of findings demonstrate the principle that displays may be learned or not learned, to a greater or lesser extent, in one form but not another, depending upon one's innate competences. These competences may be substantive, with individuals producing and understanding displays as part of maturation. Alternatively, the competences may be procedural, such that individuals innately know how to *learn* the right displays to produce and to understand (see Cosmides & Tooby, in press).

So far I've presented the genetic control of learnability as nomethetic, that is, as a species characteristic. But even within a species, individuals whose genotypes are conducive to learning certain categories or topographies (e.g., amplitudes or durations) of displays may differentially reproduce depending on the added fitness the displays confer. This "heritability of learnability"[4] has direct implications for the so-called "cross-cultural" studies of human faces, as I discuss later.

---

[4] The interaction of genetics and learning have received wide attention. The genetic control of learnability was discussed by James Mark Baldwin (1895, 1896), and Simpson (1953) and later Smith (1985) termed it the *Baldwin Effect*. Baldwin's genetic control of learnability is well established in modern evolutionary theory. Eibl-Eibesfeldt (1970) provided dozens of examples from classical ethology of the "innate disposition to learn." The Baldwin Effect was resurrected by Seligman (1970), whose "preparedness" was a propensity to acquire simple phobias with aversive conditioning. Gould and Marler (1987) and Marler (1991) provided evidence (some mentioned here) consistent with "instincts to learn." The heritability of learnability was demonstrated as early as the 1930s by Heron (1935) and Tryon (1942), who interbred rats to obtain strains that were atypically good or bad at running mazes, and by Dudai and Quinn (1980), who bred strains of *Drosophila* that either could not learn, or learned but forgot fast.

Even after one has surmised that a particular display is under genetic control and is thus one facet of a species' phylogenesis, there remains the question of how the display arose. More precisely, there is still the question of the selection pressures that caused the display's evolution. Next, I discuss the predominant mechanisms by which displays are thought to arise, those of signal ritualization and conventionalization.

4

MECHANISMS FOR THE EVOLUTION OF FACIAL EXPRESSIONS

DISPLAYS AS HYPERTROPHIED BEHAVIOR

Many of the faces we humans make are like the interjections in our speech; they are easily noticed by those around us. Human facial displays are thus like all animal signals; they are dramatic and seem optimized for signal value. The threatening cat piloerects, arches its back, and issues a hiss that would stop most interlopers dead in their tracks. The male songbird issues unmistakable calls from its arboreal perch. The human female, upon seeing an attractive male, averts her gaze coyly and strokes her hair (and he may have straightened his posture and pulled up his socks . . .). The monkey grimaces and screeches when attacked. The honeybee starts a complicated "waggle" dance on its return to the hive. These acts serve no direct biological function, but every animal produces them:

> These unusually conspicuous, even bizarre, stereotyped patterns are not actions in which food is physically uncovered, prey seized or torn asunder, or opponents or predators pushed away or beaten back. Instead they occur as animals interact, as they court, dispute over territories, or defer to or dominate one another, for example. The performing individuals are usually not dealing with other participants by physical force when they do these stereotyped acts; if one is performed and the performer's opponent withdraws it is not because he was pushed away—he elects to leave under his own steam. (Smith, 1977, p. 7)

How can we explain these odd histrionics?

One clue about these kinds of acts came, oddly enough, from observations not of behavior but of morphology. It had long struck naturalists that many animals (humans included) seemed to show the exaggerated development of certain adaptive structures, with the exaggeration merely "for show."

These exaggerated features were not gratuitous or neutral; they often appeared to handicap or even cripple normal function. Elk males fight head to head, but they develop giant antlers that are nutritional burdens and entangling impediments. Male fiddler crabs seize food with their claws, but one chela (claw), used mainly for waving, is so hypertrophied that it accounts for nearly one-third the crab's total weight. Bird feathers retain heat and aid flight, but male birds often show wayward tufts of feathers and tail feathers so long that flight is retarded. And human males, like most mammalian males, use their muscles to obtain food but have an enhanced stature and bulkier musculature whose cardiovascular load probably shortens their life spans. Figure 4.1 depicts some of these exaggerated structures.

Darwin was fascinated by these exaggerations of normally adaptive structures. In *The Descent of Man* (1871), he concluded that these mor-

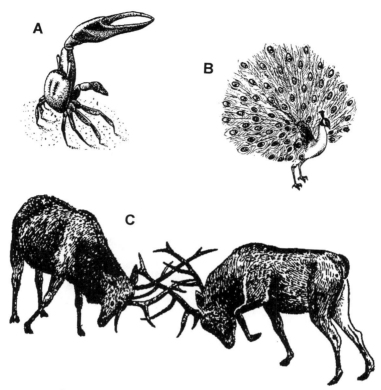

FIGURE 4.1.   Ornamental structures arising from sexual selection: (A) The fiddler crab (*Uca lactea*) with its hypertrophied chela (claw), whose size seems only for show; (B) the peacock (*Pavo*), beautifully piloerected; (C) red deer (*Cervus elaphus scoticus*) in antler-to-antler combat. Illustrations: fiddler crab and red deer from Tinbergen, 1953; peacock from Krebs and Davies, 1987.

phological caricatures were ornamental "symbols" resulting from sexual selection:

> There are many other structures and instincts which must have been developed through sexual selection—such as the weapons of offence and the means of defence—of the males for fighting with and driving away their rivals—their courage and pugnacity—their various ornaments—their contrivances for producing vocal or instrumental music—and their glands for emitting odors, most of these latter structures serving only to allure or excite the female . . . When we behold two males fighting for the possession of the female, or several male birds displaying their gorgeous plumage, and performing strange antics before an assembled body of females, we cannot doubt that, though led by instinct, they know what they are about, and consciously exert their mental and bodily powers. (p. 214)

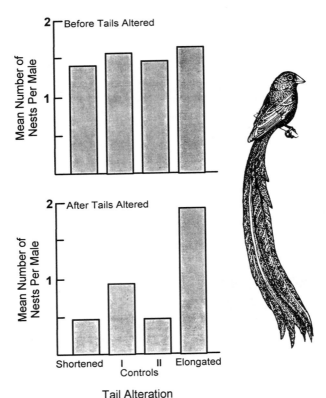

Tail Alteration

FIGURE 4.2.   Demonstration of artificial sexual selection in long-tailed widow birds (*Euplectes progne*) from Kenya (Andersson, 1982). Males normally have tails about 50 cm long. Compared to controls, nests in the birds' territories (an index of mating success) were more numerous when the birds had their tails artificially elongated, and fewer when the tails were shortened. Control I birds were untouched, whereas Control II birds had their own tails cut and reattached. Females apparently favored the supranormal tails, a preference that probably accounts for the long normal tail. Illustration adapted from Krebs and Davies, 1987.

Thus if deer antlers are for fighting, then for the deer female bigger antlers must predict better fighting, and the particularly well-endowed male is a better catch (he would be a better protector, provider, and her offspring would be more vigorous). Darwin's notion of morphological caricature as ornamentation was formalized by R. A. Fisher (1930), and placed in a population genetic model by Lande (1981). The success of the ornamental characteristics is easily demonstrated (Figure 4.2). That the exaggeration may "run amok" and become disadvantageous was discussed by Zahavi (1975, 1977), who argued that a little dysfunction goes

FIGURE 4.3.   Exaggerated behavior ritualized for display: (A) Female head-scooping during courtship feeding in the herring gull *Larus argentatus* (from Tinbergen, 1953); (B) threat posturing and piloerection in the domestic cat, *Felis domesticus* (from Darwin, 1871).

a long way: females may select males who *are* handicapped by their ornaments, because their thriving in the face of a handicap is especially prognostic.

But our interest here is in behavioral caricatures. If signals could be fashioned from the ornamental exaggeration of functional structures, could they also be fashioned from the exaggeration of *behavior*? Even the earliest investigators of displays were struck by their resemblance to the normal behavior accompanying acts like consumation or predation. For example, the tooth-baring of a threatening feline closely resembles that exhibited by an attacking one; the only difference is that the threat behavior is literally for show (Figure 4.3). It gives the other the option to escape. Similarly, a female herring gull repeatedly tosses or "scoops" its head upward when it wants to be fed by a courting male (e.g., Tinbergen, 1953); the female's movements seem to caricature how a juvenile strokes its mother's neck to make her regurgitate food (the young eat the vomitus). Again, the scooping movements are for show, because all the female is scooping is air (also Figure 4.3).

Associationist Accounts of Displays

The initial attempt to understand the formation of displays was associationist. Spencer (1855) believed that displays were overlearned habits that became "organic," that is, prewired in the nervous system through use-inheritance (i.e., Lamarckian transmission). Spencer called the elicitation of a display the "nascent excitation of psychical state," and it was strictly predicated upon contiguity:

> That the propensities to the acts are nothing else than nascent excitations of the psychical state involved in the acts, is proved by the natural language of the propensities. Fear, when strong, expresses itself in cries, in efforts to escape, in palpitations, in tremblings; and these are just the manifestations that go along with an actual suffering of the evil feared. The destructive passion is shown in a general tension of the muscular system, in gnashing of teeth and protrusion of the claws, in dilated eyes and nostrils, in growls; and these are weaker forms of the actions that accompany the killing of prey. (p. 231)

The pairing of teeth-baring with attack stamped in teeth-baring as a habit evoked when one was provoked. As I discussed in Chapter 2, Darwin (1872) appropriated Spencer's view as his *Principle of Serviceable Associated Habits*. Darwin's endorsement made the account popular; James (1890) called the same mechanism the "revival in weakened form of reactions useful in more violent dealings with the object inspiring the emotion" (p. 1092).

There are some obvious predictions from this associationist account, and the hypothetical teeth-baring display is a ready example. The display should occur only among those animals that attacked the most and which therefore had sufficient conditioning trials, *and* who lived through enough fights to have offspring and bequeath the habit (conversely, the animals who ducked fights or lost them after attacking would be much less likely to develop the habit or pass it on). After the formation of the habit by the animal (or via use-inheritance from its progenitors), teeth-baring would initially occur independent of whether or not an actual attack ensued. Indeed, over repeated provocations—whether over one lifetime or several generations—the habit should *extinguish* if it successfully deterred attack. The larger prediction, then, is that, in the absence of frank attack requiring flesh-biting, all such displays could only be vestigial. This was Darwin's conclusion, and it was a problematic one given the abrogation of Lamarckian inheritance, not to mention the panspecific existence of threat displays, and their readily observable operation as deterrents to aggression.

Selectionist Accounts of Displays

The modern selectionist account of the origins of display behavior began with efforts to formulate taxonomies for behavioral repertoires, in the tradition of species taxonomies. Two of the major figures in this early effort were Oskar Heinroth, who studied ducks and geese, and Julian Huxley, who observed the diving bird known as the great crested grebe. Heinroth (1911) found, for example, that greylag geese vocalized in one way when related members were about to walk or fly as a family, and in another just before merely walking rapidly. Because these "about-to-fly-together-as-family" and "about-to-walk" movements were often fractionated, and reliably preceded complete acts, Heinroth termed them *intention movements*.[1] Huxley (1914) detailed the grebe's complex postures and water "dances"; he suggested *display* to describe the stereotyped movements he observed. Lorenz (e.g., 1970) made numerous observations of acts (which he called *fixed action patterns*) that served as signals.

The ethologist Niko Tinbergen (e.g., 1952) is usually credited with finally forging the link between display behavior and the morphological caricatures we discussed earlier. He proposed that, like ornamental features, behavior itself could evolve for its signal value, and it did so by exhibiting the twin qualities of "conspicuousness" and "simplicity" (Tinbergen, 1953, p. 85). The behavior, in other words, became schematized or "ritualized" (after Huxley, 1923; and see Huxley, 1966), perhaps to the extent that it no longer served its original biological function (Tinbergen, 1952). Tinbergen called this *emancipation*.

The ways that ritualized behavior can become "simple" and "conspicuous" are manifold, and they include exaggeration of amplitude; lowering of the threshold for "release"; rhythmic repetition; aggregation or fusion of movements; a "freezing" of specific movements into static postures; and a coordinated morphological development that emphasizes the behavior, such as the lengthening of a tail to emphasize wagging, or the development of a mane to highlight neck movements (Eibl-Eibesfeldt, 1979, pp. 100–101).

Display modalities, topographies, and kinetics vary widely across species. Nonprimate displays may involve relatively gross body movement (e.g., tail-wagging), posturing (e.g., elevation or lowering of head), autonomic signs (e.g., piloerection and presentation of plumage, pupillary contractions, scent production), vocalization, gaze, and even electric or magnetic field emission (e.g., sharks and some eels). Discriminable *facial* displays occur in nonprimates. Examples include the open mouth, with or without baring of teeth, seen in reptiles (Andrew, 1964);

---

[1] I discern two definitions of "intention movement" in the ethology literature. The most common owes to Daanje (1950), who employed the term to refer to incipient, partial acts that predicted full-scale action (e.g., wing-flapping preceding flight). In the other definition, derived from Spencer (1855), Darwin (1872), and Heinroth (1911), an intention movement is behavior typically associated with an act, emitted while intending to (or about to) commit the act. The former definition is more restrictive than the latter, because it requires the behavior to be only a fragment of a serviceable act. In contrast, the Spencer–Darwin–Heinroth formulation includes acts that may occur by force of habit even though they are not fragmentary. Thus, deploying a smile while intending to affiliate would be considered an intention movement by the latter definition but not by the former. I employ the latter definition throughout.

Note that "intention" in this context refers to the function or "aboutness" of an act (see Dennett, 1987), not to the usual psychological definition, that is, a promise or stated purpose. By this definition, neither humans nor nonhumans have to *know* what they intend. Discussions of the issue of intentionality in human and nonhuman signaling are provided by Bekoff and Allen (1992), and Hauser and Nelson (1991).

and the teeth-baring and flattening of ears in threat or startle, seen in most mammals (Andrew, 1963a,b; Redican, 1982). Miller (1975) has shown evidence for discriminable facial displays for greeting, grooming, submission, and threat, in fur seals and walruses.

Primate displays can be facial, vocal, postural-gestural, tactile, or olfactory. Despite demonstrations of subliminal olfactory phenomena such as menstrual synchrony (McClintock, 1971), natural olfactory signals are not yet confirmed in humans (Stoddart, 1980). Many primates show a variety of highly differentiated facial displays, including apes and both New World and Old World monkeys (e.g., Kirkevold, Lockard, & Heestand, 1982; Marriott & Salzen, 1978; Van Hooff, 1969, 1972, 1976; Van Lawick-Goodall, 1971; Weigel, 1979; for reviews, see Chevalier-Skolnikoff, 1973; and Redican, 1982).

At present, students of primate facial behavior must operate like the early comparative anatomists, amassing observations, making inductions about communalities, and then exercising their intuitions about which displays are homologous or analogous. Researchers have generally argued for a few cases of homology among humans and other primates. Among those in Redican's (1982) summary are the: (1) grimace, or "silent bared-teeth face" (van Hooff, 1969, cf. human "fear" or "surprise" faces); (2) tense-mouth display, wherein the lips are compressed and drawn slightly inward (cf. human "anger" faces); and (3) play face, in which the mouth is opened wide with the lip corners barely retracted (cf. the human amusement smile). These are all educated guesses, and whether they are accurate will ultimately be decided with genetic comparisons. In the meantime, the precision of the guesses will be improved using quantitative coding systems for nonhuman facial displays; these are of increasing interest in primatology. Note, however, that cross-species comparisons of even quantified displays are vexed by uncertainties about which *muscles* comprising the displays in one species are homologous with those of another. As in morphological comparisons, even wholly similar displays can just be analogies.

I must close this section with a word about the Lorenz–Tinbergen view of behavior, as extended in Tinbergen's work on displays. This view is frequently considered synonymous with "ethology," but this is as mistaken as equating Russian reflexology with psychology. The Lorenz–Tinbergen view was valuable in resurrecting the topic of instinct, revitalizing evolutionary inquiries, and in acquainting many with the newfangled idea that nonhuman screeches, grunts, and wails were social *signals* rather than chaotic eruptions. Unfortunately—and I touched on this in the last chapter—their view was rigid and mechanistic, and it produced a needless chasm between ethologists and their potential collaborators in psychology and sociology. Displays were a kind of fixed action pattern, and the responses of the recipients were

just as fixed. Societies, whether nonhuman or human, were mechanisms themselves, like bee hives or ant colonies, with social interactions
largely a set of stereotyped instinctual dances. Both Lorenz and Tinbergen gave some weight to learning as a modifier of instinct, but the
"release" of innate patterns clearly held sway, and culture had little
formative power:

> So far as our present knowledge goes, social cooperation seems to
> depend mainly on a system of releasers. The tendency of the actor to give
> these signals is innate, and the reactor's responses are likewise innate.
> We see therefore that a community functions as a result of the proper-
> ties of its members. Each member has the tendency to perform the signal
> movements releasing the 'correct' responses in the reactor; each member
> has specific capacities that render it sensitive to the species' signals. In this
> sense the community is determined by the individuals. (Tinbergen, 1953,
> pp. 85–86)

Lorenz and Tinbergen could not have known of the context sensitivity or the syntactic and semantic complexity of so much nonhuman
and human display behavior. Moreover, their Helmholtzian training
outfit them to see stereotypy rather than variation, and mechanism rather than dynamic interaction. It is as though one concluded that human
behavior was like an ant colony's after studying passenger traffic on the
New York subways. People traverse the same routes daily, and this
makes for "stereotypy." But microsocially, riders pick different cars, talk
or don't talk to different people, and when they talk, they have conversations about many different things. Likewise, animals emit alarm calls
when threatened, and the calls seem stereotyped, but microsocially, the
calls are directed mainly to kin, and may be specific to the type of threat.
Moreover, the displays of both humans and nonhumans are often quite
plastic and modifiable with just a little experience. Suffice it to say that
the Lorenz–Tinbergen mechanistic view is now outdated ethology, and
contemporary ethologists now regard nonhumans and humans as more
than reflexive automatons, and culture as formative in its own right.

W. John Smith (1977) was one of the first ethologists to suggest replacing the Lorenz–Tinbergen model with an interactive, informational one.
Smith extended Tinbergen's conceptions of behavioral schematization to
include signals shaped not only by natural selection (i.e., those that are
ritualized; e.g., species communalities in birdsong), but also by learning
(Smith called these signals *conventionalized*; e.g., regional dialects in birdsong, learned during critical periods). All signals, whether ritualized or
conventionalized, are said to be *formalized* for display.[2] As we will dis-

[2] The Lamarckism of Spencer and Darwin is now untenable, thus the conceptual distinction between
ritualization and *conventionalization*. However, it is likely that genes that promoted conventionalizing
would proliferate, thereby causing their organisms to be rapid learners of signal systems (Rozin &
Schull, 1988).

cover later, discovering which human facial displays (or which components of them) are ritualized, versus which are conventionalized, has been one of the major questions confronting facial "expression" researchers.

DISPLAYS AS FORMALIZED INTENTION MOVEMENTS

What behavior becomes formalized for visible display? Displays probably do not originate randomly. Rather, they are elaborations upon two types of movements, social instrumental habits and protective reflexes. I discuss protective reflexes in Chapter 6.

The social instrumental habits best preadapted for display would be those behaviors likely to be made in the course of overt action toward others. As I mentioned earlier, Heinroth's *intention movement* concept was predicated upon observations that many displays were fractionations of whole acts that preceded those acts. Heinroth's concept has endured because in many cases it is self-evident, and not just in birds. A bird may peck grass just before it pecks at another bird, and it may flap its wings ineffectually just before it takes off. Similarly, we may yell at the dog just before we argue with a friend, and we may make repeated "leaving" motions just before we end a conversation. The incipient acts we emit just before we act in earnest announce our intentions.

Intention movements have been widely studied in birds (e.g., Daanje, 1950; Smith, 1977). Compelling intention-movement accounts have been offered of various avian precopulatory, aggressive, and territorial-defense displays. Many accounts of primate displays as intention movements have also been proposed (for conjectures on evolutionary origins, see Andrew, 1963a,b, 1964, 1972; Chevalier-Skolnikoff, 1973; Hinde, 1966; and Redican, 1982). As a human example, lip retraction and teeth-baring during aggression may be intention movements given that biting is often part of a full-blown attack (pulling the lips away from one's teeth protects them during a bite). Goldenthal, Johnston, and Kraut (1981), and Fridlund, Sabini, Hedlund, Schaut, Shenker, and Knauer (1990) argued for the intention-movement view of the human smile as a signal of readiness to play, affiliate, or appease (see Chapter 12 for speculation on evolutionary origins of signals such as smiling).

Modern intention-movement accounts of display differ fundamentally from the original Darwinian associationist account. In the former, displays derive directly from the partial commission of instrumental acts; in the latter, displays arise by virtue of association with the *emotions* held to cause or at least accompany the acts. This distinction will be crucial in our new understanding of the nature of so-called "facial expressions of emotion," which I discuss later in this volume.

Hypertrophy of Vigilance for Displays

Most early ethological accounts of signal systems focused on formalization of *behavior*. These accounts were incomplete because they ignored its complement, the "hypertrophied," schematized behavior of *observers*. The inattention to "receiver psychology" probably compromised our understanding of the "design" of ritualized signals (Guilford & Dawkins, 1991), and perpetuated a one-sided, adynamic view of social interaction. In the human, this hypertrophied vigilance for displays may express itself as "empathy" or "interpersonal sensitivity" (Brothers, 1989, 1990). It is a special attention to displays because they are useful in predicting others' actions.

Vigilance for displays probably evolved in three ways: in *sensitivity* to displays, in *selectivity* about particular display components, and in *skepticism* about the meaning of a display. This is because a vigilant animal must discern useful information in the presence of noise (i.e., spurious, uninformative behavior) and deception. There is evidence for each.

Sensitivity: Receptive/Perceptual Attunement

Many animals show special sensitivities to salient displays. Facial perception and discrimination of facial features may be quite specialized in nonhuman primates (Rosenfeld & Van Hoesen, 1979). Humans are certainly capable of decoding complex multivariate relationships when the variables are presented as facial features (see Figure 4.4).

Recent electrophysiological evidence from single-unit recording has demonstrated neocortical and paleocortical cells sensitive to still photographs of one's species's face; they have been isolated in several kinds of animals, including monkeys (Bruce, Desimone, & Gross, 1981; Gross, Rocha-Miranda, & Bender, 1972; Perrett, Rolls, & Caan, 1982), sheep (Kendrick & Baldwin, 1987), and probably humans (Fried, Mateer, Ojemann, Wohns, & Fedio, 1982; Heit, Smith, & Halgren, 1988). The most systematic "face cell" studies have used rhesus macaque monkeys, and there are reports of cells that respond selectively to head orientation (Perrett, Smith, Mistlin, et al., 1985a), gaze direction (Perrett, Smith, Potter, et al., 1985b), the identity of the face (Perrett, Mistlin, & Chitty, 1987), and certain facial displays (Brothers, 1992; Hasselmo, Rolls, & Baylis, 1986).

Seeing a face *in toto* depends upon a visual scan pattern that traverses the critical features of the face. Early on, human infants develop relatively fixed visual scan patterns when they apperceive live human faces. As Figure 4.5 shows, the visual scans repeatedly traverse probably the most informative sections of the face, the eyes, and mouth (see Keating

FIGURE 4.4.   The mathematician Herman Chernoff (1973) exploited our ability to decode complex information from facial features when he first used cartoon faces to represent multivariate data. "Chernoff Faces" have proven themselves quite effective (Wilkinson, 1982). The ones shown here (adapted from Systat, Inc., 1992) depict the population densities, and the property and personal crimes of six New England states, with the three variables respresented, respectively, as: (1) the curvature of the mouth; (2) the angle of the brows; and (3) the width of the nose. Like the physiognomists who divined character from morphology, or emotion researchers who divine "basic emotions" from facial muscular actions, experienced Chernoff Face users report that they "see" their favorite variables in these iconized faces.

& Keating, 1982; Maurer & Salapatek, 1976). Because this scan pattern orients the infant to the caretaker's paralinguistic facial movements, it may be crucial for the timely acquisition of speech comprehension and production (Locke, 1992; and see Chapter 12).

It is tempting to posit phyletic bases for all of these findings, but this would be presumptive. It is wholly unclear whether these studies of neuronal trigger features or visual scan patterns actually represent innate "Gibsonian" faculties or just early imprinting on salient stimuli. Certainly neurons in the visual system are quite plastic, and attune themselves to critical features in the visual field (e.g., Held & Hein, 1963; Movshon & van Sluyters, 1981; Yoon, 1979). There may certainly be "face cells," but there may also be "areola cells" that arise from feeding, or "baby bottle" cells in bottle-fed humans or lab animals. Indeed, human infants may develop "Big Bird cells" from early exposure to "Sesame Street." One study found face cells in infant monkeys (Rodman, Skelly, & Gross, 1991), but these were not neonates or isolates. Of course, that such cells may be seen early does not exclude the possibility of a native

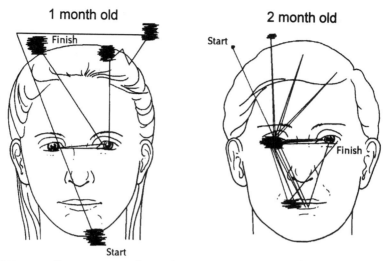

FIGURE 4.5.   Scan patterns shown by 1- and 2-month-old human infants to live faces. By two months of age, scanning traverses what are arguably the most salient regions of the face, the eyes and mouth. Reprinted with permission from Salapatek, 1975.

propensity to acquire them, perhaps during critical periods of exposure.

Because most of the face cell studies used photographed stills of faces, it is uncertain whether such cells are sensitive to dynamic displays as they occur in everyday interaction. Finding them is likely, given frequent reports of certain cells responsive to specific animate motions like hand movements and hand–object manipulation (see Brothers, 1992, for review). Resolving the issue will require the use of real-time facial displays, and recordings from neonates whenever possible and ethically defensible. Findings of "face cells" in *nocturnal* primates would provide especially strong phyletic evidence. Similar comments apply to the scan pattern studies, although real faces were used in several of the studies.

Other cautions apply to the "face cell" and scan pattern findings. Findings from clinical and experimental neuropsychology suggest overall that there is nothing special about face perception. In the rare but much-publicized deficit in face perception known as *prosopagnosia*, disruptions in face perception are but one sign of extensive defects in recognition of many familiar objects, such as animals, makes of automobiles, and buildings (Damasio, Damasio, & Van Hoesen, 1982). In lieu of dedicated processing mechanisms for faces, many have argued that humans' acuity in face perception just reflects our adeptness in perceiving complex visual figures (Kolb & Whishaw, 1990, p. 241). The converse must also be considered, however—that a selected-for capability for understanding faces led to our incidental adeptness at decoding *Ge-*

stalten of all types (e.g., Brothers & Ring, 1992). This alternative might be decided by examining the relative ease of neonatal learning of faces relative to other *Gestalten* when the visual environment is tightly controlled.

One might also wonder if these "face cell" findings are in any way surprising. When Hubel and Wiesel (e.g., 1962) posited the existence of "Grandmother" cells in the visual system, they merely meant that if *we* can identify Grandma, then there must be a cell that does the identifying. Similarly, if *we* can respond to a particular face, then we must also have a "cell"[3] that does so. Seen in these terms, the discovery of "face cells" is not surprising but altogether prosaic. I would also anticipate "dance cells" in honeybees and "sex skin" receptors in rhesus monkeys. It *will* be exciting if these face cells are shown to be innately responsive, topographically fixed, and functionally immutable.

Finally, "face cells" are typically thought to "identify" faces. The previous discussion of "Grandmother" cells assumed this. But the cells may not identify faces so much as indicate what we do when we see a face, that is, prepare oneself to interact. For example, before their "face cell" work, Rolls and his colleagues found "food cells" in the lateral hypothalamus that responded specifically to foodstuffs, but only when the animal was food deprived (Mora, Rolls, & Burton, 1976; Rolls, 1978). Do these cells "identify" food? If so, then they accord to the lateral hypothalamus a new role in visual perception. What is more likely is that "food cells" fire when feeding is initiated, and of course feeding can only occur amid an already-perceived food. Just so the "face cells." Their firing may simply be a correlate of the readiness for face-to-face interaction which, naturally, requires an already-apprehended face.

Selectivity: Cognitive Templates for Display Detection

Whether animals develop cognitive "templates" attuned to specific signal properties of salient displays is a pivotal issue. There is no doubting the existence of templates for morphological features—the classical ethologists furnished a panoply of vivid examples of behavior "released" by specific "sign stimuli" (cf. Eibl-Eibesfeldt, 1970). One human morphological template may be the classic and much-researched preference for juvenescent features noted by Lorenz (1970, and see the oft-reprinted Figure 4.6).

But behavioral displays are different. How does an animal parse the behavioral stream such that it "knows" when another is displaying? The problem may be more clearly stated in human terms. When we have dinner with a friend, we can readily tell when the friend has "made a

[3] The "cell" may of course be a cell ensemble, or just the final common pathway for an ensemble.

FIGURE 4.6.   Comparison of juvenile and adult forms of various animals. Most humans avow a preference for the juvenile form which, as Lorenz suggested, indicates an Innate Releasing Mechanism for caretaking. From Lorenz, 1970; reprinted by permission of Harvard University Press.

face" even though her facial muscles form a nonstop stream of movements from talking, biting, chewing, smelling, and breathing. How is it that her "expression" stands out in relief? Peter Marler, one of the pioneers in attacking this problem, stated it well:

> The means by which organisms achieve satisfactory classifications of things happening around them seem to me, as a biologist, to be utterly mysterious. How is it that even young organisms manage to strike an exquisite balance between taking careful account of fine variations on the one hand, and somehow also overlooking much of the variation and focussing on the invariant properties of diverse experiences? How do young children learn both to classify faces as male or female, old or young, while still being able to distinguish Uncle Joe's face from that of Uncle Harry for example? To over-stress variation in this process of perceptual classification would mean indulging in an orgy of splitting, treating every experience as unique, and leasding inexorably to a classification of the world that

would consist of an infinite number of virtually monotypic categories. (Marler, 1982, p. 87)

This is, in different form, the question asked by linguists who wish to know how the features of spoken language are decoded so quickly and accurately even though there are few gaps or silences demarcating speech units (cf. Foulke & Sticht, 1969). In a sense, there *must* be such templates that parse the behavioral stream into "natural categories," whether they are, to take a few modalities, auditory (e.g., a word like "antidisestablishmentarianism"), olfactory ("*my* teat"), electromagnetic ("attacking manta ray"), or visual (e.g., a "threat face").

Discerning the "natural categories" for perceiving displays (i.e., the nature of the templates) is for now a problem of induction, but the initial results are very promising. Most of this work has concerned birdsong, and it suggests ways to investigate human "templates." One of the most remarkable sets of findings in selectivity of response to display was provided by Marler and Peters (e.g., 1977, 1981).

Sparrow males (males are the singers) transmit their songs as cultural conventions from one generation to the next. But how do they know which song to sing? They might otherwise acquire the songs of other bird species, which would place them at distinct reproductive disadvantage. This suggests some faculty for selecting singers from one's own species. Marler and Peters audiotaped songs of two sparrow species, song sparrows and swamp sparrows, whose songs are quite dissimilar. Synthetic songs were then constructed consisting of "syllables" of the calls of each species, and juveniles of both species were then played the synthetic, intermixed calls. Regardless of the way the two species' calls were intermixed, the juveniles' first songs were distinctly those of their own species. The birds had somehow discriminated which segments of the synthetic calls were the "right" ones to learn.

The findings are all the more remarkable when one considers that there is a "critical period" from 20 to 50 days of age during which they must hear their species's song, or their later productions will all be aberrant. During this critical period, sparrow males are vocally almost silent until they give voice to their songs, so that their learning is entirely without practice. And as I reviewed earlier, isolation studies confirm that the "template" for selecting their own species's song is innate.

Sparrows clearly demonstrate the possible interactions between innate faculties and culture. Lest we rush to extend these interactions to primate and then human displays, the avian community gives caution by showing just how varied these relations can be, even within birds. For example, sparrow males who are deafened or reared in isolation and thus cannot hear mature calls develop the expected mutant songs (Marler, 1982), but this does not apply to ring doves, for example. The males sing normally even if deafened, isolated, or reared with other species (Nottebohm, 1980).

Remarkable work by Evans, Evans, and Marler (1993) shows not only a selectivity for display, but also a kind of proto-semantics in, of all creatures, domestic chickens (*Gallus gallus*). Cockerels (males) produce different alarm calls when confronted by aerial versus ground predators. First, Evans et al. secured sample calls in the laboratory; they obtained ground-predator calls by playing an audiotape of racoon sounds, and aerial-predator calls using an overhead computer-generated, televised "eagle." The cockerels' alarm calls were audiotaped and then replayed to females. The females were much more likely to run for cover after hearing the taped aerial calls, and to stand erect and hypervigilant after the ground calls.

The question of templates for display perception in nonhuman primates (again, the emphasis has been on monkey *vocal* displays) is a new one because, as Hauser (1989) stated:

> A common view of nonhuman primate vocal development has been that calls appear fully formed at birth and that experience contributes little to the modification of call structure. (p. 149)

Yet nonhuman primates may have similar species-specific templates. Zoloth et al. studied two vocalizations in lab-bound macaques, specifically two fuzzily bounded classes of "coo calls," which are distinguished by peak pitch inflections early versus late in the call. Both of these calls can begin on any frequency, however, so that a call's fundamental frequency and its point of peak inflection can be varied independently. The monkeys were placed in an operant situation in which they received tokens for discriminating recorded calls that contained early versus late peak inflections amid randomly varying fundamental frequencies, or vice versa. One species (Japanese macaques) easily discriminated inflections amid frequency shifts, but was much slower to discriminate the pitches amid varying inflection changes. The control species (pig-tailed and bonnet macaques) showed the *opposite* pattern (Zoloth, Petersen, Beecher, et al., 1979).

The calls of vervet monkeys have received the most detailed examination. The ontogeny of vervet calls is a more complex state of affairs. Vervets make many different kinds of calls in intergroup encounters, and these calls appear at different ages. Clearly, the production and comprehension of some calls (e.g., distress or "lost" calls) require social experience and auditory exposure (Hauser, 1989). The "eagle alarm" call, on the other hand, is produced early and in near-adult form, and juveniles issue it when threatened by numerous animals, but as Figure 4.7 depicts, it becomes specific to eagles as the monkeys become adults (Seyfarth & Cheney, 1986).

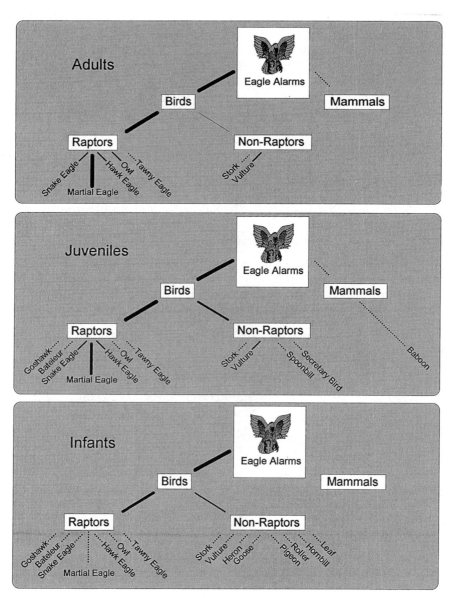

FIGURE 4.7.   Progressive specificity of "eagle alarm calls" in infant to adult vervet monkeys (*Cercopithecus aethiops*). The calls are emitted in adult form even by infants. The width of the lines denotes relative specificity of the call to the referent (predator type). Illustration adapted from Seyfarth and Cheney, 1986.

Work on human templates for *facial* displays is almost nil. Studies of congenitally blind infants roughly parallel the sensory deafferentation condition in the bird experiments, but because facial displays are not easily quantified, the evidence was anecdotal. Cross-cultural and cross-racial adoption studies could approximate conditions in which birds of one species are reared with another, but I know of none. Earlier I mentioned research on "face cells" and scan patterns, but again, these studies do not address how we discern diachronically when a "display" has occurred. A study by Leonard, Voeller, and Kuldau (1991) provides a lead on how we do it.

Leonard et al. tried to understand the temporal features of muscular contraction that determine when we "see" another smile. The human smile is a useful display for these purposes, given that it results from the action of just one (bilateral) muscle, the *zygomatic major* that attaches at, and retracts, the lip corners. We commonly infer "happiness" from smiles, but clearly not all contractions of *zygomatic major* lead to this inference, a fact readily observed in the cheesy grins produced by beauty queens or politicians, or captured by poor photographers.

Clearly there is some amplitude-time course of *zygomatic major* contraction that leads optimally to the "happy" inference, and Leonard et al. reasoned that this constituted one way to discern the trigger for the "smile" template. Smiles were videotaped, and during playback, electronic snapshots were obtained at 33-msec intervals over a 400-msec segment of each of the smiles (see Figure 4.8). Changes in smile morphology were derived by successive subtractions of one snapshot from the next. When Leonard et al. asked subjects to rate the positivity of each snapshot, their maximal ratings occurred within 100-msec (about three snaphots) of peak inter-snapshot change. The authors suggest that subjects processed the faces in 100-msec chunks, and that this figure is meaningful in light of the 80 to 140-msec response latencies of some of the neocortical (inferotemporal visual cortex) cells that may predominate in face perception.

Skepticism: Second-Guessing Displays

The term "skepticism" is anthropomorphic, but its essence is not. It is merely responding to a display according to the identity of the displayer and/or the context in which the display is issued. A clear example of skepticism from the insect and avian worlds is provided by the Batesian mimicry of monarch and viceroy butterflies. Blue jays find viceroys tasty but monarchs toxic (monarchs feast on unpalatable alkaline plants). Viceroys mimic the appearance of the monarch to deter predation. When apprehending a butterfly that is either target or mimic, blue jays have learned (and probably have evolved to learn) to peck and taste

FIGURE 4.8.   Digitized smiles from Leonard, Voeller, and Kuldau (1991). Perceptions of smiles corresponded to 100-msec windows of peak change in the shapes of the smiles, suggesting a template for smile perception. Reprinted with permission of Cambridge University Press.

before ingesting. Indeed, the birds tend to peck first at the insect's abdomen, which contains the lowest toxin concentrations (Fink & Brower, 1981).

Smith (1985) believes that mammals and birds who live in close social groups develop "calibration" skills, by which their response to a display depends on the identity of the displayer and the context of display. Smith cited supporting anecdotal data from Tinbergen (1939, 1953) on herring gulls' responses to neighbors' alarm calls.

"Calibration" (i.e., learned skepticism) has now been documented in nonhuman primates, specifically the vervet monkey. Cheney and Seyfarth (1988) repeatedly replayed audiotaped intergroup "*wrrs*" (a type of call made only when another group is present) of an individual to his group. The group habituated to the *wrr* of the target group member, but not to the *wrr*s of other group members, or to other types of intergroup calls by the target. These findings not only demonstrated calibration to the target who "cried wolf"; they also showed that vervet monkeys classify intergroup alarm calls "semantically" (also see Seyfarth, Cheney, & Marler, 1980a,b).

I know of no specific experiments demonstrating human skepticism, and they may be unnecessary. This is because nearly every human deception study (cf. Zuckerman, DePaulo, & Rosenthal, 1981a) can be recast as a skepticism study, with the subjects who are the least deceived being, in effect, the best skeptics. Humans certainly calibrate their skepticism as a function of displayer and context. We are likely to trust kin or close friends anytime, unless we discern that their momentary interests render their position antagonistic (e.g., when certain family members contest a will). Conversely, we are likely to be skeptical about anything politicians say, unless we discern that their interests do not compete with ours (e.g., when they oversee the defense of shared resources).

COMPLEMENTARITY OF DISPLAYS AND VIGILANCE FOR THEM

In contrast to associationist accounts (e.g., Spencer's and Darwin's), it is axiomatic in contemporary ethology that displays and the vigilance for them coevolve. A creature whose threat displays are especially threatening may rule the roost and hold reproductive sway, but a creature who was preternaturally vigilant might sense an aggressor's intentions and deflect them before things get out of hand.

Obviously, one could imagine a signal so obvious that little or no vigilance is required to perceive it (e.g., the proverbial hitting of a mule over the head by a 2 × 4—a "tactual display"). On the other hand, a subtler signal (e.g., an auditory one like calling the mule) might get the job done without expending undue energy (and energy, it must be emphasized, is expended on growing morphological displays as well). On the receiver's end of things, it might at first seem profitable to become more vigilant such that all conceivable signals are considered (human paranoia is a case in point). But there is a cost to pay here, as well, because one might get by with a little less vigilance and thereby have resources left for other matters. It is clear that the evolutionary costs and benefits of signaling always complement those of vigilance. Things get even thornier when deception enters the picture. This "arms race" of displays and vigilance for them (Krebs & Dawkins, 1984) is at the heart of the "behavioral ecology" view of facial displays.

It also suggests why many displays arise in intention movements. An animal that could sense another's forthcoming moves (e.g., competing for access to a female) would gain in fitness, but it would also tend to enhance the fitness of the displayer (a dominance display can establish mating priority without a costly fight). As I described in an example of territorial defense (Fridlund, 1986):

> Millions of years ago, if you crossed my turf, I might bite your head off [at some risk to me, if you decided to retaliate]. If you had advance warning, you might escape death through retreat or protective defense, and we'd both survive.
>
> But you'd need cues to retreat or protect. I'd have to give them, and you'd have to notice them. Here's the scenario: because of a lucky gene, I adventitiously bared one tooth for 1/2 second before I pounced. Your lucky gene made you look at my head. I bared my tooth, and you looked in the right place, not because I wanted to display my feelings, or because you wanted to see how I felt. We both acted out of pure dumb genetic luck. That we survived our skirmish increases the chances that our lucky genes will proliferate, and that my odd tooth-baring and your odd vigilance for it will both disseminate in our progeny.[4]

As this scenario shows, the survival of both parties follows an interaction mediated by the issuance and subsequent perception of a display. The emphasis on survivability of both parties runs afoul of a common stereotype about evolution by natural selection, that it is a have-no-mercy "survival of the fittest." The simple fact is that "survival" in evolutionary terms means long-run reproductive success, *not* a win-or-lose outcome from a fight to the death. It does one no good to win repeated fights but remain too compromised to produce young and promote their survival; winning disputes through bargaining or diplomacy is far preferable. In fact, fatal fighting should occur only if lifetime reproductive success is at stake (Enquist & Leimar, 1990). Evolution should consequently produce not Hobbesian vanquishers but good negotiators (Axelrod, 1984)—and displays are the tools that permit such negotiation (de Waal, 1989). Tinbergen (1953) stated it well:

> Since actual fighting inflicts damage as well as effecting spacing-out, a signalling system such as exists in most species, where damage is reduced to a minimum while the intimidating effect is retained, is to the species' advantage. Threat display reduces fighting in two ways: if shown by an owner (of a territory, a female, a hole, etc.) it intimidates rivals. If shown by a trespasser, it marks the latter out for attack, and thus enables an

---

[4] This model is obviously simplified. The "genes" promoting display and vigilance need not co-occur with equal frequencies, since either could occur by chance. However, the spread of one of the two genes would likely eventuate in the spread of the other. Moreover, their coevolution need not have been synchronous; it may have been "stepwise."

"Gene" here is used for clarity. Most recent models propose that evolutional novelties arise *not* from monogenesis or mutation, but either from a serendipitous blend of genes, or as a secondary effect of a pleiotropic, or multipurpose gene (Bock, 1959; Mayr, 1960). "Display" or "vigilance" genes probably arose pleiotropically. Note that my example posits random origins for the display; real-world origins are without doubt nonrandom—in other words, they originate in preadapted movements.

owner to leave harmless intruders alone. Again, these functions depend on signals. (p. 72)

Appeasement, peacemaking, diplomacy, negotiation—these actions may seem out of place in evolutionary discussions of behavior. The implicit assumption is that these are civil and therefore singularly human, whereas fighting is "natural" and "animalistic." As we will see later, this notion that one is more "basic" than the other has misdirected much research on so-called "felt" versus "false" human facial expressions, and it is erroneous. In fact, reconciliation among nonhumans (primates, at least) is well documented. It usually takes the form of affinitive interactions with opponents, or with their allies or kin, soon after an altercation. Reconciliations occur regardless of whether the species has fixed dominance relations (Kappeler & van Schaik, 1992).

The complementarity of displays and vigilance applies not only among conspecifics, but to predator–prey relations as well. Krebs and Dawkins (1984) illustrated cooperative display and vigilance between predator and prey, in an example first provided by Smythe (1970):

> Many predators rely upon surprising their prey because they cannot outrun them. Once a cat has been seen or otherwise detected by a particular bird, unless it is very close the cat has little chance of catching the bird, which simply takes to the air. To stalk a bird and get close enough to strike is a time-consuming business for a cat, only worthwhile if there is a reasonable chance of success at the end of the stalk. The interesting point is that the bird, too, benefits, from making the mind-reading easy for the cat. If he can make the cat give up and slink off, he can continue to feed uninterruptedly on the ground, rather than to have to waste time flying off or keeping himself prepared to fly off. (p. 388)

In both examples, displays are deployed when there is some ambiguity in the displayer's forthcoming actions. In the territorial defense example, the tooth-baring animal *might* have attacked, and it bared its tooth. In the predation example, the bird *might* have either stayed or flown away, and it alerted the cat. The complementarity of display and vigilance are evident, because the immediate deaths of the interloper or the feeding bird would mitigate the ritualization of either display or vigilance.

To state the point more obviously, it is very costly to display one's intentions if one is committed to enacting them; by announcing one's actions, one risks the other's heightened resistance. Natural selection should thus extinguish such automatic displays. Displaying one's intentions *can* be advantageous if one is inclined but not committed to a specific course of action, and if it is efficacious to alter or abandon one's course contingent upon the recipient's actions. Such forewarning as to how one *might* behave can garner the other's cooperation or acquiescence. For example, the best attack is a sneak attack, unless a graded, threatened attack will produce the other's submission without a fight. In the case of play, a child wanting to play with another's toys should signal with a play-face or appeasement face (usually a smile) before she touches the toys, lest a fight ensue needlessly.

Displays in general may not signal simple intentions, but indecision or conflict among several intentions (see Hinde, 1985a; or the "conflict" view of Tinbergen, 1953). From the indecision/conflict view, the threatened attack signals, "I want to attack but I don't want to have to," whereas the child's play-face or appeasement smile signals, "I want to approach and play with your toys, but not if it means that you will respond agonistically." Finally, in the case of deception, the display mimics indecision or conflict among intentions in their absence (i.e., I deploy a play-face while seeming to intend play, when in fact I am intending attack; see Caryl, 1979).

This discussion has focused on selection pressures leading to display and vigilance for display, that is, "manipulation" and "mind-reading." I expand on these in a later discussion of the "behavioral ecology" view.

Given selection pressures for the development of animal signal systems, intention movements are likely to be ritualized variants of instrumental acts. This view is consistent with the principle that in natural selection, any selection pressures must operate on the "raw material" of the current generation. This raw material is the phenotypic variance engendered by genetic variability. There are other probable sources of raw material for the formalization of facial displays. These are the facial reflexes, which I review in Chapter 6. These reflexes are embedded in the neuromuscular machinery of the facial apparatus, which I discuss next.

5

Facial Hardware: The Nerves and Muscles of the Face

THE FACIAL MASK: STRUCTURE AND NEURAL CONTROL

Actors in Greek and Roman theater often wore a comic or tragic mask (known as a prosôpon). The mask signified the actor's role, and the individual behind it was only known through the voice, that is, *per sonare* (Allport, 1937). While this mask was artifice, we are all *personas* who speak from behind a mask, even off-stage—at least off the one in the theater. This "mask" is the musculature of our face, which regulates our social roles just as surely as the Greco-Roman mask did for the actor who wore it. Figure 5.1 illustrates the facial mask. It depicts the major facial muscles from the inside out, and shows how we see, smell, taste, and speak through their portals.

Given the primacy we accord the face in our social relations, it seems prosaic to claim that the facial muscles are fundamentally just sphincters that regulate vision, olfaction, and ingestion. I have already summarized how such biological functions can be coopted for social displays, and later I will discuss the implications for understanding the human displays that have typically been termed "facial expressions of emotion."

Any treatment of human faces requires some familiarity with where the facial muscles originate, what they do, and what controls them. This is a fascinating and wide-ranging story that spans embryology, anatomy, physiology, and clinical neurology. Doing it justice would require many volumes; here, I merely highlight what will prove most important later. I exclude facial motor and sensory activities that are only indirectly related to facial displays, such as the ocular and oropharyngeal muscles, and sensory receptors for vision, smell, and taste. Much of this material is technical, so I ask your patience if your tastes don't run in this vein.

Craniofacial Embryology and Maturation

The remarkable embryonic changes that fix the structure of the human face occur within a two-week period, which begins during the fourth week of gestation. As indicated by the recent spate of interest in adult facial "asymmetry" or "laterality" in shape or movement (cf. review by Fridlund, 1988), the face only appears to be an integrated structure. It is actually tripartite, deriving embryologically from an "upper face" and two "lower face" components. The major events in the formation of the face are depicted in Figure 5.2.

By the 24th day of embryonic development, a thickening over the brain, the *frontonasal prominence*, starts to enlarge and grow forward and downward until it converges upon the developing mouth, a pit known as the *stomadeum*. The frontonasal prominence contains two thickenings, the *nasal placodes*, which differentiate to become the structures of the

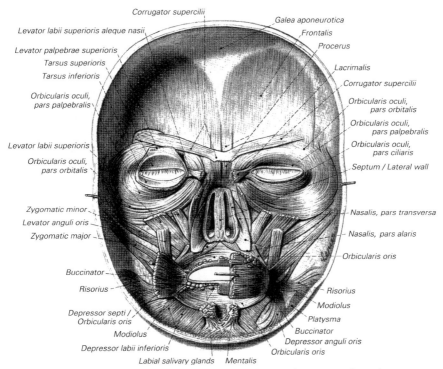

Corrugator supercilii
Galea aponeurotica
Levator labii superioris aleque nasii
Frontalis
Levator palpebrae superioris
Procerus
Tarsus superioris
Tarsus inferioris
Lacrimalis
Orbicularis oculi, pars palpebralis
Corrugator supercilii
Orbicularis oculi, pars orbitalis
Orbicularis oculi, pars palpebralis
Levator labii superioris
Orbicularis oculi, pars ciliaris
Orbicularis oculi, pars orbitalis
Septum / Lateral wall
Zygomatic minor
Nasalis, pars transversa
Levator anguli oris
Zygomatic major
Nasalis, pars alaris
Orbicularis oris
Buccinator
Risorius
Risorius
Modiolus
Depressor septi / Orbicularis oris
Platysma
Buccinator
Modiolus
Depressor anguli oris
Depressor labii inferioris
Orbicularis oris
Labial salivary glands   Mentalis

FIGURE 5.1.   The facial muscles seen from the inside out, as though one were peeling off a mask. Indeed, our faces are the masks through which we see the world, and *vice versa*. Adapted from Pernkopf (1963).

nose and the medial (centermost) part of the upper lip (Hiatt & Gartner, 1982).

During this period, the left and right sides of the lower face emerge from bilateral pouches of embryonic tissue known as the *branchial arches*.[1] There are six pairs of branchial arches, and the lower face derives specifically from the first and largest two pairs, the *mandibular* and the *hyoid* arches. Each arch contains a bar of cartilage, a muscle element, a nerve, and an artery, and these elements differentiate to become, respectively, the bones of the face, the facial musculature, the innervations to the muscles, and the vasculature supporting the facial tissues.

As these arches develop they migrate toward the midline and begin to flank the stomadeum, extending beneath it and joining portions of

---

[1] These structures are sometimes known as pharyngeal arches, visceral arches, or even gill arches. *Branchial* does mean "gill," and these gill-like pouches are indeed homologous with parts of the gill apparatus in fish and amphibians. *Contra* Haeckelian recapitulation, at no point do the branchial arches function as gills in mammalian development.

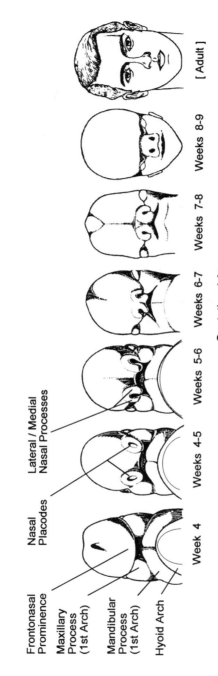

Frontonasal Prominence

Maxillary Process (1st Arch)

Mandibular Process (1st Arch)

Hyoid Arch

Nasal Placodes

Lateral / Medial Nasal Processes

Week 4   Weeks 4-5   Weeks 5-6   Weeks 6-7   Weeks 7-8   Weeks 8-9   [Adult]

Gestational Age

FIGURE 5.2.   Embyological stages in the development of the face, showing the progressive fusion of the branchial arches (the mandibular and hyoid arches, specifically) that form the mimetic facial muscles. Adapted from Hiatt and Gartner (1982) and Slavkin (1979); copyright © Lea & Febiger.

the frontonasal prominence above it. The hyoid arch develops a large muscle mass that migrates over the head and scalp, and this mass gives rise to almost all of the major facial mimetic (expressive) muscles. The mandibular arch divides into two portions: the *maxillary portion* becomes the cheek and the lateral (outermost) part of the upper lip, with the *mandibular process* the origin of the tissues of the lower jaw and temple (including the muscles of mastication, such as the masseter and temporalis).

Because the left and right sides of the lower face actually derive separately from the left and right branchial arches, they must meet and then fuse to create the lower face. Usually, the two sides fuse seamlessly, but errors are painfully evident in congenital craniofacial anomalies like cleft lip and cleft palate, a bifurcated tongue, a congenitally deviated or perforated nasal septum, or even the absence of the nose (Slavkin, 1979). Less dramatically, the nature of the lower face as a fusion product is revealed in the normal facial asymmetries observed by plastic surgeons and through photogrammetry (e.g., Gorney & Harries, 1974; Koff, Borod, & White, 1981; Sackeim & Gur, 1982).

The Facial Musculature

The facial muscles can be divided into the *superficial* muscles, which include the major mimetic muscles of the face, and the *deep* muscles, or the muscles of mastication.

Superficial Muscles

Most facial displays result from the contractions of the superficial muscles, which migrate in early embryogenesis from the second branchial arch, the hyoid arch. Although there are barely more than 20 of these superficial muscles, the potential combinations of movements resulting from their co-contractions range in the thousands. With some exceptions, the superficial facial muscles originate in bone, but unlike most of the body's striated muscles, they insert into soft tissue, specifically the dermis of the facial skin. They produce their various contractile effects upon these dermal attachments. Table I lists the major mimetic muscles of the superficial face, including their locations, actions, and innervations.

The superficial facial muscles function in one of two ways, and their etymologies (e.g., *levator*, *depressor*, *corrugator*) often suggest their functions. They act either as sphincters, constricting the area they circumscribe, or as tractors, pulling at their dermal attachments. Either way, they modify the size and shape of the slits or cavities to which they are proximal, that is, the mouth, nose, orbits (around the eyes), and, ves-

TABLE I   Major Mimetic Muscles of the Face and Scalp

Muscle	Location	Innervation (branch of CN VII except as noted)	Action
Scalp			
Frontalis	Forehead	Temporal	Wrinkles forehead and raises eyebrow
Occipitalis	Back of the head	Post. auricular	Tightens the scalp
Temporoparietalis	Temple	Temporal	Elevates the ear
Ear			
Auricularis anterior	Anterior to ear	Temporal	Pulls auricle forward and up
Auricularis superior	Above ear	Temporal	Pulls auricle up
Auricularis posterior	Behind ear	Post. auricular	Pulls auricle back
Eye			
Orbicularis oculi	Around the orbit	Temporal and Zygomatic	Closes the eye
Corrugator	Deep to the orbicularis oculi	Temporal	Makes furrows between eyebrows
Nose			
Procerus	Bony bridge of nose	Buccal	Depresses eyebrows medially
Nasalis	Cartilaginous bridge and wing of nose	Buccal	Dilates nostrils
Depressor septi	Lateral to philtrum	Buccal	Constricts nostrils
Mouth			
Levator labii superioris	Upper lip	Buccal	Elevates upper lip
Levator labii superioris alaque nasi	Upper lip and side of nose	Buccal	Dilates nostrils and elevates upper lip
Levator anguli oris	Corner of mouth	Buccal	Lifts corner of mouth
Zygomaticus major	Cheek and mouth corner	Buccal	Lifts corner of mouth
Zygomaticus minor	Cheek and mouth corner	Buccal	Elevates upper lip
Risorius	Cheek	Buccal	Draws corner of mouth laterally
Depressor labii inferioris	Lower lip	Mandibular	Depresses lower lip
Depressor anguli oris	Corner of mouth	Mandibular	Depresses corner of mouth
Mentalis	Chin	Mandibular	Wrinkles chin and protrudes lower lip
Orbicularis oris	Circumscribes mouth	Buccal	Closes, purses, and protrudes lips
Buccinator	Cheek	Buccal	Compresses cheek
Neck			
Platysma	Neck and chin	Cervical	Depresses mandible, mouth corner, and lower lip

tigially, the ears. Most of these muscles are bilateral and roughly symmetrical. Some examples illustrate their actions.

There are two main facial sphincter muscles. The *orbicularis oculi*, which shuts the eyes, is composed of two major segments. The outer *orbital* portion forcefully clamps the eyes shut, whereas the inner *palpebral* portion performs gentle closures like eyeblinks. Some observers further note a *ciliary* portion interior to the *palpebral* (Figure 5.1), but do not attribute functional specificity to it. The second major sphincter, the *orbicularis oris*, surrounds the mouth and closes or puckers the lips; the superior and inferior parts converge deep to each lip corner, at vertices known as the left and right *modiolus*.

Numerous tractor muscles enlarge or otherwise modify facial conformation. Most have antagonists in other tractor muscles. Eyelid opening is controlled by the *levator palpebrae superioris*, which antagonizes the actions of the palpebral portion of the *orbicularis oculi*. Brow movements derive from the actions of several muscles. The *frontalis* elevates the eyebrows, with *medial* and *lateral* portions raising the inner and outer brows, respectively. The *frontalis* overlies and glides over a thick fibrous sheet, the *galea aponeurotica*. Antagonizing the actions of the *frontalis* is the *procerus*, which pulls down the inner brows. The brows are pulled together by the *corrugator supercilii*, whose action induces corrugations ("furrows") in the lower forehead.

As might be expected given the precise muscular control required for feeding and speech, the tractor muscles controlling the mouth are the most varied and complex. The *buccinator* compresses the cheek and thereby constricts the oral cavity; it forms most of the muscular bulk of the cheek. Overlying the buccinator are tractors that act more directly on the lips. The *risorius* retracts the lip corners laterally, the *zygomatic minor* and *levator labii superioris* elevate them, and the *zygomatic major* retracts them toward the ears (contrary to the etymology of "risorius," which translates "smile muscle," the *zygomatic major* is most responsible for the normal smile). These muscles are antagonized directly by the *depressor anguli oris* and *depressor labii inferioris*, which depress the lip corners and lower lip, respectively. And although the *orbicularis oris* is responsible for the puckering of the lips, the *mentalis* draws up the chin and makes the lower lip protrude (a skill most youngsters have mastered).

Deep or Masticatory Muscles

The deep muscles of the face have different embryonic origins than the superficial muscles. They develop from the first branchial arch, the mandibular arch, and physically they both originate from and insert into bone. These muscles are the masticatory muscles, serving to elevate and clench the jaw. Because people also clench their jaws when they aggress,

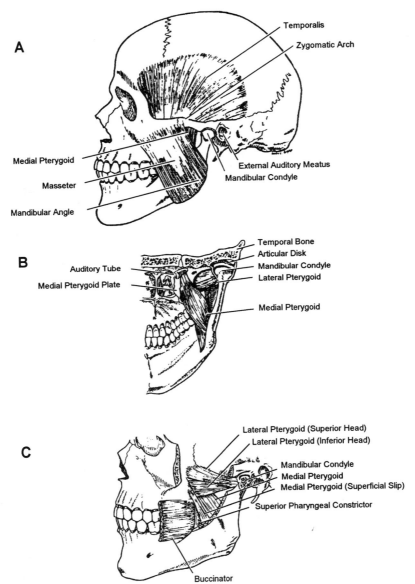

FIGURE 5.3.   The deep facial musculature of the face, which develops from the mandibular arch, and is the musculature of mastication. (A) Main jaw tractors, the *massetor* and *temporalis*; and the secondary coordinators of jaw and mouth movements of mastication in (B) frontal and (C) sagittal views. Adapted from Hiatt and Gartner (1982).

obsess, or exert effort, the deep muscles also have incidental signal value.

Four muscles comprise the deep muscles. These are depicted in Figure 5.3. The *masseter*, one of the most powerful muscles in the body, is so large that it defines the posterior shape of the jaw. It originates in the area of the cheek known as the *zygomatic arch*, and inserts into the lateral mandible (jaw bone). The second major deep muscle is the *temporalis*, which originates in the cranial bones of the temple and inserts via a tendon into the pointed *coronoid process* at the top and middle of the mandible.

The two other deep muscles are the somewhat smaller *pterygoid* muscles. The *medial pterygoid* muscle is the medial counterpart of the masseter. It elevates and clenches the jaw from the inside, originating just beside the nasal bone and inserting into the medial portion of the mandible. The *lateral pterygoid* is actually two muscles that run nearly horizontally; they originate just ahead of the cheek and insert upon the mandible in front of the ear. The superior (top) portion of the lateral pterygoid stabilizes the jaw during chewing, and unilateral contractions move the jaw from side to side. The inferior (bottom) portion opens the jaw to initiate chewing.

Together, the complex of deep muscles and the rear "horn" (*ramus*) of the mandible form the *masticatory compartment*. The forces required for incision and chewing make this compartment the site of an extraordinary convergence of intense muscular contractions. Any structural or functional misalignment within this compartment can misdirect these contractions and result in the chronic, extremely painful *temporomandibular joint syndrome*.

Facial Motor (Efferent) Nerves

Separate nerves control the superficial and deep facial muscles. The superficial facial muscles are controlled by the seventh cranial nerve (CN VII), called the *facial nerve*. During embryogenesis, as the hyoid arch's nerve element ramifies to become the branches of the facial nerve, the migrating superficial muscles drag the developing nerve fibers with them. The facial nerve makes its way from the brain to the face by coursing along the indented *facial canal* in the medial side of the temporal bone of the skull and then exiting through a hole behind the ear, the *stylomastoid foramen*. The nerve then enters the parotid salivary gland, within which it divides into six major branches. These are depicted in Figure 5.4.

The superficial muscles of the nose and lips are controlled by the largest branch, the *buccal* branch; those of the chin by the *mandibular* branch; and those of the scalp, eye, and ear by the *temporal, zygomatic,*

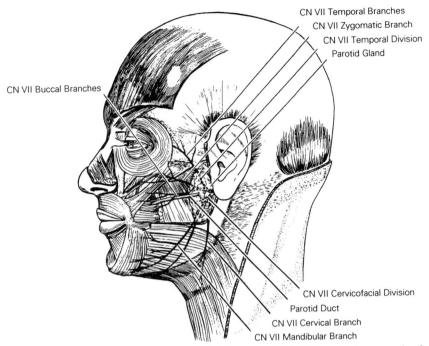

CN VII Temporal Branches
CN VII Zygomatic Branch
CN VII Temporal Division
Parotid Gland

CN VII Buccal Branches

CN VII Cervicofacial Division
Parotid Duct
CN VII Cervical Branch
CN VII Mandibular Branch

FIGURE 5.4.   The branches of the facial nerve (CN VII), which controls the major mimetic muscles of the face. From Hiatt and Gartner (1982).

and *posterior auricular* branches. Finally, the superficial muscles of the chin and anterior neck are controlled by the *cervical* branch. Minor nerve branches also appear just after the facial nerve exits the skull; these contract the stylohyoid and digastric muscle of the neck.[2] The innervations of specific superficial facial muscles are provided in Table I.

The deep, masticatory facial muscles are controlled by the largest of the cranial nerves, the fifth cranial nerve (CN V), known as the *trigeminal* nerve. All trigeminal deep-muscle control is through its *mandibular* branch, which exits a hole in deep facial bone below the eye socket called the *foramen ovale*.

Facial Sensory (Afferent) Nerves

The tissues of the face contain the gamut of sensory receptors, including those for pain, light, and deep touch, heat and cold, not to mention the

---

[2] Even before it exits the skull, the facial nerve produces branches that ligate and contract the stapedius muscle of the middle ear (the *stapedius* branch), and instigate secretions of the major salivary glands. I mention these functions cursorily because they relate only indirectly to facial movements. One exception to the facial nerve's control of the superficial musculature is the eyelid-raiser, the *levator palpebrae superioris*, which is innervated by the oculomotor nerve.

specialized receptors in the eye, ear, nose, and mouth. Additionally, the muscles and tendons of mastication contain spindle organs and Golgi tendon organs, respectively. These transduce the positions of the deep muscles and the masticatory force they exert upon the jaw. The superficial muscles insert into skin and appear to have no such proprioceptive organs.

Facial sensations of all types funnel into two main cranial nerves, the facial nerve (CN VII), and the trigeminal nerve (CN V). The facial nerve's role in cutaneous (skin) sensation is minor, being confined to its posterior auricular branch, which innervates receptors in the ear and mastoid area.

Branches of the trigeminal nerve innervate nearly every other cutaneous facial area. The *opthalmic division* receives sensory information from the upper eyelid and the conjunctiva (white) of the eye, the medial forehead and scalp, and the bridge of the nose. Nerves of the *maxillary division* innervate the lower eyelid and conjunctiva, the temple and cheek, the side of the nose, and the upper lip. Most of the sensory nerves serving the masticatory area are, like its motor nerves, part of the mandibular division of the trigeminal nerve. These sensory nerves innervate areas that include touch, pain, and pressure receptors in the temporomandibular joint, the skin and mucous membranes of the cheek, the front two-thirds of the tongue, and the chin and lower lip.

Central Nervous System Control of the Face

The facial and trigeminal nerves, like all cranial nerves, do not join the spinal cord; rather, they enter and exit the brain directly and proceed to the face by poking through *foramen* ("boreholes") in the bones of the skull. Figure 5.5 depicts the appearances of the cranial nerves at the ventral (bottom) brainstem.

The Facial Nuclei

Inside the brain, the facial and trigeminal nerves both originate in the center of the *pontine formation* (also known as the *pons*). The origins of the facial nerve are amid several discrete groups of neuronal cell bodies— from four to six, depending on the animal and the anatomist (cf. Carpenter & Sutin, 1983; Courville, 1966; Rinn, 1984). These are known collectively as the *facial nucleus*.[3] The cell groups seem to be distinct not only topographically but functionally as well.

Carpenter and Sutin (1983) presented the most common conception

---

[3] In the neurological lexicon, each discrete group of cell bodies in the facial nucleus is technically a "nucleus," but I follow convention in using the term to refer to the collective nuclei. Note that there are separate left and right facial nuclei, with each nucleus representing the facial and trigeminal nerves on the same side, that is, they represent the *ipsilateral* nerves.

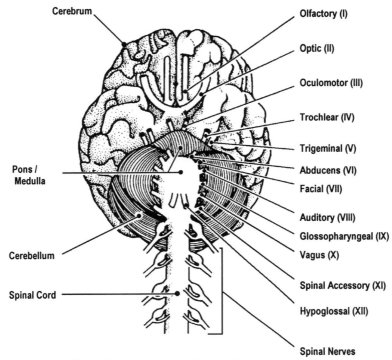

FIGURE 5.5.   Schematic depiction of the cranial nerves as they exit the brainstem bilaterally, including the trigeminal (CN V) and facial nerves (CN VII). Adapted from Slavkin (1979); copyright © Lea & Febiger.

of the organization of the human facial nucleus, in which four separate groups serve the seven facial nerve branches. As Figure 5.6 shows, the large *lateral* group is the site of origin for the buccal and mandibular branches of the facial nerve. This lateral group is especially pronounced in humans, who exhibit particularly fine-grained innervation of the buccolingual muscles. The *intermediate* group forms the origin for the temporal and zygomatic branches, and the *dorsomedial* group gives rise to the posterior auricular and stapedius branches. Finally, the *ventromedial* group is the site of origin for the cervical branch.

Like all cranial nerve nuclei, the facial nerve nuclei are not mere relay stations from cortex and subcortex to the face. To coopt some computer terminology, they are more like "intelligent controllers." This is so for two reasons. First, the neuronal cell bodies that make up the groupings in the facial nucleus are interconnected by a dense array of interneurons that can coordinate locally the actions of a configuration of facial muscles. Second, sensory information from areas such as the nucleus of the trigeminal nerve (CN V), midbrain reticular formation, and the acoustic nerve (CN VIII), also impinges upon the facial nuclei, allowing direct

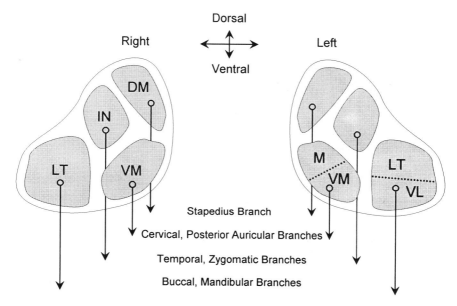

FIGURE 5.6.   The bilateral facial nuclei of the facial nerve (CN VII) located in the pons, showing the cell groups in each nucleus and the facial nerve branches that originate in each. Abbreviations for cell groupings: DM, dorsomedial group; VM, ventromedial group; IN, intermediate group; and LT, lateral group. "Left" and "Right" refer to anatomical location. Although four groups are commonly described, as depicted in the anatomical right nucleus, some anatomists bifurcate the lateral group into lateral and ventrolateral groups, and the ventromedial group into medial and ventromedial groups. This finer subdivision is depicted in the left anatomical nucleus.

elicitation of facial acts (e.g., movements associated with food ingestion or expulsion, auditory orientation and vigilance, eye closure during startle, and sneezing and yawning) and coordination of such acts once they begin (e.g., ensuring that the mouth is closed before swallowing begins). Such instigation and coordination are seen most basically in the *facial reflexes*. These reflexes may constitute the raw material (in evolutionary terms, may be "preadapted") for some common human facial displays. In the next chapter I discuss the facial reflexes and their possible role in the formation of these displays.

Laterality of Control of the Upper versus the Lower Face

If the bilateral facial nuclei control both single and some coordinated actions of the facial muscles, how do they exert this control, and how are they controlled themselves? Figure 5.7 diagrams the major motor pathways that descend from the neocortical motor strip to the facial nuclei, and from the facial nuclei to the facial muscles.

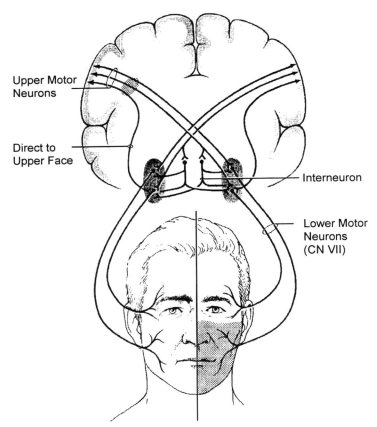

FIGURE 5.7.   Diagram of the major motor pathways controlling the facial muscles, showing predominant contralateral control with some ipsilateral control of the muscles of the upper face. The shaded areas are the facial nuclei located in the pons. Adapted from Noback and Demarest (1977).

As Figure 5.7 shows, the neural control of the facial musculature is not straightforwardly contralateral (i.e., by the opposite side); rather, it depends on whether the muscles in question are in the lower or the upper face. Control of the muscles of the lower face is decidedly contralateral. Neurons from the "motor strip" of the precentral gyrus of the neocortex—called *corticobulbar* fibers, or *upper motor neurons*—travel directly and synapse within the contralateral facial nucleus, with only indirect connections to the ipsilateral nucleus. The messages carried by these corticobulbar fibers are first modulated by and then conveyed from each facial nucleus to the ipsilateral (same-side) facial muscles. The pathways for these messages are the *lower motor neurons*, which consolidate to become the appropriate branches of the facial nerve (CN VII).

Unlike the substantial contralateral control of the muscles in the lower face, control of the muscles in the upper face is more complex (again, see

Figure 5.7). Along with the expected contralateral pathways are additional corticobulbar fibers on each side that do not cross but instead proceed directly to the ipsilateral facial nucleus. The result is that the left and right motor strips in the neocortex appear to share in control of the muscles of the upper face.

The difference in the degree to which control is lateralized in the lower versus the upper face is seen dramatically when individuals suffer unilateral damage to their corticobulbar fibers, a clinical picture known as "upper motor neuron disease." In such cases, the sufferer manifests weakness or paralysis of the muscles in the contralateral lower face, but due to the spared ipsilateral pathways, the *orbicularis oculi*, *frontales*, and *corrugator supercilii* muscles still function normally (i.e., the sufferer can still wince and raise or knit his brows). The picture is different in "lower motor neuron disease," in which the damage occurs below the facial nucleus, to one or more branches of the facial nerve. In these cases, weakness or paralysis affects the muscles of both the upper and lower face. I will discuss an important example of such a lower motor neuron syndrome, Bell's Palsy, in Chapter 8.

The impact of the differences in lateralization of control of the upper and lower parts of the face shouldn't be overdone, however. Their effects on upper- versus lower-face behavior are evident only in cases of obvious neuropathology, and are otherwise much subtler. This is demonstrated in our everyday facial movements. In the lower face, where we should be most agile at controlling separately the left and right sides of the face, most of us have trouble making smirks, smiles, or pouty down-turned mouths with equal facility on both the left and right sides—depending upon the movement, we tend to be adept only on one side or the other. And in the upper face, where we should not be at all adept at one-sided control, many of us can raise just one brow or wink with each eye.

Regrettably, to my knowledge there is no study of our comparative adeptness in contracting separately the left and right sides of bilateral muscles in our upper versus lower face. The few studies that did examine subjects' successes in making one-sided frowns, winks, smiles, and so on, suggest that we are not appreciably more adept with our lower faces (e.g., Alford, 1983; Alford & Alford, 1981; Campbell, 1982; Hager & Ekman, 1985).[4] Again, dramatic differences in the behavior of the upper and lower face seem confined to neuropathology.

Nonetheless, the reasons for the differences in upper- versus lower-

---

[4] Many studies have compared the intensities of left versus right facial muscle movements as a way to test models of cerebral hemispheric specialization for speech, gesture, emotion, and cognition, for example. These studies are beyond the scope of this chapter, but they have added little to our understanding of the face—the effects are small, easily undone, or reversed procedurally, and inconsistent with any existing model of face-brain relationships (see reviews by Borod & Koff, 1984; Fridlund, 1988; and Hager and Ekman, 1985).

face control are worth considering. It turns out that these differences are not peculiar to the face. They are actually a general feature of mammalian motor systems. First I'll discuss the general principles, followed by their implications for the face.

As Kolb and Whishaw (1990) noted, mammals are distinguished by their abilities to make independent limb movements, and primates (together with a few nonprimates like raccoons) carry this further with the independent digital (finger and toe) movements that enable clasping and grasping. These abilities stand in contrast to those of amphibians and reptiles, who have stubby limbs that largely function in stereotyped patterns like swimming, crawling, and running.

Along with the development of extremities that could be extended in space and controlled precisely were two other specializations. The first was a prehensile tail that could coil and grasp, and of which we humans retain only remnants. The second was a flexible orofacial, or mouth and nose, apparatus. This apparatus, in contrast to a beak or bony mouth, could reach out, explore and manipulate just as precisely as the limbs, and in most mammals it is flanked by vibrissae that aid these endeavors. The flexible oronasal apparatus allowed the eventual development of well-articulated vocalizations as well as nonvocal facial displays.

The explanation is one step closer, because as the neurologist Yakovlev explained, the proximity of muscles to the trunk predicts how they are controlled by the neocortex. Muscles proximal to the trunk that perform background, postural movements are controlled bilaterally. On the other hand, as one proceeds through the extremities to the fingers and toes, control becomes increasingly contralateral. This allows us now to return to the embryology of the face (Figure 5.2), and to understand the differences in neocortical upper- versus lower-face control (Figure 5.7). The upper face arises from the frontonasal prominence, which is an extension of the trunk that folds over the developing brain, and thus its control is largely bilateral. The lower face in nearly every mammal is a flexible, extensible extremity, like the arms, legs and tail, and it thus conforms to the contralateral control typical of mammalian extremities, as shown in Figure 5.8.[5]

WHY IS THERE DUAL NEUROLOGICAL CONTROL OF THE FACE?

I have already mentioned two sets of influences upon the facial nuclei. First are the upper motor neurons from the neocortical motor strip, which exert a control whose laterality depends upon whether they serve the upper or lower face. Second are various reflex-mediating neurons

[5] The human's recently developed orthognathia (discussed in Chapter 3) obscures this fact but does not alter the neurology.

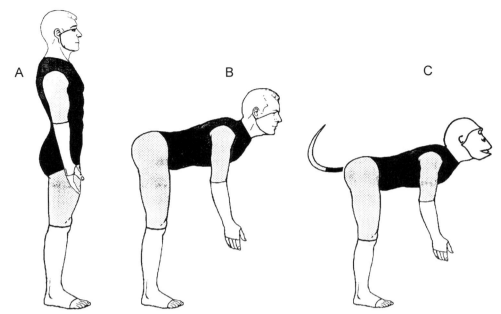

FIGURE 5.8.   The relationship between greater laterality of neurological control (lighter shades) and spatial extensibility of human body parts, depicted in (A) the standing human. The reason that certain body parts in the human are more lateralized is clarified by distorting (A) to approximate the generic quadrupedal primate form (B), including its prognathia and prehensile tail (C). The most spatially extensible body parts (lighter shades) are those capable of the most precise movements, whose controlling musculature is innervated most contralaterally, and which are under the aegis of the pyramidal motor system. Those which are less extensible perform only coarse movements and are more bilaterally innervated and extrapyramidally controlled. Spatial extensibility explains both the differences in upper- versus lower-face innervation and the types of brain damage involved in central versus reverse facial paralyses (see text).

from other cranial nerve nuclei and assorted hindbrain regions. There is probably a third major set of inputs to the facial nuclei. These inputs form apart from the neocortical pathways, hence they are called "extra-pyramidal." And by virtue of their non-neocortical origins they are termed "subcortical." But both these terms are descriptors by exclusion. Why do we posit a third set of influences?

The evidence comes from two phenomena in clinical neurology. The first is that of *central facial paralysis* (also, *corticobulbar palsy*), which occurs with a stroke or other brain lesion that damages the upper motor neurons emanating from the precentral motor strip. Individuals with this syndrome have intact facial reflexes (Chapter 6), and can produce normal symmetrical smiles when told jokes or tickled. When they are asked to move their lower facial muscles, however, their movements are dramatically weakened on the side of the face contralateral to the lesion (the upper-face muscles, which are bilaterally controlled at the facial nucleus, contract symmetrically).[6]

The second syndrome is termed *reverse facial paralysis* (and, oftentimes, *mimetic palsy* or *amimia*). As expected, those afflicted with this syndrome can make facial movements to command, but their faces are largely immobile and almost masklike, missing the apparently spontaneous faces that occur in greeting, joking, and everyday conversation. Reverse facial paralysis occurs with an intact motor strip and upper motor neurons, and thus another brain area or areas must be damaged to account for the deficient facial behavior. The inference, then, is that the third set of controls upon the facial nerve nuclei are those areas that, when lesioned, result in reverse paralysis.

What exactly is the brain locus for this third set of influences? One of the clues derives from brain autopsies from individuals who suffered reverse facial paralysis. Another derives from the disorder of Parkinson's disease, which produces the same masklike amimia, along with the preservation of movements to command. Both seem to involve the destruction of structures such as the basal ganglia (which includes structures like the caudate nucleus, putamen, globus pallidus, and the claustrum), substantia nigra, red nucleus, thalamus, the pontine reticular formation, and an assortment of other subcortical areas which, collectively, are known as the *extrapyramidal motor system*.[7] Wilson (1924) first proposed that the faces preserved in central facial paralysis were controlled by this system.

It is clear, then, that central and reverse paralysis form a classic two-by-two double dissociation between lesion and behavior (Teuber, 1955)—following lesions in one region but not another, certain faces are spared but others are impaired. But what do we call the faces that are spared and those that are impaired? This is an important interpretive problem, because many theorists use the clinical neurology findings I have summarized to answer the question, "What do facial expressions express?"

The differences between the faces spared and impaired in central versus reverse facial paralysis have variously been cast in terms of dis-

---

[6] Even lower-face control is occasionally retained in upper motor neuron damage, leading some observers to infer some amount of bilateral neocortical control of the lower-face muscles (e.g., De Jong, 1979). The same reasoning is used to account for the effects of lesions to, or removal of, the precentral "face area" of the neocortex itself. Here the syndrome is observed only acutely, and full control of both sides is typically regained within several months (Taylor, 1979). Using the reasoning from the previous section (and see Figure 5.8), the laterality of control shouldn't be categorical. It should instead be a matter of degree, depending upon the structure's spatial extensibility and resulting degree of independent movement.

[7] The assemblage of structures that forms the extrapyramidal motor system changes with the text that describes it, and some authors advocate discarding the term (Noback & Demarest, 1977). Its functions exist nonetheless, and certainly the structures I mention are involved, but their integrity as a "system" is what is controversial.

tinctions such as "nonemotional–emotional," "posed–spontaneous," "deliberate–spontaneous," or "voluntary–involuntary" (e.g., Monrad-Krohn, 1924; Tschiassny, 1953). These distinctions are cross-cutting, not strictly analogous (e.g., spontaneous faces need not be either unposed, emotional, or involuntary, as when we spontaneously pose before a camera or smile before greeting a superior).[8] Nor, it seems to me, should we necessarily take them seriously as naming the essential differences between types of faces. Rather, the distinctions are connotative, reflecting our beliefs about what kinds of behavior are "under our control" and for which we can therefore be made accountable. It is worth considering whether a more valid distinction can be made between these two kinds of faces. Let me suggest one, based on parallel findings about other movement disorders.

The first is a type of aphasia (speech disorder) known as *apraxia of speech*. Individuals with this syndrome cannot—to use J. Hughlings Jackson's term—"propositionize," or construct a speech utterance from their verbal lexicons (Head, 1926). Depending upon the severity of the syndrome, sufferers of apraxia of speech can with some effort push out words when coaxed, but most often they communicate by resorting to pantomime and other gesticulation. Curiously, some speech remains even in the most severe cases; it is usually termed *automatic speech*. What remains are utterances that require no new construction; these are over-learned phrases like rhymes and songs, exclamations, prayers, the alphabet, counting, and the days of the week or months of the year. Once cued, those with apraxia of speech can usually sound off the sequence with reasonable fluency. When asked what they just uttered, they cannot verbalize their response (Martin, 1988).

The second disorder is termed *ideomotor apraxia*, and it affects non-speech limb and finger movements (e.g., Brown, 1972).[9] As in apraxia of speech, musculoskeletal function is uncompromised, but sufferers are unable to execute even simple movements to command. For example, patients with ideomotor apraxia may be unresponsive when asked to lick their lips, purse their lips and blow, or extend one hand and turn it. And like apraxia of speech, certain movements remain. If asked to

[8] A third neurological syndrome, termed *pseudobulbar palsy*, sometimes accompanies the same corticobulbar lesions involved in central facial paralysis. In pseudobulbar palsy, sufferers show spells of laughing and/or crying that occur and remit spontaneously. Pseudobulbar palsy is sometimes interpreted as implying that "emotions" are "released" from the usual cortical controls (e.g., Brodal, 1981). Such interpretations implicitly endorse a Rousseauean reason-against-emotion view that I contest later. In fact, the syndrome occurs only with widespread brain damage accompanying multiple strokes (usually from arteriosclerosis), or from globally degenerative demyelinating diseases like multiple sclerosis (MS) or amyotropic lateral sclerosis (ALS, or Lou Gehrig's disease; see Chusid, 1976). The laughing and crying are more aptly interpreted not as a "release of emotion" but the direct instigation of smiling, paroxysmal breathing, lacrimation, and so on, by damaged pathways that have pathological irritability.

[9] Some observers consider apraxia of speech as one subtype of ideomotor apraxia. In neither disorder do deficits in responding to commands indicate linguistic compromise (Heilman & Valenstein, 1979).

drink, they show normal lip-licking after swallowing. If a lit match is held to the mouth, they will likely blow it out. If a key is pressed into one hand and a locked padlock is presented, they can place the key in the lock and turn it.

Both apraxia of speech and ideomotor apraxia are manifest by impairments in constructing movements but the retention of overlearned, habitual speech or movements. It is reasonable, then, to wonder whether central facial paralysis should be considered a type of apraxia. The same kinds of commands that fail to produce faces in central facial paralysis fail to elicit speech-related movements in apraxia of speech, or instrumental movements in ideomotor apraxia. The same kinds of routinized cues that produce automatic speech in apraxia of speech ("Recite the Lord's Prayer") and instrumental acts in ideomotor apraxia (e.g., holding a match to the lips) are duplicated in tasks designed to elicit "emotional" faces, for example, joke-telling or "emotional" interactions.

The main consequence of this analysis is important. If the types of faces inferred from neurological lesions are cast in terms of motor control in general, then there is no need to postulate ad hoc dichotomies peculiar to faces. Our faces, then, should not be construed as "nonemotional versus emotional," or any other special dichotomy cited earlier, but as "constructed versus overlearned," like other motor behavior. This general view counters the contemporary ideology that some faces, by virtue of such neurological inference, must necessarily "reflect" or "express" emotion. The validity of this ideology must rest upon other evidence, as I will discuss shortly.

Now, I turn to the possible building blocks of many facial displays, the facial reflexes.

6

FACIAL REFLEXES AND THE ONTOGENY OF FACIAL DISPLAYS

The facial reflexes are crucial to any evolutionary account of human facial displays. This is true for two reasons. First, by virtue of their certain physiological functions (either current or vestigial) they are resistant to modification or deselection (i.e., they are highly canalized). As a consequence, they probably arose early in phylogeny. Second, the origins of many facial displays may be in facial reflexes, whether they are coopted during individual development (the "ontogenetic view"), or during phylogenesis through ritualization and emancipation. I begin by cataloging the common facial reflexes and reviewing their physiology.

THE FACIAL REFLEXES

Normal adult facial physiology includes various reflexes that are generally considered innate and immutable, and characterized by few synapses. The muscles that function in the facial reflexes are innervated by the cranial nerves that directly enter and exit the base of the skull (mostly CN V and CN VII, the trigeminal and facial nerves, respectively; Chusid, 1976). These reflexes are generally protective, although some are now mostly vestigial, such as the Hering-Breuer (dive) reflex, which slows the heart when the face is cooled. Others have no known function, such as the photic sneeze reflex, in which people sneeze when they enter bright sunlight.

The facial reflexes are usually divided into three kinds. The *superficial* reflexes are those of the skin and mucous membranes, whereas the *visceral* reflexes are those of the eyes and eyelids, and the facial–cardiac reflexes. Finally, the deep or *myotatic* reflexes are reflexes of the bony joints, chiefly the jaw. Table I lists and describes the major facial reflexes.

Apart from these normal adult facial reflexes, the infant enters the world with an additional set of protective reflexes. These normally disappear by 5–7 months of age as coordinated instrumental behavior emerges, but they may reappear with neural trauma in adulthood. Because these reflexes are symptomatic of neuropathology after infancy, they are called "pathological" reflexes. They nonetheless constitute part of the reflexive repertoire from which—at least according to ontogenetic accounts—some mature facial displays may develop. The pathological facial reflexes include the

1. *Glabella reflex*, the eyeblinks made to taps to the glabella (the ridge above the eyes at the midline, over the *corrugator supercilii* muscles).
2. *Head retraction reflex*, the snapping back of the head after a sharp downward poke to the upper lip.
3. *Rooting reflex*, the initiation of sucking and turning of the head toward a stroke to the cheek.

4. *Snout reflex*, the sharp contractions of the lips produced by taps to the upper lip.
5. *Tongue thrust reflex*, the protrusion of the tongue to eject foreign matter (e.g., premature solid foods) placed on it.

Both the normal and, in infancy, the pathological facial reflexes act to facilitate more complex activities. These include: (1) language; (2) consumation; (3) regulation of oral and nasal respiration, gustation, and olfaction; (4) protection and lubrication (through lacrimation) of the eyes; (5) orientation; (6) vision; (7) audition; (8) pain; and (9) startle.

In the cat, for example, the motoneurons in the nucleus of CN VII, the facial nerve, connect to afferent fibers from the tenth cranial nerve (CN X, *vagus*), which mediates parasympathetic influences throughout the viscera. These fibers most likely participate in the interactions of eating and digestion, such that mastication itself can induce peristalsis and gastric secretion (Tanaka & Asahara, 1981). The nuclei of CN VII, the facial nerve, may receive afferent fibers directly from other pontine nuclei, such as those mediating ocular movements and facial sensations

TABLE I   Facial Reflexes

Reflex type	Name of reflex	Reflex action
Superficial	Corneal (Conjunctival)	Eyeblinks to corneal irritation
	Nasal	Sneezing to nasal membrane irritation
	Pharyngeal	Gagging to irritation of pharynx
	Uvular	Raising of uvula during speech or with irritation
Visceral	Accomodation	Pupillary contraction with ocular convergence
	Blink Reflex of Descartes	Blinking and eyelid closure to rapidly approaching object
	Carotid sinus	Bradycardia (slowed heart rate) and momentary hypotension to pressure applied over carotid sinus in the neck
	Cilospinal	Pupillary dilation to pain, e.g., a pinch to the neck
	Consensual light	Centrally mediated pupillary contraction to retinal illumination of opposite eye
	Dive (Hering-Breuer)	Bradycardia and halt in respiration to cooling of the face
	Light	Pupillary contraction to retinal illumination
	Oculocardiac	Bradycardia to pressure exerted over the eyeballs
	Photic sneeze	Sneezing upon entering bright sunlight
Myotatic (Deep)	Maxillary	Jaw closure to tap to middle chin or lower teeth or jaw

(e.g., CN V, the trigeminal nerve; and CN IX, the glossopharyngeal nerve). These connections probably coordinate the blink, rooting, and sucking reflexes during infant feeding (Bratzlavsky & vander Eecken, 1977).

I mentioned earlier the probable relations between human brow and forehead movements, and the actions of the pinnae (earflaps) that accompany orientation, vigilance, and withdrawal in nonhumans. Indeed, the articulation of head turning and pinnae protraction in orientation and auditory localization may occur directly in the nucleus of CN VII, the facial nerve (Santibanez, Espinoza, Astorga, & Strozzi, 1974).

Little is known about the neural substrates of facial actions that involve the integrated actions of multiple muscles. Stimulation of motor cortex or pyramidal tract most frequently elicits largely discrete, contralateral facial muscle movements in the monkey, although there are reports of rhythmic mouth and tongue movements suggestive of mastication (Denny-Brown, 1939). Stimulating "limbic" and hypothalamic sites produces fairly realistic threat displays in the cat, with the appropriate facial concomitants, for example, exposing of teeth, pinna retraction, hissing (see Ectors, Brookens, & Gerard, 1938; Flynn, 1967; Hess, 1954). Finally, stimulating pontine and medullar sites in the brainstem in monkeys reportedly elicits coordinated facial displays, including a "tensing grimace," a "faciorespiratory complex simulating laughter," and eyelid closure (Weinstein & Bender, 1943).

Because intracranial stimulation evoked these actions, it might be inferred that the investigators had in fact localized the neural generators that produced them. As I discussed, attempting to localize the neural generators for any behavior can be exasperating, and these inferences from stimulation studies are no exception. For example:

1. These studies rarely used anatomical descriptions of the evoked actions, and relied instead upon simple observation and imprecise emotion-related terminology. Consequently, it is always uncertain how much the actions evoked by intracranial stimulation resemble those evoked by normal exteroception.

2. In any brain stimulation study, it is never clear whether one is stimulating a neural generator for the target behavior, or the final common pathway for the generator(s), or just a collateral pathway that happens to course through a functionally irrelevant region of the brain. For example, one could imagine stimulating a part of the thalamus and obtaining facial movements, concluding that the thalamus is "responsible" for facial movements, and then finding that the electrode had merely punctured the *internal capsule*, the bundle of motor axons that exits the precentral gyrus (i.e., the "motor cortex") and traverses the thalamus on its way to the brainstem and spinal cord. This was a

lesson learned over 30 years ago by the neurophysiologists who tried to pinpoint reward, hunger, or satiety "centers" in the hypothalamus, and found themselves mired in an endless series of "center" versus "tract" arguments (see Rosensweig & Leiman, 1982).

3. The facial behavior may have been elicited only indirectly, as a by-product of some other drive like pain, hunger, or thirst. To be imaginative, the masticating movements observed by Denny-Brown might have been a reaction to stimulation-produced hunger, or even a food-related olfactory hallucination. More mundanely, electrically stimulating the motor nerves controlling the muscles of the mouth and tongue might have produced oral and pharyngeal discomfort (e.g., a burning or tingling in the mouth), and the masticating movements were the animal's attempt to reduce it. Similarly, feline threat displays, observed in the brain stimulation studies cited above and many others, may simply represent the cat's natural response to any odd sensations that accompany the brain stimulus. In other words, the cat *is* threatened, with the threat being a novel, proprioceptive one rather than the usual one "out there."

4. One other indeterminacy plagues experiments that show intracranial stimulation of multiple-muscle facial actions. The topographic mapping of the facial muscles onto different brain areas (i.e., the precentral gyrus vs. the facial nucleus) occurs at different densities. Thus the neuronal pathways for, say, the tongue and lips are closer together at the nucleus of CN VII (the facial nerve) in the brainstem than at the precentral gyrus of the neocortex. The problem is that any stimulating electrode placed into brain tissue has a current-dependent "spread of effect" around the electrode tip. If the electrode is placed into an area with a denser representation of muscle groups, then more muscles will be stimulated solely as a function of the electrode's "reach" into the surrounding brain tissue. The result would be that electrical stimulation of the facial nucleus would stimulate more muscles to act than would equivalent motor-cortical stimulation. This would lead to the erroneous inference that the facial nucleus was the site of the integration of coordinated multiple-muscle actions (Potegal, Blau, & Miller, 1980). Of course, the nucleus of CN VII may indeed be the point at which such behavior is coordinated, but supplementary evidence would be required to cinch the conclusion. The "spread of effect" confound inherent in intracranial stimulation is not mere technical arcanum; it was exactly the culprit in the controversy about whether the hypothalamus was a coordinating structure for consummatory behavior, or just a final common pathway for "higher centers" (cf. Valenstein, Cox, & Kakolewski, 1970; Olds, Allan, & Briese, 1971; Wise, 1974).

OTHER FACIAL REFLEXIVE COORDINATIONS

The face is also involved in several other stereotyped muscular or vascular actions. These actions are too complex, and their effects are too broad, to be considered typical reflexes, but their stereotypy and inertia make them reflex-like. The most important are blushing, yawning, and laughing. I discuss each.

Blushing

Blushing was, for Darwin, "the most peculiar and most human of all expressions" (1872, p. 310). It was also the most troublesome display for his antitheological account, given Victorian beliefs about what blushing signified. Janet Browne described Darwin's problem:

> All the higher qualities of man, all the Victorian virtues of modesty, innocence, and sensibility, were dramatically revealed by the flustered self-consciousness of an outright blush. Blushing showed the spiritual and moral side of human nature more clearly than any other facial display. Only blushing, it was thought, could prove that men and women had a conscience, that they could tell right from wrong and feel guilty when they overstepped the boundaries of convention. (Browne, 1985, p. 317)

Blushing signified morality, and also provided evidence for man's divinity. This Victorian view was best enunciated by Thomas Burgess (1839), who believed that blushing indicated an innate sense of guilt that restrained people from deviating from God's "allotted path" (cited in Browne, 1985, p. 318).

Blushing was thus the most important action for Darwin to explain via descent, and although demonstrating continuity was his strategy throughout *Expression*, he at once violated his own account and declared blushing uniquely human:

> Monkeys redden from passion, but it would require an overwhelming amount of evidence to make us believe that any animal could blush. (p. 310)

If Darwin could not provide a natural history account, he could at least provide a mechanistic one. Blushing was due to the flow of fresh blood into the capillary beds of the head and neck. But unlike laughter, which could be caused by tickling, or crying, which could be caused by pain, blushing could not be produced by deliberate physical stimulation; its cause had to be psychological.

Darwin's aims in *Expression* obviously did not permit him to endorse Burgess's thesis, so he was left to propose another psychological mechanism. He first argued tendentiously that attention to a body part would increase blood flow in that part:

In a large number of cases, as with the salivary and lacrimal glands, intestinal canal, etc., the power of attention seems to rest, either chiefly, or as some physiologists think, exclusively, on the vaso-motor system being affected in such a manner that more blood is allowed to flow into the capillaries of the part in question. This increased action of the capillaries may in some cases be combined with the simultaneously increased activity of the sensorium.

This mechanism allowed Darwin to supplant Burgess's uniquely human "moral sense" with a uniquely human "self-attention" that also explained why the face and neck blushed the most:

Now as men during endless generations have had their attention often and earnestly directed to their personal appearance, and especially to their faces, any incipient tendency in the facial capillaries to be thus affected will have become in the course of time greatly strengthened through the principles just referred to, name, nerve-force passing readily along accustomed channels, and inherited habit. (p. 345)

Darwin's final rejoinder to Burgess was to redefine the "guilt" that so many before him believed underlay blushing:

With respect to real shame from moral deficiencies, we can perceive why it is not guilt, but the thought that others think us guilty, which raises a blush. A man reflecting on a crime committed in solitude, and stung by his conscience, does not blush; yet he will blush under the vivid recollection of a detected fault, or of one committed in the presence of others, the feeling of blushing being closely related to the feeling of regard for those who have detected, witnessed, or suspected his fault.

Darwin's treatment of blushing was arguably the least satisfying in *Expression*. By abrogating innate guilt in favor of human self-consciousness, he merely postponed the question of blushing's natural origins. And "guilt" is only one cause of blushing. Darwin discusses other causes, such as breaches of etiquette, shyness, and modesty. But he does not deal well with cases in which people's attention to us, whether wanted or unwanted, produces not blushing but anxiety or even blanching.

Most contemporary research on the issue has focused on embarrassment and what elicits *it*. Blushing itself remains as much a mystery today as it was for Darwin. Still lacking are a satisfying theory about its evolutionary origins, a reasonable species-comparative account, and any decisive information about whether it is more a vascular reflex or a ritualized display (for a recent review, see Leary, Britt, Cutlip & Templeton, 1992).

Yawning

Yawning has been studied most systematically by Robert Provine and colleagues. It is a faciorespiratory act that includes the wide gaping of the mouth, coupled with a long inhalation followed by a short exhalation (Provine & Hamernik, 1986b). It is observed in most vertebrates (Provine, Tate, & Geldmacher, 1987), but has been studied almost entirely in humans. It is practiced throughout the life span (Gesell, 1928), and human data even show yawning *in utero* as early as 11 weeks after conception (DeVries, Visser, & Prechtl, 1982).

Yawning is also quite contagious; it can be elicited merely by the sight of a yawning face (Provine, 1989b), or even when reading or thinking about yawning (Provine, 1989a). It also occurs in boring or aversive situations (Provine & Hamernik, 1986a), and is especially frequent at the time of awakening or falling asleep (Provine, Hamernik, & Curchack, 1987a). It is so stereotyped in its timing and appearance, with specific elicitors that include yawning itself, that it may be "the best example of a stereotyped fixed action pattern and stimulus releaser in humans" (Provine & Hamernik, 1986a).

Why, then, do we yawn? The current research offers only a partial answer. The usual conjecture is that yawning is somehow restorative physiologically. Certainly when we are bored or irritated, yawning seems to make us momentarily less agitated; this may be due to its frequent association with stretching of the arm muscles and lordosing of the back (Provine et al., 1987a). When we're in danger of falling asleep (e.g., while driving), it can temporarily forestall the inevitable—even while it alerts us to our own sleepiness. These observations led to the widespread assumption that, under conditions of low blood levels of oxygen, or high blood levels of carbon dioxide, yawning is triggered and restores the normal O_2–CO_2 equilibrium. This simple hypothesis seems not to hold, because neither alterations in inhaled O_2–CO_2 concentrations nor forced breathing affects the frequency or duration of yawning (Provine et al., 1987b).

Perhaps the crucial liability of a simple respiratory, restorative hypothesis is its inability to explain the contagiousness of yawning. This has led some researchers to believe that yawning should be considered a social display that evolved to regulate the levels of arousal and vigilance of one's social group. This is an intriguing hypothesis, but it also has two liabilities:

1. It is unclear whether yawning is mediated by the presence of others, apart from its contagiousness. In other words, is each of us more disposed to yawn—even without having seen another's yawn—when we are with others? This is the question of *audience effects*, which I cover in Chapter 8.

2. A selectionist theory of yawning would require an explanation of how yawning conferred heightened personal or inclusive fitness. And confirmation would require ecological studies, most likely among nonhumans.

One final note on the display theory. It may seem odd that so many humans think it rude to expose their yawns, and instead obscure them by moving their hands to cover their mouths. This may, however, simply be a case of simultaneous displays, one (the yawn) which communicates "I am tired" or "I am bored," and the mouth occlusion, which communicates, "I don't want you to know that I am tired or bored." This lets the facts about the yawner be known, but deprives the interactant of the right to notice without being rude him or herself. In this regard, it is interesting to ponder in how many human cultures individuals occlude their yawns. Unfortunately, I know of no data on the subject.

General Relations with the Autonomic Nervous System

Many theorists are interested generally in the relations between facial actions and those of the autonomic nervous system (ANS), but the exact connections between the facial muscles and the ANS are not well mapped (for review of findings associating facial and ANS action, see Fridlund et al., 1987). Stimulation of motor-cortical tissue (e.g., that mediating facial action) typically evokes concurrent phasic ANS activity (Wall & Pribram, 1950). This phasic activity probably compensates for the energetic or circulatory demands of concurrent or impending motor activity (also see Freeman, 1948; Obrist, 1976). The relations between the face and the ANS have figured importantly in psychophysiological theories that attempt to relate emotion to facial expression, as I discuss in Chapter 8.

PROTECTIVE REFLEXES AS PHYLETIC PREADAPTATIONS FOR DISPLAYS

Andrew (1963a,b, 1964, 1972) and van Hooff (1969, 1972, 1976) have argued that many components of displays may have evolutionary origins in the facial reflexes. By virtue of their visibility, these endogenous reflexes were well preadapted for cooption as visual displays. Examples include ear protraction and retraction, which may have led to human brow-knitting and raising, respectively; and head-shaking during oral rejection, which may have led to the "No" gesture (cf. Darwin, 1872).

In other cases, the *audibility* of certain reflexes (for example, the shriek found frequently during glottal closure in startle), or their effects on vocalization (e.g., lip corner retraction during startle, which may optimize the vocal tract for transmission of shrieks), may have preadapted them for paralinguistic display, that is, they highlight, supplement, or substitute for speech. I discuss these in Chapter 12. Some displays usually taken to connote emotion may also have ontogenetic bases in reflexes, as I discuss next.

REFLEXES AS CONSTITUENT ACTIONS IN THE ONTOGENESIS
OF DIAPLAYS: FOUR MECHANISMS

The claim that complex behavior derives ontogenetically from more elementary neural components owes most to the model of brain function proposed by the foremost nineteenth-century neurologist and epileptologist, John Hughlings Jackson (1875/1958a, b). In his studies of the pathological reflexes, Jackson took a recapitulationist view of brain function. He maintained that "higher" centers in the nervous system (those developing later in phylogenesis, and appearing later in ontogeny) superordinated or integrated the operation of lower centers (i.e., those mediating the reflexes). Neural insult, Jackson believed, resulted in a regression that represented both ontogenetic reversal and phylogenetic recapitulation ("dissolution"), seen in "release signs" like resurgent infant reflexes (see Chapter 5).

Jackson's view derived directly from the popular nineteenth-century notion that "ontogeny recapitulates phylogeny," the putative "Biogenetic Law" promulgated by the ardent Darwinian and evolutionary popularizer Ernst Haeckel (Haeckel, 1874). The recapitulationism Haeckel formulated and Jackson advocated was popular in earlier neuroscience. Its most popular instantiation was Paul MacLean's "triune brain" conception (see MacLean & Rosenfeld, 1976), depicted in Figure 6.1. The recapitulation doctrine was based on misconceptions about embryogenesis (Gould, 1977).[1] McLean's recapitulationist "triune brain" model was, in turn, predicated upon a "scale" conception of phylogenesis in which the "newer" parts of the brain overlie and override the "older" parts (see Figure 6.2). In fact, all parts of the human brain are equally evolved.

It is nonetheless of interest whether in ontogenesis, mature displays are formed from infant reflexes (see Bratzlavsky, 1979; discussion by Bruner, 1973). The alternative ontogenetic mechanisms are not always made explicit. There are actually four such mechanisms for facial displays, of which three involve the facial reflexes.

Reflex Cooption during Maturation

During maturation, "higher centers" in the nervous system coopt infantile reflexes and produce subtle, graded adult displays. Logically, then, the innate "dog paddle" elicited when an infant is placed in water (lost after a few weeks of age) may be coopted to form later swimming, the

---

[1] "Misconception" is a slight overstatement. Grant (1985) notes that Haeckelian recapitulation (terminal addition of new stages) does occur, but it is atypical. von Baer's dictum that ontogeny proceeds from simple, common forms to complex, differentiated ones (von Baer, 1828) reflects the general case. The dictum does not permit asserting that, for example, emotions are more phylogenetically "primitive," a claim that will be examined more thoroughly later. The interested reader is referred to Lovtrup (1978) for a discussion of Haeckelian versus von Baerian "recapitulation," and Gould (1977) for phylogeny–ontogeny relations.

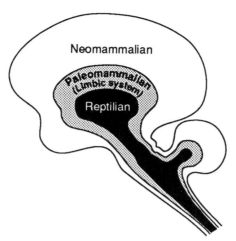

FIGURE 6.1.   The popular "triune brain" conception of psychiatrist Paul Mac-Lean (e.g., MacLean, 1967, 1968, 1970, 1990). MacLean conceived the human brain as a Jacksonian contrivance in which a "paleomammalian brain" (the limbic system) overrode and selectively suppressed the reflexive "protoreptilian brain," and was itself overridden and selectively suppressed by the intellectual and perspicuous "neomammalian brain." MacLean's view was merely the neu-rological counterpart of an outmoded nineteenth-century recapitulation. The counter to MacLean's view is shown in Figure 6.2. From MacLean (1967), re-printed with permission.

startle reflex might be coopted to make the adult "surprise" display, and the infantile rooting reflex might be the preadaptation for adult kissing (although the latter seems unlikely given that adult kissing is highly culture-bound). This mechanism is exclusively nativist. It is classically Jacksonian when the reflex is supplanted by the adult display (e.g., rooting and kissing), but not when the coopted reflexes are retained (i.e., we can be startled *and* make surprise displays).

The problem with this model is the nature of the "cooption." What does it mean to coopt a reflex? One could imagine, perhaps, that "higher centers" could interpose interneurons that dissociate some elements of a reflex and place the brakes on others, such that the reflex components could be deployed instrumentally. More fancifully, one might imagine that the "higher centers" note the kinesthetics of the reflexes whenever they are elicited, and then use them to practice instrumental facsimiles of the reflexive actions. Needless to say, whether and how ontogenetic reflex cooption occurs is open to question.

Conventionalization of Reflex Actions

Adults shape the child's developing displays, and the "raw material" shaped by this parental pedagogy is the repertoire of preexisting facial

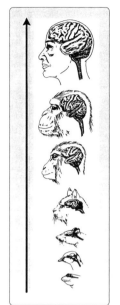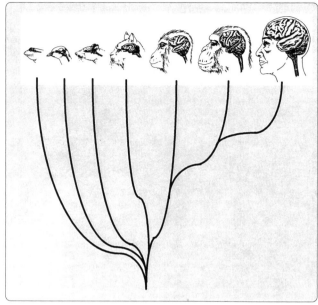

FIGURE 6.2.   Recasting of nineteenth-century phylogenetic "scale" versus modern "tree" conceptions (Figure 3.11) in terms in brain evolution. *Contra* MacLean's "triune brain"—a scale conception in disguise—the human brainstem is not reptilian, it is distinctly human, as is the human "limbic system"; all parts of the human brain, like all extant animals, are equally evolved.

reflexes. A ready analogy (though not a reflexive one) is provided by infant vocalizations. Parents wait interminably for their infant to utter "ma-ma" or "da-da," with the first passable utterance eliciting ooh's and ah's even though it may have been entirely random. Similarly, an infant whose rooting reflex was elicited may lead a caretaker to treat the child as though she were "trying to make a kiss." Young infants' faces show high base rates of seemingly disorganized reflexive activity, allowing ample opportunity for parents to shape a repertoire of conventional displays.

Imitation and Social Shaping

Children may develop mature displays by direct imitation of caretakers who model and prompt for appropriate displays. Seen in this way, the infant is *tabula rasa*, and the constant stream of words and faces that caretakers provide while looking at the child face-to-face or at each other is pure pedagogy. This mechanism is entirely independent of the form and function of the facial reflexes.

"Mimetic Theory" and the Production of Facial Analogies

"But soft, what light through yonder window breaks? It is the East, and Juliet is the sun" (*Romeo and Juliet*, Act II, Scene 2). Obviously Romeo was not identifying Juliet as an astronomical object, just likening her to one. For her star-crossed lover, Juliet was *like* the sun, that is, radiant, and Romeo's behavior was distinctly heliocentric. This is a verbal analogy,[2] and analogical reasoning is a conventional topic in cognitive psychology (e.g., Sternberg, 1977). For example, this is a typical verbal analogy:

> Sour is to lemon as sweet is to ice cream.

We automatically think of analogies as verbal, but could some be *facial*? (Here, I am talking about facial behavior, not the morphological analogies of the comparative anatomist.) This idea seems wholly unconventional but is actually quite tenable. The following sentence describes such a facial analogy:

> The face I make to you is the one I make to ice cream.

As the analogy establishes, I make the identical faces to "you" and "ice cream" because I am *likening* you to ice cream (perhaps you and ice cream are both sweet).

That some facial behavior may be explainable as analogy is actually an old idea, but it is unknown among most contemporary investigators of facial behavior. The first formulation was by Theodur Piderit (1867) in his *mimetic principles* of facial expression. Wundt independently arrived at the same conclusion, naming it the *association of analogous feelings*. The Piderit–Wundt account became known collectively as the *mimetic theory*. Floyd Allport (1924) endorsed it and described it succinctly:

> Originally evoked only by biologically prepotent stimuli (pain, noxious tastes, etc.), facial expressions come eventually to be produced in response to objects or situations, often social in character, which are merely *analogous* to the original stimuli . . . the language of facial expression is thus largely one of unconscious metaphor. (p. 216)

In the mimetic theory, the face is so important in expression because it contains so many specific sensory organs, such as the mouth, tongue, nose, and eyes, along with the sphincter muscles that open them to the world or close to protect them. The faces we make in the world of people and ideas, then, build by analogy upon our infantile intentions toward tastes, smells, and sights. Piderit, Wundt, and Allport proposed many

---

[2] Technically, Shakespeare was using metaphor, or analogy by implication (the "like" is omitted). Verbal analogies made explicit with "like" are *similes*.

such analogies, and as I discuss below, even Darwin used analogy to explain our reactions to humor.[3]

The mimetic theory can explain many facial movements that fit alternative mechanisms, whether ontogenetic (those above) or phylogenetic (ritualization), but it can also explain some facial and nonfacial movements that are refractory to alternative analyses. Why, for example, do we scratch our heads when we try to solve a complex problem? For the mimetic theorist, we react toward a vexing problem as we would toward a dermal irritant, that is, vexation is psychological irritation.

What is missing in the mimetic theory is an account of *how* we come to liken concrete sensory experiences such as sweetness or bitterness with abstractions like character attributes or moral proscriptions. Specifically, how do we come to liken personal "sweetness" to chemical sweetness, or an obnoxious idea to a noxious smell? Or are these analogies just plays on words?

Closer study may reveal the mimetic theory to be just a vacuous construction of our own figures of speech. Alternatively, the theory may prove quite the opposite. Apart from teaching us about some of our facial behavior, it may help explain how we progress from the domain of concrete objects and sensations to the abstraction and manipulation of attributes and ideas.

RESEARCH STRATEGY FOR EVALUATING ONTOGENETIC MECHANISMS

The four mechanisms are of course not mutually exclusive; they may all be involved, only for different displays. Evidence on their relative contributions is sparse.

Estimates of ontogenetic versus phylogenetic influences on displays (i.e., determining whether learning is necessary) are often based on facial displays of congenitally blind infants (see review by Charlesworth & Kreutzer, 1973). As I discussed earlier, these studies approximate nonhuman "isolation" experiments that restrict experience to test innateness. Observations from such studies suggest that smiling, laughter, and crying develop without direct imitation, and that blind infants and children are facially impassive compared to sighted children (Charlesworth & Kreutzer, 1973; Fraiberg, 1974). Given both the environmental deprivation and the unfortunate stigmatization endured by these children, some of their facial impassivity probably indicates clinical de-

---

[3] As Allport (1924) noted accurately, "Darwin's theory implies the mimetic theory in that it describes the origin of expressions to originally serviceable habit quite useless in the situations in which they later are called forth; but it does not do justice to the analogical association of certain expressions with particular situations" (p. 215). Darwin's treatment of humor may be the sole exception; his account was frankly analogical.

pression. For many of these children, the blindness no doubt reflected more general developmental immaturity or neuropathology. For example, when these studies were conducted, congenital blindness was frequent among babies whose incubators were supplied with pure oxygen, whose prolonged inhalation can cause macular degeneration. The babies who were incubated were likely to be either premature or ill to begin with. Nor were these studies definitive technically, because descriptions of the actual facial movements corresponding to these and other displays (e.g., "surprise," "anger") in blind children were vague and imprecise.

According to Eibl-Eibesfeldt (1979), it is untenable that caretakers shape the displays in blind (or blind and deaf) children, because the patterns have to occur in recognizable form to be reinforced. He does not believe that complex responses like tantrums could occur through reinforcement. I contend, respectively, that the disorganized facial movements of the neonatal face occur at frequencies high enough to allow easy reinforcement of selected actions; and that he underestimates the power of reinforcement. Certainly behavioral extinction of tantrums is typically rapid. Eibl-Eibesfeldt allows that deaf and blind children may touch their caretakers' faces and thus acquire displays via this indirect, tactile mimicry.

Eibl-Eibesfeldt argued that tactile modeling could be excluded with a study of thalidomide children tragically born deaf, blind, and without arms (Eibl-Eibesfeldt, 1973a). He reported that these children make typical displays, claiming that differential reinforcement is unlikely because the children could not touch the caretaker's face. Although his cinematographic evidence is compelling, the children still may be reinforced for appropriate displays (e.g., smiles) by caresses and hugs. Once again it is clear that the definitive test would be uniquely provided by studies of blind children who have blind caretakers. The studies would necessarily control for caretakers' touching the children's faces, or hearing their children's vocalizations (the latter would suggest at least the conformation of the mouth). The tactics necessary to approximate these conditions would be so extensive, the prospects of finding enough subjects so rare, and the possible consequences for the children so negative, that such studies are more *Gedanken* experiments than plausible ones.

Despite limitations, the thalidomide-children study, together with the problematic Sackett (1966) isolated infant monkey data, thus constitute the best evidence to date for genetic control of some infantile facial displays and this evidence is weak. Again, the nature of these infant displays is obscured by the anecdotal reportage.

The crucial issue in the study of infant displays, however, is whether these juvenile displays relate at all to *adult* displays. Their existence does not imply *anything* about adult displays, which may have been under different selection pressures during phylogeny and hence may be different neurologically. Ontogenetic accounts of adult displays *postulate* such relationships, but they may be no greater than the connections between infant and adult swimming, or the toe eversion of the Babinski reflex and the kicking of a football.

How could it be determined whether there are such relationships? The distinctiveness of the facial reflexes offers many opportunities to determining whether some adult facial displays are developmentally emancipated facial reflexes. An exhaustive research strategy would explore the following questions:

1. Are there variances in the amplitudes, latencies, and time courses of the facial reflexes, and if so, are the differences heritable?
2. Are there variances in the types and intensities of the elicitors of the facial reflexes, and if so, are these differences heritable?
3. Do the variances observed in either the reflexes or their elicitors account for the variances observed in corresponding aspects of juvenile and then adult facial displays?

These questions can be explored: (1) across species using the comparative method; and in humans, (2) across races or diverse genetic populations, also using the comparative method, and (3) at an individual level, using twin and adoption studies.

THREE ONTOGENETIC HYPOTHESES

There have been no systematic efforts to follow such a strategy, but there is much speculation and some spotty evidence. I summarize three cases of reflexes and their arguably emancipated counterparts in adult human displays: tickling and amusement displays, startle and surprise displays, and gagging and revulsion displays.

Tickling, Humor, and "Duchenne Smiles"

Although it seems farfetched, Darwin (1872) and Hecker (1873) both connected tickling to humor both by virtue of the responses they produced (laughter, smiling, etc.) and in their qualities as elicitors. As Darwin stated by analogy:

> The touch must be light, and an idea or event, to be ludicrous, must not be of grave import. It seems that the precise point to be touched must not be known; so with the mind, something unexpected—a novel or incongruous idea which breaks through an habitual train of thought—appears to be a strong element in the ludicrous. (pp. 201–202)

Fridlund and Loftis (1990) found preliminary support for the Darwin–Hecker hypothesis. Questionnaire data from 100 college students showed strong correlations between reported ticklishness and, as Darwin predicted, their propensities to: (1) giggle, (2) laugh, (3) smile, (4) piloerect, (5) blush, and (6) cry. These relationships were specific to the Darwin–Hecker view, and did not reflect general temperament or excitability.

Fridlund and Loftis also suggested the second ontogenetic mechanism to explain the findings. In their view, the clonic abdominal reflex and its autonomic and facial accompaniments seen in laughter and crying are variable and heritable (see Provine & Yong, 1991, for ethological perspective on laughter). Caretakers typically try to initiate laughter by tickling, with the infant's responding leading caretakers to try visual puns, followed by the word-play of adult humor as the child acquires language. The adult's "sense of humor," then, would depend in part upon the degree of reflexive responding to initial tickling. The cross-sectional data gathered by Fridlund and Loftis (1990) thus suggest a formal developmental test: simply, those who are the most easily tickled as infants should be the most easily humored as adults.

Much has been made recently of cases in which the smile is accompanied by wincing. Wincing is, of course, one of the responses made by people who are being "tickled," either physically or psychologically by humor. The wincing to tickling or humor is actually the continual elicitation of the protective blink reflex of Descartes, which contracts the eye sphincter muscle known as the *orbicularis oculi*. This protective wincing makes sense when one conceives of both tickling, and most kinds of humor, as tension induction (Berlyne, 1969; Spencer, 1860) or mock attack (Freud, 1938; Lorenz, 1966).

Among the first writings about wincing in smiling were those of G. B. Duchenne du Boulogne (1959), mentioned in Chapter 1 for his galvanism of the facial muscles. Ekman and Friesen (1982a) revived one of Duchenne's observations, that "genuine" smiles could be distinguished from "phony" ones by the co-occurrence of wincing. This assertion is questionable, and to see why requires some mention of the history of "genuine" and "phony" smiles.

Among Duchenne's photographs of his subjects' faces, now at the École de Beaux Arts in Paris (Browne, 1985), were those of an elderly gent who reportedly tolerated the galvanism particularly well. Darwin reprinted some of them in the *Expression of the emotions in man and animals* (1872); the two relevant ones are provided here in Figure 6.3.

From Figure 6.3, it is obvious that many cues could mark the ungalvanized face as the "natural" one, chief among them being the presence of the galvanizing electrodes upon the other photograph. In *Expression*, Darwin reported showing the photograph of the nongalvanized condition to several acquaintances. Although Darwin did not specify the question he asked them, all judged it "true to nature" (p. 203). He then showed the other photograph to 24 acquaintances, and apparently asked them what it "meant" (p. 203). Three could not fathom the expres-

FIGURE 6.3.   Photographs made by the French physician G. B. Duchenne du Boulogne, as reprinted by Darwin in *Expression of the emotions in man and animals* (1872). The man is (*left*) smiling, and (*right*) having his cheeks stimulated electrically. The apparently greater wincing seen in the ungalvanized smile, noted by Duchenne, was the basis for Ekman and Friesen's (1982a) claim that wincing was associated with "genuine" or "felt" smiles. Darwin was less convinced (see text).

sion. The remaining 18 judged the expression a smile, and made comments such as " 'a wicked joke,' 'trying to laugh,' 'grinning laughter,' 'half amazed laughter,' etc." (pp. 203–204). Notably, Darwin reported no judge who questioned the authenticity of the face, and the quotations he provided do not suggest that the judges were struck overall by its inauthenticity. Thus nothing a priori is inauthentic about "a wicked joke" or "grinning laughter." "Trying to laugh" might denote inauthenticity, but the judge might have meant that a natural laugh was being obstructed by the electrodes. Nonetheless, Darwin proceeded to accept Duchenne's wholesale judgment that the expression was "false."

Darwin did not accept Duchenne's claim that the man's wincing primarily determined the judgments of "naturalness." He himself tried to analyze the giveaway cues to "naturalness," and concluded that they were as much based on the furrowing of the brow (the galvanisms must have caused some discomfort), and the different conformations of the upper lip and the nasolabial furrow (p. 204). And Darwin notes that smiling itself can compress the lower eyelids and produce the appearance of wincing; hence, the "tight-lipped" smile under galvanization may have been insufficient to change the lower eyelids' appearance.

Despite the ambiguities Darwin noted, Ekman and Friesen (1982a) divided smiles into the "felt" versus the "false," based on the wincing that Duchenne considered so decisive. Ekman (1989) suggested replacement of the term "felt" smile with either "enjoyment smile" or the "Duchenne smile," and he and his colleagues have tried to substantiate the smile dichotomy.

In my discussion of the behavioral ecology view of signaling later in this volume, I question the claim that "felt" and "false" (or "Duchenne" and "non-Duchenne") smiles differ in their authenticity. For now, it serves to note an even more basic problem with the "Duchenne smile" formulation. It conflates two facial movements to make one "expression," and thereby obscures the nature of either.

Smiling plus wincing is just that, a combination of movements consisting of an ordinary smile (i.e., the bilateral contraction of *zygomatic major*), plus the tonic elicitation of the blink reflex of Descartes. The issue is not the illusory one of "types of smiles" and the ostensible phenomenology tied to each, but the conditions under which the protective blink reflex of Descartes coincides with smiling. Both would be expected in humor, or the psychic tickling noted by Darwin and Hecker, and indeed, Ekman et al. have solely used humorous films to elicit them (Ekman, Davidson, & Friesen, 1990; Frank, Ekman, & Friesen, 1993).[4]

Of course, one objection might be that humor inductions imply enjoyment, so that I have just redefined terms. However, humor—like tickling—is not always enjoyable. People can easily be tickled or humored past their tolerances, such that they will yell "Stop!," cry copiously, grab their sides to palpate cramps ("side-splitting humor"), or fall to the floor from cataleptic loss of postural tonus; and all the while they keep smiling and wincing. This is not enjoyment.

One should expect protective wincing to occur conjointly with many other facial displays and with elicitors besides humor. Ekman et al. (1990) and Frank et al. (1993), because they classified smiling with wincing as a conjoint single act, did not provide evidence that wincing itself was restricted to humor, that is, that it had discriminant validity. Indeed, it should not be. We wince when we threaten others with beady eyes, or ogle them with a reptilian stare. And we wince when someone chastises us and makes us cringe, tells us a harrowing story about a close call, asks us to solve a complex math problem in our heads, or tells us how much they will miss us. If we followed the logic used to discuss the "Duchenne smile," and made wincing criterial for naming new facial displays,

---

[4] The Frank et al. study used the same films as Ekman, Friesen, and Ancoli (1980), but like the published report by Ekman et al. (1980), it omitted the "ocean" condition in which subjects reported equivalent happiness but made very few smiles. I doubt whether subjects would wince in that condition, either. The importance of the selective omission of this experimental condition is discussed in more detail in Chapter 11.

Leonard et al. (1991) reported an optical illusion whereby judges examining photos of smiling subjects "saw" difference in the "expression" of the eyes when there was none: "Apparently the change in mouth shape affected the 'Gestalt' of the entire face" (p. 168). It is possible that even trained facial coders are susceptible to this illusion, and are over-coding wincing.

we would be forced to have the Duchenne threat, the Duchenne frown, the Duchenne stare, and so on. Instead, we should consider protective wincing as a normal response to nearly any strong stimulus, and not one predictive of any particular hedonic or phenomenological state.

Startle and Surprise Displays

Startle and surprise are certainly superficially similar. Both occur following an unexpected stimulus with a quick onset, and both include rapid limb movements (usually retractions).[5]

The ontogenetic question is whether components of startle combine to form the display that connotes "surprise." The usual contention about the two is that "the term *startle* is used to describe the most extreme surprise reaction" (Ekman & Friesen, 1975, p. 36).

This can be true on the stimulus end. An unexpected 80 dB tone may be merely surprising, but one at 140 dB is almost certainly startling. This generalization does not always apply, however, because we can be startled by a light tap on the back if we are preoccupied or believe that we are alone.

Apart from their elicitors, it is debated whether the reactions themselves are related (Tomkins, 1962; Vaughan & Sroufe, 1976; Wolff, 1966). There is certainly a "surprise" display, issued when we are struck by the unexpected. There is a conventionalized version that we use conversationally when we want another to believe—rightly or wrongly—that what he or she is saying is unexpected. In contrast, it is unlikely that the startle reaction itself is formalized as a social display, because it is so brief, and because others nearby are likely to be startled by the same stimulus and unable to observe one another well enough for mimicry.

In order to evaluate whether startle and surprise are related, precise measurements are required of each. Startle has been studied more closely. Ekman, Friesen, and Simons (1985) extended efforts of Landis and Hunt (1939) by examining the response topography of subjects startled by a pistol shot. Both sets of investigators found marked, reliable stereotypy (wincing, lip stretches, head and trunk movements) within 200 msec of the startle stimulus. Ekman, Friesen, and Simons also found this stereotypy to be unaffected in timing or topography when subjects were instructed to inhibit the reaction. In contrast to these data, observations of surprise are largely anecdotal, but they suggest several differences. Startled people wince, but they open their eyes in surprise. They retract

---

[5] The startle reflex is anatomically and functionally distinct from the infant's Moro reflex, sometimes called the "Darwinian grasp" reflex, which is elicited by the perception of falling and is clinically induced by letting the head drop several inches. The Moro reflex is the "fur-clinging" reflex advantageous to the infants of modern hirsute primates; in us it is vestigial.

(stretch) their lips when startled, but drop their jaws when surprised (e.g., Ekman & Friesen, 1975).

It seems obvious that the startle reaction is protective but the surprise reaction is investigative, and that their topographic differences discount the premise of a surprise-startle continuum. What they share nonetheless is that both occur to novelty, and this may make an ontogenetic analysis interesting. For example, the amplitude and latency of the startle reaction is variable from person to person, and can be manipulated experimentally (e.g., Lang, Bradley, & Cuthbert, 1990). Additionally, the heightened startle pathognomonic of Post-Traumatic Stress Disorder suggests that the reaction is characterologically modifiable over the life span (American Psychiatric Association, 1987; Archibald & Tuddenham, 1965). Thus it would be relatively easy to compare the relations between startle and surprise both cross-sectionally and longitudinally.

A final word about the nature of "surprise." That many researchers tally surprise among their "basic" emotions (e.g., Izard, 1971) is—well, surprising—because what surprises us can be either wanted or unwanted. Even Ekman and Friesen (1975) stated that "surprise itself is neutral in hedonic tone. It is, rather, the following emotion that gives a positive or negative tone to the experience" (p. 35). They still included surprise as one of their original six basic emotions. Of course, any behavior could be indicative of "emotion" given the distensibility of the emotion concept (more on this in a later chapter), but an emotion without hedonic tone is a special distention of the concept.

Instead, the facial behavior of "surprise" is best considered just one part of ordinary orientation, with the eye and mouth sphincters (the *Orbicularis oculi* and *Orbicularis oris*, respectively) relaxing as components of the investigative behavior.

Gagging and "Disgust Displays"

Another candidate for ontogenetic study is the gag reflex and its relationship to later "disgust" and revulsion displays.

The "gag" reflex is clinically evoked by pharyngeal stimulation (when it is known as the pharyngeal reflex; Table I). It is also elicited readily by ingesting unpalatable (e.g., rotten) substances. During gagging the jaw drops, the soft palate closes off the mouth airway, the nares (nostrils) close off the nasal airway, the tongue flattens and protrudes from the mouth (the "gaping" seen in numerous species) and reverse peristalsis (incipient vomiting) often ensues. Gagging is obviously protective. It is elicited through CN IX (the glossopharyngeal nerve) and enacted mostly through CN X (the vagus nerve). Mediation is substantially via the pontine brainstem, with other central mediation unclear (Nolte, 1988).

One of the clearest instances in which a facial display resembles a protective reflex is the social "disgust display." Assuming some connection, how did we get from the pharyngeal reflex to the social display? It may be that during maturation the child begins to deploy a weakened gag reflex in *anticipation* of ingesting something foul. With further development, the *idea* of something foul may deploy the weakened reflex, and what is foul may no longer be food, but aesthetics or politics (cf. Rozin, Haidt, & McCauley, 1993). This is an extended conditioning argument (e.g., Aronfreed, 1968), but it is troublesome for a Pavlovian model given that it: (1) should extinguish in a few trials without reinforcement by a direct reflex elicitor; and (2) depends on an extreme degree of stimulus generalization to explain elicitation by merely disagreeable ideas.

More likely, the social disgust display is simply a convention, a conversational icon, just like the child's use of tongue protrusion as a cocky display of defiance. It may be acquired via social shaping of reflexive rejection (the second ontogenetic mechanism), or it may simply be an analogy (the fourth mechanism).

The analogy account seems especially persuasive. Allport (1924) endorsed it, and recounted it vividly:

> The facial reaction here is that accompanying the rejection of an unsavory substance from the alimentary canal, as from vomiting; or the puckering of the nose so as to prevent the entrances of unpleasant odors into the nostrils. Originally the response was produced *only* when stimulated by such disagreeable substances; but with increasing development it becomes extended to persons, language, scenes, and proposals which offend one's aesthetic habits or moral principles. The language of the face is cruder and more frank than that of the tongue. To look at a person with contempt is to say to him, 'I can't stand your odor!' To look at him with loathing is to liken him to an intolerable substance which one is about to vomit. (p. 215)

Buttressing the analogy account are the frequent *verbal* analogies that often supplement the face or even supplant it, for example, "You make [or it makes] me sick," "Don't give [feed] me that," or among one cohort of California teenagers, "Gag me with a spoon." The disgust display, whether or not deployed with words, deters interaction (cf. Smith, 1977); it signifies "I am rejecting you [or it]."

Viewing the display has undoubted potency. Seeing another vomit food nearby can be enough to stop us from eating, or even trigger our own nausea or vomiting.[6] Admittedly, what may be aversive here is not only the face but also the sound and posture of vomiting, not to mention the sight and smell of the *vomitus*. The effect is salutary, since we are

---

[6] I am speaking strictly of the instigation of retching, which is not necessarily associated with nausea. Rozin and Fallon (1987) should be consulted on the development of disgust reactions, and on their relationship to food, contamination, and superstition.

likely to be eating from the same menu. Conversationally the consequence is similar: seeing another "spit out" us or our ideas with a disgust display is usually enough to make us either leave or change the subject (that is, the topical menu).

Like the "surprise face" above, some theorists consider the "disgust" face an "expression" of a basic emotion (e.g., Ekman & Friesen, 1975; Izard, 1971). The facts suggest otherwise. The gag reflex acts not to "express" sensory disgust but to abort it. Likewise, the social display[7] signifies not "you make me sick" so much as "I want to do with you what I do with bad food (lest I get sick)." It thereby denotes an intention rather than an "expression" of an emotion, and is therefore better named "revulsion" or even "rejection" than "disgust." As for the often-noted concurrence of the display with teeth-baring and/or nasal aversion (in these cases, sometimes labeled "contempt"), these actions simply signal the vehemence or finality of the rejection.

SUMMARY OF ONTOGENETIC ACCOUNTS AND RESEARCH STRATEGY

"Isolation studies" using the congenitally blind and thalidomide babies have been implemented to test the innateness of displays by restricting visual and tactile experience, respectively. Results from these studies suggest that neither type of experience may be required for the emergence of infant displays such as crying and distress. Because the environmental restrictions are incomplete, the results are only tentative, and may imply little about adult displays. Using infants whose sensoria are more restricted is of little use, because these infants usually suffer more general neuropathological debility, and probable secondary psychopathology as well.

The prospects are more sanguine for evaluating more specific ontogenetic mechanisms, specifically those concerning the facial reflexes. Almost nothing is known about the extent to which the facial reflexes are variable, and whether any such variance is heritable. These basic physiological data are prerequisite for evaluating the ontogenetic mechanisms I reviewed. These mechanisms differ in the degree to which they base adult facial displays upon the facial reflexes, or assume the innateness of the displays themselves. I have suggested a research strategy for evaluating the viability of these ontogenetic mechanisms.

Evaluating the specific ontogenetic hypotheses I have discussed has

---

[7] The nonreflexive "disgust" display, which I here label "social," can of course be issued when alone, as when we recall someone obnoxious or something objectionable. Here, as in many other cases I review later, the solitary face has the same status as solitary language (e.g., talking *sotto voce* to ourselves or others). It is "social" even though the referent is ourselves or an implicit interactant, as I discuss in Chapter 7.

been hampered by insistent efforts to force-fit infant facial movements into theories of "emotional expressions" with their excess phenomenological baggage, and to a priori sets of "fundamental emotions" (these theories handicap us enough in the realm of *adult* facial behavior, as I discuss next). Infant facial movements begin in muscles that are primarily sphincters gating oral, olfactory, and visual perception, and quickly come to regulate social interaction. How this happens is fascinating in its own terms.

7

EMOTIONS VERSUS BEHAVIORAL ECOLOGY VIEWS OF FACIAL EXPRESSION: THEORY AND CONCEPTS

Since Darwin, the central preoccupation of researchers on the face has been to forge the correct links between movements of the face and those ineluctable states we call emotions. The advocates of this "Emotions View" (I cite some of the more influential ones below) are not a homogeneous group in all their axioms and precepts, but they share the belief in the centrality of emotion in explaining facial movements.

The Emotions View of faces differs substantially from the "Behavioral Ecology View" that derives from modern accounts of the evolution of signaling behavior.[1] Each view has consequences for how we understand the evolution of facial displays, the findings about facial displays across diverse geographic regions, and the role of facial behavior in our everyday lives. This section contrasts the two.

THE EMOTIONS VIEW OF FACES

In this view, emotions are akin to instincts (see McDougall, 1908). They are elaborations of homeostasis, differentiated from a set of phyletically primitive tropisms or dispositions such as approach–avoidance (e.g., Izard & Malatesta, 1987; Kinsbourne, 1978a,b; Schneirla, 1959). The prototypes for such dispositions may be seen in consummation. For example, just like a water-deprived organism that appraises water positively and seeks it out (or conversely, appraises poison negatively and rejects it), so an organism appraises an "emotional" stimulus and reacts "emotionally" to it.

A term used commonly by emotion theorists is the "decoupled reflex." This is used to denote that emotions are like reflexes in their automaticity but not so fixed in their responses. Leventhal and Scherer (1987) provided a clear description of the decoupled reflex model:

> Whereas an amoeba will reflexively move if the temperature changes, a human facing bitter cold will feel distress, experience physiological changes and a strong urge to move, yet may stand fast. The ability to stand fast with distress permits a wider range of instrumental responses such as putting on more layers of clothing or burning the furniture. Emotional processes decouple automatic, reflex responses from their eliciting stimuli and provide the opportunity for more adaptive reactions. (p. 7)

These decoupled reflexes make the organism respond more flexibly in a changing environment by providing "intraorganismic signals" (Scherer, 1984) that mediate behavior. Either by habit transmitted to progeny

---

[1] I suggest the "behavioral ecology" descriptor because it connotes interdependence, and thereby underscores the coevolution of formalization and vigilance. I make this choice with some reservation, given that it is sometimes identified strictly with the slightly cynical and overstated Krebs–Davies–Dawkins exploitive view of signaling (Krebs & Dawkins, 1984; also see Krebs & Davies, 1987, for a synoptic look at behavioral ecology). I do not use the term so parochially; the terms "interactional" or "communicative" could easily be substituted.

through use-inheritance (e.g., Spencer, 1855; Darwin, 1872), or over the course of genetic evolution (Tinbergen, 1952, 1953), these tropisms or drives became differentiated and intensified. Thus, to meet environmental complexities, "approach" differentiated into, for example, happiness or lust, and "avoidance" into, for example, sadness, fear or guilt. Izard (1991) also described the supposed progression from instinct to emotion, with its apotheosis in the human:

> It is relatively easy to see why animal life developed reflexes and instincts. Reflexes are specific adaptive patterns of behavior that in some cases accompany an animal through an entire life cycle. Human beings are born with less [sic] reflexes, though a few of them, like the eye blink, remain adaptive throughout life. But reflexes and instincts are rigid and stimulus dependent; when decision-making and flexibility in strategy or performance are required, they are not enough. (p. 4)
>
> In the evolution of the human species, emotions emerged to provide new types of motivation and new action tendencies as well as a greater variety of behaviors to cope with the environment and life's demands. (p. 9)[2]

Although Herbert Spencer (1855) regarded facial behavior as a "spillover" of emotion (this position resurfaced in early ethology's releaser theory), the dominant conception in the Emotions View is that facial actions associated with these elaborated reflexes are "readouts" (Buck, 1984, 1985) of the state that occasions their instigation. As Buck (1984) stated:

> Spontaneous expression is . . . a kind of running "progress report" which involves a direct reflection or "readout" of the affective aspects of the process of knowledge by acquaintance. (p. 13)

In humans the "decoupled reflexes" become "fundamental emotions" or "affect programs" (e.g., Ekman, 1972; Izard, 1971, 1977; Tomkins, 1962, 1963), which begin to resemble the "fixed action patterns" of early ethology (Alcock, 1984). The affect programs that constitute the fundamental emotions consist of a constellation of behavioral, physiological, and experiential phenomena. As Izard described them, fundamental emotions have: "(a) a specific innately determined neural substrate, (b) a characteristic neuromuscular-expressive pattern, and (c) a distinct subjective or phenomenological quality" (Izard, 1972, p. 2). These programs are triggered by certain prototypical events, whose salience was also determined during human evolution (Plutchik, 1980). The list of fundamental emotions vary with the theorist, but most advocates of the Emotions View include: happiness, sadness, anger, fear, surprise, disgust,

---

[2] The contention that humans are born with fewer reflexes than nonhuman animals has no neurological basis. In this passage Izard appears to foreclose the possibility of nonhuman emotion, but this is not Izard's consistent position, nor is it widespread among emotions theorists.

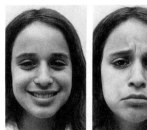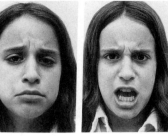

FIGURE 7.1.   Facial configurations maintained by the Emotions View to be innate, universal expressions of four fundamental emotions: (*left* to *right*) happiness, sadness, anger, and fear. Photographs courtesy of Linda Camros.

and contempt. Each is maintained to have its own prototypical expression; some examples are provided in Figure 7.1. Emotional expressions that depart from the expected prototypes are asserted *ad hoc* to be admixtures of the prototypes, resulting from the expression of "blended affects" (Tomkins, 1963; Ekman & Friesen, 1969b, 1978; Izard, 1979).

Although these fundamental emotions are innate programs, they are not immune to modification of either their instigators or their facial readouts:

> The fact that there are genetically based mechanisms for the fundamental emotions does not mean that no aspect of an emotion can be modified through experience. Almost anyone can learn to inhibit or modify the innate emotional expressions . . . In addition to learning modifications of emotion expressions, sociocultural influences and individual experiences play an important role in determining what will trigger an emotion and what a person will do as a result of an emotion. (Izard, 1991, p. 19)

For the emotions theorist, emotions are modifiable with experience, and thus infancy is where they can be observed in the raw (cf. Malatesta, 1985). It is during infancy that the various aspects of emotion, such as feeling states and faces, are innately concordant (Izard, 1978; Izard & Malatesta, 1987). Over the course of development, as the nervous system is thought to become more "corticalized," the associated displays gradually become subtler, less instinctlike, and more socialized (Izard & Malatesta, 1987). With this "corticalization" and socialization comes the possibility of deception, whether malignant lying or the benign variety seen in politeness and diplomacy. The result is that in normal social interaction, the involuntary readouts of emotion can be modified to meet the demands of enculturation. They become masked, squelched, or histrionically intensified (Ekman, 1985). In these cases, culture can be pitted against the innate emotion programs, and despite great efforts to maintain a social "mask," one's emotion can "leak" onto the face (Ekman,

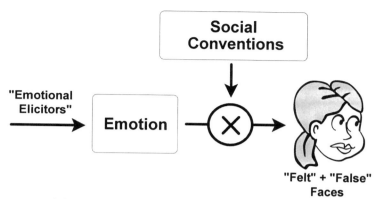

FIGURE 7.2.   Schematic of the two-factor model that underlies common emotions views of facial expressions. In this model, everyday faces result from innate, prototypical facial expressions that read out emotional state, but which can be modified by socialization.

1984); an example would be pursed lips that "leaked" anger on a determinedly impassive visage.

It is apparent that the most frequent Emotions View of faces is, as I termed it elsewhere (Fridlund, 1991a), essentially a "two-factor" model that posits two basic kinds of faces. This model is depicted in Figure 7.1. First are the innate reflexlike faces that read out ongoing emotion; these are termed "facial expressions of emotion." Second are learned, instrumental faces that connote emotion that is not occurring; these reflect everyday social dissimulation such as the smile of politeness. The facial expressions observed in everyday life represent an interaction of emotional instigation and cultural adulteration, as Figure 7.2 shows.

The origins of the two kinds of faces differ as well. The emotional facial displays, and the elicitors of these displays, are held to be substantially innate. Conversely, the supposed hiding or disguising of emotional displays, and the deployment of nonemotional displays, is held to be largely a function of training or tradition within a given culture (i.e., the putative cultural display rules of Ekman & Friesen, 1971). The learned modulation of "involuntary" emotional displays by display rules is posited by perhaps the best known of the two-factor theories, Ekman's neurocultural model (e.g., Ekman, 1972, 1973, 1977). Ekman's model had its major impact as one interpretation of findings about faces from different cultures and geographic regions. Russell reviews these studies in Chapter 10, and I discuss Ekman's model in Chapter 11.

I appropriated the "two-factor" moniker from Mowrer's earlier "two-factor" learning theory, which considered behavior to be a composition of Pavlovian conditioning and instrumental learning (Mowrer, 1960). The two-factor conception is implicit in Buck's spontaneous/symbolic face distinction (Buck, 1984). It is explicit and distinctly Mowrerian in studies that treat "emotional" and "social" faces, respectively, as conditional responses and instrumental acts (e.g., Vaughan & Lanzetta, 1980), or in views that dichotomize faces as "felt" versus "false" (Ekman & Friesen, 1982a). The two-factor conception self-consciously draws from Darwin, who proposed two classes of facial expressions: inherited habits and learned simulations of those habits. Note, however, that the Emotions View places itself in Darwin's lineage, except that Darwin's emotional expressions were useless vestiges and not adaptive readouts. The Emotions View also draws upon an implicit but familiar romanticist portrait of human nature, which I believe explains both its appeal and its persistence. I discuss this romanticist view in Chapter 11.

THE BEHAVIORAL ECOLOGY VIEW OF FACES

In contrast to the Emotions View, the Behavioral Ecology View of facial displays does not treat them as "expressions" of discrete, internal emotional states, or the outputs of modular affect programs. For the contemporary ethologist or the behavioral ecologist, displays have their impact upon others' behavior because, for reasons I outlined in Chapter 4, vigilance for and comprehension of signals coevolved with the signals themselves. The balance of signaling and vigilance, countersignaling and countervigilance, produces a signaling "ecology" that is analogous to the balance of resources and consumers, and predator and prey, that characterize all natural ecosystems.

Displays are specific to intent and context, rather than derivatives or blends of a small set of fundamental emotional displays. Indeed, simultaneously proposing a small set of fundamental affects, and then invoking "blends" of them to explain why everyday displays are so varied, is considered procrustean, tautological, and self-confirming (see Ortony & Turner, 1990, for a critique of theories of "basic emotions"). Instead of there being six or seven displays of "fundamental emotions" (e.g., anger), there may be one dozen or one hundred "about to aggress" displays appropriate to the identities and relationship of the interactants, and the context in which the interaction occurs. [3] The topography of an "about to aggress" display may depend on whether the interactant is dominant or nondominant, conspecific or extraspecific, and whether one is defending territory or young, contesting for access to a female, or

---

[3] Moynihan (1970) and Smith (1969) surveyed the literature on numbers of displays found in diverse species. Both concluded that there was an upper limit of about 40 discriminable displays in each species's repertoire. As the authors acknowledged, these kinds of frequency counts are incomplete because they do not include spatial and temporal configurations of displays. They also omit human paralanguage. The question of frequency counts of displays is extremely complicated, since display taxonomies can be structural or functional, and the functional taxonomies must also tabulate the contexts in which displays are deployed.

TABLE I   Emotions and Behavioral Ecology Interpretations of Common Human Facial Displays

Emotions view ("facial expressions of emotion")	Behavioral ecology view (signification of intent)
"Felt" ("Duchenne") smile (expression of happiness)	Readiness to play or affiliate ("Let's play [keep playing]," or "Let's be friends")
"False" smile (feigned happiness)	Readiness to appease ("Whatever you say," or "I give in")
"Sad" face	Recruitment of succor or request for restitution ("Take care of me," "Hold me," or "Please make it right [or better]")
"Anger" face	Readiness to attack ("Back off or I'll attack")
"Leaked" anger (inhibited anger)	Conflict about attacking ("I want to attack and I *don't* want to attack")
"Fear" face	Readiness to submit ("If you continue, I'll back off [slink away]")
"Contentment" face	Readiness to continue current interaction ("Everything [you're doing] is just fine")
"Contempt" face	Declaration of superiority ("I can't even bother with you")
"Poker" face (suppressed emotion)	Declaration of neutrality ("I'm taking no position [on what you're doing or saying]")

retrieving stolen food or property. Any genetic control might apply to one form but not another.

Table I compares typical facial displays as interpreted by the Emotions View and the Behavioral Ecology View. Note that I have not depicted prototype faces for each category. This is because, *contra* the Emotions View, there seem to be *no* prototype faces for each category. Rather, displays exert their influence in the particular context of their issuance; a face interpreted as "contemptuous" in one context may be interpreted as "exasperated" or even "constipated" in another (Chapter 10 provides the evidence here). The table simply illustrates the kinds of descriptors that each View applies to facial displays. Thus, in contexts in which one would try to appease another, any smile one issued would tend to be labeled a "false smile" in the Emotions View, which would connote a masking smile over some other emotion. For the behavioral ecologist, the same smile would likely be labeled an "about to appease" display, and it would deliver the same message as the words, "I give in" or "Whatever you say."

Because facial displays are the results of a formalized coevolution with vigilance for them (Chapter 4), they are not readouts but "social tools" (Smith, 1977) that aid the negotiation of social encounters. Andrew (1963b) captured the distinction when, in decrying the notion that instinctlike emotion underlies display, he stated, "It is probably truer for a man to say 'I would like to hit you' than for him to say 'I am angry'" (p. 5).[4] Andrew's quote should not be construed to say that displays *express* intent; this would be yet another "readout" view. Instead, displays are declarations that signify our trajectory in a given social interaction, that is, what we will do in the current situation, or what we would like the other to do. And this "context" depends considerably not only on the structural features of the situation, but on the succession of interactants' displays and their responses to them. Ginsburg and Harrington (1993) stated this eloquently by illustrating how a sequence of linguistic displays (i.e., utterances) arises from a current context and thereby alters it:

> Actions are components of larger acts which their successful completion helps to accomplish. For example, caustic and denigrating comments help to accomplish an argument . . . For example, in a violent argument we might find the sequence,
> "What do you take me for, a fool?
> "Yes."
> "Oh yeah? I'll show you" [followed by a knife attack].
> The last utterance and its associated violent action occur under the condition of the two prior utterances having been performed. This is similar to the notion (Clark & Brennan, 1991) that conversations are the progressive accumulation of common ground: actions at prior times in the course of an act constitute the context for current actions in that act . . . And the current actions become incorporated as part of the context for subsequent actions. (p. 4)

I have depicted my conception of the Behavioral Ecology View in Figure 7.3. It is meant to contrast with the two-factor Emotions View model in Figure 7.2. The figure makes obvious that the "facial expressions of emotion" of the Emotions View actually serve the social motives of the displayer. No distinction is made between "felt" and "false" displays issued by "authentic" and "social" selves; instead *all* displays are considered to arise from interaction, thus there is *only* an interactive self (I discuss the sociality of solitary facial displays in Chapter 8). Finally, displays are deployed and interpreted within the context of the interaction ("social context" in the figure). This context is formed from both its structural features (e.g., the setting as well as the relations of the interactants), and—as the Ginsburg and Harrington quote establishes—the accreted "common ground" that arises from any previous interactions.

---

[4] Andrew's statement is correct insofar as it grounds displays in contingent intent, but it may be misleading if one infers that one may be able to verbalize an intention in order to *have* one. Thus, we can "blurt out" faces just as we can "blurt out" words and not know why in either case; our "explanations" for these Freudian slips, and if you will, Freudian faces, are either post hoc rationalizations or reasonable accounts provided by others.

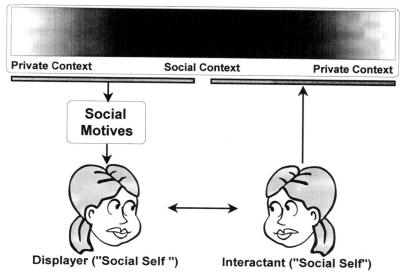

FIGURE 7.3. The Behavioral Ecology View of facial displays, showing that displays are issued in the service of social motives, and are interpretable in the context of interaction.

Finally, the "private context" of the participants consists of that set of expectations, needs, and so on, that each brings to the interaction, and these in turn result in great part from one's prior interactions. For this reason, the figure depicts the interactants' private contexts as melding with their shared social context.

In summary, the Emotions View holds that facial displays (except for paralinguistic and deceptive ones) are prepotent, involuntary readouts of emotion that emerge unless deliberately masked or suppressed (Ekman, 1984). From an evolutionary perspective, this conception is unlikely on five grounds, because it: (1) regards "emotional expression" as automatic unless volitionally managed, and thus neglects the costs of automatic display; (2) omits the recipient's coevolutionary role in display; (3) presumes that adult displays emerge from "emotional" infant displays through socialized dissimulation; (4) fails to account for the poor relationship between emotions and facial displays; and (5) takes a crypto-moralistic view of deception. I discuss each of these difficulties in detail, and indicate the resolutions afforded by the Behavioral Ecology View.

The Emotions View Neglects the Costs of Automatic Expression

As I mentioned earlier, any reasonable account of signaling must recognize that signals do not evolve to provide information detrimental to the signaler. Displayers must not signal automatically, but only when it is beneficial to do so, that is, when such signaling serves its motives. Automatic readouts or spillovers of drive states (i.e., "facial expressions of emotion") would be extinguished early in phylogeny in the service of deception, economy, and privacy. Thus, an individual who momentarily shows a pursed lip on an otherwise impassive face is not showing "leakage" of anger but conflicting intentions (cf. Tinbergen, 1953), for example, to show stolidity *and* to threaten.

The Emotions View Omits the Recipient's Coevolutionary Role

The second reason that the reflexive, emotion "readout" conception of emotion theories is improbable is that it neglects the indispensable role of the recipient in the process of formalization. Recipients of displays should only attend to cues that provide predictions about the future behavior of the displayer, regardless of how the displayer "feels." This does not imply that recipients can *only* use formalized cues; everyday behavior in a given context also allows prediction of the others' next moves (Argyle, 1972; Kendon, 1981). Nonetheless, only those cues to which recipients reliably attend *can* become formalized. Social intentions must therefore drive displays, and one's emotional state bears no necessary relation to how one is moved to act.

Although I reviewed mechanisms whereby some displays may have their origins in formalized reflexes, the stereotypy and "automaticity" of displays connoting emotion (Ekman, 1984) do not necessarily imply reflexive origins. To the contrary, "automatic," instinctlike displays may have arisen from skilled social instrumental acts. This is because genes that produce functional acts would be expected to proliferate, creating better performers of those acts. Over the course of evolution, natural selection would produce better and better learning of these acts such that they would resemble reflexes or tropisms, in due course losing their instrumental character. Thus skilled acts, not only reflexes, may have been preadapted as displays. Our progenitors may have been *less* reflexive displayers than we.

The components of any complex display, then, may reflect a mixture of two mechanisms: the emancipation and formalization of reflexes, and the automatization and "instinctualization" of instrumental acts. For example, human threat displays are often marked by a tightened jaw and narrowed gaze, with clenched fists and rigid arms. I believe that the gaze may be an emancipated and ritualized protective reflex, whereas the jaws, fists, and arms are "instinctualized," formerly instrumental acts associated with attack.

The Emotions View Presumes That Adult Faces Are Dissimulated Variations of Infant Faces

The most reflex-like human faces are seen in infants, and in the Emotions View they are held to reflect an "innate expression-feeling concordance" (cf. Izard & Malatesta, 1987). In the Behavioral Ecology View, the seeming reflexiveness of infant displays just reflects the selection pressures upon the infant. The altricial human infant's social milieu is relatively simple; the infant merely needs to garner caretaker attention, and the caretakers discern the required response. Thus the primary selection pressures on children are to capture and hold the attention of caretakers (especially if competition originally occurred among infants of multiple caretakers, i.e., if early hominids were polygynous; see Alexander, Hoogland, Howard, Noonan, & Sherman, 1979). In appreciating this view, it would be well to conceive of the infant not as an innocent bundle of joy (although, sentimentally, it often is!), but as a servomechanism cleverly shaped by natural selection to emit the displays that will optimally promote and maintain parental care. Evolution should thus equip infants with displays specialized to be intense attention-grabbers.

What displays should evolution "choose" to grab adult attention? Conceivably, infants may have evolved merely to be good emulators of the requisite adult displays. Those infants who are good emulators can better parasitize the extant adult signal system. Thus by virtue of the fact that adults succor other adults who are crying, those infants who produce loud cries will receive more reliable care. Because adults are engaged when other adults smile, then babies who produce "flashbulb" social smiles will more readily engage caretakers and obtain similar advantage. Because infants who did not emit pronounced cries or smiles would have been comparatively neglected and less viable, natural selection should directly shape the production of exaggerated, plangent, canonical infant displays.[5]

When should infants display? In the case of crying, infants should of course cry when hungry, tired, in pain or in need of diapering, and so on. The so-called "distress" cries of the newborn, in this account, are

---

[5] The emulation may be due to natural selection (i.e., the infant is a hard-wired emulator), and/or it may occur via early imitation of the caricatured faces caretakers make toward neonates (Meltzoff & Moore, 1977).

A disguised, erroneous recapitulationism is contained in the belief (cf. Rousseau and Freud) that human displays connoting emotion reflect the upwelling of our "animal" pasts. As many observers have remarked, humans may be *more* histrionic than their progenitors. Lorenz (1970) first noted that humans may be especially reactive not because of regression (i.e., Jacksonian dissolution) but because of their neoteny (retention of juvenile traits due to developmental retardation). In other words, the human adult's similarity to the infant is not only morphological—it extends to the behavior of the adult form as well. Lorenz attributes to behavioral neoteny other human qualities such as close family life and adult curiosity.

protolinguistic protests which mean, "Fix it!" or just "Get me outta' here!" These displays are "honest," that is, occurring when the infant needs a caretaker's direct intervention. The infant, however, cleverly shaped by natural selection, should issue additional cries, or convincingly urgent ones, periodically and unpredictably. These "deceptive" cries[6] should be issued often enough to insure steady caretaker attention, but not so often or so needlessly that the attention diminishes or even extinguishes. Caretaker attention is a risky commodity, as suggested by the high rates of child abuse and infanticide worldwide, and most likely it is infants' ingratiation strategies (e.g., acting cute and issuing endearing smiles) that explain why so many manage to thrive.

Is the displaying infant "emotional"? Prerequisite to any answer is a definition of emotion,[7] but for the behavioral ecologist the question is moot. Individuals of any age who show the right displays at the right time will survive, even if they are anhedonic (arguably, the psychopathic adult fits this criterion). Displays function as manipulations, and infant cries and smiles are manipulations that merely serve to garner caretaker attention and intervention. No emotion is implied or required; whether infants are emotional when they issue displays is a separate problem whose resolution requires evidence independent of the displays.

Compared to infants, older children begin a trend toward more subtle and variegated displays. In the Emotions View, the change from plangency to subtlety of display reflects learned dissimulation, that is, "socialization of emotion" (cf. Lewis & Michalson, 1982, 1985) or the internalization of "display rules" (Saarni, 1978), the effect of which is the

---

[6] From a mechanistic standpoint, one could well imagine that infants would evolve a set of semistochastic generators that are wired to separate displays, and whose firing rates have evolved for optimal caretaker attention.

That infants might be deceptive is at first blush hard to accept. As I describe in Chapter 11, the Emotions View of the infant is an ill-disguised derivation from Rousseau, reinforced by the musings of poets and insistent pop-culture propaganda. In this conception, infants are naive and untainted by worldly duplicity until they are corrupted by culture—their displays are no longer "authentic" (i.e., emotional) but become distorted by the demands of society ("display rules").

My claim that infants have social motives but not emotions is opposite to the usual view. Again, my use of "motive" and "intention" implies no necessary awareness or volition. Instead, the intentionality is programmed by natural selection (cf. Dennett, 1987). In other words, the "sin" of signaling to one's own advantage is original. Nor does deception imply corruption, *if* displays are seen as deployed in the service of social motives. Thus the infant's distress cry sometimes signifies "diaper me," whereas at other times it signifies "attend to me even though I don't need it" (i.e., need it biologically). There is no basis for assigning ontological primacy to either.

Wolff (1969) asserted based on spectrographic data that infants have different cries for different needs. His assertion has led to the burgeoning research on infant "cry psychophysics" (Green, Jones, & Gustafson, 1987). There may be different cry types, but infants whose cries *all* seemed to signal biologic need would be at an advantage (notably, parents may not be able to discriminate cry types; see Muller, Hallien, & Murry, 1974).

[7] Throughout this chapter and the next, I use the word "emotion" freely, in the variety of ways used by proponents of the Emotions View. In fact, proponents provide no agreed-upon way to determine whether one has an emotion or is being emotional. I discuss these problems with definition in Chapters 8 and 11.

uncoupling of the innate expression-feeling concordance (Izard & Malatesta, 1987). In the Behavioral Ecology View, the increased subtlety of more mature displays may be due to either maturation or socialization.

Conceivably, increased variation in facial display with maturation would simply reflect normal developmental differentiation of both morphology and behavior, a trend seen even in early embryonic development and known as von Baer's Law of Differentiation (von Baer, 1828). More likely, the increased subtlety of display *is* social, but it is not dissimulation. Rather, it results from the fact that the child apperceives more complex social relations, which engender more complex social motives. Thus the infant merely has to cry or smile to garner the attention of a caretaker who discerns how to respond. In contrast, the adult rarely has an attentive, discerning caretaker. Satisfying needs requires sophisticated signals to negotiate a complex social terrain that includes one's relatedness to those present, and a context of interaction that may involve varying social roles, past interactions, modes of reciprocation, and moral notions of entitlement.

The Emotions View Fails to Account for the Poor Relationship between Emotions and Facial Displays

Adults are certainly considered to "have emotions," but the relation of adult display to emotion, as usually defined, is adventitious. Displays serve social motives, which themselves may depend little upon whether, for example, people say that they are emotional. Everyday smiling is illustrative. We may be courteous, loving, amusing, or reassuring, and smile accordingly, if we are so moved—regardless of whether we feel happy, sad, angry, or fearful. I know of no evidence that we smile more when we are happy, but if we do, it is likely so for two reasons. We may simply prefer (and report being "happier") in situations that engender such motives. More likely, social motives served by smiles (e.g., humor, play, affiliation) may arise more frequently during those periods when we say that we're happy, and at these times, our impulse is to tell someone. This impulse may reflect personal disposition or cultural tradition about whether one "shares one's happiness" with another or simply thanks God quietly for one's blessings.

It is clear as well that people often do *not* show facial behavior when the emotions theorist would predict it by nearly any criterion. When people feel immensely wounded by another, or praised overwhelmingly by an audience, their faces will remain motionless—except, perhaps, for moist eyes. In fact, it is altogether common to say that a person is especially "moved" because her face isn't!

The multiple determinants of other prototype "emotional expressions" also vitiate the Emotions View. In emotion theories, the display characterized by wincing, downturned mouth, and frequently tears (i.e., the "cry" face), is thought to express sadness. Nonetheless, we also cry when we would say that we are happy, angry, frightened, or relieved. From the Behavioral Ecology View, the function of the cry-face display in all cases is to signal readiness to receive attention or succor, regardless of one's emotional status. Similarly, the display comprised of a knit brow, pursed lips or retracted lip corners with bared teeth, and fixated gaze (i.e., the "about to attack" face), is held in emotions theory to express anger. For the behavioral ecologist, making an "about to strike" face functions to repel an interactant, and acting this way can occur for many reasons and amid circumstances that could connote many emotions. Indeed, we make this face not only when we are angry, but when we are helpless, frightened ("defensive"), frustrated, exasperated, bored, or engaging in a fit of bravado.

The social-motive analysis of threat displays follows that for smiles. I know of no evidence that we make threatening "attack" faces more when we are angry. If we do, it may be because when we are angry we often seek out another to provoke. We make threat faces in the process, but the faces serve the provocation rather than the anger occasioning it (again, anger is just *one* emotion that can lead us to provoke another). Moreover, our attacking another in anger may occur only if we believe that events that anger us mandate confrontation and retaliation; alternatively, our anger should occasion smiling if we believe that anger mandates supplication or even a sly con. These beliefs may be individual or cultural.

Threat displays deserve special attention, because they have been a major focus within modern ethology. Analyses have been provided by Caryl (1979), Maynard Smith (1974, 1982), and Hinde (1985a); these analyses underscore threat's indirect relation to emotion. Maynard Smith argued that threat displays may not only indicate intent to strike, but also the displayer's abilities to fight if provoked (i.e., features such as size, strength, and endurance, known as the organism's *Resource Holding Potential* or RHP; see Parker, 1974). Human males often engage in such bluffs and demonstrations of "potency."

Hinde (1985a) maintained that an organism intending fight or flight should do so immediately; threat displays should only occur in, and depict, conflict or ambivalence (i.e., one's attack is contingent upon the next move of the other). Similarly, Tinbergen 1953) argued that threat displays always stemmed from simultaneous drives to escape and to attack. The reasoning is compelling. To enhance fitness, displays should be shaped by evolution toward finely graded signals that one intends but is not committed to a course of action; the displays should of course occur mainly in circumstances of risk or conflict (Hinde, 1985a).

Displays should thus be more likely with conflicts in intent; in no case would the display be a simple readout. This axiom runs counter to the

Emotions View that there are prototypic displays that read out "pure" emotion. In fact, one can reasonably argue that displays generally should not necessarily occur when one is emotional at all, but when they will do the most good for the displayer. (Predicting such optimality mathematically is the focus of the "game-theoretic" analysis of displays in modern ethology; see Caryl, 1979.) Thus a loud bellow when conditions are *not* threatening—or, for that matter, every fifteen minutes around the clock—may alert others of one's RHP and forestall predation far better than one issued contingent upon another's attack. To continue the logic: (1) one should not cry whenever one is saddest, but when succor is most readily available; (2) one should not produce a "fright" display when afraid unless submission is advantageous or rescue is desired, and these conditions may hold even when one happens not to be afraid. The form and intensity of a display, and the alignment of the display with personal resources or intentions, would depend on contextual factors such as common interests, availability of resources, and presence of kin, intruders, and predators (Ricklefs, 1979).

The Emotions View Takes a Crypto-Moralistic View of Deception

It is a canon within the Emotions View that what is "hidden" in deception is ostensibly detectable through "leakage" from unmanaged behavior (Ekman, 1981; Ekman & Friesen, 1969a). Various studies have claimed to show leakage of emotion in deceit (for reviews see Zuckerman, De-Paulo, & Rosenthal, 1981a, 1986; Zuckerman & Driver, 1985), but these studies have found only signs of agitation or "displacement behaviors" like lip-biting (covered more fully in Chapter 12). True demonstrations of "leakage" require not only that the "leaked" emotion be detectable, but that it be *decodable* (i.e., what one "leaks" must predict the emotion one is attempting to hide).

For the behavioral ecologist, the leakage conception is a Freudian atavism, and again, "leakage" reflects conflict among intentions, that is, "I want to indicate X and I *don't* want to indicate X." That many researchers have retained the view that deception *qua* deception produces leakage results from the studies they have designed, which typically required that subjects deceive by stating counterfactuals or taking morally objectionable positions. Consequently, for most subjects, *deception was confounded with conflict about deceiving*. This conflict can be moral (wanting to comply by lying vs. believing that one shouldn't anyway) or pragmatic (wanting to comply by lying vs. expecting nonetheless that there will be hell to pay). I know of only one study that included the obvious controls to rule out conflict as the source of "leakage"—the inclusion of situations contrived such that subjects both deceive *and* endorse their deception.

Bavelas and colleagues devised such a situation, and thereby established the importance of the conflict view (Bavelas, Black, Chovil, & Mullett, 1988). Subjects had to lie in order to keep secret a friend's surprise birthday party. They lied perfectly but showed no "leakage." Moreover, the authors discovered that when subjects were faced with the choice to lie or tell a hurtful truth, the subjects rarely lied. Rather, they *equivocated*, supplying "meanings implied but not claimed," like verbal "arrows aimed to miss" (p. 4). For example, when friends ask us to appraise their wretched new piece of art, we tend neither to damn nor to deceptively praise it. Instead, we utter equivocal comments like, "Very interesting. Who's the artist?"

Recent findings thus suggest that: (1) lying per se does not "leak"; rather, conflict about lying simply generates conflict in facial behavior; (2) in the real world, we may equivocate far more than we lie. If these initial findings are substantiated, then it is reasonable to question the ecological validity of nearly all studies of facial deception.

In the Behavioral Ecology View, deception is regarded as omnipresent and potentially highly advantageous for the displayer. Krebs and Dawkins (1984) provided a cynical model of the evolution of signal systems that was influential but regrettably oversimplified. It was based on deceptive control and countercontrol by "manipulators" (displayers) and "mind-readers" (those under the potential control of displays). Manipulators, in displaying, run a risk in revealing their resources, weaknesses, or intentions, but they may gain advantage by the ability of their displays to control mind-readers. Mind-readers gain by predicting what manipulators will do, but have much to lose if they are too easily manipulable. They must become more vigilant, empathic, *and* skeptical. The evolution of signal systems is thereby held to be one of intrinsically competitive "salesmanship" confronting "sales resistance" (Krebs & Dawkins, 1984).

Krebs and Dawkins unfortunately emphasized an exploitive view of signal systems. Their emphasis on deception did much to turn attention to the flexibility and sociality of nonhuman displays, one that is now quite instantiated in modern ethological conceptions of signaling (e.g., de Waal, 1982; Cheney & Seyfarth, 1988). But as Smith (1986) and others have indicated, relationships between manipulator and mind-reader, that is, seller and buyer, are often cooperative. Moreover, signal systems would not evolve were they not in the long run advantageous for both (Alcock, 1984). Sometimes, as in business, long-term good will is worth more to the seller than a quick swindle, even though one is vulnerable to an occasional con. Similarly, "openness" in one's affairs (i.e., public display) lubricates social interaction, but is constrained by an increased vulnerability to eavesdroppers who "illegitimately" detect the displays. The dynamic equilibrium between cooperative signal systems, and exploiters who devalue the signals by mimicking them (i.e., deceit), has been analyzed in terms of the game-theoretic model known as Evolutionary Stable Strategy (ESS) theory (Axelrod, 1984; Maynard Smith, 1974, 1982; Maynard Smith & Price, 1973; Slatkin, 1978). The minimax problem presented by eavesdroppers can be analyzed similarly. Regrettably, I know of no research applying ESS analyses to human signal systems.

Can one predict when signals would be exploitive? "Manipulation" and "mind-reading" should be more frequent or more extremely exploitive when individuals are nomadic or asocial (e.g., in singles bars, although the "victim" in the bar scene may often be a willing one). They should be much more mutually beneficial when individuals are social (i.e., living in troops, families, or herds), and cooperation would enhance inclusive fitness because one's interactants are likely to be kin, or those with whom one expects future social relations (Boyd & Richerson, 1985). A variety of studies support this generalization (Smith, 1986).

SUMMARY

The Emotions View proposes a small set of fundamental emotions that are "decoupled reflexes" differentiated by natural selection, triggered by releaser-type stimuli, and accompanied by prototypic facial displays. Variations from the prototypic emotional expressions are explained as reflecting the elicitation of blends of the fundamental emotions, or the effects of culture-specific conventions.

In the Behavioral Ecology View, there are neither fundamental emotions nor fundamental expressions of them. Displays do not "differentiate" from primitive tropisms, because the tropistic progenitor is evolutionary fantasy. Rather, they evolve in particulate fashion in response to specific selection pressures, and they necessarily coevolve with others' responsivity to them. That signals serve social motives does not imply that they are learned; an innate social cognition that mediates juvenile or adult displays is more reasonable than the supposition of "affect programs" that must be developmentally unlearned or culturally constrained. Displays have meanings specifiable only in their context of occurrence, and they are issued to serve one's social motives in that context. These motives bear no necessary relation to emotion, and indeed, a range of emotions can co-occur with any social motive. As manipulations serving intent, displays are issued when they will optimally enhance cultural or genetic inclusive fitness. Display deployment depends upon the intent of the displayer, the topographic features of the niche, the behavior of the recipient, and the context of the interaction.

What would evidence be for one view over the other? That is the topic of Chapter 8.

8

EMOTIONS VERSUS BEHAVIORAL ECOLOGY VIEWS OF FACIAL EXPRESSION: THE STATE OF THE EVIDENCE

Several lines of investigation allow us to compare the validity and validity of the emotions and behavioral views I presented in Chapter 7. These lines of evidence include the: (1) complexity of display over phylogenesis; (2) amount of deception and phylogenesis; (3) the dependence of displays upon sociality; (4) the implicit sociality of solitary displays; (5) the presence or absence of common "fundamental emotion" circuits underlying disparate displays; and (6) the manner in which facial actions relate to nonfacial physiological activity. I discuss each, and then consider the viability of the concept of "emotion" central to the Emotions View of facial behavior.

RAMIFYING OF DISPLAYS IN PHYLOGENY

John Dewey (1894) is most responsible for the idea that emotion derives phylogenetically from undifferentiated tropisms:

> Upon evolutionary principles, [emotion] must be a differentiation, selected and perpetuated because of its utility in the struggle for life, out of an original more diffuse and irradiating wave of discharge. (p. 194)

Dewey's idea carries a testable implication. If primitive drives or tropisms differentiated into discrete, fundamental emotions with accompanying displays, then species that are extinct must have had less differentiated displays than those that are extant. In other words, ramifying of an emotion should parallel the arborizing of the phylogenetic tree.

What evidence can we adduce for this? Of course, little is known about the behavior of extinct species, but I know of no data to suggest a correspondence between display repertoire and place in phylogenesis. Even simple multicellular animals have elaborate defensive repertoires. Sexual reproduction evolved very early. With it came sexual selection, as we can discern from hypertrophied secondary sexual characteristics in the fossil record. It follows that all the attendant intersexual and intrasexual behavior—particularly female incitement patterns and the ubiquitous male-to-male fights, bluffs, and contests—must have evolved simultaneously (Arnold, 1983; Darwin, 1871; Emlen & Oring, 1977; Trivers, 1972). Early sexual creatures certainly required a signal system for the negotiation of copulation. As Figure 8.1 shows, by the early Jurassic Period (about 200 million years B.C.), fossil tracks suggest that dinosaurs traveled in herds, with large animals at the periphery and juveniles at the center (Gould, 1980). Crests, frills, and horns in these dinosaurs were probable specializations for sexual and agonistic display (Gould, 1980). A "social cognition" in the service of dominance and kin selection was therefore likely as well (see Cheney, Seyfarth, & Smuts, 1986).

FIGURE 8.1.   A herd of *Centrosaurus* in a defensive circle, exhibiting a social organization substantiated from fossil track records. It is now known that, at least by the early Jurassic Period, circa 200 million years B.C., animals like these ceratopians must have developed the display repertoires required to negotiate dominance and sexual selection within the herd and to make alarm calls that exploit herd action in the service of self-protection. Illustration Copyright (1993), Tim Gardom with Angela Milner from *The Book of Dinosaurs*, by Prima Publishing, Rocklin, CA.

I belabor this point, because it is inconceivable that even a very primitive animal line could have survived without signals relating to copulation and sexual selection, the acquisition and protection of territory, and the deterrence of predation. The notion of the tropistic progenitor that just approaches or avoids is fanciful but wholly improbable. As Arnold (1960) stated:

> One wonders how the dumb animal could survive if a stimulus simply aroused "a diffuse wave of discharge" . . . an animal would be quite unable to learn even the most primitive coordinated movement of fight or flight, let alone hunting for food, or mating. (p. 115)

Differentiation of display in any evolutionary line is mostly a function of niche factors such as sociality (e.g., solitary vs. family or troop existence; formation of dominance hierarchy), modes of sexual selection and reproduction (e.g., monogamy vs. polyandry or polygyny), and prevalence of predators. It has little to do with place in phylogeny, and a tropistic view of display evolution is just fancy.

DECEPTION IN PHYLOGENY

According to the Emotions View, facial displays innately read out emotion but become dissimulative as soon as one becomes sufficiently "corticalized," thereby acquiring the cognitive capability to deceive and to learn when it is advantageous. By this view, then, creatures with lower encephalization quotients, and juveniles of each variety, should show less deception. In the Behavioral Ecology View, deception would be present throughout the phylogenetic tree, and not just in displays of more encephalized animals or in the adults of each species.

The evidence here decidedly favors the Behavioral Ecology View. It is now clear that interspecific deception spans the animal and botanical kingdoms, and that the deceptions are implemented both morphologically and behaviorally. Common morphological deceptions include mimicries in structure or coloration. These were formerly thought to predominate in plants (e.g., specializations of bee orchids in the service of pseudocopulation with bees) and insects (e.g., Batesian or Mullerian mimicries), but motoric mimicries in insects are now frequently reported. One example is the exploitation of male–female flash signals by predatory *femme fatale* females in the firefly *Photinus* (see Lloyd, 1975). Behavioral mimicries (i.e., deceptive motoric displays) are widely reported in fish, birds , and marsupials. Examples are rife. The cleaner fish exhibits a natural shimmy that momentarily "hypnotizes" its host fish and thereby allows it to clean the host's gills. The shimmy is mimicked by the predatory "false" cleaner, who hypnotizes the host and gobbles a healthy chunk of gill instead. Similarly, healthy birds manifest "crippled-wing" displays, and opossums play dead, all to deter predators. Even crustaceans may show such deceptive behavior (Adams & Caldwell, 1990). Needless to say, deception (bluffs and cons) is commonplace among mammals generally, including the great apes (e.g., Chevalier-Skolnikoff, 1973; de Waal, 1982), and—need I add—humans (Ekman, 1981, 1985).

I know of no systematic comparisons of amount of deception throughout the phylogenetic tree, but it is an generally considered by botanists and zoologists that deception inexorably coevolves with display itself. Ontogeny-phylogeny relations would predict that deception is not confined to highly encephalized animals or to the adult forms of animals; the amount and form of deception shown by any animal would depend more on the predominant signal systems of the animal and the specific features of its niche. For example, animals whose interactions are governed by olfactory displays would be expected to trade in olfactory deception; those who interact using language (humans) would be expected to deceive with their language. One should not expect that humans deceive more than other animals, or that human adults deceive more than human juveniles (although adult deception, like all adult display, probably has the edge in subtlety). Humans and human adults may in fact deceive *less*, given that language allows one to equivocate and evade a response rather than offering one that is counterfactual (Bavelas et al., 1990).

FACIAL DISPLAY VARIATION WITH SIBLING COMPETITION

I argued above that selection pressures specific to juveniles, not "unsocialized emotions," drive infants toward attention-grabbing displays. I further speculated that during the course of evolution, infants may have come to emulate the adult signal system and "selfishly" gain caretaker attention. Sibling competition might further intensify infant displays. The "selfish infant" account is compatible with existing evidence concerning infant displays, but evidence is needed to show its superiority to the Emotions View. It would be gathered using the comparative approach, among human societies with different family sizes or numbers of caretakers per child (e.g., monogamous vs. polygynous mating systems), and across species with different litter sizes. With increased competition for caretaker attention, infants should generate more intense displays, or alternative tactics like ingratiation.

THE DISPLAYS OF SOCIAL VERSUS SOLITARY SPECIES

Assuming that facial displays are predominantly social and instrumental implies the emission of fewer displays in relatively solitary species. In making such a comparison, one assumes that there is no difference in *emotionality* between nonsocial and social species. I know of no basis for asserting such a difference. A proponent of the Emotions View might argue that if there are fewer displays in relatively solitary species, then these species are *ipso facto* less emotional. This argument is tautological without verification of emotionality independent of display.

There is only limited research bearing on this comparison. In general, the existing data indeed suggest that animals with more limited social behavior show fewer displays. For example, the nocturnal nonterritorial frog shows only 10 displays; they relate to location, species and sex identification, attack, and precopulation (Rand, cited in Smith, 1977). One might wish to investigate so-called "solitary species" as limiting cases, but the notion of a solitary animal species is a zoological fiction. All animal species are social to some degree; even the "lone wolf" is finely attuned to the olfactory displays of other wolves that mark territorial boundaries, has a defensive display repertoire, and must engage in the precopulatory displays necessary to propagate his line.

AUDIENCE EFFECTS AND THE CONTEXT-DEPENDENCY OF DISPLAYS

If displays simply read out fundamental emotions (deception notwithstanding), then across species the displays should largely be a function of emotional elicitors. As I discussed earlier, the idea that nonhumans must be emotionally driven without the constraints of civilization follows from Hobbes and Freud. It is now part of popular culture, as witness our calling those who commit heinous crimes "animals." It surfaces in the Emotions View of faces through the popular but recapitulationist notion of the modular human "limbic system," as exemplified by the paleomammalian portion of MacLean's fanciful triune brain (Chapter 6). The Emotions View uses this view of nonhumans, together with our shared phylogeny, to suggest that human facial displays are automatic, quasi-reflexive readouts that are outgrown with socialization (Ekman, 1972; Izard and Malatesta, 1987).

Alternatively, if displays serve social motives throughout phylogeny, then across species their occurrence should be a function not only of the proximal elicitors, but of those who are present, one's aims toward them, and the context of the interaction. In highly social animals, displays should conform to social structure. Moreover, because displays can enhance inclusive fitness, the behavioral ecology view predicts that, controlling for elicitors, individuals will display more when nearby interactants are genetic relatives than when they are unrelated.

Recent research in animal signaling suggests that many nonhuman facial and vocal displays vary considerably with the presence of interactants, and with the relationship of those interactants to the displayer. These findings are known collectively as "audience effects." Studying audience effects requires the presence of a triad of experimental participants: a displayer, the object of the display (either animate or inanimate), and an audience. I have depicted this triad in Figure 8.2.

In formal terms, the signaler is the *referrer*, the object is the *referent*, and the audience constitutes the *referee(s)*. Within this triad, one can change the size or composition of the audience, and an audience effect is confirmed if the referrer's display changes. In essence, the audience creates the context for the emission of a display; and audience effects, when observed, show that displays are context sensitive, even if the elicitor of the display (which is often, but need not be, the referent) is held constant. Note that audience effects, because they require a triad of participants, are not synonymous with social psychological constructs such as "social facilitation" (Geen & Gange, 1977; Zajonc, 1965) or developmental ones like "social referencing" (Feinman & Lewis, 1983; Klinnert, Campos, Sorce, Emde, & Svejda, 1983). These are inferred from observations of *dyads* (an individual and an audience, in the first, and an infant and a caretaker in the second).

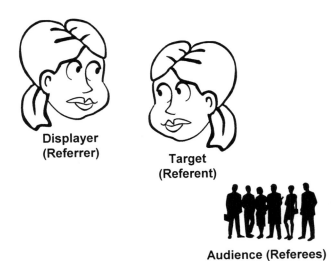

**Displayer
(Referrer)**

**Target
(Referent)**

Audience (Referees)

FIGURE 8.2.   The experimental components necessary to study audience effects on nonhuman or human displays. An audience effect is confirmed if the displays of an actor (the *referrer*) toward an object (the *referent*, either animate or inanimate), vary as a function of an audience (the *referee*). Audience effects demonstrate the sensitivity of displays to the social context of their emission, and have been noted widely in both nonhumans and humans.

Demonstrations of audience effects in nonhuman displays have been of special interest because they "provide an empirical means . . . to explore . . . intentionality in animal communication" (Marler & Mitani, 1988).[1] These demonstrations render implausible the assertion that human facial displays must be "emotional readouts" because of their common origins with other animals. Below I recount the evidence on the sociality of nonhuman displays, followed by the comparable evidence on human facial displays.

Nonhuman Audience Effects

The dependence of display on social context is corroborated by data on both vocal and nonvocal displays from other nonhuman species. One of

[1] The issue of intentionality is a thorny one, in great part because its formal philosophical usage (i.e., intention is function) is at odds with its everyday usage, which equates intentions with promises. Here Marler and Mitani refer to formal intentionality, which implies neither that the displayer premeditate its display, make a promise to the object, be conscious of emitting a display, nor that it "know" its display's effects on the object. These issues have been explored by Dennett (1987), and Cheney and Seyfarth (1990) paid them special attention in the context of audience effects. In their discussion they question just how much vervets and other animals "know" about what they are doing, just what they "mean" when they display, and whether receivers and audiences "know" the intended effects of the displays. I have circumvented these "levels of intentionality" issues in the interest of space, and use intentionality in a purely functionalist sense, that is, one discerns intent from the effects of displays, and from the efforts of displayers to obtain those effects.

the earliest and still among the most important studies of nonhuman audience effects was that of Moore and Stuttard (1979; and see Bolles, 1979). They sought to replicate Guthrie and Horton's (1946) classic experimental adaptation of Thorndike's studies of cats in puzzle boxes. Guthrie and Horton had wanted to show, *contra* Thorndike, that all learning occurred on one trial and that the "instrumental response" was always the last response emitted before reinforcer delivery.

In the original study, Guthrie and Horton stood outside a glass-fronted puzzle box and used flash photography to capture each cat's posture at the instant it opened the puzzle box. The posture betrayed a stereotypy predicted by the contiguity theory: the cats typically used their necks and flanks to "nuzzle" the vertical bar that opened the box. Moore and Stuttard repeated this procedure, but with two conditions. First, like Guthrie and Horton, the experimenters stood outside the box awaiting the cat's exit. The cat issued the expected stereotyped nuzzling in order to escape the box. Some examples of this posturing are shown in Figure 8.3. In the second condition, the experimenters left the puzzle box room, and the stereotypy nearly disappeared. Moore and Stuttard made the obvious ethological interpretation—the stereotypy did not reflect one-trial learning, but rather the typical feline "flank-rubbing" social greeting, directed toward the experimenters visible outside the box.

Experiments with other nonhuman species support the sociality of display. In the Belding's ground squirrel (Sherman, 1977), threatened females are much more likely to give alarm calls when kin are present. The "altruistic" female caller enhances her inclusive fitness (i.e., survival of her genes through her relatives) by her calling, even though by alerting a predator she risks her own life. (Male Belding's ground squirrels move once per year, have few nearby relatives, and seldom give alarm calls when threatened). Results similar to Sherman's have also been found in spider monkeys, who alter the duration of their alarm calls in proportion to the number of kin in the vicinity (Chapman, Chapman, & Lefebvre, 1990). These findings provide powerful support for the regnant view that many "animals give costly alarm calls only when they have relatives near them to benefit from their altruism" (Alcock, 1984, p. 479).[2]

Dorothy Cheney and Robert Seyfarth have documented in the field dependency of display on intent and context in the vervet monkey (*Cercopithecus aethiops*), found throughout Africa. Vervets are small Old

---

[2] Alcock's statement is extreme, because animals do call in the presence of nonrelatives, and sometimes they act with "reciprocal altruism" toward them. There are insufficient data now to specify how many species: (1) show kin selection in calling, (2) in what contexts it is practiced, and (3) whether calls in the presence of nonrelatives largely represent errors in discrimination, or "hidden" kin selection (e.g., juveniles out of range may benefit because predators are diverted by adult calls).

FIGURE 8.3.   Cats in puzzle boxes showing the typical flank-rubbing "greeting display" toward the rod that actuates the puzzle box door. *Contra* Guthrie and Horton, Moore and Stuttard (1979) showed that cats make this stereotyped movement only when the experimenter is visible outside the box door. Illustration from Guthrie and Horton (1946), reprinted with permission.

World monkeys; as adults, they are about the size and weight of an average house cat. They divide their days between life on the ground and in trees, and show a distinctive social structure consisting of several related females and their offspring, plus a transient set of males who have wandered in from other groups. One such family of vervets is depicted in Figure 8.4. Cheney and Seyfarth's studies have mostly been in East Africa, in Kenya's Amboseli National Park. I have already discussed Cheney and Seyfarth's work on the ontogeny of vervets' predator-specific vocal calls in Chapter 3. Their field studies show clearly a display semantics that does not conform to an emotional view of the vocalizations.

Other findings by Cheney and Seyfarth suggest that a vervet's displays refer to the identities of the recipients and the place of the displayer in the social structure (for the fullest discussion, see Cheney & Seyfarth, 1990). For example, the scream of a misbehaving vervet juve-

FIGURE 8.4.   A family of vervet monkeys (*Cercopithecus aethiops*), whose calls constitute the best evidence for referential, semantic signaling in nonhumans. Photograph courtesy of Marc Hauser.

nile moves adults in the troop to glare at the juvenile's *mother* (Cheney & Seyfarth, 1980). Captive vervet females produce more alarm calls under threat when in the presence of their own infant rather than an unrelated infant (Cheney & Seyfarth, 1985). When a vervet is threatened by another, the victim often "redirects" threat displays to an uninvolved third party. However, this third party is not selected randomly, tending instead to be a relative of a vervet previously in conflict with the victim (Cheney & Seyfarth, 1980, 1982)! Moreover, data by Keddy Hector, Seyfarth, & Raleigh (1989) show that subordinate but not *alpha* vervet males deploy more affiliative displays toward infants when they can see that the mother is observing. Thus, issuance of displays in vervets depends not only on the direct interactants, but also on who is observing.

The most systematic studies of audience effects have been conducted by Peter Marler and his colleagues, using domestic chickens (*Gallus gallus*). Typically, two chickens are placed in adjacent cages, where each can hear and see the other. One bird is provided a referent for a display, and the other constitutes the audience for the potential displayer.

One series of studies used food as the referent, with the food calls emitted by cockerels (males) as the display in question. These calls were traditionally considered signs of emotional arousal due to the presence of food. Marler, Duffy, & Pickert (1986a,b) discovered, however, that cockerels preferentially emit food calls in the presence of females, but fewer food calls in presence of familiar rather than strange females,

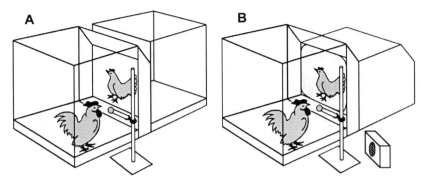

FIGURE 8.5.   One apparatus used by Peter Marler and colleagues to study audience effects. Domestic chickens (*Gallus gallus*) hear calls over a loudspeaker, with another chicken (the audience) present either physically (A) or on television (B).

fewer still when alone, and the fewest of all in the presence of another male. Other data suggest that males emit deceptive food calls when food is absent and females are distant; these calls tend to elicit female approach (Gyger & Marler, 1988). One is tempted to consider the food call as a strategy to induce female attention and approach.

The same kind of effect applies to cockerels' alarm calls. Males also sound more alarms in the presence of their mate or another female (Karakashian, Gyger, & Marler, 1988). This selectivity does not depend on the audience's countering the actor's behavior, since, as depicted in Figure 8.5, the audience may just consist of a televised image; indeed, videotaped audiences work as well as live ones (Evans & Marler, 1991).

Couldn't the enhanced calling just result from increased "emotional arousal" due to a female's presence? Obviously such an explanation could make the findings compatible with an Emotions View. Evans and Marler (in press) tested this alternative explanation by arranging for a male to receive food only after pecking an operant key, and then only during signaled periods of food availability. When males were placed in their cages adjacent to a female, they tended to produce a stereotyped courting dance. However, they did not issue food calls until the signal light came on and indicated food availability. Still, food calls might be interpreted as independent conditional responses from previous key-pecking trials, but one other manipulation counters this explanation. Males made substantially more food calls when females were present, but their operant rates at key-pecking for food were unchanged. The obvious interpretation is referential; the males' food calls "referred" to the food independent of their level of "emotional arousal."

Marler and Evans (1993) formalized a model by which they interpret nonhuman audience effects (see Table I). The model obviously applies not only to their own research, but to audience-effect studies *writ large*.

TABLE I   Marler's Contrast of Affect vs. Referential Views
of Animal Signaling

	The affect hypothesis of animal signaling	The referential hypothesis of animal signaling
Input specificity	Each animal signal is a response to a wide range of eliciting stimuli. Referents for animal signals are always global.	Some animal signals are specific responses to a limited class of eliciting stimuli. Referents for animal signals are global or restricted, depending upon functional requirements.
Conditions of production	Animal signals occur as obligatory members of suites of emotional responses to eliciting stimuli.	Some animal signals are potentially separable from other responses to eliciting stimuli, and can be emitted or withheld, depending upon social circumstances.

From Marler (1993); reprinted with permission of P. Marler.

As the table shows, the Marler–Evans model compares "affect" versus "referential" hypotheses of animal signals, which map closely on my Emotion versus Behavioral Ecology dichotomy. The hypotheses stipulate two ways in which affect-based and referential signals should differ. First, they should differ in their *input specificity*. Signals that are emotional outbursts should be elicited by a range of stimuli that would be expected to evoke the emotion. For example, if a particular signal arose from fear, then any elicitor that would reasonably evoke fear should elicit the same signal. On the other hand, signals that conform to the referential hypothesis should have much more specific elicitors, or more properly here, referents. These referents would only influence the animal to signal if, in context, it would be functional to do so. Second, the two kinds of signals should differ in their *conditions of production*, which here denotes the pattern of behavior comprising the signal. Signals that are emotional outbursts should consist of a stereotyped and invariant pattern of behavior. Thus, a signal of fear might include piloerection, agitation, and vocalization—and it should always include these if fear has been evoked. In contrast, the pattern of behavior comprising referential signals should be more variable, with the animal capable of producing some components while withholding others. Thus an animal that is threatened by a predator may indeed piloerect and become agitated, but may not vocalize if it is disadvantageous to do so—if, for example, a pack of similar predators is nearby.

The model is intriguing because it is so pragmatic. It enables researchers to test the involvement of "emotion" in displays without needing to define emotion. It does this by being connotative rather than essentialist. That is, whatever "emotion" is, most researchers from an Emotions View would probably endorse the proposition that affect-based signaling would be elicited by a range of stimuli and manifest as a nondissociable configuration of responses. Likewise, most would probably agree that the combination of specificity of referents and context-dependent dissociability of responses would not follow from an affect-based account. Note, however, that the model's strength—its neat sidestepping of the definitional issue—is also its Achilles heel, because it relies on agreements about what "emotion" connotes. As I discuss further at the end of this chapter, advocates of the Emotions View have themselves failed to define "emotion," and instead have rendered it so elastic that it can encompass nearly any behavior. I would anticipate no failures of imagination in attempts to retain affect-based explanations even of signals that unequivocally belong on the "referential" side of Table 8.1.

Nonetheless, in terms of the Marler–Evans model, and certainly in my own view, the nonhuman audience-effect studies demonstrate that the occurrence and topography of many animal signals are highly dependent on the nature of the interactants and the context of interaction. They thus mitigate the earlier Lorenz–Tinbergen view that they are readouts or spillovers of emotion or drive. In fact, the displays are more like language than the emotional outbursts assumed in the conjured phylogeny of the Emotions View. I discuss further the linguistic aspects of vocal and facial displays in Chapter 12. Again, the most important consequences of findings that many nonhuman displays are referential is to undermine the implication that human faces must be themselves reflexive and "emotional" because it is assumed that animals are.

Human Audience Effects

Several studies of audience effects in humans now provide strong support for the interactive nature of facial displays. Smiles have received the most attention.

Smiling

One of the best known human audience effect studies was a set of field experiments conducted by Kraut and Johnston (1979) that provided strong support for a social-motive view of the human smile. The authors recounted four experiments.

In the first two experiments, observers watched the behavior of bowlers at Ide's Bowling Lanes in Ithaca, New York. Bowling represents an interesting naturalistic situation in which to discern audience effects, because the signaler (the bowler) is interposed between the referent for a display (the pins she intends to topple), and the audience (her friends in the waiting pit at the head of the lane). Direct interaction is minimal during the roll and maximal just afterward. First, Kraut and Johnston had observers chart the behavior of bowlers from a vantage point behind the waiting pit. The list of acts charted by the observers included not only the bowlers' facial displays, but also their head movements, laughing, gaze, grooming, and vocalizations. The results, computed using elaborate temporal and factor analyses, suggested that

> Bowlers smiled when they were being social, when they were being playful, or when they were otherwise communicating an emotional statement to an audience. Both close-mouthed and open-mouthed smiling shared a nonemotional, social motivation. (p. 1546)

The authors' interpretation may have been a bit tendentious given its dependence upon the outcomes of complex multivariate analyses, but it was buttressed substantially by a second, much cleaner study. In this study, observers were positioned both behind the waiting pit and in back of the pin-setting machine at the end of the lane. This allowed the charting of bowlers' behavior as they rolled the ball and watched their roll, and as they pivoted to face the members of their bowling party. The observers also tracked the outcome of each roll. Figure 8.6 (A) tabulates the findings from 116 rolls by 34 bowlers. As the figure shows, subjects rarely smiled while facing the pins, but did so frequently when they pivoted to face their friends in the waiting pit. And the outcome of each roll—which would reasonably be expected to affect bowler's emotions—bore little relationship to the emission of smiles.

Kraut and Johnston obtained similar findings in two subsequent field studies that exploited situations in which the extent of social interaction and subjects' presumed emotional state could vary independently. In the third study, groups of fans were photographed at Cornell hockey games, and the photographs were scored for whether, based on posture and gaze, the fans were part of a social group (e.g., friends who had come together to the game) or were "uninvolved." The photographs were taken after good and bad plays by either team (good plays for Cornell and bad plays for the opposing team were pooled, and vice versa). The outcome of each play was thought, reasonably, to represent an emotional stimulus. These results are depicted in Figure 8.6 (B). Here, smiling was related to the outcome of each play, but was substantially dependent upon whether the fan was with friends. Finally, people were observed either alone or interacting (the social factor) on either sunny or rainy days (the emotion factor). Here the results were even more dra-

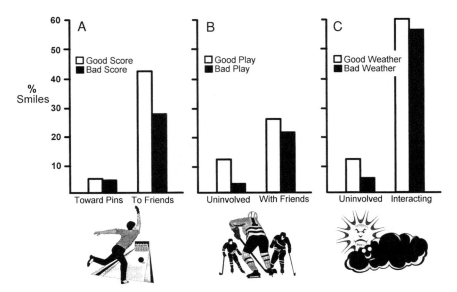

FIGURE 8.6.   The sociality of public smiling exhibited by bowlers, fans at a hockey game, and passersby on a city street. Bowlers (A) exhibited substantial smiling toward friends but little toward the pins, regardless of the outcome of a roll. Fans at a hockey game (B) smiled much more when they were with friends, regardless of the outcome of their team's plays. Finally, passersby (C) smiled much more when interacting than when uninvolved, regardless of the weather. Data from Kraut and Johnston (1979).

matic (Figure 8.6, C). Smiling depended overwhelmingly upon whether the subjects were interacting, and very little upon the pleasantnesss of the weather.

Additional anecdotal data illustrate the indirect link of smiles to display. One does not smile upon opening a gift, but rather when catching the gaze of the gift-giver. As Darwin (1872) knew, a child will smile and look excited when expecting candy from an adult, but consume it impassively after obtaining it (though she may smile toward the adult who gave it to her). Indeed, children's smiles nearly always occur in social contexts (Bainum, Lounsbury, & Pollio, 1984) as indeed do those of adults (Provine & Fischer, 1989). Similarly, lovers smile during flirtation but smile much less during prolonged sexual foreplay or copulation. Indeed, smiling during coitus probably would not indicate enjoyment, but rather the wish that the partner *think* that one was enjoying oneself, whether true or not.

Unlike the emotional readout view, functional accounts of these instances are readily available. The smile of the gift recipient signals that the relationship (e.g., friendship, love) is affirmed by the gift; this affirming smile can occur regardless of the recipient's mood. In the candy and flirtation examples, the smiles are solicitations. The copulatory smile signals reassurance or affirmation. When two lovers greet, they may each smile to the other. The smiles may occur even when each is independently unhappy. The lovers' smiles affirm readiness to behave in accordance with the existing set of relations (love).

Faces to Odors and Taste

Other faces are viewed as reflexive manifestations of basic pleasures such as odors or tastes, and Steiner (e.g., 1974, 1976) suggested that there were olfactory-facial reflexes that read out hedonic taste and odor appraisals (of course, many tastes are actually distinguished through the corresponding odors). There is no doubt that with strong oropharyngeal irritation, expulsive facial reflexes act to clear the nose or mouth (e.g., the trigeminal irritation produced by ammonia). These are brainstem-mediated, protective reflexes (Chapter 6) whose actions imply neither hedonics nor emotion. So the issue is whether, apart from such supra-normal stimulation, patterned faces automatically accompany the he-donics of odor or taste.

The contention that reflexive, hedonic readout faces occur during gustation was undercut in studies by Brightman, Segal, Werther, and Steiner (1975, 1977). Brightman et al. videotaped subjects who were eating sweet or salty sandwiches, either alone or in triads. Judges view-ing the videotapes of the solitary subjects could not guess which type of sandwich the solitary subjects were eating, even for the most intense tastants. In contrast, judges viewing the videotapes of the triads easily guessed the type of sandwich the subjects were eating.

Most studies have concentrated on olfaction, and here, too, the evi-dence for this "hedonic/reflexive" view is rather weak. Steiner himself described a study (Steiner, 1977) in which neonates were exposed to five odorants: butter, banana, vanilla, shrimp, and rotten eggs. Judges were asked to classify the neonates' facial responses as either accepting, indif-ferent, or rejecting. Although the modal responses were in the predicted direction for all odors, the variability was considerable. At least 40% of the neonates departed from prediction on four of the five odors; only the rotten eggs produced "rejection" faces in all the neonates. These results are ultimately uninformative because we cannot know the neonates' individual appraisals of the odors, and the appraisals may indeed have departed from Steiner's predictions. For example, some neonates may have liked vanilla and shrimp while others disliked them. Nor did Stei-ner equate the odorants for intensity, so that the uniform rejection of the rotten eggs may have been due to the intensity of the stench. But one finding was especially notable: the judges had considerable difficulty in agreeing on the type of face the infants had shown: their average correla-tions of their classifications were .62 if the rotten eggs were included and only .47 if they were not (calculated from Steiner, 1977). This fact leads to the conclusion that the neonates' facial behavior was either too weak or too complex to code reliably. Neither interpretation favors an account based on olfactory-facial reflexes.

Similar ambiguous findings arise from studies of adults' faces to odors. Kraut (1982) had subjects sniff various odors while their faces were being videotaped, and then had judges try to discern which odor subjects were sniffing based solely on their recorded facial behavior. The findings were analogous to those obtained by Steiner (1977); the judges' ability to determine the odors was largely confined to the strong unpleasant ones—specifically, high concentrations of pyridine, butyric acid, and acetic acid (Ehrlichman & Bastone, 1992)—each of which is likely to produce the kind of oropharyngeal irritation I mentioned earlier. From my perspective, there is an additional problem with the Kraut (1982) study. Subjects knew that they were being videotaped, making the conditions of occurrence implicitly social. As I indicate later in this chapter, this casts in doubt the "hedonic" nature of any faces that Kraut's subjects did produce.

One exemplary study of faces and odors meets the twin objections of stimulus nonequivalence and open videotaping that compromise the earlier findings by Steiner (1977) and Kraut (1982). Tassinary (1985) fastidiously equated the perceived strengths of varying concentrations of 17 consensually pleasant and unpleasant odors using magnitude estimation, exposed a total of 13 subjects to controlled doses of the odorants using an automatic olfactometer, covertly videotaped the subjects, and then scored their moment-to-moment facial behavior using an abbreviated version of Ekman and Friesen's Facial Action Coding System (Ekman & Friesen, 1978). These methods were, in theory, capable of discerning any patterns of visible facial movement that corresponded to the subjects' hedonic ratings of the odors.

Tassinary's findings were complex but, overall, they paralleled previous ones. Subjects showed earlier, more intense, more varied, and longer-duration facial behavior with strong rather than with weak odors; but the unpleasant strong odors accounted for most of this difference. Overall, facial behavior did not discriminate pleasant from unpleasant odors (p. 132). Further exploratory analyses showed that when the odor judgments and facial behavior were compared for individual subjects, facial responses like nose wrinkling and snarling tended to occur with strong unpleasant odors, and smiling tended to occur more with weakly but not strongly pleasant odors (p. 133). In fact, only two subjects smiled to strong pleasant odors (p. 144). These analyses were post hoc explorations, and we therefore cannot know how many other tests showed *no* differences. But with respect to "olfacto-facial reflexes," Tassinary was blunt about his findings: "The facial responses to these odors simply don't behave like reflexes" (pp. 144–145). The only possible exception Tassinary allowed was the quicker facial response to strong odors, and this difference was mostly due to unpleasant odors—precisely those that, once more, would elicit the protective reflexes I discussed earlier.

Thus, apart from reflexive rejections of strong unpleasant odors, there is little evidence that facial actions automatically track the hedonics of taste or odors. What is clear, however, is the predominance of demand over hedonic readout, at least in adult faces. This was demonstrated by Gilbert, Fridlund, and Sabini (1987), who had subjects pose facial responses to odors so that raters could easily identify the type of odor (good, bad, or neutral) from the poses. However, subjects showed few facial responses to the odors when smelling them in private, despite dramatic differences in their hedonic ratings of the odors. These findings were replicated using facial electromyography by Jäncke and Kaufmann (1944).

Motor Mimicry

Another behavior previously considered a readout of inner state is that of *motor mimicry*. We cringe when we hear of another's fear, and grit our teeth with their anger. Bavelas and colleagues, in especially provocative research, have now documented the communicative nature of motor mimicry. Bavelas, Black, Lemery, and Mullett (1986) found that the pattern and timing of wincing at an experimental confederate's pain was strongly dependent upon eye contact with the ostensible sufferer.

In a second study (Bavelas, Black, Chovil, Lemery, & Mullett, 1989), subjects who listened face to face to stories told by confederates predictably mimicked the movements of the storytellers. The authors reasoned that if the listeners' movements were empathy-induced readouts of internal state, then they should be identical in form to those of the storytellers (i.e., when storytellers moved left, so should the listeners). Instead, listeners' movements were mirror-reflections of the storytellers'! (In other words, when storytellers moved left, listeners moved *right*.) The authors made the compelling interpretation that

> Motor mimicry is not the manifestation of a vicarious internal state but a *representation* of that state to another person . . . just as a word is not the object or state it represents, motor mimicry should not be equated with the state it represents.
>
> We do not agree with theories that, in effect, assume that the overt behavior is a "spill over" from an inner vicarious experience. We propose that it has a function of its own, a communicative one. (p. 8)

Sociality of Solitary Faces

That social species should deploy fewer displays when alone should of course apply to humans. Yet the assumption that solitary humans make far fewer faces when alone seems contrary to the rationales of experiments that isolate subjects in order to measure putatively "uncensored"

faces. Chovil (1988) reviewed several such studies conducted by advocates of the Emotions View, and found that, indeed, many subjects
show very few faces, and she sardonically called this the "problem of
nonexpressive subjects." Chovil documented that in many experiments
these subjects' data were withheld from analysis because the subjects
were "nonexpressive."

There is no doubt that humans make fewer faces when alone. In the
olfaction and gustation studies cited previously, Gilbert et al. (1987)
found few spontaneous facial displays to odors, even though subjects
appraised the odors as clearly smelling good, bad, or neutral; and
Brightman et al. (1975, 1977) found few spontaneous faces while solitary
subjects ate sweet versus salty sandwiches, even though they observed
many evaluative faces when subjects ate the sandwiches in triads.
Nonetheless, solitary faces do occur. This fact is often touted as definitive evidence that the faces (or at least some faces) are by nature readouts
or expressions of emotion rather than social, communicative displays
(see Buck, 1984, 1985; Cacioppo & Tassinary, 1987). As Buck (1984) put it,

> When a sender is alone . . . he or she should feel little pressure to
> present a proper image to others, and any emotion expression under such
> circumstances should be more likely to reflect an actual motivation-
> al/emotional state. (p. 20)

Ekman took the same tack when he described a study of differences in
facial displays among Japanese and Americans (cf. Ekman and Friesen's
"display rules" study, reviewed in Chapter 11). Ekman stated,

> In private, when no display rules to mask expression were operative,
> we saw the biologically based, evolved, universal facial expressions of
> emotion. (Ekman, 1984)

The most pointed declaration of the reliance of the Emotions View
upon the supposed emotional nature of solitary faces was provided by
Ekman et al. (1990), who stated,

> Facial expressions do occur when people are alone . . . and contradict
> the theoretical proposals of those who view expressions solely as social
> signals. (p. 351)

The belief that faces observed in solitude constitute the definitive
evidence for "facial expressions of emotion" is instantiated in the experiments conducted by proponents of the Emotions View. Experimental
subjects are typically isolated in a laboratory room and exposed to various kinds of "emotional" elicitors. Many of these are depicted in Figure
8.7.

These include: (A) face-to-face contact; (B) contact through a window,
partition or laboratory wall; (C) watching television; (D) imagery tasks;

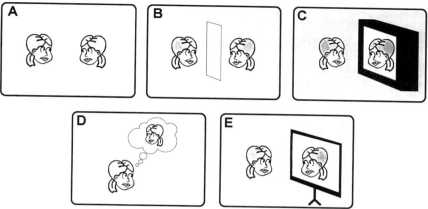

FIGURE 8.7.   Common methods of eliciting "facial expressions of emotion" in the laboratory, arranged to show that they are implicit manipulations of sociality. Depicted by subjects: (A) interacting face to face; (B) interacting through a glass or partition (or with the experimenters through a laboratory wall); (C) watching a televised image; (D) imagining others, including themselves, as actors in their imagery; and (E) viewing a slide, usually of other people. The implicit sociality in manipulations (B–E) mitigates the assumption that the facial displays issued by subjects who are physically alone are pure "facial expressions of emotion" unaffected by social convention.

and (E) viewing slides. Because subjects are physically alone in panels B though E, any facial displays elicited in subjects are considered "expressions of emotion." The exception is panel A, face-to-face contact, which is considered "social" and is therefore held to produce a combination of both emotional and conventional faces.

Contrary to this categorization, I contend that a binary view of what is "social" and what is "nonsocial" is too absolutist; I suggest instead that the manipulations in Figure 8.7 vary in their sociality. Everyone considers face-to-face contact (A) the most social, but does speaking through a glass or partition (B) make it nonsocial? I think not, but then what if the glass is a CRT faceplate (C)? Asserting that watching a televised image is not social would be news to soap opera lovers who consider the characters to be intimate acquaintances, and to sports fans who throw things at the screen. And what if the image is not on the CRT, but in my mind's eye (D)? Finally, what if I freeze a frame of an image and show a photo (E)? Would this make viewing a face nonsocial? Not necessarily, as sales of baby and family albums would attest; the photos in them are not mere silver halide spots; they are cues to the reconstruction of interactions (i.e., panel D). In this sense, a still image of a face is a projective stimulus. When a patient examines a TAT card and begins to shake, blanch, and then burst into tears, it's not the ink on the card. Ditto for still images, but their use has nevertheless been formalized as the "slide-viewing technique" (Buck, 1979), and pictorial depictions were used in nearly all studies of "facial expressions of emotion" among different populations (see Chapter 10).

I believe that it is reasonable to consider the varying types of "emotional elicitors" as representing simply different kinds of sociality. Unfortunately, in the facial expression literature sociality is treated as though it conformed to the All-or-None Law. If the interactant is not physically in the room, then by the two-factor logic of the Emotions View, social factors have been excluded, any faces that occur must be emotional faces, and the stimuli must therefore be labeled emotion elicitors. This absolutism is, I think, absurd. Ascribing faces to readouts of emotion and not social motives is legitimate only *if* sociality is controlled, whether the sociality is implicit or explicit. Even when steps are taken to make subjects believe that they are "unobserved" (e.g., using a hidden camera), the experimenters still constitute an implicit audience; this is because the wall of the laboratory—with the experimenters behind it—constitutes a *de facto* partition condition just as in Figure 8.7 (B), with the power of such an arrangement commonly acknowledged in the social-psychology literature on social impact and evaluation apprehension (Latané, 1981).

In contrast to this axiom of the Emotions View, it seems obvious to me that the physical presence of others is one of the *least* important criteria for ascertaining the sociality of facial displays. I believe this for five reasons:

1. When we are alone *we often treat ourselves as interactants*. We talk to ourselves; reward or punish ourselves; hit, touch, and stroke ourselves; and deploy facial displays in the course of these acts. Can it be said that talking to ourselves is not communicative, but a "readout"? If so, what is being read out? In the same sense that words said to oneself are communicative, then the faces made to oneself are communicative as well.

That we are social interactants with ourselves at first seems absurdly solipsistic, but it is entirely consistent with views that emphasize the "private, authentic self" as a social construction (Mead, 1934), and the dialogical nature of thought as internalized speech (Bakhtin, 1981; Vygotsky, 1962; Wertsch, 1985). As Vygotsky stated,

> The very mechanism underlying higher mental functions is a copy from social interaction; all higher mental functions are internalized social relationships . . . their whole nature is social . . . In their whole private sphere, human beings retain the functions of social interaction. (cited in Wertsch, 1985)

That we are audiences to our own productions is evident in speech acquisition. As early as 18 hours prenatally, infants can discern their own cries from those of other infants (Martin & Clark, 1982), and by one week of age, crying is severely disrupted if infants hear it delayed electronically (Cullen, Fargo, Chase, & Baker, 1968). When they start babbling to caretakers, they begin to repeat those sounds to themselves, try out new ones, and even giggle at their own productions. Further, Locke (1990) reviewed evidence that babbling is delayed and distorted if infants cannot hear themselves talk (i.e., in congenitally deaf infants). Given the close relations between vocalization and facial movements (Chapter 12), infants' shaping of their own speech sounds may be influential in determining the facial displays they develop.

2. *We often act as if others are present when they are not.* We curse them, or utter words of love to them, or rehearse what we will say to them when we see them. In many of these acts we deploy facial displays. Our acting as if others are there when they are not is usually done with prior knowledge of their absence (e.g., practicing for a play, talk, or interview). Occasionally it is done without prior knowledge of others' absence, as when we speak to, and make faces to, a person we believe is in the next room—when the other has in fact departed, and can no longer hear us. With or without prior knowledge, these faces, too, are communicative, although they are emitted when we are alone.

I attempted to document empirically the importance of this kind of implicit audience as a mediator of solitary faces (Fridlund, 1991a). Subjects watched an amusing videotape in one of four viewing conditions: (A) alone; (B) alone, but with the belief that a friend nearby was engaged in an irrelevant task; (C) alone, but with the belief that a friend nearby was viewing the same videotape in another room; and (D) when a friend was physically present. Viewers' smiles were measured using facial electromyography (EMG; see discussion below) over the *zygomatic major* muscles responsible for smiling. The results are shown in Figure 8.8.

Smiling among solitary viewers who believed a friend was viewing nearby was equal to that shown in the actual presence of the friend, but greater than that shown by subjects who simply viewed alone. Self-ratings of happiness did not differ among the viewing conditions, and within conditions rated, happiness correlated negligibly with smiling. The findings confirmed audience effects for human smiles, demonstrated that the effects do not depend upon the physical presence of the interactant, and suggested that the smiles did not result from altered emotional experience.

These findings run counter to assumptions by proponents of the Emotions View. That the findings were counterintuitive was established using a "pseudoexperiment" technique taken from mental imagery studies (Kosslyn, Pinker, Smith, & Schwartz, 1979). The technique uses pseudosubjects to whom are explained, or who simulate, the experimental procedures experienced by the actual subjects. The pseudosubjects are then asked how they *would* respond to the procedures. We used

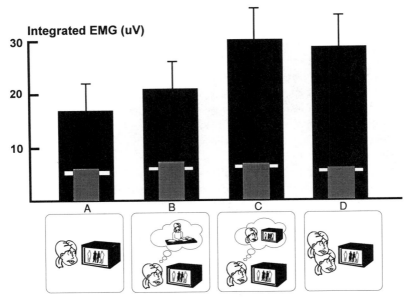

FIGURE 8.8. Smiling, measured using the facial electromyogram (EMG) over the *zygomatic major* muscles, of subjects who viewed amusing videotapes in one of four conditions of varying sociality. The first condition (A) had the lowest sociality, with subjects arriving to the laboratory and viewing alone. In conditions B through D, subjects arrived with same-sex friends who either (B) went to another room "to complete psychological tests"; (C) went to another room to "view the same tape at the same time"; or (D) sat with and viewed the tape along with the subject. Subjects showed a monotonic increase in smiling from A to D, even though in conditions A through C they were physically alone. Data from Fridlund (1991b).

both naive raters and a group of graduate students in an established emotion seminar at a major East Coast university. When provided with a description of the experiment, both groups of raters made predictions that accorded with the Emotions View but not with our results.

Similar findings emerged from another study involving gradations in sociality. Chovil (1991) studied the types of gestures made in different social contexts. Her subjects (here, all females) heard stories about close calls in one of four conditions: (A) alone, from an audio tape recording; (B) from another subject across a partition; (C) alone, over the telephone; and (D) talking to another subject face to face. Subjects' facial displays— largely wincing and grimacing—were scored using visible facial coding. Chovil then obtained sociality ratings for the four conditions by asking a separate group of raters to estimate the "psychological presence" afforded by each. The conditions were ordered according to their esti-

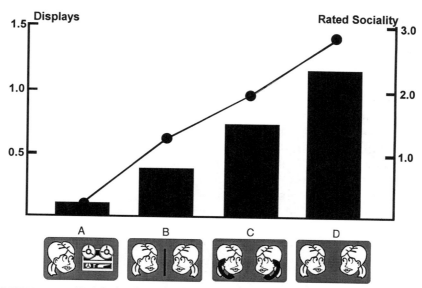

FIGURE 8.9.   Facial displays (bars) displayed by subjects who heard stories about close calls in one of four listening conditions varying in sociality: (A) alone, over a tape recorder; (B) from another subject across a partition; (C) over the telephone; and (D) face to face. Independent judgments of the level of sociality in each condition produced a trend (superimposed line) that conformed to the number of displays in each condition. Data from Chovil (1991).

mated sociality. Her results (Figure 8.9) revealed a monotonic trend for facial displays as a function of sociality, mapping nearly identically onto those provided by Fridlund (1991a). Her data also extend implicit audience effects to faces other than smiles, using visible coding rather than facial EMG recording. Chovil did not collect self-report data as a measure of emotion, and one counterargument to her sociality finding is that subjects may have been more emotional when their context of interaction was more social. As our own data showed (Fridlund, 1991a), there is no necessary relation between emotionality and sociality. Indeed, if there were, people would never suffer abandonment depression or feel happy when someone left the room (Chovil & Fridlund, 1991). As part of this study, Chovil also constructed a system for classifying her subjects' facial behavior. In line with the Behavioral Ecology View, an overwhelming proportion of the behavior conformed with communicative, paralinguistic categories. In Chapter 12 I discuss Chovil's classifications and, more generally, the close relations between face and language.

3. *We often imagine that others are present when they are not.* In our imagination we engage in interactions with others who are not there, that is, we "simulate" interaction with them. We imagine talking to them, arguing with them, making love with them, and throughout these acts, we

deploy facial displays (e.g., Fridlund, Schwartz, & Fowler, 1984). As in the previous example, we usually have prior knowledge that the others are absent. However, we sometimes become lost in reverie, and we momentarily forget that the imaginary others are actually absent. The facial displays made in reverie are also social and communicative, both when we are lost in reverie and *believe* they are there, and when we know that they are not. When we imagine a lover, and then smile and become sexually aroused, if we say that the smile was nonsocial, would we say that the arousal was nonsexual?

Fridlund et al. (1990) employed standard affective imagery procedures and established the role of imaginary audiences in mediating private faces. Subjects provided, and were then asked to imagine, situations that they enjoyed either alone (low-social) or with other people (high-social). Subjects' smiling during the imagery was again estimated using facial EMG overlying the *zygomatic major* muscles. Following each trial, subjects used emotion scales to report how happy they felt during the imagery. These happiness ratings were then controlled statistically. The results are depicted in Figure 8.10. Subjects showed more EMG activity in their *zygomatic major* sites in high-social than in low-social imagery, even when their happiness ratings were equalized. Fridlund et al. interpreted the smiling in the high-social imagery as influenced (in this case, potentiated) by the larger cast of imaginary interactants, and believed that subjects were displaying to the "people in their heads." Fridlund, Kenworthy, and Jaffey (1992) later replicated these findings and extended them to dysphoric imagery using a standard imagery protocol.

In several of the studies I have reviewed that contain sociality manipulations, face-to-face interaction resulted in maximal facial behavior. This should not always be the case, however, because in many contexts we do *not* issue communications to others. One important determinant of our facial behavior is our social role with respect to our potential interactants. Commuters on a subway may be within inches of each other yet pretend not to notice; if they are friends, however, their talk and facial behavior may be incessant. Just this kind of finding was reported by Wagner and Smith (1991), who videotaped pairs of subjects while they "rated their emotions" to slides. The facial behavior of the subjects was more discernible if the two were friends than if they were strangers. In the Behavioral Ecology View, the subjects' faces were no more than a running commentary on the series of slides. Had they been permitted, the friends would have chatted while they made faces; and the strangers would have done neither. And it is hard to strip an experiment of the influence of such social roles. To the solitary subject, the experimenter is a judge and the subject is in temporary solitary confinement, awaiting parole for "good behavior." Two male or two female subjects in the same

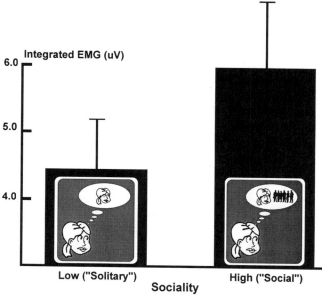

FIGURE 8.10.   Smiling as measured by facial electromyography over the *zygomatic major* muscles, while subjects were imagining doing something pleasurable either: alone (*left*) or with others (*right*). Smiling was greater when the imaginary cast of characters was larger, even after controlling for rated happiness. Data from Fridlund et al. (1990).

room may make a contest out of the experiment, whereas an experiment with a male–female pair may become a "blind date."

It also stands to reason that if strangers were placed in an "implicit sociality" study such as that conducted by Fridlund (1991a) or Chovil (1991), then increasing the directness of sociality should merely produce the increasing alignment of facial behavior with that expected in or observed for the corresponding face-to-face interaction. Friends sharing a humorous experience face to face should exhibit greater facial behavior than if they are separated by a partition; friends asked to play poker should exhibit less. Strangers would probably issue little facial behavior regardless of the sociality condition or the type of experimental task. This is because, in most cases, we have less to say to strangers than to our friends, and our faces follow accordingly. There are exceptions, as when we "spill our guts" to a total stranger on a plane, and here, our faces pour out with our words. (Again, I detail the intimate links between faces and voices in Chapter 12.)

4. *We often forecast interaction and deploy displays appropriately*, consciously or not, even though no interactant is immediately present. These displays function in the service of seeking or shunning interaction. Most species have displays that function to deter potential interac-

tants. In both gorillas and humans, a tongue-showing display deters others (Smith et al., 1974; Dolgin & Sabini, 1979). If we are in a bad mood, we scowl upon entering the office in the morning; the scowl discourages potential greeting. On the other hand, solicitation of inter-action is omnipresent (cf. the "readiness to interact" displays described by Smith, 1977). We deploy a smile seconds before greeting a neighbor at the front door. As T. S. Eliot stated, "I must prepare a face to meet the faces that I meet." Like the bird who calls continuously in case a suitable mate should fly past (Smith, 1977), the human infant solving a problem deploys a "cognitive mastery" smile (Sroufe & Waters, 1976). The smile usually seduces any potential pedagogues who may encounter the in-fant.

This was confirmed by Sue Jones and colleagues, who developed an infant analog to Kraut and Johnston's (1979) bowling observations. In-fants were positioned such that they could look either at toys or at their mothers, and Jones et al. observed their facial behavior toward each. As early as 10 months of age, infant smiling was almost entirely dependent upon visual contact with the caregiver (Jones & Raag, 1989; Jones, Col-lins, & Hong, 1991).

5. *We often treat nonhumans, and animate and inanimate objects, as interac-tants.* That we often treat nonhuman animals as humans is self-evident to any pet owner. We talk to them, confide in them, praise and curse them, and make faces and gesture to them. Most people have no diffi-culty according pets agency and treating them as autonomous interac-tants. What is more reluctantly acknowledged is the extent to which we accord agency to inanimate objects and regard *them* as interactants. Dev-otees of indoor gardening talk, gesture, and make faces to their house-plants. Children do the same to their stuffed animals, dolls, or toy soldiers. In outbursts of animism, most of us have pummeled intransi-gent soda machines that "stole our money" or television sets that "lost our station," and in so doing we scolded them, called them names—and in the act, we made faces and gestures. Again, the faces and gestures we make to objects are no more readouts of emotion than is our flattery toward our houseplant or our derisive remarks to the malfunctioning soda machine or television. All are social communications, with the interactant an object that we have anthropomorphized to have eyes, ears, language, and intentions.

Viability of the Implicit Sociality Account of Solitary Facial Displays

In the implicit sociality view, implicit or imaginal interactants can never be excluded. Subjects' thoughts will always be populated, whether by thoughts or images either of the experimenter, or the others in their lives, or even themselves, and moreover, we convert inanimate objects into interactants. I call this process *restitutional interaction.*[3] Achieving pure "aloneness" is thus a *reductio ad absurdum* that would require narcotization so complete that daydreaming stops, and this would terminate most overt subject behavior, not just facial movement.

This fact carries a major implication for the laboratory study of facial behavior: it undercuts any presumption that isolating subjects or minimizing their physical contant with others actually "purifies" their facial productions in any way. In other words, our solitary faces are just as conventional as our "social" ones. When subjects are alone versus in the presence of others, what differs is not the "amount" of sociality, but its directness, or the degree to which one's social engagement is entrained to *specifiable* others, that is, those planted in the room by the experimenter.

It might be objected that the implicit sociality view, then, is non-disconfirmable. In fact, it probably is unfalsifiable *in extremis*, but this is no impediment to its viability as a scientific concept. This feature is shared with many useful and established theories whose limiting cases are unattainable. There are several examples. Superconductivity theory is alive and well. Despite the fact that the temperature of absolute zero is probably unattainable, potent and useful superconductivity effects can be observed as one approaches it. Similarly, special relativity theory holds that traveling at the speed of light is unattainable, but relativistic effects are well documented as the velocities of experimentally induced particles approach it. And scientists of all ilks—including psychologists themselves—exploit daily the utility of the natural logarithm, even though ln(0) is entirely undefined. Like these well-established theories and entities, implicit sociality can be studied quite easily within experimentally manipulable ranges.

The strict falsifiability objection is also instructive, in that it reveals the extent to which we view most animals (especially humans) atomistically, instead of as components of, and agents within, an encompassing web of social relations—even when alone (see Mead, 1934). Indeed, "solitude"—not implicit sociality—may be the odder concept.

Nor is the implicit sociality view novel. Wundt, Piderit (see Piderit, 1858, 1886), Gratiolet (1865), and Ribot (1897) all proposed "imaginary object" accounts of solitary faces made toward absent others. Gratiolet, for example, provided the case of the indignant man who clenches his teeth (and, perhaps, his fists) toward an absent adversary. B. Apfelbaum (personal communication, June, 1989) has reminded me that people

---

[3] The "restitution" concept is a psychiatric one borrowed from Bleuler, who proposed that hallucinations of others were a restitutional symptom of patients (e.g., schizophrenics) who had actually withdrawn from others.

often *blush* in private, a fact difficult to explain without imagining embarrassment in front of fantasized others. As Piderit (1858) stated,

> The muscular movements of expression are in part related to imaginary objects, and in part to imaginary sensory impressions. In this proposition lies the key to the comprehension of all expressive muscular movements.

Darwin knew this argument. Unfortunately, he disposed of it peremptorily (Darwin, 1872, pp. 6–8). I believe that this was due to his overriding interest in building a Lamarckian, reflexive model of faces as emotion-instigated serviceable habits (Chapter 2). In fact, Darwin had settled on the three principles of expressions before he had completed many of his observations; they were contained in his *M* and *N* notebooks, which he began as early as 1838 (Gruber, 1974). With Darwin's success in explaining evolution in terms of natural selection, his "latest hobby horse" (Browne, 1985), an emotional-reflexive view of expressions, became popular. This popularity led to the rise of the Emotions View of faces as readouts, the "decognitivizing" of solitary faces, and a long-standing neglect of imaginary objects accounts.

But Darwin's disposal of implicit sociality in the *Expressions* volume may have been strategic. In that volume he aimed to show continuity by likening human faces to nonhuman movements. In *The Descent of Man*, he took the reverse tack, and tried to show that nonhumans were strikingly similar to humans (i.e., they had dreams, memories, imagination, pride, shame, etc.). In this volume, he *endorsed* the concept of implicit sociality. It was an endorsement ignored by subsequent emotion theorists:

> Now with those animals which live permanently in a body, the social instincts are ever present and persistent . . . So it is with ourselves. Even when we are quite alone, how often do we think with pleasure or pain of what others think of us—of their imagined approbation or disapprobation; and all this follows from sympathy, a fundamental element of the social instincts. (Darwin, 1871, p. 114)

DO "FUNDAMENTAL EMOTIONS" UNDERLIE FACIAL DISPLAYS?

In the classical Emotions View, there are several fundamental emotion "circuits" (see Ortony & Turner, 1990) whose activation produces prototypic, iconic facial displays, unless contravening social demands force deployment of a deceptive mask. This view would be demonstrated if the emotions or "affect programs" were isolated phenomenologically and physiologically (i.e., localized neurally), independent of the occurrence of facial displays. Any display held to portray "anger," for example, would require the unitary "anger" program to be activated and causal. Classical emotions theory posits that the relation would be necessary for infants and probabilistic for adults. For the behavioral ecologist, there may be no fundamental affect programs to activate. Rather, signal movements arise in particulate fashion because of specific environmental and interactional demands, and the movements have meaning only in the social context of their issuance.

THE RELATIONS OF FACIAL DISPLAYS TO EMOTION AND PHYSIOLOGY

Whether "fundamental emotions" exist is thought by many to be resolvable psychophysiologically. The debate was often cast as one between two distinctively nonevolutionary views: the peripheralism of W. James (1884, 1890), who argued that somatomotor changes *were* the emotions, to the centralism of W. Cannon (1929), who believed that emotions differed physiologically only in the accompanying degree of general arousal (see Goldstein, 1968, for review of physiological theories of emotion). Cannon's centralism was the forerunner of contemporary "cognitive" theories that argue against instinctlike, elicitable, discrete emotions (Mandler, 1984).

Do Emotion Inductions Produce Distinctive Physiological Patterns?

If discriminable physiological correlates or "signatures" were discovered for each hypothetical emotion, then it is arguable that "fundamental emotions" theories would be bolstered. This is because the peripheral (i.e., muscular, cardiovascular, and glandular) emotion signatures would be indices that central affect circuits or programs were activated. Numerous studies have suggested that if individuals are placed in situations designed to induce "happiness," "sadness," "anger," "fear," and so on, they show situation-specific changes in autonomic responses like electrodermal activity, heart rate, blood pressure (e.g., Arnold, 1945; Averill, 1969; Ax, 1953; Funkenstein, 1955, Schachter, 1957; Schwartz, Weinberger, & Singer, 1981), or in facial electromyographic patterns (e.g., Fridlund et al., 1984; and review by Fridlund & Izard, 1983). "Emotion" manipulations have included affective imagery, social inductions such as threat or provocation, and stimuli such as loud noise.

The first of several studies to explore induced patterns of facial actions and their relations to autonomic activity was conducted by Ekman, Levenson, and Friesen (1983), who instructed subjects to recall instances when they felt happy, sad, angry, disgusted, fearful, or surprised. Subjects then performed facial actions comprising displays thought to connote these emotions. On both tasks, skin temperature and heart rate patterns discriminated "happy" from "anger" and "fear" instructions.

On the directed facial action task only, the "anger" and "fear" conditions were discriminable. According to the authors' interpretation of these changes, "it was contracting the facial muscles into the universal emotion signals which brought forth the emotion-specific autonomic activity" (p. 1210). (Notably, Wall and Pribram, 1950, had previously confirmed that stimulation of motor cortex elicited autonomic activity concurrent with movement, but they did not ascertain whether the pattern of activity was related to the type of movement.)

Do these studies lend support to the existence of "fundamental emotions"? There are two other criteria that must be met: (1) any physiological changes must not reflect mere differences in general arousal; and (2) such changes must be attributable to emotion and not just display.

First, patterns of physiological change specific to the emotion situations corroborate "fundamental emotions," but generalized arousal does not. This is because it is trivial to show, for example, that our heart beats faster and we sweat more when "angry" than when "sad." The difference may simply be due to the extra exertion entailed in raising our voice, clenching our fists, and gritting our teeth, with such exertion eventuating in a greater cardiovascular and thermal load. The effects of exertion may explain the data of Schwartz et al. (1981). Subjects imagined and then "expressed the emotions" of happiness, sadness, anger, fear, and relaxation while performing the Harvard Step Test (a common stress test in which one repeatedly steps up and down upon a wooden platform). Subjects showed differences in heart rate, and in diastolic and systolic blood pressure, specific to the "emotion" trials. Are these findings attributable to emotion? Not necessarily, because differences in posture and footstrike force may account for the cardiovascular effects during the Step Test. Ruling out this hypothesis requires a control condition in which the topographies of posture and footstrike were cued without reference to emotion, and in which control subjects did not become angry while behaving like the angry subjects.

Demonstrating "fundamental emotions" requires physiological patterns specific to emotion and not just exertion. Moreover, a physiological pattern that discriminates among indications of emotion may still be attributable to general arousal. As I showed in the case of facial EMG activity (Fridlund, 1988), differences in the rates of change in different physiological systems can make general arousal differences among emotions look like "patterning."

Second, visceroautonomic changes, whether patterned or not, may occur in preparation for intended action, regardless of emotional state. Thus, cardiovascular change in an aggressive individual may not indicate activation of an emotion circuit, but the intent to strike, whether or not the individual is angry. To restate the issue, "deceptive" (or more aptly, "pretended"; Bavelas, 1989) displays may elicit the same patterns as "honest" ones. Thus studies that assay physiological changes in emotion all require simulated-emotion (i.e., deception) controls. A case in point is the classic experiment by Ax (1953). Many autonomic differences occurred when subjects were frightened by an "inexperienced" experimenter versus angered by an abusive one. The appropriate control procedure would have required trained actors briefed about the experiment, and told to feign without "real emotion" the reactions of experimental subjects. In the Behavioral Ecology View, the same autonomic patterns should be obtained in subjects who pretended.

That autonomic change may be more a function of display than one of emotion was in fact suggested by the Ekman et al. (1983) data. The authors regarded the autonomic changes they observed as related to emotion, but they also observed similar autonomic differences when *requesting* various facial actions without intentionally mentioning or cuing emotion. There are three possible explanations for these findings:

1. In Stanislavski fashion (i.e., by tacitly assuming the role cued by making the face; see facial feedback section, below), subjects became emotional during the facial mimicry and thereby produced the changes. Self-ratings of emotion for the requested facial action task were unfortunately not reported.

2. The autonomic changes may have resulted from subjects' reactions to being *asked* to make particular faces (Ekman & Friesen, 1975).

3. The autonomic changes may not have related to emotion, but to facial displays *qua* displays. This is Ekman et al.'s (1983) interpretation of their directed action data. This account, of course, is consistent with the Behavioral Ecology View that deception is omnipresent, and that displays serve social motives, any of which may occur regardless of one's emotional state.

Because no physiological study of induced emotion has included a pseudoexperimental ("pretend") control group, there is no evidence that emotion per se relates to autonomic functioning. That autonomic activity relates to impending or ongoing exertion is undeniable (Cannon, 1929; Freeman, 1948). The implication can be stated simply: whether an organism *is* angry—whatever one means by the term—should have less bearing on autonomic functioning than the fact that it *acts* angry.

Is Facial Electromyography a Royal Road to the "Readout?"

Whether as cause or effect, the assumption that facial behavior is an index of mood or emotion underlies many recent studies that sample EMG activity of the face. In the facial EMG technique, tiny electrodes attached to the skin over facial muscles detect the secondary pulse trains

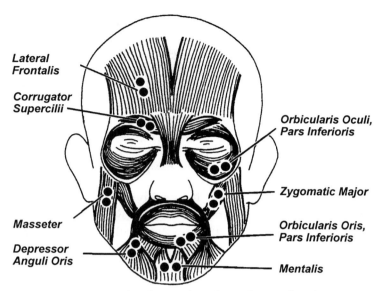

FIGURE 8.11.   Placements for skin surface electrodes used in electromyographic (EMG) studies of facial behavior. Twin recording disks overlie each muscle of interest, and the electrodes detect the electrical signals generated by the contracting muscle tissue underneath. Two electrodes per muscle site are required for the "differential recording" of these signals in order to achieve the cancellation of extraneous electrical noise. Properly conducted, facial EMG recording can accurately and precisely capture the level of contraction of the underlying muscles (see Fridlund & Cacioppo, 1986; Fridlund & Fowler, 1978).

created by contracting facial muscle tissue (see Fridlund & Cacioppo, 1986; Fridlund & Fowler, 1978). Figure 8.11 shows facial muscles over which EMG electrodes are usually attached, and the attachment points for those electrodes. Typically, subjects' facial EMG activity is monitored while they are alone watching movies or slides, or imagining social interactions (Fridlund and Izard, 1983, provided a review and description of types of studies).

Facial EMG activity in many of these studies is assumed to be uncontaminated by social roles and contexts, and thus it must reflect "pure" mood or emotion. This is assumed for two reasons: (1) the subject is alone while viewing or imagining; and (2) the facial EMG activity is below or at the edge of visibility. Indeed, we were mistaken in making an emotional interpretation of our early facial EMG findings (Fridlund et al., 1984).

By my earlier reasoning, the fact that facial EMG activity occurs when subjects are alone does not mitigate the sociality of the muscular actions. That the actions are incipiently visible or entirely covert is irrelevant to their sociality. Our talking to ourselves, or imaginally to others, is also incipiently visible or entirely covert, and it is often measurable only with psychophysiological methods (McGuigan, 1978). Talking in any form is certainly social and communicative. Because most human facial actions are paralinguistic (Fridlund & Gilbert, 1985), most covert faces should occur with covert language detectable using laryngeal EMG. This possibility remains to be investigated.

The facial EMG technique promised the opportunity to get beneath the "social mask" of visible faces, and to detect and quantify "real" emotion. In the Behavioral Ecology View, the facial EMG technique *can* enable investigators to pierce the overt social mask—and ascertain the covert social mask! (This is not an uninteresting prospect; see Fridlund et al., 1990; Fridlund, 1991a,b.)

In summary, that facial displays occur when one is alone does not constitute evidence that some faces are readouts of mood or emotional state. It is conceivable that there are some "readout" faces, but the requisite evidence would obtain from studies (electromyographic or otherwise) correlating faces with emotional state when there is no obvious interactant, *and* when we are not: (1) treating ourselves as social interactants; (2) acting as though others are present when they are not; (3) imagining that others are present when they are not; (4) forecasting interactions with others who are not immediately present; and (5) anthropomorphizing nonhuman animals—or animate or inanimate objects—as interactants.

Does Facial Feedback Determine "Emotional Experience?"

Psychophysiologists have also wondered whether the face, rather than being a "readout" of emotional experience, instead *determines* it. The putative effects of facial displays are usually attributed to proprioceptive feedback. (Other researchers hold that the "feedback" provided by faces occurs via perceiving the reactions of others, but these variants are merely restatements of social interaction theories.)

The origins of this belief are dramaturgical. As the eighteenth-century German playwright Lessing conjectured:

> . . . I believe that when the actor properly imitates all the external signs and indicators and all the bodily alterations which experience taught him are expressions of a particular (inner) state, the resulting sense impressions will automatically induce a state in his soul that properly accords with his own movements, posture, and vocal tone . . . . (Lessing, in *Theatrische Bibliothek*, 1767, cited in Robertson, 1939, p. 475; translation by H. Gleitman, 1985)

Wundt (1896) extended Lessing's reasoning:

> Just as expressive motion appears to us the reflection of an internal psychological state, it has the quality of being able to affect it again . . .

School psychologists have scarcely paid attention to the alternating relationship between sensation and internal emotion. But a deeply knowledgeable thinker like Lessing did not overlook this. 'The average actor,' he states in the third part of the *Hamburgische Dramaturgie*, 'if he has learned the most basic expressions of rage from an actor with genuine emotion, and has learned to imitate them accurately—the hasty walk; the stomping foot; the rough, partly screaming, partly suppressed tone; the movement of the eyebrows; the trembling lips; the grinding teeth, etc.—if he, I say, only learned these things which can be imitated at will, does so accurately, then his soul will be affected by a feeling of a dark sense of rage which again reflects back into his body, producing reactions that do not depend on our will alone: his face will glow, his eyes will glisten, his muscles will swell, in short, he will appear as a really enraged being without understanding why that should be the case . . . ' Lessing might have said it even better: he will not only appear to be a man in rage, he will become such.

Darwin is often claimed to have believed that the feedback inducing such "a state in the soul" might be physiological, a claim that would presumably bestow upon it the evolutionary imprimatur. The inference is based on a brief passage at the conclusion of Darwin's *Expressions* volume (1872):

> The free expression by outward signs of an emotion intensifies it. On the other hand, the repression, as far as this is possible, of all outward signs softens our emotions. (p. 365)

Using this statement as evidence that Darwin believed that expression determines emotion is, however, a misinterpretation of the text. It is clear from the passage's context that Darwin was advocating moderation in "expressing emotions," lest one lose control. He was also suggesting that general exertion acts to effect in the brain a hypermetabolic state, which results in a Spencerian spillover of heightened subjective excitation. He was not speaking of proprioceptive feedback from muscles or skin distension. Darwin's comment has more to do with the phenomenon known in contemporary social psychology as "transfer of excitation" (Zillman, 1983) than facial feedback.

That facial expressions may determine some intense emotions (or "coarse" emotions, as James termed them) is also explicit in James's emotion theory (James, 1884, 1890):

> The bodily changes follow directly the perception of the exciting fact, and . . . our feeling of the same changes as they occur *is* the emotion. (James, 1890, p. 463)

For James, willful termination of an expression also terminated the emotion:

Refuse to express a passion and it dies . . . If we wish to conquer undesirable emotional tendencies in ourselves, we must assiduously, and in the first instance, go through the outward movements of those contrary dispositions which we wish to cultivate.

Darwin's assertion that "emotional expression" intensifies the emotion, and James's that physiology *was* feeling, though superficially palatable, run counter to everyday intuitions about emotion and catharsis. As Spencer (1863) stated,

> It is commonly remarked that the suppression of external signs of feeling, makes feeling more intense. The deepest grief is silent grief . . . People who conceal their anger are habitually found to be more revengeful than those who explode in loud speech and vehement action . . .
>
> On the other hand, all are familiar with the truth that bodily activity deadens emotion. Under great irritation we get relief by walking about rapidly. Extreme effort in the bootless attempt to achieve a desired end, greatly diminishes the intensity of the desire. Those who are forced to exert themselves after misfortunes, do not suffer nearly so much as those who remain quiescent. If any one wishes to check intellectual excitement, he cannot choose a more efficient method than running till he is exhausted. (pp. 456–457)

Spencer's view was sensible, and Freud affixed it firmly within the tenets of psychoanalysis (Freud, 1921/1946). But Spencer's and Darwin's anecdotes suggest *opposite* effects of actions on emotions (negative vs. positive feedback, respectively). That both are plausible *prima facie* suggests that there is no compelling, clearcut relation that would call for research aimed at mechanistic explanation.

Despite these equivocal relations, many researchers have pursued the issue. They have generally neglected the cathartic phenomenon Spencer described and focused on the Jamesian positive-feedback account.[4]

---

[4] A related theory implying a negative-feedback relationship was provided by Jones (1935), after Allport (1924), who posited a hydraulic but noncathartic "internalizer–externalizer" trait which distinguished individuals who were putatively expressive and "internally" (i.e., autonomically) quiescent from those who were impassive and autonomically reactive. In Jones's trait autonomic activity was *not* predicated upon facial feedback. Several researchers have nonetheless used an inverse relationship between facial behavior and autonomic reactivity (usually estimated from electrodermal response and heart rate) to propose the face as the mediator of the reactivity (e.g., Buck, 1977; Buck, Miller, & Caul, 1974; Buck, Savin, Miller, & Caul, 1972; Lanzetta & Kleck, 1970; Notarius & Levenson, 1979; but see negative or contrary results reported by Ekman et al., 1983; Tourangeau & Ellsworth, 1979; Kleck, Vaughan, Cartwright-Smith, Vaughan, Colby, & Lanzetta, 1976; and Zuckerman, Klorman, Larrance, & Spiegel, 1981b). Kleck et al. (1976) maintained that an inverse relationship between facial behavior and autonomic activity does not necessarily reflect Jones's trait, but rather the fact that anxious people are often stirred to action but nonetheless remain immobilized.

My own belief is that the mechanism that accounts for "internalizer–externalizer" findings is just thermoregulation. To put it simply, the thermoregulatory demands of autonomic arousal force the immobilized (i.e., "unexpressive") subject to shift from locomotor cooling to evaporative cooling via sweating with tachycardia. This dual-cooling mechanism is a well-established feature of mammalian thermoregulation (see Satinoff, 1978).

How could one test a Jamesian account? James himself offered two methods, but was characteristically dismal about the utility of either:

> The only way coercively to *dis*prove it . . . would be to take some emotion, and then exhibit qualities of feeling in it which could be *demonstrably* additional to all those which could possibly be derived from the organs affected at the time. But to detect with certainty such purely spiritual qualities of feeling would obviously be a task beyond human power.
>
> A positive proof of the theory would, on the other hand, be given if we could find a subject absolutely anaesthetic inside and out, but not paralytic, so that emotion-inspiring objects might evoke the usual bodily expressions from him, but who, on being consulted, should say that no subjective emotional affection was felt. Such a man would be like one who, because he eats, appears to bystanders to be hungry, but who afterwards confesses that he had no appetite at all. Cases like this are extremely hard to find.

Indeed so. The first method must fail because—without a high-tech "phenomenoscope"—it relies upon superhuman (and unbiased) introspectionism. And the second fails just as surely, because absolutely anesthetic subjects do not exist. Furthermore, obtaining the "qualities of feeling" of partially anesthetic or deafferented humans places one in the initial introspective quagmire (e.g., Hohmann, 1966).

Rather than testing the stricter and slipperier Jamesian formulation, most researchers have focused on a simpler derivative which proposes the *face* as the major determinant or mediator of emotional experience. Tourangeau and Ellsworth (1979) termed this proposition the "facial feedback hypothesis," and documented its peculiar scientific status as an idea with an uncertain genealogy and a multiplicity of variants. Most sources nonetheless attribute the original hypothesis to Tomkins (Tomkins, 1962).

Under different versions of the "facial-feedback hypothesis" (see reviews by Buck, 1980; Ekman, 1982; Izard, 1990; Laird, 1984; Matsumoto, 1987; Tourangeau & Ellsworth, 1979; and Winton, 1986), "facial expressions which are associated with the fundamental emotions" (Lanzetta & McHugo, 1986, p. 2) are either *necessary* or *sufficient* to produce emotional experience.

In the "necessity" version, emotional experience cannot occur in the absence of the appropriate facial displays. The necessity version should not be seriously entertained, because there are so many counterexamples in which emotional experience persists in the absence of facial display.

The clearest case is provided by individuals with peripheral facial-nerve pathology that results in facial paralysis (e.g., Bell's palsy). They show neither emotional dyscontrol nor anhedonia. If facial feedback determined emotion, then the sufferer should show one of the two. In fact, the onset of Bell's palsy is often quite sudden; the patient wakes up one morning and finds that one-half of his/her face does not work. The victim is typically terrified, despite the fact that the *lateral frontalis*, which raises the brows in "fear" (i.e., submissive threat) faces, is functionally denervated. After such a rude awakening, the Bell's palsy patient must come to accept a dissociation between what is displayed and what is intended. The following passage is taken from a letter written to me by a psychologist whose mother suffered from Bell's palsy:

> My mother had a temporary case of Bell's palsy about five years ago, during which time the left side of her face was paralyzed. But that's not all: the left corner of her mouth was frozen in a slightly raised position, and her left eye often blinked despite conscious effort to control it. In short, she presented a highly flirtatious display!
>
> After reading your paper I decided to ask her about her emotional states during that period (she's pretty frank). She recalled feeling slightly embarrassed in most cases, but not sexy. (In fact, she experienced moments of revulsion at the thought that she was making such a face toward her boss, whom she despised.) Yet with my father it was all a joke, and she apparently camped it up with him.
>
> In short, she was able to experience a range of emotional responses with her facial display held constant, so to speak. Her external flirtatiousness was uncorrelated with a variety of internal states ranging from disgust to more pleasant emotions. (Perhaps there were even times when emotional states matched displays, but one hesitates to ask one's mother directly about such things.)
>
> Part of my mother's discomfort stemmed from knowing that what she displayed was incongruent with her internal state of mind. This is also the dilemma of people who laugh during sad occasions such as funerals. Like my mother, they believe that others are going to read their displays in terms of underlying dispositions.

It might be objected that the Bell's Palsy case is inconclusive because: (1) it is based on pathology, and (2) the paralysis is unilateral. Yet dramatic evidence that strong emotion persists in normal individuals despite total paralysis is provided by three further examples.

The first example is the obvious one of dreaming. In dreams, individuals can have experiences that range from euphoria to stark terror, despite the striate muscle paralysis that ensues at the onset of REM sleep. This evidence could of course be contested, if it is maintained ad hoc that the facial-feedback hypothesis applies only to "conscious emotion" and not the "unconscious" variety in the dream.

Mitigating this ad hoc objection is the second example, that of sleep paralysis, a parasomnia that most people experience occasionally but others suffer chronically (see Hauri, 1977, for clinical description). This condition usually occurs on awakening from sleep, when consciousness returns before the normal REM sleep-related muscle paralysis remits. One is paralyzed, and manifestly aware of it. If facial feedback determined emotion, then the individual with sleep paralysis should be momentarily anhedonic. Not surprisingly (and *contra* the necessity version), most first-time sufferers are instead horribly panicked; they often believe they are about to die, or will never move again.

The third example of the persistence of emotion despite paralysis is described vividly by Altmann (1987). He relates the courageous experiment by the British physician Prescott, who in furthering research on muscle relaxants, self-injected the paralytic drug *d*-tubocarine (the pharmacologically active ingredient in curare). In the middle of the experiment, Prescott felt he was drowning in his own saliva. His colleagues assumed everything was fine.

> There was nothing he could do about it. He could not move a limb, finger, or toe. . . . He was terrified. His blood pressure and pulse rate, which had raised dramatically, showed his fear, but his colleagues failed to realize how frightened he was. . . . Minutes later, doctors injected Prescott with an antidote. (p. 79)[5]

The counterexamples to the necessity version are, by strong inference (Meehl, 1978; Popper, 1962), fatal to it, and leave one to consider only weakened variations.

In the "sufficiency" version, simulated or "managed" displays should modulate emotional experience. Logically, a "sufficiency" version implies that emotional experience need not require a facial expression, but a facial expression does imply production or alteration of emotional experience. This view is not compelling primarily because it cannot explain the omnipresence of deception. If facial displays determined emotion, then individuals could not lie with their faces, play poker, sell used cars, or "stonewall" at news conferences. If liars' faces affect their sentiments, the effect is surely small.

Several investigators have nonetheless sought to find *some* effect of facial behavior in inducing emotion, and this effort has result in numerous social psychology experiments that have had subjects either: (1) maintain simulated, fixed displays during inductions of emotional arousal (for example, smiling vs. teeth-clenching at slides of Ku Klux Klan members; see Laird, 1974); or (2) modulate (strengthen or weaken) the facial displays they make while emotionally aroused.

These experimental tests of the hypothesis that involve simulated or modulated displays are all problematic, in four ways:

1. They are inextricably confounded with implicit suggestions to subjects about how they should act. A subject instructed to move facial

---

[5] A traditional objection to curarization findings is that "facial feedback" could be provided from central motor to central sensory centers despite end-organ (i.e., muscular) paralysis. In this condition, however, the face would be obviated, and the "facial feedback hypothesis" would become centralist.

muscles to form a smile at Ku Klux Klan slides is being asked implicitly to take an amused stance toward them; one instructed to jaw-clench is being cued to posture aggressively. Thus in these studies the experimenter is actually a director, and the subject a Stanislavski actor who "slips into role." The actor-subject may indeed be using sensations from the face to assume role, as he would his gestures or tone of voice, for example, were he so coached. But it is the role or "set" taken in the given social context that determines the emotion, not the displays themselves, whether facial or otherwise (Stanislavski, 1936, 1965). Seen in this way, simulation manipulations are, as Lessing would have maintained, pure dramaturgy.[6] This skeptical account was cogently stated by Piderit (1886):

It is hardly possible for someone unskilled to imitate a certain expressive gesture, for instance rage, completely accurately and true to nature, without transporting himself into the role of an enraged person. And when someone more experienced wishes to maintain this expression, immediately—through association of ideas—more or less vivid memories of similar psychic states and experiences arise out of habit, then there may appear the self-deception that "the sensory feeling of muscular contraction" is alone capable of arousing the affect.

Piderit continued by noting an obvious problem with the "facial feedback hypothesis" which has escaped its modern proponents:

Additionally, the delusion that expressive motions can produce the corresponding affect is more likely to occur with rage, since it is very easily induced through the production of anger-evoking imagery, and can be done deliberately even without all the accompanying muscular movements. If, on the other hand, a less frequent affect is imagined, such as ecstasy, then it must be conceded that even the most expressive facial gestures and movements—enthusiastic waving of the arms, a sweet smiling mouth, adoring glances, etc.—will not be able to arouse in us the feeling of ecstasy when the correct mood is missing, so that, for example, a musical composition, a painting, or a poem may leave us indifferent, and our best efforts at external muscular motions cannot change our mood, much less make us ecstatic. On the contrary, the more zealously we try to use contrived external movements and force to attain an emotion not already felt, the more obvious will be the failure of our efforts. This is true not just for expressive gestures, but also for certain symbolic gestures which have become rote, such as those practiced habitually during prayer, because those who perform them mechanically without the appropriate mood will feel no reflective effect upon religious feelings.

[6] This performative, dramaturgical analysis may be especially applicable to the experiment by Ekman et al. (1983), in which many of the subjects were *actors*, and the directed facial actions were obtained using a "coach" (i.e., a director) and a mirror. Together, these make for an audience and thus a performance.

2. The simulation manipulations violate social contexts in ways that may be awkward, embarrassing, or silly (e.g., Strack, Martin, & Stepper, 1988).[7] For example, it is silly to maintain a fixed smile under most circumstances, regardless of what state the investigator intends to elicit; hence, any increments in "happiness" with smiles may stem from amusing incongruity.

3. It takes effort to make faces or alter the faces one is already making. Because smiles require the contractions of only one muscle, the *zygomatic major*, and because they are omnipresent, they are easy to make and sustain. In contrast, any face chosen for its putative relations to "negative emotions" requires more than one muscle, and by implication the coordination of these muscles. Making or sustaining such a face will usually require more attention and effort than making a smile. Thus, any subject asked to move muscles such as to make smiles versus "negative" faces is likely to rate the smile movement more pleasant.

4. Subjects may alter their cognitive strategies for coping with the demands of the experiment such that the effects look like facial feedback. For example, a few studies of the "sufficiency" hypothesis had subjects modulate displays they were making during experimentally induced emotion (e.g., Lanzetta, Cartwright-Smith, & Kleck, 1976). Findings such as these studies may be confounded by "indirect" Stanislavski effects; that is, subjects told to display more or less are being told implicitly to be more or less emotional. Subjects will comply by *being* more or less emotional. They will accomplish this not via facial feedback, but by attending more or less to the emotional stimuli, distracting themselves, re-framing the situation, and so on. Subjects' introspections regarding their experimental performances would be informative.

Facial feedback researchers have attempted to control for many of these artifacts and confounds, and these efforts are laudable. Regrettably, to my knowledge no study has yet controlled adequately for the implicit demands of the social context engendered by the experimental manipulations. Among the requisite controls is the one I employed in

---

[7] The Strack et al. (1988) study is typical of manipulation studies, and it was lauded widely as having "done the best job of meeting the challenge of manipulating subjects' facial expressions without the subjects' being aware that their facial expressions are the focus of the investigation" (Sabini, 1992). Strack et al. had subjects view cartoons while holding a felt-tip pen either with clenched teeth (producing a smile) or their lips (producing a pucker). Those who puckered rated the cartoons less amusing. I suspect that subjects felt sillier putting on a forced grin than puckering. Moreover, from a performative perspective, Strack et al. merely used a prop (the felt-tip pen) to lead subjects to smile in the experimental situation, and higher amusement ratings would be consistent with the subjects' performances. The Strack et al. study is also dubious ecologically: if the findings were general, then humans would find pleasure in neither kissing nor playing brass instruments.

my audience-effects study (Fridlund, 1991a), the pseudoexperiment technique adopted from mental imagery studies (Kosslyn et al., 1979). As applied to facial feedback studies, the pseudosubjects would engage in all aspects of the experiment except that they would not perform the face manipulation. If pseudosubjects cannot reproduce the data provided by real subjects, then experimental demand can be ruled out.

Three additional problems for both the necessity and sufficiency versions of the facial feedback hypothesis are those of (1) "first cause"; (2) autocatalysis; and (3) the primacy of the face. To elaborate:

1. The "first cause" problem is the usual Aquinian one. If faces relate so intimately to emotion, and emotion results or is modulated by facial feedback, what moves the face in the first place?

2. The problem of autocatalysis stems from the positive-feedback model presumed by most investigators. In proposing such positive feedback from emotion-instigated faces upon emotion, mechanisms must be posited and demonstrated which dampen runaway escalation of both emotion and facial action.

3. The third problem is in according primacy to the face, a view originated by Tomkins (1962). Critical new data suggest that induced *postures* equal facial movements in influencing reports of emotion (Duclos, Laird, Schneider, Sexter, Stern, & Van Lighten, 1989). At the very least, these data vitiate Tomkins's assertion of facial primacy, and they logically force proponents to rename their object of study the *somatic feedback hypothesis*. The Duclos et al. data also corroborate my Stanislavski account, which would hold that almost *any* movement could alter emotionality if it induces the subject to "slip into" the role engendered by the behavior. Indeed, in the Behavioral Ecology View, faces may have no intrinsic meaning apart from the social context or role in which they are deployed. The smile of a party-giver and that of a sadist have different meanings, as do the cry-face of one in grief and one who has won a lottery. Facial-feedback studies treat them as univocal indicants of discrete emotions.

I believe that construing the facial feedback hypothesis as one for social psychology was unfortunate, and it has resulted in a plethora of indeterminate experiments. The facial feedback hypothesis is essentially a problem for other disciplines—neurophysiology, because the putative feedback mechanism relies on proprioception or exteroception; and psychophysics, because differences in facial actions are claimed to determine or titrate quantities of felt emotion. Realistically, these kinds of investigations are painstaking, and because the face's effect upon emotional state must be minuscule, their yield will likely be low.

Current versions of the facial feedback hypothesis are not compelling.

There are no everyday phenomena that require it for their explanation. Any relations between emotion and facial display are readily explained by the mediation of social motives. It is of course possible that *some* facial displays may play *some* contributory role in felt emotion, but any scientifically useful facial feedback hypothesis must be seriously delimited so as to specify types of displays, those circumstances under which they may be contributory, the nature of their contributions, and the mechanisms by which they contribute.

IS AN EMOTIONS ACCOUNT OF FACIAL DISPLAYS VIABLE?

Throughout my discussion of facial displays and my comparison of the Emotions and Behavioral Ecology Views, I have treated "emotion" as a given and contested its importance in understanding faces. The studies I have discussed show that nonhuman and human faces depend upon social context, and suggest that "facial displays of emotions" are manifestations of social intent.

One might question whether this is just an issue of definition. Certainly if emotion is defined broadly enough, then faces must "express emotion." For example, why isn't it reasonable just to say that emotions are, or can include, the expression of social motives? If we define terms such that smiling in order to be friendly while feeling happy *is* happiness, and crying in order to obtain succor while feeling sad *is* sadness, then the distinction between the Emotions and Behavioral Ecology Views becomes moot. This solution, though diplomatic, is problematic, for reasons I outline below.

The Inadequacy of Action as a Criterion

It is obvious, *contra* peripheralist views, that we can act one way and feel another. Moreover, it is now clear that the experience of emotion is separable from bodily action. We know this from several phenomena, chiefly curare experiments such as the one I cited above, in which people feel terrified despite total paralysis. So what do we call emotion, feeling happy or acting happy, feeling sad or acting sad? Suppose, for example, that I decided to con someone, and slyly put on a sad face in order to bilk them of some of their money. What then is my emotion?

To continue the argument, suppose that someone smiles because she is sad and lonely but desperately wants to be friendly. What is her emotion? Or suppose someone bursts into tears and wants a hug because they've just won the lottery and they're gloriously happy? What's the emotion there? To save an emotions theory of faces, we'd have to say that smiles mean you're happy and want to be friendly except when you're sad and lonely and want to be friendly. And we'd have to say that crying means you're sad and want a hug except when you're happy and want a hug. Why this circumlocution? It is more sensible just to say that the smiling signifies the desire to be friendly, and crying the desire to be hugged.

There are other problems in trying to lump social motives with emotions. First, which social motives would be included and which would be excluded? For example, if we perceive that we have been slighted, we may be inclined toward revenge, and one might call this social intent an "emotion." On the other hand, suppose we construe that we are slighted, and instead want to negotiate? If wanting revenge is emotional, then why isn't wanting to negotiate?

The Inadequacy of Self-Report as a Criterion

If action does not imply emotion, then perhaps the criterion of emotion should be phenomenological. That is, whether one *feels* emotional should be the signifier of emotion. My wanting revenge thus reflects an emotion if and only if I "feel angry," my wanting to be friendly is happiness if and only if I "feel happy," and my crying and wanting a hug is sadness only if I "feel sad." The problem here is manifold. One concerns scientific validation. Can I take a subject's report as indicating something *true*? For example, suppose the same subject who stated, "I am happy," also stated, "I have a personal relationship with God." Forgetting the report of emotion for the moment, how would we verify her relationship with God?

We cannot directly establish her personal relationship with God for several reasons, including the requirement that we first establish God's existence independent of her testimony. We might resort, then, to the usual tack of validation by convergent evidence. So we find that our subject goes to her church twice per week and double-tithes her income to it, has religious icons scattered throughout her house, repeats and acts in accord with the moral precepts of her religion, stresses the importance of her relationship with God with others outside the laboratory, and encourages others to develop one of their own. She also prays six times per day and shows a characteristic physiological pattern when she does so. Does all this convergent evidence get us closer to validating her claim? I suggest that her report of emotion is no more useful and no easier to validate. In fact, the whole metaphor of "reporting one's emotion" is a misplaced journalistic metaphor. When our subject "reports" her relationship with God or "reports her emotion," what she is doing is *making a claim* for the former, and I submit, for the latter as well. The claim cannot itself validate the subject of the claim, whether it be of emotion or God.

The Inadequacy of Physiology as a Criterion

One might be tempted to flee the worlds of variously interpretable overt actions and murky phenomenology and rely instead upon the biological bedrock of "involuntary" physiological activities. But this proves no solution, either. If it was unclear earlier which subset of social intentions could be considered "emotions," so biological theories are unclear about which types of *un*intentional actions constitute them. For example, tachycardia (elevated heart rate) and sweating (measured using the electrodermal response) do not signify emotion if they occur because I am hot, but they do if it occurs because I have heard thunder. Similarly, a subtle wrinkling of my nose—for our purposes, detectable only with facial EMG—does not signify an emotion if I have sniffed pollen, but it does if I have sniffed stale vomit. I must then qualify *when* each autonomic or facial EMG signal signifies emotion, and when it does not. This merely sidesteps the issue by diverting the criterion of "emotion" to the elicitors of the autonomic changes, thereby forcing ad hoc declarations about which elicitors are *de jure* "emotional," for example, thunder and stale vomit are, but heat and pollen are not. The problem is no better if one shifts the criterion to a certain pattern of physiological activities, because the same elicitor issue prevails.

The Nonexistent Consensus about What Constitutes "Emotion"

Among the proponents of the Emotions View, one looks in vain for some agreement about what constitutes both the inclusion and exclusion criteria for emotion, that is, those signs that indicate the presence of emotion, and those that indicate its absence. The stated definitions are not helpful in specifying the term. For example, here is one from a recent undergraduate emotion text:

> Emotion is a genetic and acquired motivational disposition to respond experientially, physiologically, and behaviorally to certain internal and external variables. (Carlson & Hatfield, 1992, p. 5)

The problem with this definition is obvious. It could cover anything, such as asking someone to pass the salt at the dinner table, or knowing to come in out of the rain. The nonspecificity is rife. Here, for example, is Izard's capsular description of the phenomenon of emotion:

> An emotion is experienced as a feeling that motivates, organizes, and guides perception, thought, and action.
> All aspects of this description are critical to understanding the nature of emotion. Emotion motivates. It mobilizes energy, and, in some cases, the energy buildup is experienced as an action tendency. Emotion guides mental and physical activity, channeling energy in selective directions. . . . Emotion also acts as a regulator or filter for our senses. (Izard, 1991, p. 14)

Here, the logical question is what *isn't* emotion. Emotion has, in fact, replaced Bergson's *elan vital* and Fliess's and Freud's *libido* as the energetic basis of all human life. Note that I have not selected these passages as particularly easy targets; they are representative of definitions of the term "emotion." Nor am I faulting the present cohort of proponents of the Emotions View. Emotion has been defined in nearly every imaginable way, so as to encompass every conceivable human phenomenon, as Hillman's profoundly scholarly review of emotion concepts attests (Hillman, 1972).

Nor is frustration with the term new. One of the reasons William James turned to a peripheralist account of emotions was his contempt for essentialist views that asserted their fundamental, categorical nature:

> The . . . descriptive literature of the emotions is one of the most tedious parts of psychology. And not only is it tedious, but you feel that its subdivisions are to a great extent either fictitious or unimportant, and that its pretenses to accuracy are a sham.
>
> The trouble with emotions in psychology is that they are regarded too much as absolutely individual things. So long as they are set down as so many eternal and sacred psychic entities, like the old immutable species in natural history, so long all that *can* be done with them is reverently to catalog their separate characters, points and effects. (James, 1890, pp. 1064–1065)

Early on, this led to wholesale disenchantment among many onetime emotion researchers. Many began to note how the concept of "emotion" figures so large in human life, yet crumbles like so many ashes when examined with a little care:

> The whale has a twofold distinction among the fishes: first, when seen from a distance, it looms large among them; and second, on close examination, it is found to be no fish at all. Something like that I predict for the theory of emotions among the theories in psychological textbooks and periodicals. (Meyer, 1933, p. 292)

Others have no hope that anything can come of attempts to define the term:

> An attempt to define emotion is obviously misplaced and doomed to failure. (Mandler, 1975, p. 10)

The arguments I review are all old and well crafted (again, see Hillman, 1972), but they have made no dent in the professional enthusiasm for the term. How can "emotion" seem so important if it is so vexing scientifically? One reason may be because it is so socially convenient. Using an emotions vocabulary is itself a "social tool"; it is advantageous precisely because it is polite. Instead of calling someone who's hurt us a "worthless piece of human excrement," we can say that we are "angry" toward them. Culturally, emotions language has probably replaced the language of demonic possession, and we can capitalize on this fact. Instead of saying, "I am angry" to the person who hurt us, we can say "I can't help but have these angry feelings toward you." This lets us both off the hook. Our emotions just happened to us, so the conventional accountability goes, and we also don't have to comment on the other's actions. And if *we* do something we wished we hadn't, we can just claim that we were "being emotional."

We must still evaluate the sensibility of any Emotions View of faces. Throughout this volume, I suggest that facial displays can be understood without recourse to emotions or emotion terms, and I show that certain tenets of the Emotions View of faces are improbable or unworkable. What cannot be done is to show that emotions have no role in facial displays, because excluding emotion would require a definition that allows it. At present, arguing against "emotion" in any form is shadow boxing.

In the end, emotion may be to the face as Ryle's "ghost" (Ryle, 1949) was to the machine. "Emotions" and homuncular "ghosts" may both be constructions borne of a transcendentalist wish for something more than function or mechanism. If psychology's "Cognitive Revolution" dispatched the need for a managerial homunculus in the nervous system, so then must we finally dispatch the notion that the face mirrors the passions of the soul. But this conclusion may be premature. For the time being, the only rejoinder to those who question whether any facial display might be related to emotion is, "What do you mean by emotion?"

9

INTRODUCTION: CROSS-CULTURAL STUDIES OF FACIAL EXPRESSIONS OF EMOTION

Explicit in the classical Emotions View of facial expressions is the assumption that "fundamental emotions" correspond with genetically controlled prototype faces. This assumption derives chiefly from early cross-cultural comparative data on those displays traditionally considered "facial expressions of emotion." In the last 20 years, the cross-cultural studies of facial expressions have been well publicized, and the claims of "universality" by their authors became the common wisdom about facial expressions. Brief descriptions of these studies began to appear with representative photographic stimuli in nearly every introductory psychology and anthropology text. It is thus enlightening to note the sociopolitical context in which they arose.

When the cross-cultural studies of facial expressions were conducted in the 1960s, the *Zeitgeist* was a pronounced cultural relativism. It had begun with antiuniversalist attacks by two anthropologists, Margaret Mead (e.g., 1928) and Bronislaw Malinowski (e.g., 1961). Both had challenged universality with counterintuitive findings about psychosexual development in non-Western cultures. The anthropological concensus that "universals" were fictive was also visible in work by the linguist Benjamin Whorf, who argued that the Hopi Indians had no conventional sense of time (Carroll, 1956). Some anthropologists even argued that color perception was culturally based (cf. Brown, 1991).

The basis for the cultural relativism movement was linguistic: language determined cognitive categories, and cultures would therefore be as different as their languages. The emphasis on language was consistent with the then-fashionable Marxist axiom that all consciousness was "class-consciousness," and "human nature" was an artifact of social structure. Whorf's mentor Edward Sapir (1929) stated the presumption precisely:

> The 'real world' is to a large extent unconsciously built up on the language habits [of a society, and thus] the worlds in which different societies live are different worlds.

Such relativism extended to human facial expressions, which were considered linguistic and, by implication, just as culturally variable as language. Anthropologist Weston La Barre (1947) argued that "there is no 'natural' language of emotional gesture" (p. 55), a position continued by Ray Birdwhistell (1963, 1970).

Brown (1991) reviewed the impact of the relativistic era, and documented the pro-universalist resurgence that began in the 1960s and successively overturned relativist dogma. For example, Berlin and Kay (1969) found that color classifications across cultures were surprisingly similar. Malotki (1983) discovered that the Hopi sense of time was indeed as fully developed as ours. Spiro (1982) reanalyzed Malinowski's own data and found that, as expected, the matrilineal Trobriand Islanders *did* manifest an Oedipus Complex. Finally, amid a political firestorm, Derek Freeman (1983) showed that the venerated Margaret Mead had grossly misjudged the supposedly peaceable and libertine Samoans because she was unfamiliar with both the culture and the language.

The cross-cultural studies of human facial expressions were thus part of the counterreaction to the prevailing relativism. They were designed explicitly to provide evidence for universality, and thus their a priori limitations were not considered sufficiently. Any findings of universality, it was assumed, would imply innateness of facial expressions when, in fact, whether any displays are universal is *independent* of whether they are innate. This is true because:

1. Assuming that innateness even *required* universality was a fundamental error. Displays of a certain kind would not necessarily occur in all cultures, given that a phyletic trend need only be statistical (Eibl-Eibesfeldt, 1972).

2. Any communalities across cultures may reflect not innateness and shared phylogeny, but convergent evolution *or* learning common to all. For example, nearly all cultures believe in God (or a set of gods) and have some kind of currency or standards of reciprocity, but this does not imply that either is innate; both may arise due to the universal exigencies of life.

3. Any findings of *non*universality would not exclude innateness of facial displays, because the *differences* among cultures may be due either to founder effects *or* genetic drift, not just culture-specific convention. Thus, congenitally light skin is entirely innate, as is congenitally dark skin, but the fact that cultures differ widely in skin color does not at all mitigate the innateness of skin color. Indeed, labeling as "cultural" the variations in the faces used by people in disparate areas of the world biased the debate. These variations might not have been "cultural" but "regional," determined genetically just as much as the purported universals.

Consequently, the cross-cultural studies could *never* answer the question posed by their proponents. The studies were conducted nonetheless, and the post hoc claims have typically been hyperbolic. The following passage is typical:

> The early work of Darwin (1872/1965, 1877) and the more recent work of Ekman, Friesen, and Ellsworth (1972) and Izard (1971) have shown that certain emotions, referred to . . . as *fundamental emotions*, have the same expressions and experiential qualities in widely different cultures from

virtually every continent of the globe, including isolated preliterate cultures having had virtually no contact with Western civilization. The data . . . provide a sound basis for inferring that the fundamental emotions are subserved in innate neural programs. (Izard, 1991, p. 17)

What do these studies *actually* show? In an earlier manscript, I summarized evidence of cross-cultural communalities in facial displays connoting emotion by paraphrasing my earlier review with Ekman and Oster (Fridlund et al., 1987). These reviews repeated the oft-cited claims of universality of "facial expressions of emotion." While preparing this volume, I learned that a colleague, James Russell, had just completed the most careful analysis to date of the cross-cultural studies. His analysis is both particularly astute and singularly disturbing, and it suggests that the assumption of universality of human "facial expressions of emotion" was premature.

I now present this review (Russell, 1994), and discuss its implications directly afterward.

10

Is There Universal Recognition of Emotion from Facial Expression? A Review of the Cross-Cultural Studies

"Everyone knows that grief involves a gloomy and joy a cheerful countenance. . . . There are characteristic facial expressions which are observed to accompany anger, fear, erotic excitement, and all the other passions" (Loveday & Forster, 1913, p. 805, 808). These words are Aristotle's. Aristotle was not proposing a new idea, but was cataloging what was known on the topic of physiognomy. The theory was that a person's physical appearance, especially in the face, reveals deeper characteristics: poor proportions reveal a rogue, soft hair a coward, and a smile a happy person.[1]

Today, few psychologists share Aristotle's belief about the meaning of poor proportions or soft hair, but many share his beliefs about facial expression and emotion. Oatley and Jenkins (1992) observed, "by far the most extensive body of data in the field of human emotions is that on facial expressions of emotion" (p. 67). Recent reviews of those data (see Table I) have agreed that the face reveals emotion in a way that is universally understood: happiness, surprise, fear, anger, contempt, disgust, and sadness—these seven emotions, plus or minus two, are recognized from facial expressions by all human beings, regardless of their cultural background.

As Matsumoto (1990) said, "the universality of facial expressions of emotion is no longer debated in psychology" (p. 195). Rather, it is a "fact," the implications of which are debated. Defending the idea of basic emotions against Ortony and Turner's (1990) criticisms, Ekman (1992b) and Izard (1992) pointed to universal facial expressions. Turner and Ortony (1992) replied, "We do not (and did not) dispute the fact that there are universal facial expressions associated with certain emotions" (p. 566).

If universality is a fact, then the implications are far reaching indeed. Brown (1991) and Buss (1992) cited the existence of universal facial expressions as one of six key cases for bringing back the concept of human nature. For some theorists, universality is deeply revealing about the nature of emotion. For others, universality is a finding that must be accounted for by any viable theory of emotion (e.g., Oatley, 1992). Izard (1971, p. 188) wrote, "emotion at *one level is* neuromuscular activity of the face" (emphasis Izard's). DePaulo (1992) wrote, "the fact that facial expressions of basic emotions are fundamentally the same across cultures (e.g., Ekman, 1972; Izard, 1971) is consistent with the position that there may be automatic links between the experiencing of the basic emotions and the expression of those emotions" (pp. 205–206). Oatley

Reprinted from *Psychological Bulletin, 115,* 102–141. Copyright © 1994 by the American Psychological Association, Inc. Reprinted with permission.

[1] Although the book quoted in this paragraph has been attributed to Aristotle, it may have been written or compiled by his students (Evans, 1969). See also Chapter 1.

TABLE I   Conclusions from Recent Reviews of Research
on the Universality Thesis

Source	Conclusion
1. Ekman (1980)	"Are facial expressions of emotion the same for all human beings?" (p. 91); "Definitive data are now available on the question of universality" (p. 93); "There is conclusive scientific evidence to resolve the question of universality" (p. 96); "There are some facial expressions of emotion which are universal" (p. 137)
2. Izard (1980)	"Impressive evidence for the innateness and universality of six of the fundamental emotions: enjoyment (happiness), distress (sadness), anger, disgust, surprise, and fear" (p. 201); "Since all human beings recognize these expressions and attribute to them the *same* experiential significance, it is reasonable to infer that they are genetically based or preprogrammed" (p. 185)
3. Frijda (1986)	"Many facial expressions occur . . . throughout the world in every human race and culture. The expressions appear to represent, in every culture, the same emotions" (p. 67)
4. Fridlund, Ekman, & Oster (1987)	"Observers label certain facial expressions of emotion in the same way regardless of culture." (p. 157)
5. Gudykunst & Ting-Toomey (1988)	"The research cited indicates that facial expressions representing the basic emotions are recognized universally." (p. 182)
6. Buck (1988)	"Research on the communication of emotion via facial expression suggests that certain displays appear and are correctly recognized in widely different cultures." (p. 351)
7. Izard & Saxton (1988)	"The evidence for the innateness and universality of the expressions of the fundamental emotions is sufficiently robust to consider Darwin's hypothesis an established axiom of behavioral science." (pp. 651–652)
8. Oster, Daily, & Goldenthal (1989)	"Conclusive evidence for the universality of certain facial expressions has come from studies in which observers were asked to identify the emotions shown in photographs of facial expressions" (p. 114)
9. Brown (1991)	"The conclusion seems inescapable: There are univeral facial expressions" (p. 26)
10. Mesquita & Frijda (1992)	"Certain facial expressions of emotion appear to be universal across cultures" (p. 14); "There appears to exist a universal human set of emotion reaction modes [including] facial expressions" (p. 21)
11. Carlson & Hatfield (1992)	"Ekman and other psychologists have uncovered compelling evidence that six basic emotions are expressed in much the same way in all cultures" (p. 221)

and Jenkins (1992) pointed to facial expressions when they argued for the discreteness of emotions: "Investigators have found expressions specific to discrete emotions. Emotions may be considered discrete in the sense that they are produced and recognized pan-culturally" (p. 67). According to one proposal (although subsequently modified, Ekman, 1992a), whether or not a particular state is an emotion can be determined by that state's association with a universal facial expression: "There is a distinctive pancultural signal for each emotion. . . . If there is no distinctive universal facial expression associated with a given state, which functions as a signal, I propose that we not call that state an emotion" (Ekman, 1984, p. 330).

The theories and ideas mentioned so far, their logical relations, and their evidential base are an important part of the psychology of emotion. The present chapter focuses on one basic assumption: that emotions are universally recognized from facial expressions. After a brief historical sketch of and several comments on this thesis, I describe the key evidence on which it rests and raise questions about the methods used to gather that evidence. I then describe various alternative accounts of the data.

A PARTIAL HISTORY

My view of the history of this topic is somewhat different than that usually presented. Most recent articles on facial expression begin, not with Aristotle, but with Charles Darwin. The history of research on the universality thesis was described by Ekman (1980) in terms of Darwin's (1872/1965) ideas, challenges to Darwin, the rejection of Darwin, and, finally, "a conclusive answer to one of Darwin's questions, and an answer in agreement with Darwin's own conviction. There are some facial expressions of emotion which are universal" (p. 137). In his review, Izard (1971) referred to the universality of facial expressions as "Darwin's hypothesis" (p. 225). Izard (1971) wrote that some researchers agreed that "Darwin was right," others that "Darwin was wrong." Izard (1971) described one major review of the available evidence on facial expressions as "anti-Darwinian" (p. 225).

Darwin was not the originator of the universality thesis. Before Darwin's book appeared in 1872, facial expressions of emotion were a topic of great interest (Bain, 1855, 1859; Bell, 1806; Duchenne, 1859/1990; Piderit, 1867; Spencer, 1855) and were apparently assumed to be universal. For instance, in a book written before Charles Darwin was born, Bell wrote, "The violent passions mark themselves so distinctly on the countenance, both of man, and of animals, that we are apt in the first instance to consider the movements by which they are indicated, as certain signs or characters provided by nature for the express purpose of intimating the internal emotion; and to suppose that they are interpreted by the observer in consequence of a peculiar and instinctive faculty" (1806, p. 84).

Duchenne de Boulogne (1859/1990) referred explicitly to universality. He attributed facial expression to a creator and wrote that "once this language of facial expression had been created, it sufficed for Him to give all human beings the instinctive faculty of always expressing their sentiments by contracting the same muscles. This rendered the language universal and immutable" (p. 19).

In turn, Duchenne drew on even earlier work, such as that of the artist Le Brun (1702/1982). Nor was Le Brun the originator of the idea of universality. Aristotle's words quoted at the beginning of this article express an idea that can be found in Greek and Roman writers of antiquity (Evans, 1969). Darwin (1872/1965) drew on the work of his many predecessors (Montgomery, 1985), and stated himself that the universality of facial expression "has often been asserted," although "without much evidence." As a first step in his research program, Darwin thus sought evidence for the universality thesis "with all the races of mankind" (pp. 14–15). Still, Darwin's principal goal was not to establish universality, but to provide an evolutionary rather than creationist account of the origins of facial expressions. In short, the universality thesis predates Darwin by several thousand years. That facial expressions might not be universal appears not to have occurred to most people. Both evolutionists and creationists believed in universality. Universality is a background assumption, a part of common sense, at least in Western cultures. Whether in other cultures is the topic of this chapter.

In the twentieth century, the scientific study of emotion and facial expression was taken up by experimental psychologists. The earliest work (e.g., Feleky, 1914; Langfeld, 1918a,b) did not cite Darwin, but attributed to common sense the idea that emotions can be seen in the face. For example, Langfeld (1918a) commented, "It did not need this experiment to prove the well known fact that emotions and attitudes could be judged from pictures" (p. 183). Although some of the results agreed with this common sense view, there soon appeared evidence that questioned whether emotions could be reliably judged from pictures of faces, even within our own culture. Different observers provided different emotion labels for the same expression (Buzby, 1924; Feleky, 1922). Observers were found to be swayed by the label the experimenter suggested (Fernberger, 1928). The emotion attributed to a face could be altered by training (Allport, 1924; Guilford, 1929). When actual rather than simulated emotions were studied, the resulting facial expressions did not seem to reveal that emotion (Landis, 1924). The emotion attributed to infants depended more on the infant's situation than facial behavior (Sherman, 1927). The 1920s were a low point in the fortunes of the universality thesis.

In 1938, a review and reanalysis of some of these data convinced

Woodworth that disagreements over what emotion is shown in a particular face were more apparent than real. Earlier researchers had assumed that each emotion would have a unique facial expression. Woodworth first grouped together synonyms and words for closely related emotions (such as *wonder, astonishment, amazement, surprise,* etc.). He then joined the groups into even broader clusters (e.g., joining the love, happiness, and mirth groups into one cluster, fear and suffering into another). Scoring any response within the resulting broad cluster as correct eliminated much of the disagreement. When the six clusters were then ordered by similarity into a linear scale, most of the remaining disagreement was found to be minor. For example, disagreements in labeling the expressions of fear and suffering were not spread evenly across the five remaining clusters, but tended to be only one step away: they were most often labels either from the surprise cluster on one side or from the anger-and-determination cluster on the other. When Feleky's (1922) seemingly negative judgment data were reanalyzed by Woodworth's method, the correlation between the emotion intended and that judged was 0.92.

Schlosberg (1941, 1952, 1954; Woodworth & Schlosberg, 1954) pursued Woodworth's approach, first altering the linear scale to a circular one. Schlosberg asked what the members of the broad clusters formed by Woodworth had in common. What, for example, unites love, happiness, and mirth, or fear and suffering? Schlosberg's suggestion was such things as degree of pleasantness versus unpleasantness. In his final version, Schlosberg (1954) suggested three such underlying dimensions: pleasant–unpleasant, degree of activation, and attention–rejection. Triandis and Lambert (1958) and Osgood (1966) took Schlosberg's idea cross-culturally and found similar dimensions.

The history of this topic has sometimes been presented as if it were a conflict between two opposing camps. For example, Ekman (1984, p. 319) wrote,

> For more than 100 years scientists argued about whether facial expressions are universal or specific to each culture. On one side Darwin (1872/1965), and, more recently, Lorenz (1965) and Eibl-Eibesfeldt (1972), argued that facial expressions are innate, evolved behavior. On the other side, Birdwhistell (1970), Klineberg (1940), LaBarre (1947), Leach (1972), and Mead (1975), argued that facial expressions are instead like a language, socially learned, culturally controlled, and variable in meaning from one setting to another. (p. 319)

Various positions have actually been taken on these questions. Undoubtedly, writers of one extreme persuasion or the other can be found, but middle views can be found as well. As important examples of a middle view, I cite Klineberg (1940), Woodworth and Schlosberg (1954),

Bruner and Tagiuri (1954), Triandis and Lambert (1958), and Osgood (1966).

First, consider Klineberg, the only psychologist cited in the quotation above and whom Ekman (1980) had earlier listed as one of Darwin's chief antagonists. Klineberg (1938) had reported that people in other cultures sometimes used unfamiliar facial expressions to signal their emotions, as when a Chinese novel described a character as sticking out his tongue in surprise. In his textbook, Klineberg (1940) detailed evidence of cultural variation, but he also wrote that "undoubtedly certain types of expressive behavior . . . are common to all human societies" (p. 176). He mentioned laughing with joy and tears in grief. He kept faith in the universality thesis in the face of cultural variation through three propositions. First, even if some facial expressions (such as the Chinese tongue protrusion) are culture specific, other expressions (such as laughing and crying) could still be universal; thus the culture specificity of one expression does not speak against the universality of another. Second, culture might determine whether natural expressions are permitted, inhibited, or exaggerated. To illustrate, he cited large cultural variation in weeping from grief. This normative control later came to be called a *display rule*. Third, culture could determine what emotion occurs in a given situation. For example, having her husband take a second wife might be a source of pride in one society, jealousy in another. Thus, witnessing their husbands' second marriage, the wives in these two cultures need not show the same facial expression because they would not be experiencing the same emotion.

As further examples of a middle view, consider Woodworth and Schlosberg (1954) and their colleagues. In their concluding paragraph on facial expression, they disagreed with Klineberg's (1938, 1940) emphasis on cultural variation. They then wrote: "One emerges from a study of this topic with the conviction that there *are* certain basic emotional patterns in man" (p. 132, emphasis in the original). Triandis and Lambert (1958) and Osgood (1966) offered cross-cultural evidence for this conviction.

As a final example, consider Bruner and Tagiuiri's (1954) review, characterized by Izard (1971, p. 225) as "anti-Darwinian." Bruner and Tagiuri (1954) pointed to the sobering negative findings that had accumulated, mainly in the 1920s, but they also pointed to positive findings:

> Other [researchers] have shown that emotional expressions were labeled with considerable accuracy (e.g., Darwin, 1872; Schulze, 1912; Feleky, 1914; Langfeld, 1918; Ruckmick, 1921; Stratton, 1921; Goodenough, 1931; Woodworth, 1938; Munn, 1940). (p. 635)

Bruner and Tagiuri (1954) emphasized Woodworth (1938) and Schlosberg's (1941) analysis of these conflicting findings, apparently agreeing with the conclusion that "as a whole, judges of emotions from posed photographs do strikingly well" (p. 365). Their final assessment was not an extreme position:

> After considering the four technical problems, . . . we return finally to the question 'To what extent are emotions recognizable?' We must come to the chastening conclusion that the literature is sufficiently haphazard to preclude a simple answer to this question. It depends . . . That one can provide a multitude of situations in which accurate and consensual judgments can be obtained—of this there can be no question, if ever there was one. (p. 639)

In 1962, Tomkins published the first volume on his theory that was to mark the beginning of the modern era in the study of facial expression. Tomkins (1980) declared that "affect primarily is facial behavior." Tomkins (1962, 1963) provided the list of so-called basic emotions that, with minor modifications, stands today and provided evidence that these emotions are easily read from facial expressions (Tomkins & Mc-Carter, 1964). Tomkins inspired and tutored Izard and Ekman, who provided the most widely cited cross-cultural studies, including studies in isolated, illiterate societies (Ekman, Sorenson, & Friesen, 1969; Ekman & Friesen, 1971; Izard, 1971). Ekman and Izard also reviewed the relevant literature, describing their own vision of the history of the field (Izard, 1971; Ekman, Friesen, & Ellsworth, 1972). For example, Ekman (1992b) wrote of the state of affairs in 1962: "Facial expressions were then considered to be an inaccurate source of culture-specific information" (p. 552). Ekman and Izard's ideas and cross-cultural studies entered introductory psychology texts in the late 1970s (Braun & Linder, 1979; Kagan & Havemann, 1976; London, 1978). In 1987, Ekman and his colleagues concluded that most psychologists had shifted to their position.

THE UNIVERSALITY THESIS

Precisely what is meant by saying that emotions are universally recognized from faces? Before any thesis along these lines can be verified, it has first to be formulated in a clear way. This universality thesis can be found asserted in textbooks, chapters, and journal articles, but it is not always clear exactly what is being asserted.

For example, precisely how did the conclusions regarding universality reached by Ekman (1972), Izard (1971), and their colleagues differ from the conclusions of Klineberg (1940), Bruner and Tagiuiri (1954), and Woodworth and Schlosberg (1954)? Ekman (1972) acknowledged the evidence of cultural variation and defended the universality thesis against such evidence through the same three ideas used by Klineberg (1940): cultural variation can be accounted for (1) through some gestures being culture specific, others universal; (2) through cultural norms that regulate when to mask, inhibit, or exaggerate natural facial expressions; and (3) through cultural influence on the cause of emotion. Their predecessors' conclusions were cautious and complex, the new tone was more confident, but the substantive difference is surprisingly difficult to state. It appears to consist of two assertions: (1) certain facial expressions are "easily recognized" (Izard, 1977, p. 501);[2] and (2) recognition is in terms of discrete, "specific emotion categories" (Izard, 1977, p. 502)—such as happiness, surprise, fear, anger, disgust, contempt, and sadness—rather than the overlapping broad clusters and dimensions suggested by Woodworth (1938) and Schlosberg (1941, 1952, 1954).

But even these differences are not perfectly clear. What amount of agreement constitutes easy recognition? Under what circumstances is recognition predicted to be easy? And what is the precise difference between recognition in terms of discrete, specific emotion categories and recognition in terms of broad clusters? Izard (1971) counted a fair range of freely generated emotion labels as supporting his hypothesis. In contrast, Ekman and Friesen (1988) criticized Izard (1971) for this broad range and seemed to presuppose a one-to-one correspondence between a specific emotion term and a specific facial expression. Ekman (1992b) argued that the number of basic emotions can thus be revealed by studies of facial expression. Asking how to cut nature at the joints in the domain of emotion, Ekman (1992b) wrote, "I am tempted to say that those joints are nakedly exposed by the findings on universality in expression." Yet, Ekman (1992a) also wrote not of specific discrete emotion categories but of emotion families, thereby returning toward Woodworth's (1938) view.

Who said what on which occasion is less important than the question of what conclusion is warranted by the evidence. My focus in this chapter is not on the position of any one writer, but rather on how far the evidence takes us. Let me propose therefore that the universality thesis be thought of as a family of hypotheses. Variations arise in three principal ways.

Specificity

First, the phrase *universality thesis* could describe propositions of varying specificity. At the nonspecific end of the continuum would fall the vague claim that some facial movements have some sort of emotional meaning, which is understood at above-chance levels by some human beings in

---

[2] Secondary sources have read this message clearly. For example, according to Carlson and Hatfield's (1992) textbook on the psychology of emotion, "sadness is a universal emotion easily recognized by all peoples, in all times, and at all places [p. 266]. . . . It is easy to recognize the face of anger. . . . The look is unmistakable [p. 350]."

most cultures. At the other end of the continuum would fall the claim that, for example, exactly 7 separate specific facial configurations signal the corresponding number of separate specific emotions, which are easily recognized as such by all human beings. The conclusions reached by Klineberg (1940), Bruner and Tagiuiri (1954), and Woodworth and Schlosberg (1954) fall toward the nonspecific end of the continuum; conclusions by Izard (1971) and Ekman (1972) appear to fall toward the more specific end. More recently, Izard (1990) and Ekman (1992a,b, 1993) may be taking somewhat different positions.

Ecological Relevance

The universality thesis could be taken to have various degrees of ecological relevance. A narrow interpretation would be that emotional facial signals can occur and can be recognized, but only under limited circumstances. A broader, more ecologically relevant interpretation would be that unless there is a deliberate attempt at deception, the face naturally expresses the emotions that occur in everyday life and that observers routinely recognize the emotions expressed. In other words, this distinction is between competence and performance. Older evidence emphasized ecological relevance (Landis, 1924; Munn, 1940; Sherman, 1927); more recent evidence less so (Izard, 1971). Older, more cautious reviews were more concerned with ecological relevance (Bruner & Tagiuiri, 1954); more recent, more optimistic reviews less so (Ekman et al., 1972; Izard, 1971). C. Izard (personal communication, November 10, 1992) emphasized a more narrow interpretation of his version of the universality thesis. In contrast, Ekman and Friesen (1975) emphasized the relevance of their findings to everyday situations, and Ekman, O'Sullivan, and Matsumoto (1991a) emphasized the question of ecological validity in evaluating research on facial expression.

Substance: Four Propositions

The universality thesis is ambiguous in yet another way. Four related propositions can be distinguished: (1) universality of facial movements: specific patterns of facial muscle movement occur in all human beings; (2) expressiveness of facial movements: certain facial patterns are manifestations of the same emotions in all human beings; (3) universality of attribution: observers everywhere attribute the same emotional meaning to those facial patterns[3] (in a commonly seen phrase, those facial pat-

---

[3] The word *attribution* is to be taken in as neutral a way as possible. There is no consensus on just what sort of process occurs when the observer "sees" an emotion in the face of another. Writers have used words such as *label, categorize, identify, see,* and *recognize*. The process might be innate or learned, conscious or unconscious, propositional or nonpropositional. On such questions, my review is noncommittal.

terns have universal "signal value"); and (4) correctness of attributions: observers are correct in the emotions they (consensually) attribute to those facial patterns. The last proposition, of course, presupposes the first three.

In much of the writing on this topic, these four propositions are not distinguished. Indeed, our everyday language invites their being confused. The phrase *facial expression* implies that facial movement has a meaning, which it expresses. The word *recognition* implies that what is recognized is really there. English words for facial movements, such as *frown*, are so imprecise that researchers are forced to speak instead of the "facial expression of fear," the "facial expression of anger," and so on. Thus, the words we have for facial movements imply their expression of specific emotions, which are there to be recognized or not.[4]

Less often, distinctions are noted, and an explicit argument is offered for combining these propositions. For example, Oster, Daily, and Goldenthal (1989) argued that:

> if observers from very different cultures—including isolated, preliterate cultures—see the same emotions in the same faces, we can confidently conclude that these expressions have universal meaning. We can also infer that this meaning is derived from the observers' experience with spontaneous expressions observed in real-life, emotion-arousing situations in their own cultures. That is, we can infer that the expressions themselves are universal. (p. 114)[5]

Of course, these four propositions may be related empirically, and specific theories can predict links among them. But for the purpose of analyzing the evidence, I believe that these four propositions are best kept separate, until proven otherwise. After all, it is at least conceivable that emotions are expressed by the face universally, but that some cultures have failed to recognize this fact. Perhaps attribution of emotions to faces is a cultural achievement, which in our culture is partially correct

---

[4] To maintain some helpful distinctions, a convention is adopted in this chapter whereby emotion words used by observers are italicized (e.g., the word *happy*), but emotion labels used by researchers to refer to specific patterns of facial movement are in quotation marks (e.g., an expression of "happiness"). On the other hand, the words *recognition* and *facial expression* are used for lack of a simple alternative. *Recognition* simply means here a judgment that conforms to prediction. *Facial expression* simply means here *facial movement*.

[5] Caution rather than confidence is required in considering such arguments. Imagine that a man rubs his abdomen and, with both hands, rapidly pushes imaginary food into his mouth, or cups his hands, throws back his head, and pretends to pour something down his throat, or closes his eyes and places the side of his head on his joined hands. It is possible that observers from very different cultures— including isolated, illiterate cultures—would see hunger, thirst, and sleep in these pantomimes. If that is so, would we then infer that the pantomimes have meaning derived from spontaneous actions observed in real-life situations and that the pantomimes themselves are universal? The pantomimes presumably capture something of real-life action, but in an exaggerated, stylized form. We would not infer that the exact actions of the pantomine ordinarily accompany hunger, thirst, and sleep. Of course, facial expressions are not pantomimes, and my point here is a logical one. But this example does coincidentally underline a question that arises in the cross-cultural studies: do the photographs of facial expressions typically used represent spontaneous, naturally occurring facial actions?

but not perfect. Some other cultures might do better, some worse. Alternatively, it is also at least conceivable that people falsely attribute emotions to facial movements. "Recognition" might be a widespread but false belief. Even when they are universal, folk beliefs need not be correct. It might not be wise for me to argue that any of our current folk beliefs are false, but it should be easy to see that widespread folk and even scientific beliefs of the past were false. Consider the belief, probably once universal, that the sun rises and sets on a stable earth, or the belief that physiognomy reveals character. Consider the initial clash between common sense and scientific theories, such as the conception of space and time in modern physics, or the age of the earth in geology, or the evolution of life in biology.

THE SCOPE OF THIS CHAPTER

A review of all the evidence potentially bearing on the universality thesis is beyond the scope of this chapter. I chose instead to focus on the evidence that has convinced past reviewers. Statements of the universality thesis found in journals, chapters, and textbooks are often followed by references to *secondary* sources. My review of this topic therefore began with secondary sources (Izard, 1971; Ekman et al., 1972; Ekman, 1972, 1973; Ekman & Oster, 1979; plus the more recent reviews listed in Table I) from whom I extracted citations of primary evidence for universality. Their emphasis was clearly on modern cross-cultural judgment studies,[6] which are therefore the topic of my review.

By "modern," I refer to studies beginning with Ekman et al. (1969). I excluded pre-1969 articles because Izard (1971) and Ekman et al. (1972) reviewed them in detail, often coming to conclusions different from those of previous reviewers and of the authors of the original articles. More recent reviews often ignore the earlier studies, or cite the interpretations offered by Izard (1971) and Ekman et al. (1972). Further review of these disputed studies seemed less useful than a critical examination of more recent ones.

The principal limitation of my review is the focus on judgment studies. As implied by Oster et al.'s (1989) argument, evidence that all "ob-

---

[6] Various kinds of additional evidence were cited: naturalistic observation of facial movements in various cultures (Eibl-Eibesfeldt, 1972; Ekman, 1980), laboratory observation of facial movements of members of two different cultures (Ekman, 1972), correlation of facial movement with self-reports of emotion (Ekman et al., 1980, but see Fridlund, 1991a), observation of facial communication in infants (Izard & Malatesta, 1987; but see Camras, 1992; Nelson, 1987; Oster et al., 1992), observation of facial movements in children born blind (Eibl-Eibesfeldt, 1972; Goodenough, 1932; Thompson, 1941), and studies of the accuracy of judgments based on observation of facial movements (Ekman, 1982). Altogether, such studies suggest, to me, support for the first proposition listed above (specific patterns of facial movement occur in all human beings), but are neutral for the other three. For the purposes of this chapter, I assume that the first proposition is essentially correct. This assumption leaves open the meaning of facial behavior and the status of the last three propositions.

servers see the same emotions in the same faces" (i.e., the cross-cultural judgment studies) has been taken as evidence for the entire universality thesis. Judgment data are offered to support the emotional meaning of facial behavior (e.g., Matsumoto & Ekman, 1988). In the following passage, Ekman (1980) captured the importance of the judgment study: "Definitive data are now available on the question of universality" (p. 93). "The judgment study of the face . . . is the method employed in all but one of the experiments which have finally settled the issue of universality of facial expression" (p. 96).

I review studies of modern, literate cultures next and studies of isolated, illiterate cultures in a later section.

JUDGMENT STUDIES IN LITERATE CULTURES

For literate cultures, the widely quoted high "recognition" scores come from eight studies. Different studies included slightly different lists of basic emotions, but all had six emotions in common. All results concerning these common six are listed in Table II, separately for 20 Western (Europeans plus English-, Spanish-, or Portugese-speakers in North or South America) and 11 non-Western (Asian and African) samples. "Recognition scores," which are the percentage of subjects who agreed with prediction, were greater than that expected to be by chance for each type of facial expression in each study. Happiness achieved the highest averages, with a median of 96.4% in Western and 89.2% in non-Western cultures. Surprise achieved the second highest, 87.5% in Western and 79.2% in non-Western cultures. Among the negative emotions (sadness, disgust, anger, and fear), the range of medians was from 77.5% to 82.6% in Western and from 63.0% to 76.0% in non-Western cultures.

Three further studies have been cited, but were not included in Table II. First, Winkelmayer, Exline, Gottheil, and Paredes (1978) asked American, British, and Mexican observers to judge facial expressions of "happiness," "anger," and "sadness." Percentages of agreement were not reported for the emotions separately, however, and therefore are not reported in Table II. The overall mean recognition score was 39.3%, where the figure expected to be by chance alone would be 33%.

The second study (Ekman & Friesen, 1986) concerned a single emotion, contempt. Across 10 cultures, recognition averaged 75%. Results for individual cultures were not reported and therefore are not listed in Table II. The basic result was subsequently replicated in six more cultures (Ekman & Heider, 1988; Matsumoto, 1992b). Although Ekman and Friesen's (1986) claim created controversy (Izard & Haynes, 1988; Ricci Bitti, Brighetti, Garotti, & Boggi-Cavallo, 1989; Russell, 1991b,c), Ekman and his colleagues defended their claim (Ekman & Friesen, 1988; Ekman et al., 1991a,b; Matsumoto, 1992b).

TABLE II   Recognition Scores from Eight Studies with Literate Subjects

Culture	N	"Happy"	"Fear"	"Disgust"	"Anger"	"Surprise"	"Sadness"
				Facial expression			
Western cultures							
American[a]	99	97	88	82	69	91	73
Brazilian[a]	40	97	77	86	82	82	82
American[b]	89	96.8	76.0	83.2	89.2	90.5	74.0
English[b]	62	96.2	67.0	84.5	81.5	81.0	74.5
German[b]	158	98.2	84.0	73.0	83.2	85.5	67.2
Swedish[b]	41	96.5	88.8	88.0	82.2	81.0	71.5
French[b]	67	94.5	83.5	78.5	91.5	84.2	70.5
Swiss[b]	0.36	97.0	67.5	78.2	91.8	85.5	70.0
Greek[b]	50	93.5	67.8	87.5	80.0	80.2	54.5
Chilean[c]	119	90.2	78	85	76	88.3	90.9
Argentine[c]	168	94.0	68	79.3	71.6	93	87.6
Estonian[d]	70	88.0	60.2	89.0	77.7	82.5	84.7
American[e]	53	96.7	69.8	71.7	64.6	85.9	72.6
American[g]	40	100	67.5	92.5	90.0	92.5	87.5
Estonian[h]	85	90	91	71	67	94	86
German[h]	67	93	86	61	71	87	83
Greek[h]	61	93	74	77	77	91	80
Italian[h]	40	97	82	89	72	92	81
Scottish[h]	42	98	86	79	84	88	86
American[h]	30	95	84	86	81	92	92
Median		96.4	77.5	82.6	81.2	87.5	80.5
M		95.1	77.3	81.1	79.1	87.4	86.5
Non-Western cultures							
Japanese[a]	29	87	71	82	63	87	74
Japanese[b]	60	93.8	58.2	55.8	56.8	79.2	66.8
African[b]	29	68.0	49.0	55.0	50.8	49.0	32.2
Kirghizian[d]	80	89.2	51.3	86.0	47.2	71.3	89.2
Malyasian[e]	30	95.8	45.6	59.2	49.8	69.8	66.4
Ethiopian[f]	100	86.8	58.8	54.8	37.3	50.5	52.0
Malaysian[g]	31	100	66.5	97.5	86	95	100
Chinese[h]	29	92	84	65	73	91	91
Japanese[h]	98	90	65	60	67	94	87
Sumatran[h]	36	69	70	70	70	78	91
Turkish[h]	64	87	76	74	79	90	76
Median		89.2	65.0	65.0	63.0	79.2	76.0
M		87.1	63.2	69.0	61.8	77.7	75.1

Note: Izard's (1971) term for "sadness" was *distress*, but it was defined as synonymous with *sadness*.

[a] Ekman et al. (1969).

[b] Izard (1971).

[c] Ekman (1972).

[d] Niit & Valsiner (1977).

[e] Boucher & Carlson (1980); figures given are unweighted average across two stimulus sets.

[f] Ducci, et al. (1982).

[g] McAndrew (1986).

[h] Ekman et al. (1987).

The third study provided another Chinese sample. Chan (1985) showed nine of Izard's (1977) photographs of facial expressions to 124 medical students at the Chinese University of Hong Kong. The study was conducted in both Chinese and English. Subjects were allowed to select one or two words from the forced-choice list; the judgment was scored correct if either choice was as predicted. These data were not included in Table II because this criterion for recognition was more lenient than that used there. Chan's obtained recognition scores were "happiness" 97.6, "surprise" 66.9, "sadness" 61.3, "anger" 96.0, "disgust" 62.1, and "fear" 66.9.

Some further judgment studies exist, but for various reasons were not cited in the secondary sources as evidence for the universality thesis.[7] Some failed to report sufficient information to be useful. Some were criticized for their sample of facial expressions (Matsumoto, 1992a); for example, two (Cüceloglu, 1970; Kilbride & Yarczower, 1976) used line drawings of faces and are not reviewed here. Nevertheless, two sets of studies are useful.

First is additional data from Africa. Only two samples from Africa are shown in Table II, and both suggested a noticeable discrepancy between African and Western results. Izard (1971) found an overall recognition score of 49.0% from a sample of Africans tested in France. This score contrasts with 83.4% in his normative, American group. He excluded the African data from most of his analyses (because the subjects were not tested in their native language). Ducci, Arcuri, W/Georgis, & Sineshaw (1982) obtained an overall recognition score of 51.9% from Ethiopians (no normative figure was reported, but the set of photographs was supplied by Ekman and Friesen). To estimate the reliability of this African–Western difference, it is helpful to look at additional data, which appear to replicate the difference even when the Africans were tested in their native language. Wolfgang and Cohen (1988) obtained an overall recognition score of 48% from Ethiopians (in contrast to 75% in their normative, Canadian sample). Kilbride and Yarczower (1980) obtained an overall recognition score of 62.5% from Zambians (in contrast to 94.2% in their normative, American group). Kilbride and Yarczower (1983) provided further data on Zambians. Although they did not report overall recognition scores and their set of facial expressions has been criticized (Matsumoto, 1992a), their results were informative. Given the same set of facial stimuli, which included both American and Zambian posers,

[7] Undoubtedly, unpublished data also exist. M. K. Mandal (personal communication, March 12, 1993) gathered unpublished data from 100 subjects in India who were shown Ekman and Friesen's (1976) standardized set of photographs. The experiment was conducted in English. The results for the normative American sample and for the Indian sample, respectively, were: 98.5 and 87.0 for "happiness," 92.3 and 75.1 for "surprise," 88.6 and 73.0 for "sadness," 87.8 and 73.3 for "fear," 92.3 and 75.1 for "disgust," and 88.9 and 74.5 for "anger."

Americans obtained significantly higher recognition scores than did Zambians.

Second is additional data from Japan. Izard (1971) and Ekman et al. (1987) had found a similarity between American and Japanese "recognition" for the hypothesized expressions of non-negative emotions, but a discrepancy on the "fear," "disgust," and "anger" expressions. Fortunately, three more studies have recently been published (Matsumoto, 1992a; Matsumoto & Ekman, 1988, 1989). Table III combines the earlier results, seen in Table II, with the new ones. The additional data showed a similar pattern to the old. Moreover, Matsumoto (1992a) found a statistically significant interaction between culture and type of facial expression.

I now turn to a critical analysis of these studies. The results have already been summarized in Tables II and III. The methods used are summarized in Table IV. The similarity of method across studies allows me to consider the studies as a whole rather than individually. For con-

TABLE III   Recognition Scores from Six Comparisons of Japanese and American Observers

Culture	N	"Happy"	"Surprise"	"Sadness"	"Fear"	"Disgust"	"Anger"
Ekman et al. (1969)							
American	99	97	91	73	88	82	69
Japanese	29	87	87	74	71	82	63
Izard (1971)							
American	89	96.8	90.5	74.0	76.0	83.2	89.2
Japanese	60	93.8	79.2	66.8	58.2	55.8	56.8
Ekman et al. (1987)							
American	30	95	92	92	84	86	81
Japanese	98	90	94	87	65	60	67
Matsumoto & Ekman (1988)							
American	235	98.0	93.3	93.0	77.7	80.9	87.4
Japanese	154	98.0	89.2	75.6	37.6	70.1	68.1
Matsumoto & Ekman (1989)							
American	124	98.0	94.4	94.5	71.1	78.5	87.1
Japanese	110	97.6	88.0	77.1	30.8	68.2	69.6
Matsumoto (1992a)							
American	41	97.6	92.0	92.6	81.8	91.1	89.6
Japanese	44	98.3	92.0	71.9	54.6	74.7	64.2
Averages							
American							
Median		97.3	92.0	92.3	79.8	82.6	87.3
M		97.1	92.2	86.5	79.8	83.6	83.9
Japanese							
Median		95.7	88.6	74.8	56.4	69.2	65.6
M		94.1	88.2	75.4	52.9	68.5	64.8

TABLE IV Methods Used in Studies with Literate Subjects

Source	Subjects	Facial stimuli	Design	Order of presentation	Response format
1. Ekman et al. (1969)	College students	30 preselected still photos of posed and spontaneous expressions	Within-Ss[a]	Unspecified	Forced choice, 6 alternatives
2. Izard (1971)	College students	36 preselected still photos of posed expressions	Within-Ss	1 random order, same for all Ss	Free label and forced choice, 9 alternatives
3. Ekman (1972)	Unspecified	Same as used in Ekman et al. (1969)	Within-Ss	Unspecified	Forced choice, 6 alternatives, and Intensity Rating
4. Niit & Valsiner (1977, Expt. 1)	College students	35 preselected photos from Ekman and Friesen	Within-Ss	Unspecified	Forced choice, 7 alternatives
5. Winkelmayer et al. (1978)	College students	60 silent film clips, unselected spontaneous expressions	Within-Ss	1 semirandom order, same for all Ss	Forced choice, 3 alternatives
6. Boucher & Carlson (1980, Malay Sample)	High school and college students	47 preselected still photos from Ekman and Friesen	Within-Ss	1 random order, same for all Ss	Free label and forced choice, 6 alternatives
7. Ducci et al. (1982)	High school students	28 preselected still photos from Ekman and Friesen	Within-Ss	2 random orders, each counterbalanced	Forced choice, 7 alternatives
8. McAndrew (1986)	College students	30 preselected still photos from Ekman and Friesen	Within-Ss	1 random order, counterbalanced across Ss	Forced choice, 6 alternatives
9. Ekman & Friesen (1986)	College students	24 preselected still photos of posed muscle configurations	Within-Ss	1 random order, same for all Ss	Forced choice, 7 alternatives
10. Ekman et al. (1987)	College students	18 preselected still photos of posed and spontaneous expressions	Within-Ss	1 random order, same for all Ss	Forced choice, 7 alternatives, and Quantitative Rating

[a] Ss, Subjects.

venience, I call the combination of typical features the *standard method*. In the remainder of this section, I discuss first the results and then the individual features of the standard method. In doing so, I do not dispute the formal statistical finding in each study of an association between facial expression and emotion label. I do not seek one feature of method that is a fatal flaw. Rather, in light of this discussion, the evidence as a whole is later evaluated for what it says of universality and against the criteria of ecological, convergent, and internal validity. I focus on four questions:

First, are recognition scores uniform across cultures? Second, are the results generalizable beyond the specific experimental context in which they were obtained? Third, is recognition in terms of specific emotions or broader clusters of emotions? And fourth, how easy is recognition and is it possible that recognition scores were inflated by the method itself? One focus is thus the precise magnitude of the recognition scores. Evidence that agreement is lower than expected, even if still above chance, allows various alternative explanations. For example, agreement with prediction would be low but still greater than chance if observers could simply distinguish positive expressions from negative ones. Higher, but still less than perfect, agreement is predicted by Schlosberg's (1952, 1954; Woodworth & Schlosberg, 1954) model or its more modern variants (Russell & Bullock, 1986).

Results

Recognition scores from the eight studies of Table II were analyzed with a two-factor analysis of variance with a between-within design. Each sample was treated as a single case ($n = 20$ for Western cultures and $n = 11$ for non-Western cultures). Culture (Western, non-Western) was a between-subject factor. Type of expression ("happy," "surprise," "sadness," disgust," "anger," "fear") was a within-subject factor. Adjustments due to lack of sphericity were used where needed.

The main effect of culture was significant, $F(1, 29) = 15.36$, $p < .001$. The main effect of type of expression was significant, $F(5, 145) = 25.57$, $p < .001$. Their interaction was also significant, $F(5, 145) = 2.39$, $p < .05$. A simple-effects analysis pursued the interaction effect obtained. When experimentwise alpha level was determined by Bonferroni's method, there were no significant effects due to culture for "happy," surprise," and "sadness" expressions, but there were for "disgust" [$F(1, 104) = 9.17$, $p < .01$], "anger" [$F(1, 104) = 18.94$, $p < .001$], and "fear" [$F(1, 104) = 12.55$, $p < .001$] expressions.

A discriminant function analysis of the recognition scores showed significant [$c^2(1) = 15.99$, $p < .001$] discrimination based on culture. Twenty-seven of the 31 groups were classified correctly. Four were misclassified. The Argentine and Estonian samples were misclassified with the non-Western set. (Estonian is a non-Indo-European language, and Estonia was a member of the Soviet Union at the time of the study.) The Turkish sample and McAndrew's (1986) Malaysian sample were misclassified with the Western set. Turkey straddles Asia and Europe and could have been included with the Western set. McAndrew's Malaysian sample was living in the United States.

Bonferroni matched-sample t tests with overall alpha set at .05 were used to explore the reliability of differences between recognition scores for the different types of expressions. Among the Western samples, "happy" differed from each of the others; "surprise" differed from each of the others, except "disgust." Among the non-Western samples, "happy" differed from "disgust," "anger," and "fear."

A parallel set of analyses was conducted for the American–Japanese comparisons shown in Table III. In this analysis, the number of samples was even smaller, $n = 6$ within each culture, but the statistical results were similar. There were significant main and interactive effects in the main analysis: for culture, $F(1, 10) = 54.00$, $p < .001$; for type of expression, $F(5, 50) = 24.89$, $p < .001$; and for their interaction, $F(5, 145) = 4.50$, $p < .01$. The simple effects analysis did not yield significant effects due to culture for the "happy," "surprise," or "sad" expressions, but did for "disgust" [$F(1, 21) = 12.21$, $p < .01$], "anger" [$F(1, 21) = 19.40$, $p < .001$], and "fear" [$F(1, 21) = 38.49$, $p < .001$].

The discriminant function analysis was significant [$c^2(1) = 12.00$, $p < .001$] and correctly classified all 12 samples on the basis of culture.

Again, Bonferroni matched-sample t tests with overall alpha set at .05 were used to explore the reliability of differences between recognition scores. Among the American samples, "happy" differed from each of the others except "sadness" and "anger." Among the Japanese samples, "happy" and "surprise" did not differ from each other, but each of them did differ from the rest. "Fear" also differed from "sad."

The analyses of the Japanese–American comparisons from Table III nicely complement the analyses of the more general comparisons of Table II. Unlike the latter, the Japanese–American comparisons equate the number of samples, the stimuli, and other details of method. Altogether, the finding of reliable differences due to culture, to type of expression, and to their interaction appears to be robust. These analyses do not challenge the original researchers' conclusion that recognition scores are greater than chance, but they do show that recognition scores are not uniform. Recognition varies in a reliable and systematic fashion. The scores on the "happy expression" provide a baseline comparison of these observers' performance on the task per se. Therefore, reliable differences from this baseline in scores for other expressions in different cultures require examination.

Subjects

In all studies described in Tables II and III, subjects were students: high school students in two samples and college students in the rest. Wolfgang and Cohen (1988) tested a sample of 96 volunteers from Central and South America living in Canada. The stimuli consisted of 40 posed facial expressions from a standardized set. Recognition scores varied with education level: overall recognition was 81% from those with a university education, 66% from those with a high school education, and 43% from those with a primary school education. These differences were statistically significant.

There is also a question of how much the studies provided a strict test of universality. The non-Western cultures included often had extensive contact with the West. The cross-cultural aspect of the studies is mitigated by the possibility that in these non-Western societies, students receive more exposure to Western culture than does the general public. To cite one of countless possibilities, students might be exposed to Western drama, and since the ancient Greeks, tragedy and comedy have been symbolized by frowning and smiling masks. Students might have seen Western books, magazines, newspapers, films, television, and other media; they might also have had more direct contact with Western students or faculty. The extent of this problem undoubtedly varied from study to study. Boucher and Carlson's (1980) Malaysian sample had no personal contact with Westerners, but McAndrew's (1986) Malaysian sample lived in the United States.

One study directly explored the effect of contact. Ducci et al. (1982) compared urban with rural high school students in Ethiopia. The urban students were in nearly continuous contact with Western culture, whereas the rural students were relatively isolated. Other than contact, most other relevant factors such as age and education were similar in the two groups. All subjects spoke Amharic and were equally familiar with the emotion terms used. Recognition scores were reliably greater for urban than for rural students.

For the more recent studies, the use of college students also raises an even more troubling possibility: the universality thesis or even the specific hypothesis proposed by Izard (1971) or Ekman (1972) could have been taught to some of the subjects used to test that thesis. Through their coursework or general reading, college students might have learned which specific expressions had been hypothesized to be associated with which emotion. Books on drawing techniques describe how to draw a facial expression for each emotion (Faigin, 1990; Peck, 1987). Popularized books teach students how to recognize specific emotions from specific facial expressions (Ekman & Friesen, 1975). Darwin's (1872/1965) book might have been encountered in a psychology or biology class. The extent to which student subjects in each study were trained in the universality thesis is difficult to estimate. This problem would be greater if the subjects were drawn from psychology courses. For students enrolled in psychology courses up to the late 1970s, their textbook might have taught that situational information dominates over facial information in the judgment of emotion. After that time, some popular introductory psychology textbooks began to include material supporting the universality thesis with photographs of the hypothesized universal facial expressions (Braun & Linder, 1979; Kagan & Havemann, 1976; London, 1978). Table II shows no noticeable shift in recognition scores around the late 1970s, and only the Ducci et al. (1982) study directly supports these musings about training and cultural influence. Still, no evidence rules them out. In any future studies, the relevant background and training of the subjects should be examined and reported. As acknowledged by Izard (1977) and Ekman (1980), the question of cross-cultural universality is best answered by the study of cultures more isolated from Western influence than those of Tables II and III.

Presentation of Stimuli

Psychological theory and research are unequivocal in proclaiming the dependency of a response to a given stimulus upon other stimuli presented. This principle applies to responses as simple as recordings in single cells and to responses as complex as global judgments of happiness, morality, or beauty (Helson, 1964; Parducci, 1965). In accord with this general principle, the judgment of a given facial expression has consistently been found to depend upon what other faces are presented (Manis, 1967, 1971; Russell, 1991c; Russell & Fehr, 1987; Tanaka-Matsumi, Nelson, Attivissimo, & D'Urso, 1993; Thayer, 1980a,b). Judgments of expressions claimed to be signals of basic emotions are no less relative: When particular stimulus contexts were created, the "contempt" expression was judged as disgust, the "surprise" expression was judged as a surprise-fear blend, and the "anger" expression was judged as sad. In addition, expressions claimed to be neutral have been found judged as happy when seen embedded in one stimulus set, and as sad when embedded in another. The question then is how much the results summarized in Tables II and III depend on the particular stimulus context created by the experiment. Stimulus context might have exerted an influence through previewing, within-subject design, and order of presentation.

Previewing

In some studies (e.g., Winkelmayer et al., 1978), the subjects were first shown the entire set of facial expressions, after which each stimulus was redisplayed for the subjects to rate. Whether a preview was offered in other studies was not specified. Winkelmayer et al. (1978) reported that a preview was necessary for their subjects to achieve a reliable degree of agreement. Presenting subjects with the full range of facial expressions highlights both similarities within expression type and differences between expression types. Presenting an equal number of broad smiles, wrinkled noses, sneers, and so on further highlights similarities and differences.

Within-Subject Design

All studies in Tables II and III used a within-subject design: each subject was asked to judge the entire set of facial expressions within a relatively short period of time. A within-subject design creates the same kind of problem as does previewing. It invites a more direct comparison between the various facial expressions than would be available in a between-subject design (or in everyday encounters with facial expressions). Responding to a set of stimuli creates a series of complex assimilation and contrast effects.

Results from a within-subject design need to be be verified with a between-subject design. And one attempt to do so failed: The facial expression published by Matsumoto and Ekman (1988) as a signal of contempt was judged *contempt* in a within-subject design, but was judged as *disgust* in a between-subject design (Russell, 1991b). According to Ekman and Friesen (1986), a "contempt" expression is a unilateral raising and curling of the upper lip; a "disgust" expression is a wrinkling of the nose. Seen separately (between-subject design), these facial movements are both most typically labeled as *disgust* (Russell, 1991b). But, when both expressions are presented to the same subject (within-subject design), then the subject might feel called upon to notice the difference between the two expressions and (especially when the response scale calls for a distinction between *disgust* and *contempt*) to assign different labels to them. That they do so in a consensual manner is still informative, but the point is that method appears to influence the results obtained. Of course, contempt is the least well established of the "basic" emotions and, as noted, has aroused the most controversy. (In addition, Ekman et al. [1991a] argued that the ecological validity of the Russell [1991b] finding has yet to be established. Russell agrees, but believes that the finding nevertheless has methodological implications.)

Ekman et al. (1991b) recently revealed that "in our early studies (Ekman, 1972) we found unreliability in initial responses when subjects had to judge expressions. . . . We have found that subjects better understand what is expected of them after trying it a few times" (p. 294). Ekman et al. (1991b) reasoned that their subjects were initially unfamiliar with the task and that a few trials were required to understand the instructions. The high recognition scores for "happy" expressions in Table II speak against this interpretation. Ekman's (1972) and Izard's (1971) theories would seem to predict that this would be an exceedingly simple task. (After all, the observer simply had to select one word from a short list for universal, biologically based signals.) In any case, if subjects must be trained on the task per se, then they should receive that training with neutral material (such as matching names to color patches) so that training does not influence the results of the experiment. The relevant point is that an initial response constitutes a between-subject design, and this passage from Ekman et al. (1991b) therefore reveals that recognition scores were not as high (were not as reliable) in a between- as in a within-subject design.

There are several more indications. Tanaka-Matsumi et al. (1993) obtained a recognition score of 44.2% for Ekman and Friesen's (1976) "sad expression" with a between-subject design. Recognition of the "sad" expression rose to 58.3% when it was preceded by a single "happy" expression and to 72.1% when it was preceded by a single "anger" expression. They obtained a recognition score of 41.7% for Ekman and Friesen's (1976) "anger" expression with a between-subject design. Recognition rose to 53.1%, 66.7%, and 57.9% when it was preceded by a single "happy," "sad," or "surprised" expression. Finally, Russell (1993b) compared a between-subject design with the combination of preview plus within-subject design. Although there was only one example of each expression and the dependent measure was free label rather than forced choice, the results (shown in Table V) were consistent with the other evidence.

In all, what little evidence we have suggests that something about the within-subject design produces higher recognition scores than would a between-subject design. I believe that the size of the effect varies with the type of expression. It was large for the "contempt" expression, but was small for the six types of facial expressions included in Table II (given the other aspects of method). Nevertheless, the within-subject design, like previewing, may have increased the recognition scores there a bit.

Order of Presentation

For a within-subject design, order of stimulus presentation becomes an issue. Order should be varied systematically, or a separate random order should be created for each subject. However, the studies listed in Tables II and III sometimes used one or two orders of presentation. Different subjects are thus not responding simply to a particular facial expression alone. Rather, they are responding to that expression embedded within an identical context consisting of the preceding series of other facial expressions.

TABLE V   Recognition Scores and Stimulus Presentation

Facial expression[a]	Design		χ^2
	Preview + within subject	Between subject	$(1, N = 224)$
"Happy"	99.1	91.1	7.74[b]
"Surprise"	92.8	87.5	1.81
"Disgust"	79.5	66.1	5.07[c]
"Sad"	71.4	59.8	3.34
"Fear"	69.6	50.9	8.22[b]
"Anger"	60.7	40.2	9.45[b]
"Contempt"	1.8	0	
M	67.8	56.5	

Notes: Each recognition is based on 112 observations. χ^2 was used to assess the effect of design, separately for each facial expression. The dependent measure was a free label. Data are described by Russell (1993b). For "contempt," expected frequency was too low to calculate a chi-square.

[a]Label is that provided by Matsumoto & Ekman (1988).

[b]$p < .01$.

[c]$p < .05$.

Giving different subjects the same order of presentation could inflate the amount of agreement among them. Inflation of the amount of agreement does not necessarily translate into increased agreement with prediction (indeed, it could do the opposite). Like the within-subject design itself, order of presentation alone challenges validity only insofar as increased agreement tends toward the hypothesis. Therefore, only in combination with other factors already sufficient to produce very high agreement with prediction could order of presentation exaggerate that agreement.

Conclusion

Exposure to the entire stimulus set, through previewing or a within-subject design, confronts the subjects with what might appear to them to be a puzzle: how to assign, for example, seven labels to seven types of facial expression. If so, subjects might be guided in providing their responses or might even form a rough idea of the experimental hypothesis. Thus, stimulus presentation might account for some part (although not a large part) of the results generally offered in support of the universality thesis: that subjects give the same label to expressions of the same type and different labels to expressions of different types. Of course, if the facial expressions were completely meaningless to the subject, then the puzzle would remain unsolvable. But, if a subject already had a fair idea of their meaning (such as appropriate labels for some of the expressions, or whether the expressions are positive or negative, or their values on Schlosberg's [1954] dimensions, or labels for several expressions learned from the textbook), then previewing, within-subject design, and constant order of presentation could inflate the amount of agreement with prediction on some or all of the expressions shown.

Facial Stimuli

The facial expressions shown to subjects were unrepresentative of the population of facial expressions. In all studies of Tables II and III, the stimulus expressions were preselected and, for the most part, posed. The researchers naturally had reasons for this approach, and responses to preselected posed expressions could address some questions. But it is also important to ask about the possible consequences of preselection and posing. A full understanding of emotion and facial expression would include information about unselected spontaneous expressions.

Preselection

The exact degree of preselection is difficult to specify, but was extreme. Ekman and Friesen (1971) described selecting their stimuli from over 3000 photographs. Some of these 3000, in turn, had been gathered by previous researchers, with each probably culled from still others. Izard's (1971) selection procedure was complex, beginning with a pool of about 1000 posed expressions to which new ones were added. Photographs were eliminated from the pool if they failed to satisfy Izard himself or the original poser, or if they failed to achieve 70% agreement with prediction from a panel of 25–30 judges. All but one of the remaining studies listed in Table II used photographs supplied by Ekman and Friesen, although not necessarily the same ones.

When the stimulus material is not so highly preselected, then recognition scores might not be as high.[8] Winkelmayer et al. (1978) used all their stimuli and found considerably lower agreement with prediction than did any of the studies in Table II, an average of 39.6% where chance would be 33%. Malatesta, Fiore, and Messina (1987) asked 14 elderly persons to pose facial expressions of happiness, fear, anger, sadness, and a neutral state. All 70 photographs (14×5) were then shown to 30 graduate students who were given a forced-choice response scale. Overall, 41% of judgments were correct. This figure was influenced greatly by the happy poses, which were "almost always correct." With happy

---

[8] C. Izard (personal communication, November 10, 1992) reported that 34 of the photographs excluded by his procedure were subsequently shown to American and French subjects with a procedure similar but not identical to the standard method. "The mean percentage agreement for [these excluded] expressions was 31%. This contrasts with the agreement of 80% or better for American and French subjects viewing the photographs selected for the cross-cultural research." American and French observers agreed in their modal response for 17 of the 34.

poses set aside, 28% of judgments were correct for the fear, anger, sadness, and neutral poses, where presumably chance would be 25%.

Posed Expressions

All studies cited in Table II used mainly or entirely posed rather than spontaneous expressions. The universality thesis is not, at least not directly, about posed faces. Posed faces do not express the emotion of the poser but what the poser chooses to pretend and in a manner most likely to be understood by the observer. According to the notion of display rules, voluntarily posed expressions are culturally influenced, and have been said to originate in a different region of the brain than do spontaneous facial expressions (Rinn, 1984). Posed expressions have been found to be more asymmetric than are spontaneous expressions (Skinner & Mullen, 1991). Reuter-Lorenz and Davidson (1981) found that subjects could tell that some of the expressions shown were posed. Posed expressions might be exaggerated or stylized. The poses for each type of expression might be more similar to each other, and more discriminable from poses of other types of expression, than spontaneous expressions. Posed expressions can be useful to answer some questions, but concerns of ecological validity raise the question of whether observers recognize the emotion conveyed by spontaneously produced facial expressions.

There is evidence that, at least in our culture, observers can accurately judge whether someone is feeling pleasant or unpleasant, or is in pleasant or unpleasant circumstances, on the basis of spontaneous facial expressions (Buck et al., 1972, 1974; Howell & Jorgenson, 1970; Nakamura, Buck, & Kenny, 1990). Can observers go beyond a distinction between pleasant and unpleasant? Three studies have addressed this question.

Ekman (1989)   Ekman (1989) raised this question but cited only indirect evidence based on a single unpublished study. Emotion-inducing films were shown to 25 Japanese and 25 American viewers, whose faces were secretly videotaped. Specific facial movements such as smiling or lowering the brow were found on the videotapes in similar frequency in the two samples. Two segments from each videotape, one taken while the viewer watched a "neutral" travelogue and the other taken while the viewer watched a "stress" film (industrial accidents and the like), were then shown to a sample of judges. Judges were asked to guess whether the viewer was watching the travelogue or the stress film. According to Ekman (1972), "about 60% of the judgments" (p. 243) were correct (chance would have yielded 50%). Ekman (1972) argued that "these findings provide strong evidence in support of our position that there are universal facial expressions of emotions. . . . It is reasonable to expect that the judges would make [their judgments] by a reasoning process in which they judged facial behavior as showing a particular emotion, for example, disgust, and disgust as being an emotion which would be more likely to occur during a stress film than a neutral film" (p. 244).

However, the slight increase in accuracy might have been achieved without such reasoning. For example, judges might have interpreted facial expressions simply as positive or negative and guessed that negative expressions occurred during the stress film or positive expressions during the travelogue. Or, the 60% accuracy might have been achieved with no reliance on facial expression at all. If the original viewers had, for example, averted their gaze more during the scenes of accidents than during the travelogue, then the judges might have exploited this difference. A test of Ekman's interpretation would require that judges agree on the specific emotional meaning of specific spontaneous facial expressions.

Motley and Camden (1988)   Candid photographs of the facial expressions of four subjects were taken while they participated in six elaborately plotted interpersonal exchanges each designed to elicit a different emotion. That the anticipated emotions were actually elicited was checked by retrospective report and physiological recordings. The same four subjects then posed facial expressions for the same six emotions (happiness, surprise, anger, disgust, sadness, and confusion). The resulting 48 photographs (6 spontaneous and 6 posed from each of four subjects) were then shown to 20 judges. For each photo, the judges were asked to select one emotion from a list of the six. For posed expressions, 81.4% of judgments were accurate, but for spontaneous expressions 26.0% were accurate. The difference was highly significant. Analysis of judgments of spontaneous expressions for individual emotions showed that judgments did not differ from random selection, except for happy expressions.

Wagner, MacDonald, and Manstead (1986)   Wagner et al. (1986) videotaped the spontaneous facial expressions of persons viewing emotion-eliciting slides. The viewers indicated their response to each slide by selecting one of seven emotion words. Fifty-three judges then attempted to guess the viewers' emotions from the videotape by selecting one of the same seven emotion words. From their analysis of the results, Wagner et al. (1986) concluded that "overall accuracy was significantly greater than chance, although it was not impressive in absolute terms. Only happy, angry, and disgusted expressions were recognized at above-chance rates" (p. 737).

I believe that their modest conclusion is overly optimistic. Their three significant recognition scores were 48.4% for "happiness," 22.69% for "disgust," and 12.67% for "anger." As their level of comparison (what they called "chance"), Wagner et al. (1986) used the percentage of times a given label was used overall—that is, its base rate. Thus, 12.67% correct for "anger" was considered significant because it was reliably greater than 8.27%, the base rate with which the word *anger* was selected across all stimuli. Given the forced-choice response format and the nonrepresentative sample of stimuli, I find this comparison level necessary but insufficient. (Thus judges might not so much have associated the label *anger* with facial expressions of "anger" as they did not find the word *anger* appropriate for smiles, for the wide open eyes of "surprise," and so on.) A more conservative approach would require judges to exceed not only base rate, but random choice. This is because observers could exceed base rate through a random process. For instance, imagine that for one type of facial expression the judges had no idea whatsoever what emotion label to pick. If, on these trials only, judges in effect selected their responses blindfolded from a hat, then 14.3% of their responses (one out of seven) would be expected to be correct by chance alone. Return now to the three "significant" findings. Although happiness (48.4%) was well above this level of random choice, disgust (22.69%) was only somewhat above, and anger (12.67%) was slightly below. The obtained results cannot allow us to reject the possibility that subjects selected the words *anger* and *disgust* for the appropriate facial expressions as often as they did in a random process. (Wagner, 1993, subsequently proposed more sophisticated ways of assessing recognition.)

Even if performance exceeds both base rate and random choice, judges still might not associate specific facial expressions with specific emotions. Let us assume that the judges can tell positive from negative facial expressions reasonably well. This assumption is consistent with the markedly higher success on happiness both in this and in the Motley and Camden (1988) studies. In addition, other studies of spontaneous facial expressions show that judges can guess whether the eliciting circumstances were pleasant or unpleasant with accuracy greater than chance. The question then becomes whether judges discriminated among negative emotions—that is, beyond a positive–negative distinction.

Table VI examines this question by focusing on those cases in which the viewer indicated a negative emotion and the judge rated the face as showing a negative emotion. Part 1 shows the figures reported by Wagner et al. (1986, Table 4). Part 2. converts those figures to percentages of negative responses. The simplest null hypothesis—that for these cases, choices among the four negative response alternatives were random—predicts that 25% of the responses in Part 2 would be correct. Overall,

TABLE VI   Responses to Negative Expression

Facial stimulus	Response word				
	Fear	Sad	Disgust	Anger	TOTAL
Part I. Percentage of all responses					
"Fear"	10.28	20.55	12.65	15.42	58.90
"Sad"	8.90	16.74	22.88	8.05	56.57
"Disgust"	5.26	18.69	22.69	9.98	56.62
"Anger"	9.67	18.33	19.00	12.67	59.67
Mean	8.53	18.58	19.31	11.53	
Part II. Percentage of negative responses					
"Fear"	17.50	34.90	21.50	26.20	100.0
"Sad"	15.70	29.60	40.40	14.20	100.0
"Disgust"	9.30	33.00	40.10	17.60	100.0
"Anger"	16.20	30.70	31.80	21.20	100.0
Mean	14.68	32.05	33.45	19.80	

Notes: Percentage of "correct" responses is underlined. Data are from Wagner, MacDonald, & Manstead (1986).

27.1% of responses were correct. Percentages for "fear" and "anger" expressions fell below, "sad" and "disgust" expressions above, this level. The seemingly better performance on "sad" (29.6%) and "disgust" (40.1%) expressions can now be compared with the base rates. Looking across the rows, we can see that the modal response was *sad* to the "fear" expressions, and was *disgust* to the "sad," "disgust," and "anger" expressions. There was no differential labeling of "sad" and "disgust" facial expressions but a greater willingness to use the labels *sad* and *disgust*. The label *sad* was not more likely to be used for the "sad" expression than for any other negative expression, indeed, less likely. The label *disgust* was applied equally often to the "disgust" and "sad" expressions.

Conclusion   We have no cross-cultural studies of recognition of emotion from spontaneous facial expressions. Even in Western cultures, too few studies exist to draw firm conclusions. (Some earlier studies exist [Landis, 1924; Munn, 1940; Sherman, 1927], which were reviewed by Izard [1971] and Ekman et al. [1972].) The available studies demonstrate the need to consider carefully the criterion by which performance is evaluated (Wagner, 1993). Apparently significant performance could be due to high base rate for specific labels, to random choice on certain trials, or to a positive–negative discrimination. (A further problem in these studies, to be discussed shortly, is their use of a forced-choice response format.) Beyond such factors, the available results (Motley & Camden, 1988; Wagner et al., 1986; Winkelmayer et al., 1978) do not demonstrate a recognition of specific emotions from spontaneous facial expression.

Conversely, the available studies do not allow us to conclude that the fault—if *fault* is the right word—lies in the observer. In these studies, the person feeling the emotion might not have produced any facial expression in the first place. A study reported by Ekman, Friesen, and Ancoli (1980) suggests that at least some of the difficulty may indeed have arisen at the encoding stage. Something is amiss in spontaneous communication, but it could be either an encoding or decoding problem. Perhaps further information on this question could come from scoring the available records of spontaneous expressions with one of the objective facial scoring systems (Ekman & Friesen, 1982b; Izard, 1983).

Response Format

The results of Tables II and III are all derived from asking subjects to select one word from a prespecified list of emotions. For instance, a subject might have been asked to select one of the following: *happy, sad, afraid, angry, surprised, disgust,* and *contempt.* This type of forced-choice response format is a common instrument in research on emotion and has been advocated as the method of choice in the study of facial expression, although other response formats have also been used.

In this section, I first use a recent study to demonstrate that problems can arise when forced-choice format is used—quite different kinds of facial expressions can all be placed in the *same* emotion category, and one and the same expression can achieve consensus on quite *different* emotion categories, depending on the choices given to subjects. Then I examine two alternative methods of collecting subjects' responses: freely chosen labels and quantitative ratings.

Forced Choice

A forced-choice format clearly alerts the subject to the experimenter's expectation that the facial expression is to be interpreted in terms of emotion and even which emotions. After the first trial, the set of category choices is "primed" and might influence subsequent perception (Wyer & Srull, 1981). Subjects were not given the option of saying *none of the above* or of choosing a nonemotion. For example, they were not allowed to give *frustration, seeing a friend, attending to something novel,* or some other situational interpretation to the face. They were not allowed to describe the face as part of an instrumental response, such as *threatening, staring,* or *avoiding.* They were not given the option of choosing a more general emotional state, such as *unhappy, distressed,* or *aroused.* Oster et al. (1992) criticized judgment studies of babies' faces for lacking just such nonspecific alternatives.

Given the list of options generally used, a forced-choice format is at odds with the properties of the emotion concepts presented (Russell, 1989b). For instance, forcing the observer to choose exactly one option treats the set of options as mutually exclusive, which they are not: Subjects place the same event (a facial expression, the emotion of another, or their own emotion) into more than one category. Forced choice treats each option as an either–or (present–absent) choice, which it is not: subjects reliably rate different events as belonging to a given category to different degrees.

Potential problems stemming from forced choice have not been widely discussed in connection with the study of facial expression. If observers find on the prespecified list the precise emotion label they had already spontaneously thought of, then no serious problem arises. However, consider the situation in which the list of response options fails to include a label for the observer's spontaneous categorization. It might be thought that such a situation would be immediately obvious because it would result in idiosyncratic and thus random responses. Such an outcome is possible, but, as will be shown, not inevitable.

A small study recently showed that forced choice *can* lead to consensus on results rather different from those reported in Table II (Russell, 1993a). The "wrong" expressions were categorized as a particular emotion when a different forced-choice response format was used. By "wrong," I mean not simply expressions slightly different from the prototype. I mean expressions previously claimed as expressing fundamentally different emotions: the "sad" expression categorized as *fear*, the "fear" expression categorized as *surprise*, and so on.

There were 12 conditions, or demonstrations. In each condition, subjects were shown one photograph of a facial expression from the Japanese and Caucasian Facial Expressions of Emotion (JACFEE) set, developed by Matsumoto and Ekman (1988). The subject was then asked to select one emotion label from a list of options. (Slightly different methods were used for the first six and last six conditions; five options vs. six and the placement of the predicted option.) In each condition, the predicted option was not a synonym for the emotion name supplied by Matsumoto and Ekman (1988) but was predicted from a circular model of the judgment space for emotions (Russell, 1980; Russell & Fehr, 1987). The options available in each condition are shown in Table VII where the predicted option is highlighted. In the first condition, for example, the options were *happiness, surprise, contempt, fear,* and *interest*. The subjects were shown an "anger" expression and predicted to select *contempt*.

The percentage of subjects selecting the various options in each condition is also shown in Table VII. Of course, some response will be modal, but the results were not *quantitatively* different from those seen in Table II. The range of the twelve modal responses was 46.3 to 96.3%, the

TABLE VII Percentage of Judges Choosing Various Response Options

Five choices

Facial expression[a]	Option	%	Option	%	Option	%	Option	%	Option	%
1. "Anger"	Happiness	1.2	Surprise	6.3	<u>Contempt</u>	76.2	Fear	5.0	Interest	11.2
2. "Disgust"	Happiness	0	Disgust	7.5	<u>Contempt</u>	90.0	Fear	0	Interest	2.5
3. "Sadness"	Happiness	1.2	Anger	1.2	<u>Contempt</u>	46.3	Fear	36.3	Interest	15.0
4. "Anger"	Happiness	0	Relax.	0	<u>Frustration</u>	96.3	Fear	1.2	Interest	2.5
5. "Contempt"	Happiness	2.5	Surprise	0	<u>Boredom</u>	88.8	Fear	0	Interest	8.8
6. "Contempt"	Happiness	1.2	Anger	1.2	<u>Disgust</u>	77.5	Fear	1.2	Interest	18.8

Six choices

Facial expression	Option	%	Option	%	Option	%	Option	%	Option	%	Option	%
7. "Anger"	<u>Contempt</u>	70.0	Joy	0.0	Surprise	0.0	Fear	5.0	Fear	10.0	Interest	15.0
8. "Anger"	Joy	0.0	Relax.	0.0	<u>Surprise</u>	93.8	Fear	0.0	Fear	0.0	Interest	6.25
9. "Fear"	Joy	0.0	Relax.	0.0	Contempt	5.0	Surprise	8.75	<u>Disgust</u>	71.25	Disgust	15
10. "Sadness"	Joy	5.0	<u>Fear</u>	73.75	Surprise	2.5	Excitement	11.25	Fear	0.0	Interest	7.5
11. "Disgust"	Joy	0.0	Relax.	0.0	Anger	12.5	<u>Fear</u>	75.0	Fear	7.5	Interest	5.0
12. "Surprise"	Joy	3.75	Relax.	0.0	Contempt	0.0	Disgust	6.25	Disgust	11.25	<u>Fear</u>	78.75

Notes: Predicted response option is underlined. For each condition, a separate χ^2 test ($N = 80$) examined whether response labels were chosen at random. For conditions 1–6, the degrees of freedom were 4. For conditions 7–12, the degrees of freedom were 5. For each condition, this null hypothesis was rejected at α of .001.

[a] Label is that given the photograph by Matsumoto & Ekman (1988).

median of which was 76.8%. In each condition, responses were far from what would be expected by random assortment and the predicted option was the modal choice in each case.

In the first condition, subjects were shown an "anger" expression and found to categorize it as *contempt*—at least 76% did. This figure can be compared with previous results reported by those who found the same expression categorized as *anger*. For example, Ekman and Friesen (1986) found that 73% of their subjects categorized "anger" expressions as *anger*. In Table II, the median percentage of agreement for "anger" expressions was 81.2% for Western subjects, 63.0% for non-Western subjects. Or, the present result can be compared with Ekman and Friesen's (1986) claim that a very different expression, a unilateral lip curl, is "unique to contempt": the percentage of their subjects selecting *contempt* for the lip curl averaged 75% across 10 cultures.

In a subsequent condition, the "anger" expression was labeled as *frustration*, and, in another condition, as *disgust*. The "disgust" expression was labeled *contempt* in one condition and *anger* in another, the "sad" expression as *contempt* in one and as *fear* in another, the "contempt" expression as *boredom* in one and as *disgust* in another, the "fear" expression as *surprise*, and the "surprise" expression as *fear*.

In no case did subjects select a category label at random, and the use of the labels therefore implied no idiosyncratic selection. Forced choice could yield random selection, of course, but the list of options used here was carefully constructed to allow the modal response to be predicted. Even so, it should be clear that these data do not show that the "anger" expression really expresses contempt, that the "surprise" expression really expresses fear, and so on. Nor do these results even say that observers necessarily attributed *contempt* to the "anger" and "disgust" expressions, and so on. If that is so, then the same reasoning shows that the results of Table II cannot be used to say that the various expressions really express the emotions claimed in those studies nor that the subjects necessarily attributed those emotions to those expressions.

The method in this study is not advocated for general purposes. One anonymous reviewer commented that the response format used here was "as rigged" against the traditional hypothesis as the traditional format was "rigged in support." The purpose of this study was to expose potential problems. Given other options, they would have chosen other category labels. Given still other options, they would not be able to agree on one label as best. Thus, given different lists of options, forced choice *can* yield anything from random choice to a consensus, even on, from what researchers have generally concluded, the wrong answer.[9]

---

[9] C. Izard (personal communication, November 10, 1992) rightly points out that forced-choice format alone could not guarantee consensus. He pointed to unpublished data (see Footnote 8) on facial expressions that failed his selection criteria for inclusion in his set. Even with forced-choice response format, the mean percentage agreement on these photographs was 31%.

Therefore, consensus achieved through forced choice need not point to subjects' unique response.

The question might be raised whether the odd results here were due to the list of response options being overly restrictive. In general, any short list, including the ones used in the studies of Table II, should be suspected of being overly restrictive. The results presented show that the occurrence of near consensus is no evidence to the contrary. The question might be raised whether the odd results here were due to the list of response options failing to include the "correct" option. One problem is that we would need independent evidence to know the "correct" label, and such evidence is lacking for the studies of Table II.

These results raise the question whether observers would still prefer the "correct" (predicted) label when plausible alternatives are available. For example, shown Matsumoto and Ekman's (1988) "anger" expression, would observers select *anger* when the options are *anger, determination, frustration, hostility, hatred, jealousy,* and *pain*? This question is relevant to whether observers interpret facial expressions in terms of specific emotion categories or broader clusters and was explored in a final study by Russell (1993a).

The study used two examples of Matsumoto and Ekman's (1988) "anger" expression and the seven response options listed above. These seven options had been chosen to be close to anger in Russell and Fehr's (1987) judgment space for emotions. Still, a semantic analysis leaves the word *anger* as the only option that unequivocally denotes the emotion of anger. *Hostility, hatred,* and *jealousy* refer to emotions qualitatively different from anger, according to Johnson-Laird and Oatley's (1989) semantic analysis. *Pain* refers to a complex sensation or perception rather than to a prototypical emotion. *Frustration* and *determination* refer to conditions of having a goal blocked and the resolve to do something. The results are shown in Table VIII. The two photographs yielded somewhat different profiles—an important result itself because the photographs were predicted by Matsumoto and Ekman (1988) to signal the same emotion. And *anger* was not the modal choice for either expression.

In sum, forced choice *can* produce apparently contradictory results. For some facial expressions and some circumstances, subjects can consensually pick different emotion labels for the same expression. The universality thesis cannot be demonstrated solely through forced choice, and corroboration must be obtained with other response formats. In the next section, I examine two alternatives: freely chosen labels and quantitative ratings.

Freely Chosen Labels

If recognition of emotion is easy and in terms of separate discrete emotion categories, then a list of emotions supplied by a researcher should

TABLE VIII   Percent Selecting Different Labels
for Two Facial Expressions Reported
to Be of Anger

| Response option | Expression | | |
	A	B	Total
Frustration	45.0	35.0	40.0
Determination	40.0	23.3	31.7
Anger	5.0	20.0	12.5
Hostility	6.7	11.7	9.2
Hatred	0.0	5.0	2.5
Jealousy	1.7	3.3	2.5
Pain	1.7	1.7	1.7

Notes: $N = 120$. Sixty judges saw each photograph. Data from
Russell (1993a).

not be necessary for recognition to occur. An observer's freely given
response should reveal that recognition. However, when observers are
given freedom to choose their own label, they don't always specify an
emotion. This result was obtained by Darwin (1872/1965) when he asked
over 20 persons to comment on still photographs. Darwin did not report
the details of his results, but Frijda (1953) repeated this open-ended
approach, and found a variety of responses. The majority of responses
did not mention emotions at all, but rather situations: "She looks as if
she is looking at a small child playing." Another subject said that the
person in the photograph appeared "as if looking at something with
fixed attention, a game or something, tense, two cars which almost get
into collision, but nothing happens. Then she says, 'Gosh, who would
do anything so stupid!'" (p. 314). Of course, these respondents might
have used such situational descriptions to convey an emotional interpretation. But, some might not.

Subsequent "free label" studies have been less free. They required
subjects to restrict their response to a word or two; the subject was told
that the word or two should describe an emotion. Of the five studies
that obtained "free labels," I discuss four here (Izard, 1971; Boucher &
Carlson, 1980; Russell, 1991b; Russell, Suzuki, & Ishida, 1992) and one
more (Sorenson, 1975, 1976) in a later section.

Izard (1971)   Izard (1971) obtained freely chosen labels from American, English, French, and Greek college students for 32 still photographs
of 8 different types of facial expression. These same students then provided the forced-choice judgments already cited in Table II. (The degree
of overlap in results from the two judgment tasks was not reported).
"Recognition" scores resulting from the two response formats are shown

TABLE IX   Recognition Scores from Forced Choice and Free Labels

Facial expression	American Forced	American Free	Greek Forced	Greek Free	Number words correct[a]
"Interest"	84.5	36.9	66.0	35.8	22
"Joy"	96.8	89.8	93.5	80.2	28
"Surprise"	90.5	88.2	80.2	56.4	13
"Distress" (Sadness)	74.0	60.1	54.5	49.6	28
"Disgust/Contempt"	83.2	49.0	87.5	48.7	20
"Anger"	89.2	66.4	80.0	47.1	13
"Shame"	73.2	11.6	71.0	26.2	9
"Fear"	76.0	59.6	67.8	70.8	8
M	83.4	57.7	75.1	51.9	
N	89		50		

Notes: Figures given are percentages of responses considered correct. Samples were 89 Americans and 50 Greeks. Data from Izard (1971).

[a]Number of words scored as correct in the free-label task; see Izard (1971) for the list. Izard (1971) reported separate results for men and women, which were combined here.

in Table IX for two of the samples. Similar results were obtained from the remaining two samples.

Izard (1971) first told his subjects that the photographs were of people "who were trying to express an emotion. Some of the people tried to express a certain emotion; others tried to express another emotion, others still another, etc." (p. 268). Instructions then asked the subject to "decide which *one* emotion is expressed most strongly" (p. 268). Despite these instructions, some of the labels subjects produced did not refer to an emotion (*deliberating, observation, clowning, smile, about to cry, bad news, skepticism, sneer*). The total number of occurrences of such responses was not reported. Izard reported the responses I just listed because he considered them to be correct, and we do not know the nature of the responses (about 47% of the total) not counted as correct.

Ignoring words given by only one subject, Izard still found 224 different words or phrases produced (at least twice) for the 8 types of expression. Izard therefore devised a scoring key in which, for example, 8 of the words were considered correct for fear, 28 for joy, and so on (the number correct for each emotion is given in Table IX). In all, 141 different words or phrases were scored as correct for the 8 emotions. Not all words considered correct for a given emotion were synonyms (e.g., *distress, loneliness, pain, pity,* and *worry* were considered correct for the "sad" expression; Izard's term for this expression was "distress" but *distress* was considered a synonym for *sadness*). As noted, among the correct responses were also words not denoting emotions (*laugh, smile, clowning,* and *sees something pleasant* for "joy"; *bad news* and *crying* for "sadness"; *smirk* and *sneer* for "disgust/contempt"; *revenge* for "anger";

repentance for "shame"). The scoring method undoubtedly reflected the subjects' responses, but an issue that arises from the scoring is what version of the universality thesis the obtained results support. It is not clear how these results support Izard's contention that recognition occurs in terms of "specific emotion categories" rather than Woodworth's (1938) broad clusters.

The results were not described fully. For example, the frequency with which specific labels were chosen was not reported, and it is therefore not clear whether the modal response for the proposed facial expression of "sadness"/"distress" was *distress, sadness, loneliness, worry*, or another response. Nonetheless, the results reported showed several clear trends. First, no marked differences appeared due to culture or language. Second, although a majority of free-label responses (about 53% overall) was considered correct, a large minority (from 42.3% of American responses to 48.1% of Greek responses) was considered incorrect. Third, recognition scores from free labeling were lower than from forced choice for every type of facial expression. Fourth, the difference between forced choice and free labeling varied with the type of expression. "Joy" replicated well; "shame" replicated poorly; and the other types of expression fell between. There was a statistically significant main effect due to expression type (emotion, in his terms) for the correctness of free-label responses.

Boucher and Carlson (1980)   Boucher and Carlson (1980) obtained both forced-choice (six options) and free-label responses from the same subjects, 30 Malays. Observers were shown facial expressions posed by Americans and Malays. With forced choice, the overall mean recognition score was 68.8% on the American and 60.0% on the Malay facial expressions. These figures were lower than had been obtained with the normative group of American subjects, but were statistically significant for each emotion.

The free-label data were not described fully, but Boucher and Carlson (1980) did report that expressions for each emotion, except "fear," obtained recognition scores greater than chance, and that free label had resulted in "an apparent lower level of accuracy" than had resulted from the forced choice. Thus, the "recognition" scores must have been lower than 60.0–68.8% but significantly greater than zero, except for the "fear" expression. It is therefore impossible to say how well the results supported the conclusion of high recognition. In this analysis, as in Izard's (1971), a response was considered correct if it was one of a set of words or phrases Boucher and Carlson considered similar to the label for the target emotion. Responses considered correct were not specified, and so it is impossible to say if the results more strongly supported recognition in terms of specific emotions or broad clusters.

The degree to which the results from the free-label format replicated those from the forced-choice format varied with the type of expression. Boucher and Carlson asked how often the free label corresponded to the same subject's subsequently given forced choice to the same face (regardless of its correctness, that is, of what emotion the poser intended). The freely chosen label was considered equivalent to the forced-choice response if it fell in the cluster of related terms. The proportion of forced-choice responses that coincided with freely chosen labels was as follows: *happy* 89.9%, *surprise* 60.7%, *anger* 60.4%, *sad* 47.7%, *disgust* 39.7%, and *fear* 7.7%.

Russell (1991c)   In neither of the studies just reviewed were the freely chosen labels reported in full. For example, it would be helpful to know the frequency with which different labels were chosen. Russell (1991b) reported freely chosen labels for the Matsumoto and Ekman (1988) facial expressions of "contempt." These data, along with comparable data for the Matsumoto and Ekman (1988) "anger" expressions, are summarized in Table X. Each subject provided an emotion label of his or her own choice to 1 of 16 photographs (8 of "contempt" and 8 of "an-

TABLE X   Frequency of Free Response Labels for Expressions Reported to Be of Anger and Contempt

Anger expression			
Frustration	49	Perturbed	2
Anger	41	Perplexed	2
Mad	18	Irritable	2
Constipated	4	Doubt	2
Upset	3	Pissed off	2
Confusion	2	Scorn	2
Making a decision	2	[Idiosyncratic]	27
Contempt expression			
Disgust	16	Anger	3
Bored	10	Stupid	2
Disappointment	9	Depression	2
Puzzled	6	Indecisive	2
Confusion	6	Impatient	2
Frustration	5	Dissatisfaction	2
Indifference	5	Pain	2
Smug	5	Troubled	2
Contempt	3	Arrogant	2
Perplexed	3	Disbelief	2
Pissed off	3	Perturbed	2
Cynical	3	Amused	2
Disgruntled	3	[Idiosyncratic]	46
Sarcastic	3	Other	9

Note: $N = 160$ for each type of expression.

ger"). Twenty subjects responded to each photograph; total number of subjects was therefore 320. They responded to the question, "What *mood* or *emotion* is the woman [man] in the photograph feeling?" (p. 284).

Subjects were often reluctant to choose a single word; their initial responses were often a phrase or story, and the experimenter had to say "If you had to choose a single word, what would that be?" (Even then, 9 subjects in the "contempt" condition claimed they could not find a single word.) Single-word responses were tabulated. The result was 121 different responses, 40 for the "anger" expressions, 81 for the "contempt" expressions. (In this count, syntactic form was ignored.) The different labels produced by at least two subjects, and the frequency with which they were produced, are given in Table X.

For the "anger" expression, the modal response was *frustration*, chosen by 30.6% of the subjects. The word *anger* was chosen by 25.6%. If *anger, mad, perturbed, irritable,* and *pissed off* are considered synonyms, then 40.6% gave the expected label. If *frustration* is added to the list of correct responses, then 71.2% of responses would be counted correct. On the other hand, including *frustration* raises a problem. Although frustration can lead to anger, it might also lead to sadness, shame, surprise, or some other emotion. (This point could be especially important in cross-cultural comparisons—for example, the Semai typically react to frustration with fear, Robarchek, 1977.) Neither Tomkins and McCarter (1964) nor Izard (1971) included *frustration* as a correct response for their "anger" expression. The word *frustration* is not a synonym of *anger*. It is not clear that *frustration* refers to an emotion rather than to a situation. Oster et al. (1989) argued that frustration and anger have separate facial signals. The important point is not so much whether *frustration* is counted as correct or not, but that a trade-off is implied by either course. If *frustration* is included, then more observers agree with the hypothesis (but the hypothesis has become less precise). If *frustration* is excluded, then the hypothesis being tested is more precise (but fewer observers agree with it).

For the "contempt" expression, the modal response was *disgust*, given by 10% of the sample. Only 2% of the sample gave *contempt*. More consensus would appear if terms were clustered. Any grouping of terms that would include responses from a majority of subjects would have to include terms that are more likely to refer to a different emotion (*disgust, anger, sadness*), a nonemotion (*puzzled, disbelief*), or to be so vague as to refer to almost any negative emotion (*troubled, dissatisfied*).

Russell, Suzuki, and Ishida (1992)   Russell, Suzuki, and Ishida (1992) obtained free emotion labels from 50 English-speaking Canadians, 38 Greeks, and 50 Japanese who were members of the general public rather than students. Observers were shown seven of Matsumoto and Ekman's

TABLE XI Free-Label Judgments of Seven Facial Expressions

Predicted label of photograph[a]	English speaking			Greek			Japanese		
	Forced[b] %	Free[c] %	Mode	Forced[d] %	Free %	Mode	Forced[d] %	Free %	Mode
"Happy"	98.74	100	Happy	97.36	92	Hara (joy)	97.36	84	Tanoshii (delight)
"Surprise"	95.34	96	Surprise	90.26	55[e]	Ekplixi (surprise)	90.26	94	Odoroki (surprise)
"Sadness"	94.48	70	Sad	96.11	75	Lipi (sad)	96.11	80	Kanashimi (sorrow)
"Anger"	91.92	78	Angry	70.36	63	Thimos (anger)	70.36	48[e]	Ikari (anger)
"Disgust"	75.25	66	Disgust	74.45	68	Aidhia (disgust)	74.45	56	Iya (dislike, disgust, disagreeable)
"Fear"	77.11	62	Fear	37.66	87	Fovo (fear)	37.66	14[f]	Odoroki (surprise)
"Contempt"	47.85	2	Indifferent	64.94	0	Skeptikos (skeptical or thoughtful)	64.94	0	My hyoujou (expressionless)
M	67.7			62.9			53.7		

Note: A chi-square test was used to compare the free-label judgments from the Canadian sample with each of the other two, spearately for each photograph.

[a]Label is that predicted by Matsumoto & Ekman (1988).

[b]American normative sample, Matsumoto & Ekman (1988).

[c]Canadian sample.

[d]Japanese normative sample, Matsumoto & Ekman (1988)

[e]$p < .05$.

[f]$p < .01$.

(1988) photographs reported to show universal facial expressions of basic emotions.

Responses again included nonemotions: *smile* for the "happiness" expression, *speechless* for "surprise," *disappointment* for "sadness," *frustration* for "anger," *having failed* for "disgust." To create a scoring system similar to that used by Izard (1971) and, presumably, Boucher and Carlson (1980), words reasonably close to the predicted term were scored "correct." The percentages of correct responses obtained are shown in Table XI. For comparison, although not a rigorous one, also given in Table XI are Matsumoto and Ekman's (1988) normative figures from an American and from a Japanese sample for the same photographs. These normative figures had been obtained with forced-choice. For the "happy" and "surprise" expressions, free label replicated (indeed, surpassed) the forced-choice results. For the remaining expressions, forced-choice recognition scores were higher by from 9 to 45 percentage points in the English-speaking sample and by from 13 to 65 percentage points in the Japanese sample.

The English-speaking group gave the highest recognition scores based on free labeling to date: 67.7%, including 100% for the "happiness" expression and 96% for the "surprise" expression, indicating that subjects clearly understood the task. Overall agreement with prediction was 62.9% for the Greeks and 53.7% for the Japanese. (Because the "contempt" expression is controversial, we might want to set aside the results for that expression. If we do so, the free-label results from this study would be higher, with median scores of 74%, 71.5%, and 68% in the Canadian, Greek, and Japanese, respectively, samples.)

As in previous studies, recognition scores varied with type of expression. Overall, agreement was highest for the "happy," "surprise," and "sad" expressions. Agreement was low for the "contempt" expression, parallel to the Russell (1991*b*) result, and intermediate for "anger," "disgust," and "fear" expressions. For four of the seven expressions, amount of agreement varied with the culture of the observer. Greeks produced similar scores to the Canadians, although the "surprise" expression was given a label from the *fear* cluster by 25% of the Greek respondents. The non-Western culture, Japan, yielded similar scores with two exceptions. The Japanese scores for "anger" (48%) and "fear" (14%) were significantly lower than in the Canadian normative group. The modal response to the "fear" expression was *odoroki* (surprise).

Conclusion   Four studies of freely generated labels yielded reasonably consistent results. Although "recognition" was generally lower than that obtained with forced choice, it was high enough for Izard (1971) and Boucher and Carlson (1980) to see the results as support for their hypotheses. In the Izard (1971) study, recognition was 53% overall including happiness; for Boucher and Carlson (1980), the actual figure was not reported but was less than 60–68%, again including happiness; recognition of the "fear expression" was no greater than chance. In Russell et al. (1992), recognition was 67.7% from Canadians, 62.9% from Greeks, and 53.7% from Japanese.

These average figures must be interpreted carefully. First, responses considered correct were not synonyms. When a certain percentage of subjects was reported to categorize a particular facial expression as, for example, *anger*, the more accurate statement would be that that percentage of observers used some word from a broad cluster related to *anger*. In their manner of scoring their data, Izard (1971) and Boucher and Carlson (1980) were defining the universality thesis in a way reminiscent of Woodworth (1938) and his followers (Schlosberg, 1952, 1954; Woodworth & Schlosberg, 1954). Scoring freely produced labels creates a trade-off: higher recognition scores can be obtained at the cost of broadening the cluster of emotion words that count as correct. The experimenter can specify one particular emotion attributed to a given facial expression, but at the cost of reduced recognition scores. The amount of reduction appears to vary with the type of expression.

Second, "recognition" scores were not the same for every type of expression and culture. Recognition scores ranged from high for the "happy" expression to negligible for "shame" or "contempt." Scores for the negative emotions of anger, fear, and disgust were intermediate. Results were similar among Western samples (American, Canadian, English, French, and Greek) but lower in non-Western cultures (the Japanese and apparently the Malaysians). For both Japanese and Malaysians, the "fear" expression was rarely labeled as fear.

Lower recognition scores with free-label format has been attributed (Izard, 1971) to the difficulty of free labeling (a production measure) rather than to problems with forced choice (a recognition measure). But, Izard (1971) provided no comparison task that would allow an assessment of the difficulty of free label.[10]

Moreover, free label is not without its own problems. The instructions and procedure emphasized that the label should describe an emotion. Free label, like forced choice, presupposes that the number of labels needed is *one* and that emotion labels apply to facial expressions in a dichotomous fashion. That is, judges are forced to choose one label (albeit from an unrestricted set) as applying completely and thereby

---

[10] In unpublished data (Russell, 1993b), I sought some baseline with which free labels for facial expressions could be compared. I asked subjects to label photographs of three types: facial expressions drawn from Matsumoto and Ekman (1988), vehicles, and animals. The recognition scores were as follows: facial expressions: happy 91.1%, surprise 87.5%, fear 50.9%, sad 59.8%, anger 40.2%, disgust 66.1%, and contempt 0%; vehicles: motorcycle 100%, truck 98%, boat 100%, bus 100%, train 96%, airplane 100%, and automobile 80%; animals: elephant 100%, duck 89%, horse 100%, cow 100%, dog 100%, chicken 96%, and pig 100%.

implying that all other labels do not apply. These restrictions imposed on observers happen to correspond to the assumptions of certain versions of the universality thesis. Relaxing these constraints would allow a judge to say, for a particular face, that more than one label applies and that a given label applies only to a certain degree.

Quantitative Ratings

Given the problems just mentioned, quantitative ratings on multiple scales are a needed complement to the forced-choice and free-label formats. Quantitative ratings would not be biased against any specific hypothesis, but would simply be more neutral. If a specific facial expression is a highly recognizable, pancultural signal unique to a specific emotion, then subjects could use quantitative scales to judge it as expressing that emotion to a high degree, and as expressing all other emotions to a low degree.

Ekman et al. (1987) acknowledged that problems might exist with the standard forced-choice format and therefore gathered additional data from each subject. They hypothesized that similar results would occur "even when observers were allowed to choose more than one emotion" (p. 714). Each observer was *first* given the standard forced choice (among seven alternatives) and *then* asked to make quantitative ratings on any of the seven that were present in the face. Ekman et al. (1987) analyzed these judgments by considering only the highest rating given on each trial. They reported:

> We determined whether the emotion with the most intense rating was the emotion predicted by Ekman and Friesen and was the same across cultures. [The hypothesis] was supported; in 177 of 180 times, the emotion rated strongest by the largest number of observers in each culture was the predicted emotion. This is the first evidence of cross-cultural agreement about the most intense emotion when observers can choose more than one emotion. (p. 715)

No further details were reported for these data. As analyzed, these data do not go far beyond the forced-choice data. Just before giving the quantitative ratings for each face, each college student subject had been asked to choose one of the emotion terms as best. It is not surprising that the same subject would then give his or her highest intensity rating to that same emotion term. In a subsequent study, Matsumoto and Ekman (1989) eliminated this problem but still did not report the full set of quantitative ratings for each type of facial expression.

Analysis of other quantitative ratings shows that subjects do not interpret facial expressions dichotomously. Rather than rating one emotion high and all others low, subjects report that labels vary gradually

TABLE XII   Mean Rating on Accuracy of Category as Descriptor
of a Facial Expression

| Category label | Facial expression | | | | | |
	"Interest" 22	"Sadness" 14	"Disgust" 16	"Anger" 17	"Fear" 10	"Surprise" 7
Excited	4.5	3.0	4.3	3.4	3.5	3.6
Happy	5.1	2.1	2.3	1.7	2.2	3.8
Calm	5.2	4.0	3.1	4.4	3.6	5.0
Sleepy	2.5	3.1	2.2	3.0	3.3	2.4
Bored	3.2	3.3	3.1	4.4	3.4	3.5
Sad	3.1	5.9	3.2	5.3	4.5	4.0
Disgusted	3.1	4.6	6.8	5.6	4.4	3.0
Angry	2.9	4.8	5.7	6.0	5.2	2.9
Afraid	3.3	5.8	3.7	4.9	5.8	4.3
Surprised	4.8	4.2	3.6	3.0	4.7	6.6
Reliability	.89	.95	.96	.95	.93	.85

Notes: Ratings were made on a scale from extremely inaccurate (1) to extremely accurate (8).
Label ws that provided by Ekman. The plate number in Ekman's (1980) book for each facial
expression is as follows: "interest" 22, "sadness" 14, "disgust" 16, "anger" 17, "fear" 10,
and "surprise" 7.

from the best descriptor to the worst. Russell and Bullock (1986, Study 4)
asked 50 subjects to provide quantitative ratings for six photographs
taken from Ekman (1980), with the results shown in Table XII. The
highest mean ratings were as Ekman (1980) predicted, but subjects did
not give low ratings to all other labels. One example is provided by the
column for Photo #17, presented by Ekman as "anger." On a 1–8 scale,
this face was rated 6.0 for anger, but 5.6 for disgust, 5.3 for sad, 4.9 for
afraid, and so on in a reliable order. Similarly, the "sadness" expression
was rated 5.9 on sad, but 5.8 on afraid; the "disgust" expression was rated
6.8 on disgust, but 5.7 on angry; the "fear" expression was rated 5.8 on
afraid, but 5.2 on angry.

Russell (1991b) reported quantitative ratings on 6 emotion scales for
the Matsumoto and Ekman (1988) "contempt" expressions. Mean ratings, along with comparable results for the Matsumoto and Ekman
(1988) "anger" expressions, are shown in Table XIII. For the "contempt"
expressions, ratings on contempt were not high, either in an absolute or
in a relative sense. Absolute ratings on a 1–4 scale for the contempt label
were low: the mean, 2.2, was just above "slightly" and below "moderately." The contempt ratings were also low relative to some others. Although contempt ratings were higher than anger ratings, they were not
higher than ratings on the remaining labels and, indeed, were lower
than on disgust and boredom.

For the "anger" expressions, the mean rating on anger, 2.8, was also
between "slightly" and "moderately." Although anger ratings were high-

TABLE XIII   Quantitative Ratings of Facial Expressions Reported to Be of Contempt and Anger

Label	"Contempt" expressions			"Anger" expressions		
	Mean	SD	t^a	Mean	SD	t^b
Boredom	2.75	1.14	3.04[c]	1.17	.52	11.87[d]
Disgust	2.58	0.92	3.01[c]	2.19	.81	3.83[d]
Frustration	2.30	0.90	0.79	3.06	.92	1.40
Contempt	2.17	0.79		2.17	.92	4.97[d]
Scorn	2.05	0.98	0.96	2.44	.97	2.72[c]
Anger	1.64	0.84	4.15[d]	2.83	.97	

Notes: N = 64 for each type of expression. The stimuli were 3 × 5 color prints of photographs from the set, Japanese and Caucasian Facial Expressions of Emotion (JACFEE), developed by Matsumoto & Ekman (1988); eight were of "contempt," and eight were of "anger." The response scale was labeled *not at all* (1), *slightly* (2), *moderately* (3), and *extremely* (4). A repeated-measures analysis of variance (ANOVA) showed that subjects responded differently to the different labels, $F(5, 315) = 12.09$, $p < .001$, for the "contempt" expressions and $F(5, 315) = 39.55$, $p < .001$ for the "anger" expressions.

[a] t test ($df = 63$) examined the difference between ratings for each label and those for *contempt*.

[b] t test ($df = 63$) examined the difference between ratings for each label and those for *anger*.

[c] $p < .01$.

[d] $p < .001$.

er than on most the other labels, they were lower than on *frustration*. The result for *frustration* replicates the free-label result of Tables X and XI.

Conclusions on Response Format

The methods used so far to collect observers' judgments are highly reactive, and each has problems. We know little about the observer's spontaneous response. Knowing more about the spontaneous response, important in its own right, would also help answer some of the questions raised here about the interpretation of available results. For observers in our own culture, of course, each reader has his or her own response as a guide, but the issue is troubling when observers are from another culture.

Only one method, forced choice, supports the conclusion that, across (literate) cultures, a very high proportion of subjects agree on one specific emotion for each of the hypothesized facial expressions. Of course, forced-choice format has its place, but we must be careful in exactly what conclusions we draw from results gathered with forced choice. For example, the question arises whether this method has created a false impression that most subjects would spontaneously use the same specific emotion label for a given face.

When subjects were allowed to choose any label they wanted, they did not restrict themselves to synonyms for the 7 + 2 words used in forced choice, or even to an emotion label. For some types of expression, the "recognition" scores from free labeling were repeatedly lower than those from forced choice. Forced choice might funnel a range of genuinely different interpretations into one choice, thereby inflating the appearance of consensus. When the same subject responded with both forced choice and freely chosen labels, the results corresponded in from 89.9% of cases to as low as 7.7%, depending on the expression (Boucher & Carlson, 1980). A similar conclusion comes from contrasting the various results across the studies of the "contempt" expression: recognition scores from forced choice were high, those from free label were low. The free-label format thus *can* give results different than those given by forced choice, reinforcing the argument earlier that results from forced choice *can* be specific to that method.

If we are to disregard results from the other methods and to base our conclusions solely on results from forced choice, then we would need a convincing argument that forced choice is indeed the method of choice. Various considerations argue in the opposite direction. One study showed that the forced-choice method can produce apparently conflicting or contradictory results, depending on the experimenter's a priori choice of just which emotions to include on the list of options. In addition, the assumptions underlying the forced-choice format (all-or-none, mutually exclusive options) have not been verified by studies with other formats or by studies of the mental concepts for emotion expressed by the words observers are forced to choose among (Russell & Bullock, 1986; Russell, 1989b). Needless to say, forced choice can be useful in certain circumstances. But conclusions about the judgment of emotion from facial expression cannot rely on this one method alone.

The second most commonly used method has been free label. Most of the data on free label are from Western cultures. In the two non-Western cultures studied, the recognition scores were high for some expressions, moderate for some, and negligible for some. Recognition of the "contempt" and "fear" expressions was probably not significant. Such results might appear to offer at least a partial replication of the forced-choice results. But, like forced choice, free label forces subjects to respond in terms of emotion and to choose one emotion label as applicable in an either–or manner.

Importantly different results occur with still different response formats. The most open-ended approach has been used infrequently but did suggest that some subjects might not respond in terms of an emotion. Facial expressions might sometimes be interpreted as parts of instrumental action or in terms of the situation. Quantitative ratings help clarify the freely chosen labels, which appeared to suggest large individual differences; but quantitative ratings and freely chosen labels together indicated that *each* observer finds a range of labels applicable to a given face, to different degrees (Russell & Bullock, 1986, pursue this point). The applicable range includes not just synonyms of one basic emotion but what have been claimed to be distinct emotions. In short, as we move from more restrictive to less restrictive attempts to capture the observer's response, a different interpretation of that response emerges. There appears to be little justification for claims that a facial expression is interpreted in terms of one specific emotion category rather than a broad range of overlapping categories.

Lack of Contextual Information

In the studies listed in Tables II and III, observers knew nothing about the expresser except what was shown in the face. They knew nothing about what caused the facial expression, about the setting in which it occurred, or about the expresser's other behavior, past or present. In folk wisdom, this additional information (collectively known as the expresser's context) is useful in interpreting the facial expression. Thus, whereas a smile in the context of just having received a gift might be interpreted as a sign of pleasure, a smile in the context of just having spilled soup might be interpreted as a sign of embarrassment, and a smile in the context of greeting an adversary might be interpreted as an act of politeness. To refer to a specific facial expression as a "signal" requires that the expression communicate the hypothesized message not only when the face is seen alone, but when seen embedded in a reasonable range of naturally occurring contexts. This prediction of the universality thesis has received little attention, but is important for the hypothesized communication function of facial signals and for the hypothesized evolutionary origin of those signals.

Ekman et al. (1972) reviewed the early studies on this topic, but focused on a different question than the one being raised here. They asked the question of dominance: when both the facial expression and the context are known and when the two are discordant (i.e., when face alone and context alone would suggest different emotions), which source of information is the more influential? They found no simple answer to this question: "There seems to be no question that either source, face or context, can, on given occasions, be more salient or more useful or more of a determinant of the combined judgment than the other" (p. 150).

The results of the early studies are more consistent if the question of dominance is set aside and the question of generalizability is asked: Does the emotion attributed to the expresser when his or her face is seen alone generalize to attributions made when the face is seen in context? The early studies showed consistently that contextual information influences the observer's judgment (Frijda, 1958; Goldberg, 1951; Good-enough & Tinker, 1931; Munn, 1940; Vinacke, 1949). More recent studies also focused on the question of dominance. But again, if the question of generalizability is asked, then the answer is the same. Although the recent studies found mixed results on the question of dominance, all studies found that contextual information influenced the observers' judgment (Fernandez-Dols, Wallbott, & Sanchez, 1991; Fernandez-Dols, Sierra, & Ruiz-Belda, 1993; Knudsen & Muzekari, 1983; Motley & Camden, 1988; Nakamura, Buck, & Kenny, 1990; Spignesi & Shor, 1981; Wallbott, 1988; Watson, 1972).

Studies reviewed in the last two paragraphs can provide only a weak indication on the issue of generalizability. Ekman et al. (1972) pointed to various technical ambiguities in the early studies. But for present purposes, a more important problem is that of sampling. The set of contexts studied was not always representative of the contexts that actually surround facial expressions. In some studies, the pairing of face and context was dictated by a factorial design (all faces paired with all contexts) rather than by the likelihood of that pairing occurring in the nonexperimental world. The judgment process invoked by an unusual pairing might not be the same as that invoked by a more usual pairing. The available evidence therefore provides no strong conclusion, but does demonstrate that context *can* influence the judgment of emotion from the face and therefore that the research strategy of focusing exclusively on judgments of the face alone is of questionable generality to naturally occurring situations.

JUDGMENT STUDIES IN ISOLATED CULTURES: THE EVIDENCE FROM "THOSE ASSOCIATED BUT LITTLE WITH EUROPEANS"

> For six emotions—happiness, fear, anger, sadness, disgust, and surprise—universality of facial expression has been established by showing that members of cultures having no visual contact can correctly recognize one another's expressions. (Brown, 1986, p. 522)

This quotation from an undergraduate textbook underscores the importance attached to the studies of visually isolated cultures, to which I now turn. All of the studies reviewed here so far suffer from one widely acknowledged problem. As Darwin (1872/1965) noted, the question is what occurs with "those who have associated but little with Europeans" (pp. 14–15). Although non-Western subjects were included in the studies cited in Table II, all were students who probably had contact with Westerners in person or through films, television, books, drama, magazines, and so on. The degree of this contact is difficult to estimate, but the possibility exists of their having learned some culture-specific West-

TABLE XIV Five Methods Used with Isolated Cultures

Method	Culture	Reference
1. Standard	Sadong of Borneo	Ekman, Sorenson, & Friesen (1969)
	Fore of New Guinea	Ekman, Sorenson, & Friesen (1969)
2. Free labels	Fore of New Guinea	Sorenson (1975, 1976)
	Bahinemo	Sorenson (1975, 1976)
	Sadong of Borneo	Sorenson (1975, 1976)
3. Dashiell	Fore of New Guinea	Ekman & Friesen (1971); Sorenson (1975, 1976)
	Grand Valley Dani	Unpublished, reported by Ekman (1972)[a]
4. Posing emotions	Fore of New Guinea	Unpublished, reported by Ekman (1972)
5. Selecting photographs	Temuan of Malaysia	Boucher & Carlson (1980)

[a] In a footnote, Ekman et al. (1972) reported, "In a study of another preliterate culture in New Guinea (the Dani), which is considerably more isolated than the Fore, essentially the same results were found (Ekman, 1972; Ekman, Heider, Friesen, & Heider, in preparation)" (p. 162).

ern facial gestures, or a Western interpretation of a given facial pattern. This problem of cultural contact motivated the study of people isolated from Western culture who would provide the most telling answer to this problem.

The evidence on isolated cultures comes from two sources: (1) a series of studies organized and guided by Ekman, Friesen, and Sorenson and carried out from about 1967 to 1970 and (2) a single study conducted by Boucher and Carlson (1980). The principal methods used, the groups studied, and references are given in Table XIV.

The Ekman, Friesen, and Sorenson Studies

This research began when Ekman and Friesen saw films taken by Sorenson and others of two isolated societies in New Guinea (Ekman, 1972, p. 210). The three researchers then traveled to New Guinea and organized a series of studies. The same questions, same concepts, and same stimulus materials reappear in each of the studies, although the studies were conducted with different methods, by different experimenters, and in different places. Thirty-two of the photographs used were published by Sorenson (1975, 1976).

No single account of this entire research program has been published. Lack of a published overview has unfortunate consequences. We do not know the precise original hypothesis: for example, in some studies contempt and disgust were treated as separate emotions, in others as one emotion. Some of the studies were never published in full, but reported in secondary sources, with neither method nor results fully detailed.

Some studies were apparently never reported at all. For instance, Ekman et al. (1969) mentioned that their report concerned data only from the most westernized Fore subjects and that further data were available from less westernized subjects—data that were "similar" with the "exception of the sadness category." Apparently these data were never published. These investigators also reported that South Fore facial expressions were shown to South Fore observers, but apparently these data were never published. It is therefore unclear how many studies were conducted altogether, precisely what hypotheses were tested, in some cases exactly what methods were used or results obtained, and how selective the published reports have been.

In this research program, experimental control appears to have been low. Such problems are not surprising in cross-cultural work of this sort, but they are important nonetheless in evaluating the results. Sorenson (1976) commented,

> Neither Ekman nor Friesen, who participated in this part of the study, knew Melanesian-Pidgen or Fore. My own Melanesian-Pidgen was good; but I was not up to following native discourse or making myself understood in Fore beyond the simplest messages. Therefore, for the least acculturated Fore we had to rely on Fore translator-assistants to explain the task and to relate the stimulus stories. We were not able to monitor this communication. In view of the Fore communicational conventions, it was likely that at least some responses were influenced by feedback between translator and subject. The Fore, even those trying to be most Western, could not be expected to have internalized our Western concepts of a testing situation sufficiently to avoid "leaking" information. The suggestion that free exchange of information was "cheating" was quite incomprehensible to the Fore and alien to their view of language as an element of cooperative interaction among close associates. The best we could do was to impress our assistants continually with the importance of not discussing the pictures with the subjects, and particularly, not telling them which pictures to select or suggesting key features for which to watch. The effect of our cautions could not be determined. . . .
>
> Both native assistants and subjects were generally very eager to do things in the Western way. Like other things Western, our pictures and procedures were the subject of considerable interest and active discussion by the behaviorally alert Fore. They were quick to seize on the subtlest cues for an indication of how they should respond and react. This undoubtedly skewed our results. (pp. 139–140)

Four principal methods were used to gather data from four separate cultures, as outlined in Table XIV. I consider each method in turn.

Standard Method

Two of the reported studies (Ekman et al., 1969) used the standard method already discussed: subjects were shown preselected still photo-

TABLE XV   Percentage of Agreement with Prediction for Isolated Cultures

	Standard method			Dashiell method	
Culture:	Fore		Sadong	Fore[a]	Dani
Language:	Pidgin	Fore	Bidayuh	Fore	Dani
N	18	14	15	130	34
Facial expression					
"Happiness"	99	82	92	92	98
"Fear"	46	54	40	88[b]	80[b]
"Anger"	56	50	64	90	68[b]
"Disgust/Contempt"[c]	29	44	<23[d]	85	91
"Surprise"[e]	38[d]	19[d]	36	98	89
"Sadness"	55	—[d]	52	81	77

Note: For the Standard Method, there were six response options; 16.7% is the level due to chance.

[a]This was a group of Fore children. Similar results were obtained with Fore adults.

[b]Median values given by Ekman (1972).

[c]There is no Neo-Melanesian Pidgin word for disgust or contempt, and therefore a phrase was used: "looking at something which stinks."

[d]Modal choice was another emotion, and no figure of percentage correct was given, although it must be less than the figure given.

[e]There is no Neo-Melanesian Pidgin word for surprise, and there a phrase was used: "looking at something new."

graphs largely of posed facial expressions and then were asked to choose one of six alternatives. The results are summarized in the left half of Table XV. The three cases involving facial expressions of "happiness" obtained high agreement with prediction (82–99%)—the subjects apparently understood the instructions and could perform the task. Of the remaining 15 cases, modal responses were as predicted in 12, although the proportion of subjects agreeing with prediction was greater than 50% in only 6. The range was from 29% to 56% for Pidgin-speaking Fore, from less than 19% to 54% for the Fore-speaking Fore, and from less than 23% to 64% for the Sadong. Statistical tests compared obtained results with completely random selection of labels, which would result in 16.7% agreement. No statistical test was offered to show that results for negative emotions were reliably greater than what would be expected by random selection among negative labels (25%). The Fore-speaking Fore chose *anger* for the "sad" faces 56% of the time, a greater degree of agreement than for any other set of faces except "happiness."

Overall, with the notable exception of happiness, the results were less in agreement with prediction than were those obtained from non-isolated, literate cultures, summarized earlier in Table II. Of course, the illiterate and isolated subjects were unfamiliar with being questioned and with the idea of a scientific experiment. Even if the 12 of 15 cases for nonpositive emotions did yield results greater than chance, the results must be viewed in light of the problems already described with the standard method and the likelihood "that at least some responses were influenced by feedback between translator and subject" (Sorenson, 1976).

Another fact to remember about these two studies is that the subjects "had extensive contact with Western culture" (Ekman & Friesen, 1971, p. 125). The Fore for whom data were reported were the "most Western-ized" (Ekman et al., 1969, p. 87). They were "most influenced by con-tacts with Westerners (government, missionaries, and others)" (p. 87). Of the Sadong, "many had seen a few movies" (p. 88). As Ekman and Friesen (1971) later acknowledged:

> because all the cultures [that Ekman et al., 1969] compared had expo-sure to some of the same mass media portrayals of facial behavior, mem-bers of these cultures might have learned to recognize the same set of conventions, or become familiar with each other's different facial behavior. (p. 125)

Freely Chosen Labels

Freely chosen labels were reported for two groups by Sorenson (1975, 1976): 100 Fore and 71 Bahinemo (who were more isolated than the Fore).[11] The Bahinemo showed no consistent association between facial expression and emotion label, except for a tendency to see all the (Cau-casion) faces as angry.

Separate results were reported for those Fore with most, intermedi-ate, and least contact with Western culture; and a summary is provided in Table XVI. The data from the Fore that Sorenson provided do not always allow calculation of the percentage agreeing with prediction, but do give some indication. For "happiness," "anger," and "fear" expres-sions, the modal response was as predicted; consequently for these three, the median "recognition" score is available: 67% for "happiness," 49% for "anger," and 30% for "fear" expression, respectively. Figures are also available for two of the three groups for the "contempt" expression; therefore 28% would be the median. For the "surprise" expression, one group selected *surprise* 26% of the time; the median would be somewhat less. For "sadness" and "disgust" neither the first nor second choice was as predicted; percentage correct would therefore be less than the figures shown in Table XVI. In addition, a clear violation of prediction occurred when a majority in each of the three Fore-speaking Fore labeled the

---

[11] Sorenson (1975, 1976) also presented results from 15 members of the Sadong and seemed to imply that the response measure was a freely chosen label. However, the same results had been presented earlier and it was clear that the response measure was forced choice (Ekman et al., 1969).

TABLE XVI   Freely Chosen Modal Label and Percentage to Facial Expressions of Emotion

Facial expression	Fore-speaking Fore					
	Most contact		Intermediate contact		Least contact	
	Label	%	Label	%	Label	%
"Happiness"	Happiness	82	Happiness	67	Happiness	60
"Surprise"	Fear	45	Fear	31	Happiness[a]	31
"Sadness"	Anger	56	Anger	57	Anger	53
"Anger"	Anger	50	Anger	49	Anger	48
"Fear"	Fear	54	Fear	30	Fear	23
"Contempt"	Anger[b]	36	Contempt	28	Anger	27
"Disgust"	Contempt	39	Happiness	24	Happiness	23

Note: Response, when as predicted, is underlined.
[a]The second most common response was the one predicted, surprise (26%).
[b]The second most common response was the one predicted, contempt (29%).

"sad" expressions as *anger*. (Recall that the majority of the Fore chose *anger* for the "sad" expression in the forced-choice method as well.)

Overall, agreement with prediction among Fore was less than in free-label data in less isolated cultures. It is also not known how subjects' actual responses were clustered together to produce the results shown in Table XVI. In light of previous reports of freely chosen labels, I doubted that the Fore observers had limited themselves to precisely six labels. When asked this question, Sorenson (personal communication, July 6, 1991) wrote that the subjects produced "hundreds of words . . . stories and all kinds of things." Presumably, the results of Table XVI indicate the amount of agreement obtained on fairly broad clusters of responses.

The Dashiell Method

Because of disappointing results produced so far, the researchers turned to a method introduced by Dashiell, in which each emotion is represented by a story. On the trial for happiness, for instance, the subject was told that someone has just met a friend and is happy. The subject was then asked to select a facial expression for the story protagonist. A summary of the results is shown in the right half of Table XV. Much higher "recognition" scores were obtained with the Dashiell method than had been obtained earlier with the standard method or with free labeling. It is especially unfortunate that these studies have not been published in full. The Dashiell method has most of the features of the standard method, but some unique features as well, which are worth considering in detail.

First, these experiments were conducted in the field rather than in a laboratory, and it is unlikely that the experimenters were able to control precisely the information given to the subject. For example, it is difficult to tell an emotional story without altering one's tone of voice and facial expression. The kind of leakage described by Sorenson (1975) might have similarly played a role.

Second, the response measure reduced the number of choices: all Dani subjects and all Fore children were given 2, and all Fore adults 3, photographs to choose from. Random response selection would therefore produce 50% or 33% correct, respectively. The results reported with this measure were not corrected for guessing. An even higher level could sometimes be produced by simply distinguishing positive from negative responses. If a sad story was given to a Fore adult, for example, and the choice was among 3 options, a "sad," an "angry," and a "happy" facial expression, then 50% recognition would be achieved by distinguishing positive from negative expressions (eliminating the "happy" expression and choosing randomly between the other two).

The overall results also depend on just which faces subjects were shown on a given trial, and not all possible pairs or triads were included. Indeed, some important ones were omitted. For the Fore sample given the disgust story, an "anger" expression was never one of the possible choices. For the Fore children given the fear story, a "surprise" expression was never a possible choice; for those given the anger story, a "disgust" expression was never one of the possible choices. Therefore, the precise alternatives the subjects were given must be considered. For example, the median recognition score given in Table XV for the Dani responses to the anger story (68%) derives from four judgments: anger–happiness 94%, anger–fear 76%, anger–sadness 61%, and anger–disgust 48%, where random choice would be expected to yield 50%. If we set aside the anger–happiness result because it could be based on a simple positive–negative discrimination, then the median would be 61% (22% when corrected for guessing). This apparent ability to associate the anger story with the predicted face varies (whether reliably is not known) with the alternative. Similar examination of specific alternatives for the fear story showed that Fore adults were as or more likely to choose the "surprise" expression as the "fear" expression. (Fore children were not asked to make this discrimination.)

Third, over the course of the experiment, subjects could have learned to associate faces and stories in something like a "learning to learn" procedure. Each subject participated in a number of trials, and for each trial for a given emotion story, exactly one of the expression options recurred, namely, the "correct" expression. Some subjects might have noticed which kind of facial expression always appeared with a given story. For example, suppose that on the first trial a Dani hears the story about disgust (the protagonist smells something bad) and is shown two pictures, a frown and wrinkled nose. Suppose further that this subject has no idea which facial expression to choose for the disgust story, and so chooses randomly. Now, on the next trial that concerns the disgust story, the wrinkled nose reappears, this time paired with a different alternative. Whatever alternative is offered, that subject, eager to accommodate the experimenter, might remember the wrinkled nose from the first trial—if so, that subject will have learned that the wrinkled nose goes with the disgust story. Moreover, now suppose that the next trial concerns, say, the surprise story, and that the choice is between the "surprise" expression and the wrinkled nose of "disgust." Our subject might now guess that the wrinkled nose is *not* correct for this story. Thus, he or she could select the other (appropriate) face. On later trials for other emotions, this same subject could begin to guess the correct facial expression by eliminating alternatives previously associated with other stories. Of course, no evidence shows that anything like this fictional reconstruction actually occurred. But, that some such "learning to learn" could have occurred on some trials for some types of facial expression for some subjects cannot be ruled out. The appropriate control conditions were not included that would allow us to do so.

Fourth, the story and the emotion were confounded. For happiness, it is unclear whether the Fore or Dani subject selected the smile as indicating happiness or as the response to meeting a friend. Or, whether they selected the wrinkled nose as indicating disgust, or just a response to foul odors. Thus, the story alone, with no emotion presented or inferred by the subject, might have accounted for or contributed to the selection of a facial expression. Ekman's (1980) photographs of the Fore show various facial movements, but the question is whether the Fore interpreted these movements as expressions of emotion.

Imagine you are the subject in this experiment and that you know nothing about emotions. You are told the "anger" story concerning a protagonist about to fight. You might reasonably select the face with glaring eyes and set jaw. You are told a surprise story concerning someone looking at something new and unexpected. You might reasonably select the face staring at something. You are told a "fear" story concerning someone who sees a dangerous wild pig. You might reasonably pick a face that is tense, or where the eyes are staring, or where the mouth appears about to yell. With the data available, it is impossible to disentangle face-emotion knowledge from face-situation knowledge. Conceivably, the results might have little or nothing to do with emotion per se.

It is undoubtedly informative that people in isolated, illiterate cultures associate the same facial movements with greeting a friend, fighting, and smelling something bad, as do we in the West. The question is how to interpret the information. It might be argued that the only plausible interpretation is in terms of emotion. If these stories captured pan-cultural antecedents of emotion, as specified a priori by the experimenter's theory (and no other methodological problems occurred), or if we knew that the Fore associated each story with a specific emotion, then emotion would remain a compelling interpretation. Unfortunately, this line of defense is undermined by the way in which the stories were developed in prestudies (Fernandez-Dols, 1991): "Simple stories were developed within each culture to be relevant to that culture" (Ekman, 1972, p. 271), and emotion played no role in generating the stories. For example, in the prestudy of the Fore, some members were shown the photographs of facial expressions and asked to make up a story about the person shown. The subjects were shown a smile, and they said that the smiling person was greeting a friend. They were shown a wrinkled nose, and they said that the person was smelling something bad. Later, in the actual study, this process was simply reversed. That is, other Fore were later told the story of someone greeting a friend and asked to select the face most associated with that story; they selected the smile. Told the story of someone smelling something bad, they selected the wrinkled nose. In neither phase was emotion necessarily involved.

We Westerners seem to infer readily that happiness must have been involved in the association between the smile and greeting a friend, or that disgust was involved in the association between smelling and wrinkling the nose. But we have no evidence it was something that the Fore inferred or even thought about. We Westerners find it plausible to suppose that the Fore think in terms of happiness, disgust, and other emotions, but the purpose of this study was to gather evidence on this question. Peoples of other cultures speaking other languages may conceptualize psychological states somewhat differently than those of Indo-European cultures (for a review, see Russell, 1991a). Some cultures do not have a word equivalent to *emotion*, nor do they appear to categorize emotions in the same manner as that demonstrated in English.

The Dashiell method creates several uncertainties. Some of these uncertainties arise from the features it shares with the standard method. Some arise from its unique features and field setting. Each of its associated problems separately could have inflated the amount of agreement with prediction. When the various problems all co-occur in the same study, it is impossible to estimate their joint influence. The within-subject design of this experiment coupled with the small number of emotions studied (and perhaps the kind of leaking described by Sorenson, 1976) may have provided subjects with clues to solving a puzzle. Even a partial solution could have inflated the percentage of agreement. It is therefore impossible to know how much, if at all, the obtained results were due to subjects' associating emotions with facial expressions.

Posing Expressions

In a review of the literature, Ekman (1973) referred to a Study 2 in Ekman and Friesen (1971). Ekman and Friesen reported this study in a single sentence: "Visually isolated members of the South Fore posed emotions, and college students in the United States accurately judged the emotion intended from their videotaped facial behavior" (p. 128). Elsewhere, Ekman (1972) gave more detail. The videotapes were of 9 members of the Fore (the number taped was not specified). The American judges were 34 university students each of whom viewed videotapes of all 9 Fore and apparently chose one emotion label from a list of six. The "recognition" scores were as follows: happiness 73%, sadness 68%, anger 51%, disgust 46%, surprise 27%, and fear 18%. The last two figures did not differ significantly from those expected by chance.

As in the Dashiell method, the Fore were given stories to help them pose the facial expressions: a wrinkled nose was produced in response to the story of smelling something bad. Once again, it is unclear whether the Fore could pose a facial expression for disgust per se, or could simply show what happens when they smell something bad. The judgment task given the American subjects was within subject and used a forced-choice response format, with all the problems entailed.

The Boucher and Carlson Study: Selecting Photographs

Boucher and Carlson (1980) studied 31 Temuans, a forest-dwelling group of proto-Malay aboriginies. "While these people are by no means the cultural isolates studied by Ekman in New Guinea, their contact with Western culture is quite limited" (p. 276). Each Temuan was shown 25 photographs of five American men, each posing from 4–6 facial displays the authors believed expressive of basic emotions. The subject first saw all photographs (4–6) posed by a single actor. The subject was asked to choose the one photo where the American poser looked, say, angry. The subject was then shown the next poser and asked to select a different emotion, and so on through the five posers. This procedure was repeated until the subject had selected a photograph for each emotion available from each poser. The observer was not asked to select any emotion not present for a given poser.

On trials in which the subject was asked to select an "expression of happiness," 90.3% of responses were as predicted. The corresponding figures were 84.5% for "disgust," 79.8% for "surprise," 74.0% for "sadness," 72.9% for "anger," and 53.2% for "fear." Each of these figures exceeded chance to a reliable degree.

The facial stimuli were posed and preselected, the design was within subject, and each subject was shown the entire set of stimuli at least 5 times. Although the usual role of word (e.g., *happy*) and photograph (e.g., smile) was reversed in this study, the method is again forced choice, this time between 4 to 6 alternative faces. The method would therefore be subject to some of the same problems as those created by the standard method, including forced-choice response format. In addition, the number of trials for each emotion varied from 2 (because only 2 posers posed "fear") to 6 (because all 6 posers posed "anger," "disgust," and "happiness"). Thus the subject was asked to select fear on only 2 occasions, namely those in which the hypothesized fear face was present. Some subjects might have noticed this fact. If so, then this clue might have allowed those subjects to eliminate the "fear" alternative when another emotion was the target. Suppose, then, that on one trial the subject was asked to select the angry person among 4 alternatives, but could eliminate the "fear" and "happiness" faces. Then, the number of alternatives actually relevant would be half the nominal number. It is therefore difficult to estimate actual base-rate probabilities.

Conclusion

Recognizing that studies of literate societies in the modern world of mass communication could not answer the question of universality, Ekman et al. (1969) turned to isolated, illiterate societies. Ekman et al. (1969) hypothesized that sadness, like other basic emotions, has a biologically based, universally recognized facial signal. Photographs of the hypothesized facial signal for sadness were shown to Fore-speaking observers reared in a culture relatively isolated from outside influence. When asked what emotion the person with the "sad" expression was feeling, over 50% replied *anger*. Shown the "sad" expression, and asked more directly whether the person was happy, surprised, afraid, angry, disgusted, or sad, 56% said *angry*. Told a story about someone who was angry *and about to fight* and shown two photographs, the hypothesized anger expression and the hypothesized sad expression, 61% selected the anger expression, 39% the sad. This pattern of results from the Fore is not easy to reconcile with the original hypothesis.

Even if the pattern of results were more clear cut, the methods used with isolated societies leave many uncertainties. Although several different methods were used, some design features remained the same. For example, all studies used the same still photographs of mainly posed facial expressions. In most cases, observers provided their response in some sort of forced-choice format, either choosing among words or photographs. All were within-subject designs. No information was provided on whether the facial stimuli used corresponded to naturally occurring facial expressions in the culture studied. No information was provided that the emotion response categories correspond to indigenous concepts. The lack of an indigenous word for *surprise* among the Fore reinforces this concern.

The easiest comparison across cultures is with studies using the same method. In the isolated cultures, the standard method showed a nonrandom association between some facial expressions and emotion labels. Nevertheless, because the particular subjects had at least some contact with Westerners and Western mass media, because of the problems associated with the standard method, and because of poor experimental control, these studies could not provide a strong test of the experimenter's hypothesis. These technical problems aside, the specific hypothesis that happiness, surprise, fear, anger, disgust, and sadness were highly recognizable from facial expression fit the data clearly only for happiness. This negative result has not received the attention it deserves. The data on happiness demonstrated that the subjects understood the task per se, which in any case was quite simple. Highly selected intense facial expressions were shown one at a time. A list of six emotion names was read to each subject. Each name on the list supposedly represented one discrete basic, universal emotion. The list remained the same for every photo and was "repeatedly read to them after each photo" (Ekman, 1973, p. 210). Other than happiness, the emotion label was not associated with specific facial expressions in the manner and to the degree predicted.

Studies of freely chosen labels did not produce much support either. One group, the Bahinemo, showed no consistent pattern except a tendency to label all facial expressions as *anger*. The other group, the Fore, gave partial agreement with prediction. How their free labels were clustered together was not specified, and therefore no strong conclusions are possible.

The researchers then changed methods. The results that agreed most with prediction (Boucher & Carlson, 1980) were apparently obtained with the most Westernized subjects, and their method had problems associated with within-subject design, preselected posed still photographs, and forced-choiced response format, as well as potential internal problems of its own. The other results that agreed with prediction were gathered with the Dashiell method. This method had the most serious problems, the combination of leakage from translator to subject, a design that allows learning to learn, and a confounding of emotion with story. Moreover, the story had been generated within the culture in response to the facial expression. Even so, fear was not distinguished from surprise, nor anger from disgust. Technical problems aside, this last result indicates that if the Fore and Dani interpret facial expressions in terms of emotions, they might do so in terms of broader clusters than those indicated by the English words *surprise, fear, anger,* and *disgust.*

TABLE XVII   Median Percentage Agreement for Forced Choice

Culture group	"Happy"	"Fear"	"Disgust"	"Anger"	"Surprise"	"Sadness"
Western	96.4	77.5	82.6	81.2	87.5	80.5
Non-Western literate	89.2	65.0	65.0	63.0	79.2	76.0
Illiterate, isolated	92.0	46.0	29.0	56.0	36.0	52.0

Note: Figures are median values from Tables II and XV for results gathered with the standard method. The number of groups was 20 for Western, 11 for non-Western, and 3 for illiterate isolated cultures.

The focus of these studies was on agreement with an a priori hypothesis, but some unexpected but important results were also obtained, such as the Fore labeling the "sad" photographs as *anger*, both in the free label and in the standard forced-choice task. Because this result was not anticipated, it is less likely to be accounted for by experimental demand or help from the translator. None of the studies were aimed at revealing the role of culture in interpreting facial expressions—quite the contrary. Nevertheless, such evidence suggests that culture does play some role in the interpretation of facial expressions.

The data on isolated cultures are also consistent with the hypothesis that degree of contact with Western culture is directly related to the amount of agreement with the predictions of the Western investigators. The most straightforward comparison relies on studies that were conducted with the standard method. A clear trend is shown in Table XVII for all types of facial expression except "happy." Although the college students who served as subjects might have obscured cultural differences, the amount of agreement with prediction from non-Western literate cultures was reliably lower than that from Western cultures. In turn, more isolated cultures provided even weaker agreement with prediction. And this decrement occurred despite a softening of methodological control mentioned by Sorenson (1976) to accommodate illiterate subjects unfamiliar with experimental procedures. In addition, only among the isolated cultures were there strong contradictions of the experimenter's predictions, as when the Fore consistently labeled the "sad" expression as *anger*.

Further evidence for the same trend can be seen across the studies of isolated cultures. The greatest agreement with prediction was obtained by Boucher and Carlson (1980), whose subjects were apparently the most westernized. Among the groups given the standard method, Pidgin-speaking Fore were the only group to produce above-chance agreement on all six types of facial expression, and Pidgin is a language created for communication between cultures. In the studies of freely chosen labels, again greater agreement with prediction came from the Fore, who had more contact with Westerners, and less agreement—indeed no agreement—with prediction came from the Bahinemo, who had less contact with Westerners.

With the important exception of the Ducci et al. (1982) study, the comparisons just offered to suggest the role of culture are after-the-fact interpretations. Cultural contact was confounded with education, language, and familiarity with experimental procedures. On the other hand, the cultural differences in Tables II and III are reliable, and the emergence of cultural variation in a set of studies specifically designed to demonstrate universality should encourage researchers to follow Ducci et al.'s (1982) important lead by exploring the role of culture directly. If cultural variations are reliable, then the question arises, how do people in non-Western cultures interpret facial movements?

VALIDITY OF THE JUDGMENT STUDIES

I now turn to a summary evaluation of the evidence. Do the studies show what previous reviews have claimed they show? I consider ecological, convergent, and internal validity, although the concerns are somewhat overlapping.

Ecological Validity

Little information is available on what facial expressions occur naturally in the various societies studied and in what frequency and in what contexts. Little information is available on what interpretations observers naturally make of the facial expressions they actually encounter and in what contexts those interpretations occur. It seems unlikely that the facial expressions used as stimuli, the limited options sometimes given subjects for making their judgments, and the experimental contexts in which judgments were made were representative samples of naturally occurring stimuli, responses, and judgmental contexts.

Even if the results reviewed in this chapter are internally valid, they would not necessarily tell us what occurs in everyday situations. Preselected posed facial expressions, forced-choice response format, within-subject design, and lack of contextual information are potential challenges to ecological validity. For example, with a forced-choice response format under experimental conditions, subjects might associate soft hair with cowardice, or coarse hair with bravery, as suggested by Aristotle. Even if they do, that result would not tell us that when soft hair is encountered in everyday events, it is noticed or so coded. Soft hair would be embedded in many other features, especially behavior, which might so overwhelm the judgment that the effect of soft hair is negligible. To return to faces, suppose that facial expressions rarely or seldom occur in the intensity and clarity portrayed in the photographs shown to subjects, or that observers rarely or seldom have the time to study the face as they do when shown a still photograph. Then, their degree of recognition of specific emotions from the kind of photographs used in the experimental context might not tell us what happens in most everyday face-to-face encounters.[12] This concern is reinforced by the decline in recognition when features of method are altered.

The preceding comments carry no implication of criticism of the original researchers. Providing such information was not their purpose. However, I want to argue that ecological validity must be or must become a concern. I have three reasons in mind. First, as is evident in Table I, reviewers of this literature have not limited their conclusions to the experimental context (see also Footnote 2). Apparently, reviewers assumed the available evidence to be ecologically valid. Writers in this field have not sufficiently emphasized the lack of available information concerning ecological questions. For example, in summarizing their findings, Ekman and Friesen (1975) wrote,

> This book is about faces and feelings—your own and those of the people around you. The first focus is on what the feelings look like, in other people's faces and in your own. Photographs show the facial blueprints of the major emotions. . . . You can use this information about the blueprints of facial expression to better understand the feelings of others, even when they are trying not to reveal their feelings. Or you can use the knowledge of the blueprints of facial expression to learn about your own face, to become more aware of what your face is telling you about how you feel and what your face is telling others. . . . This book is for psychotherapists, ministers, physicians and nurses, trial lawyers, personnel manag-

---

[12] Researchers had their reasons, of course, for not attending to ecological questions. For example, facial stimuli were posed and carefully selected because natural expressions were said to be often inhibited or modulated by display rules (Ekman, 1972; Izard & Malatesta, 1987). The word *often* raises questions. If "pure" (uninhibited and unmodulated) expressions are rare but nevertheless do occur, then it still should be possible to obtain photographs of them for scientific purposes. So, the question is, why not? In the extreme case that uninhibited, unmodulated expressions are so rare that no photographs are possible, then the question is, do people ever see the pure facial expressions? If not, how on Ekman and Friesen's (1975) theory, do children acquire the ability to associate emotions and faces? And what is the purpose of a theory about a phenomenon that so rarely occurs? Izard (1977) argued that at least infants show the pure facial expressions, but this argument has been disputed by Oster et al. (1992) and Camras (1992).

It has also been argued that still photographs fail to capture the full impact of a facial expression because actual facial expressions are moving. Thus, exaggerated poses merely compensate for having still rather than moving expressions. One problem with this solution is that a moving expression might be interpreted not just more easily, but in a different manner than still expressions. In any case, the solution is not to compensate for one problem by introducing another but by studying moving expressions. Shimoda, Argyle, and Ricci Bitti (1978) used videotapes of posed facial expressions and obtained overall recognition scores of 50.3% from English, 47.4% from Italian, and 51.0% from Japanese observers.

ers, salesmen, teachers, actors . . . The psychotherapist . . . must be alert to what the face may tell him about his patient's feelings. The patient's face may show the emotion being experienced even when it is too upsetting to put into words. . . . The trial lawyer often can't trust the words of a witness or client. He needs another source, such as the face, to tell him how the person really feels. (pp. 1–3)

Ekman (1989) later pointed out that "there are no data about how many expressions for each emotion are universal. Nor is it known how often these universal expressions are seen in social life" (p. 154).

The second reason concerns those theories of emotion that have been said to be supported by this evidence. The theories of Ekman (1972), Izard (1971), and Tomkins (1962, 1963) consider the advantages of an emotion-signaling system so great as to have affected the course of human evolution. This aspect of their theories implies that universal facial expressions occur and are recognized in natural settings (or at least were in the past).

Ekman and Friesen (1975) wrote that in every generation children must learn anew the emotional meaning of each facial expression:

> no one taught you how to read those signals . . . you were not born with the knowledge. You have to pick it up. . . . [When you follow] the rules for translating a particular set of facial wrinkles into the judgment that a person is angry, afraid, etc., you do so automatically, on the basis of habits established long ago. [pp. 7–8].

This mechanism of acquiring the ability to recognize emotions from facial expressions presupposes that each child is exposed to enough examples of the facial expressions and sufficient cues to the associated emotion.

My final reason for emphasizing ecological validity is that interpretation of the kind of results reviewed here may depend on implicit assumptions about ecological distribution. Let me illustrate this dependency with an imaginary study on perception of height. The stimulus set consists of 15 men: 3 men 3'6", 3 men 5'1", 3 men 5'10", 3 men 6'5", and 3 men 7'2". Every subject responds to the full stimulus set. Responses are gathered with a forced-choice format with the options *midget*, *short*, *average*, *tall*, and *giant*. I would guess that subjects would assign the 15 stimuli to the 5 response options with very high agreement, and that cross-cultural studies would show high if not perfect agreement. If so, the results would then appear to show 5 discrete specific categories of height, easily and universally recognized. The results would appear to refute the dimensional view of a single continuum from *short* to *tall*. Of course, no one would design or carry out such a study. If carried out, the study would not be published. If published, it would not be believed. Readers would notice that the method had produced a misleading result. The ecological distribution of height is violated; the response options are designed to fit the stimulus categories. No one would find the study valid because everyone knows that height is distributed as a continuum, not 5 discrete categories. In this study of height, the flaws of method are obvious, because we know the ecological distribution. Of course, emotions and facial configurations do not form one simple obvious continuum and this imaginary study is too simple when applied to the ecology of emotion. The implicit assumptions in the design of the studies reviewed here might be correct—or, they might not be, especially as we move to more distant cultures.

To summarize, the studies reviewed in this chapter were not designed with the question of ecological validity in mind, and those who advocate the universality thesis did not always emphasize its ecological assumptions and implications. Nevertheless, the universality thesis is ultimately about what happens in natural situations. Moreover, inferences drawn from the available evidence and interpretation of that evidence rest on assumptions about the ecological distribution of expressions and the spontaneous interpretation of those expressions. Therefore, ecological questions must be raised. On most such questions, little or no information is available. What little information we have on spontaneous expressions, on unselected expressions, on freely given responses, and on judgments of the face in context raise the possibility that results from the standard method may not tell us what happens in natural settings. This possibility exists in all cultures, but is especially troubling in less familiar cultures.

Convergent Validity

The studies of Table II as well as of Ekman and Friesen (1986), and Ekman and Heider (1988) used methods similar enough to define a *standard method*. The similarity in method in the studies cited raises the question of generalizability to other methods. From responses of college students, we cannot necessarily infer how other samples would respond. From judges' responses to the forced-choice list, we cannot necessarily infer their responses gathered in other ways.

What's more important, there are good reasons to question the generalizability of results gathered with the standard method. Student subjects in more recent studies might have been familiar with the universality thesis. Previewing and the within-subjects design allows subjects to compare and contrast the stimuli. The forced-choice response format has been shown capable of producing the appearance of consensus even in the absence of the predicted emotion category.

Some degree of convergent validity has been demonstrated. The various studies listed in Table II did use slightly different procedures, stimuli, and lists of response options. For some facial expressions, freely generated labels produced results near those produced by forced choice and therefore demonstrated convergent validity across these two response formats. However, this result was limited to some types of facial expression and largely to Western cultures; for other expressions, convergence was reduced or even failed. Two studies used the Dashiell method (in which a story is substituted for the emotion label) (Ekman & Friesen, 1971). And Boucher and Carlson (1980) reversed the standard procedure and asked observers to select a photograph in response to the emotion label. Although the Dashiell method and Boucher and Carlson's method introduce their own problems of interpretation, their use is also a step toward demonstrating convergent validity.

In the above studies, one element of the standard method was altered, but other elements generally remained. For example, in the studies of freely chosen labels, the design was within subject, the stimuli were preselected posed expressions, and so on. Several studies are available on what happens when two elements of the standard method are altered. First, when spontaneous rather than posed expressions were studied, and when all the expressions rather than preselected ones were studied, no convincing evidence for anything beyond a positive–negative discrimination was found. Second, Knudsen and Muzekari (1983) examined the combination of context and forced choice. They allowed subjects an option: subjects could choose from the usual list of emotions or they could write in their own response. Half the subjects were given the usual no-context standard procedure. The other half were given a one-sentence description of the expresser's context. These latter subjects were significantly more likely to choose the write-in option. Thus forced choice may be less adequate when context is known. Third, Motley and Camden (1988) used spontaneous rather than posed facial expressions in a study on the relative influence of facial and contextual information. Unlike other studies on this question, here contextual information dominated in every case. In other words, lack of contextual information combined with posed facial expression may produce a unique result.

To summarize, convergent validity requires that any proposition be supported by results from an array of methods. Some convergence has been demonstrated, but the question of convergent validity is not really what results obtain when the standard method is kept intact except for one or two elements. Rather, the question is whether the same results occur across a broad range of methods. Little evidence of this sort is available. Generally less supportive results occur in studies where even one feature of the standard method is altered. Moreover, the results are consistent with lower recognition and recognition in terms of broader categories. Thus, the conclusion of easy recognition in terms of specific emotion categories currently rests on what I have called the standard method. The validity of that method is the next topic.

Internal Validity

It might be argued that the evidence reviewed here is like much of the evidence available in psychology today. Questions of ecological and convergent validity can be raised, but they should not be allowed to undermine the importance of what has been learned. It might be argued that the available studies on the universality thesis demonstrate competence rather than performance—what observers *can* do, if not what they actually do in natural settings or even in other experimental settings. If valid, such a demonstration—especially across a range of cultures—would be of theoretical importance, because it would reveal a human capacity. That such a demonstration was the goal of Izard's (1971) studies can be inferred from his explanation for using preselected posed facial stimuli. Indeed, some points raised here so far, such as preselection of stimuli, posed expressions, and lack of contextual information, do not directly bear on the internal validity of such a demonstration.

Potential threats to internal validity varied from study to study. These included the instructions to subjects, the forced-choice response format, previewing, the within-subject design, the possibility that subjects were familiar with or trained in the experimental hypothesis, confounds, feedback between translator and subject, learning to learn, and experimenter expectancy.[13] Still, I would not argue that any one of these features alone provides a complete alternative explanation of the full array of results seen here.

A more general problem arises from the *combination* of several of the standard design elements that recurred in many of the studies. For example, the forced-choice response format combined with the stimulus set and the within-subject design might alert the subject to what is expected. Preselection of posed facial expressions creates a special stimulus set: maximally similar within types of expression and maximally discriminable between types. The within-subject design then invites subjects to notice the composition of that full stimulus set. In the standard method, the subject could easily notice if, for example, there were three nearly identical wrinkled noses, three beaming smiles, three glaring frowns, three sneers, and so on—or whatever number of each type is used. Whatever the number of types of expression, the forced-choice

---

[13] The articles provided no discussion of any precautions taken regarding experimenter expectancy or demand effects and no debriefing of subjects on the possibility of such effects. Ekman et al. (1991b) recently commented that they "always thoroughly explained the task and then encouraged subjects to ask questions about the task before proceeding. . . . we have found that subjects better understand what is expected of them after trying it a few times" (p. 294).

response format then typically provided a corresponding number of emotion labels; if seven types of facial expression were shown, then generally seven alternative emotion labels are provided. And judges attempt to use each response category option equally often (Parducci, 1965).

But the greater threat to internal validity may come from a simpler mechanism. No one feature of method or combination of features need be a fatal flaw; rather, various features all pushing in the same direction could have had a cumulative impact. Suppose that each element of the standard method adds only a small increment to the total recognition score, each element nudging the observer in the direction of the experimental hypothesis. That is, suppose that having a within-subject rather than between-subject design increases the recognition score by a few percentage points; similarly for previewing, fixed order of presentation, experimenter expectancy, instructions to observers, and forced-choice response format. As already described, what evidence we have suggests that some of these method factors may have had a large impact on recognition scores, but suppose that the impact of each element is only modest. If so, as we subtract the influence of each method factor in turn, the recognition score would decline. Until more evidence is gathered, one can only guess what the final result would be.

For such a cumulative effect to be worrisome, it need not have influenced results for every facial expression to the same degree. For example, suppose that everyone effortlessly and spontaneously labeled the "happy" expression as *happy*. If so, changes in method would leave its recognition score high. Similarly, suppose that everyone recognizes an unpleasant expression. But would they discriminate *within* the set of negative expressions—"anger," "disgust," "fear," and "sadness"? For these four expressions, the median recognition score from the standard method was about 82% for Western literate cultures, about 65% for non-Western literate cultures, and about 49% for the isolated, illiterate cultures. All of these figures are well above the level (25%) that could be achieved by choosing randomly among these four labels. Nevertheless, replacing the forced-choice response format with free label was generally found to lower recognition scores. Replacing the within-subject design with a between-subject design lowered recognition scores. What would be the recognition scores for these four expressions when the study is between subject and includes no previewing, no experimenter expectancy, and no forced-choice response format?

Available evidence suggests that the final result would vary with culture and with type of expression. For Western cultures, I do not believe that recognition for the "anger," "disgust," "fear," and "sad" expressions would decline to the level of chance, but evidence does not convince me that recognition would remain at 82%. The more important question is what would happen in non-Western societies. For non-Western literate cultures, recognition scores might hold for some expressions, but fall lower for others. Overall, recognition might not remain at 65%. And for cultures isolated from the West, such as the Fore, recognition scores might not remain at 49%. Recognition scores for some of these facial expressions might decline to the level of chance; recognition scores for others might fall to a low but nonrandom level. For isolated cultures, current evidence does not demonstrate reliable discrimination within the set of negative expressions when the threats to internal validity are removed.

A similar argument applies to the studies of freely generated labels. Although these studies eliminate some of the problems surrounding forced choice, they yielded lower initial recognition scores. Again, focus on "anger," "disgust," "fear," and "sadness" expressions. The median score (based on a liberal scoring scheme) for the hypothesized expressions of these four negative emotions was 61% for Western cultures, 54% for Japanese (based on only one sample), less than 30% for the Fore, and still less for the Bahinemo (see Table XVIII). From these scores, we sub-

TABLE XVIII   Recognition Scores Estimated from Free-Label Responses for Four Negative Expressions

| Culture | Facial expression | | | |
	"Sadness"[a]	"Fear"	"Disgust"[b]	"Anger"
Western				
American[c]	60.1	59.6	49.0	66.4
Greek[c]	49.6	70.8	48.7	47.1
English[c]	63.5	58.9	46.4	56.6
French[c]	59.3	62.3	46.8	53.7
Canadian[d]	70	62	66	78
Greek[d]	75	87	68	63
Median	61.8	62.2	48.9	59.8
Literate non-Western				
Japanese[d]	80	14	56	48
Isolated non-Western				
Fore[ef]	Negl	30	Negl	49
Bahinemo[e]	Negl	Negl	Negl	?

Note: Negl indicates that the figure was not reported by the original investigator, but was apparently negligible.

[a]Izard's term was *distress.*

[b]Combination of disgust and contempt in Izard's (1971) data.

[c]Izard (1971); weighted average.

[d]Russell, Suzuki, & Ishida (1993).

[e]Sorenson (1976); see Table XVI and text for discussion.

[f]Figure is median of three Fore groups.

tract the influence of previewing, within-subject design, fixed order of presentation, experimenter expectancy, and other aids in conforming to the experimental hypothesis. Again, until more evidence is gathered, one can only guess what the final result would be. A baseline of chance cannot be as easily estimated here as in the case of forced choice. One baseline might be the base rate of generating a "correct" label when asked simply to name a negative emotion. In any case, for Western cultures, I do not believe that recognition scores would decline to such a baseline, but evidence does not convince me that recognition scores would remain at 61%. In non-Western cultures, the final recognition scores might be less high.

When recognition scores sink into the low or even moderate range, then new issues arise. If recognition scores drop below 50%, the possibility exists that the predicted interpretation is not the most common interpretation. (Such was the case in the Japanese free-label data: the modal response to the "fear" expression was *surprise*.) Wagner (1993) surveyed the way in which recognition has been calculated and analyzed, finding that "almost all papers published between 1979 and 1992 . . . suffer from one or more of three errors" (p. 2): inappropriate measurement of recognition, the use in statistical analyses of inappropriate chance levels, and misapplication of χ^2 and binomial statistical tests. When recognition scores are high, corrections for these errors are minor and do not alter the final conclusion. The lower the recognition scores, however, the greater the relative role of these errors in the results, and the more likely the final conclusion would be altered.

Recognition scores for some facial expressions in some non-Western cultures might not exceed chance. Nevertheless, let us suppose that, even when properly assessed and analyzed, recognition remains greater than chance for most facial expressions for all cultures. If so, the observer must provide some initial association between facial expressions and emotion labels. Method factors then could combine to guide that association into a consensual and clear pattern. Given the design of the standard experiment, even a vague beginning could result in a pattern that looks like the universality thesis. Note that on this account, method factors do not account for the results *completely*. In other words, if observers had no idea whatsoever about how to associate facial expressions with emotion labels, then the puzzle would remain unsolved. Method factors alone would not manufacture the associations. The standard method could help the subject think about questions that would not otherwise have arisen, and it might turn a vague idea into a highly consensual choice. But some association between face and emotion must be provided by the observer. So, as great as the problems of method are, they cannot be used to dismiss the evidence entirely. Rather, alternative explanations of that evidence must be examined.

ALTERNATIVE INTERPRETATIONS

The studies reviewed here have been said to support specific theories of facial expression proposed by Ekman (1972, 1989) and Izard (1977). Strictly speaking, what these various studies did was rule out the null hypothesis of no agreement whatsoever about what emotions to attribute to various facial expressions. Ruling out random choice is not the same as confirming any particular theory. A study on the interpretation of facial expressions that pits the null hypothesis of random choice against any reasonable substantive hypothesis is likely to find in favor of that substantive hypothesis.

An explanation of the available evidence need not account for high consensus on the 7 ± 2 emotion categories. Rather, it need only provide an initial association between some facial configurations and some emotion labels. An initial association then provides a preliminary solution to the puzzle presented in the experiment. Method factors can then help shape this solution into the amount of agreement seen in the particular study. Various possibilities exist on just what this initial association might be, on how people spontaneously interpret facial movements. Here are several alternatives (these are alternatives to each other rather than alternatives to the universality thesis—indeed some are versions of the universality thesis):

1. One possible explanation is an account along the lines proposed by Tomkins and McCarter (1964), Izard (1971, 1977), or Ekman and Friesen (1986). As I have attempted to demonstrate, the available evidence neither proves nor disproves these hypotheses. Their account might hold for some facial expressions, but not for others.

2. The observer might spontaneously interpret facial expressions in terms of a list of categories somewhat or completely different from those proposed in alternative 1. For example, the list might consist of four broad categories, roughly *happiness, surprise/fear, disgust/anger*, and *sadness*. This list might have the most cross-cultural viability. Or, the list might be *calm, excited, surprised, distressed, frustrated, disgusted*, and *depressed*. Or, the list might be much longer—studies of freely chosen labels suggest several hundred categories. On any of the alternatives, an observer would spontaneously interpret a particular facial expression in terms of a category often different from that supposed by the researcher. Given the standard forced-choice response format based on the researcher's hypothesis, the subject chooses the word on the list of options provided that is most similar. In this way, subjects' initial categorization would be channeled into the hypothesized categories.

The present alternative represents an uncountable number of specific hypotheses. The most interesting possibility is that the list of categories varies from one language to another, from one culture to another, or even from one individual to another. Consider the Balinese, for whom "the face is taken to be the physical manifestation of hidden forces of major significance—the heart" (Wikan, 1990, p. 52). The categories into which the Balinese divide facial expressions are in some ways similar to but in some ways different from what is done in English. Balinese distinguish *cerah muka* (clear, bright, happy) faces, *layu* (withered, sad) faces, *muram* (gloomy, cloudy, shamed) faces, *ny ebong* (grave, stern) faces, *sinis* (cynical) faces, and *galak* (jealous, furious) faces. More generally, the mental categories into which emotion is divided vary to some degree with language (Russell, 1991a; Wierzbicka, 1992).

3. The observer might initially interpret a facial expression in terms of bipolar dimensions rather than specific discrete categories. Recall that when observers are asked to judge pleasure–displeasure from spontaneous facial expressions they tend to be accurate. In a study such as Wagner et al.'s (1986), the results could be accounted for in terms of a single pleasant–unpleasant discrimination. More powerful still would be two- or three-dimensional accounts. Recall that Woodworth (1938) analyzed both agreements and disagreements, and found that interpretation of facial expression could be understood as placement within broad clusters, which, in turn, fell along a single dimension. Schlosberg (1952, 1954) later proposed two and then three underlying dimensions. Subsequent researchers have found bipolar dimensions a useful way of accounting for aspects of how people conceptualize emotion (Daly, Lancee, & Polivy, 1983; Russell, 1980; Watson & Tellegen, 1985) and facial expressions (Abelson & Sermat, 1962; Russell & Bullock, 1986; Russell, Lewicka, & Niit, 1989). A review of cross-cultural evidence suggested that pleasantness–unpleasantness, arousal–sleep, and potency–submissiveness are candidates for universal dimensions in the conceptualization of emotion and feeling (Russell, 1991b). Young preschoolers categorize facial expressions in terms of the same broad dimensions (Russell, 1989a).

To illustrate this type of account, imagine that subjects' initial interpretation of a face is in terms of degree of pleasure and degree of arousal. If the subject is given a forced-choice response format, then the subject chooses the option that comes closest in terms of pleasure and arousal. Even the simple two-dimensional account just described provides an explanation for various aspects of the data. Thus, consensus appears highest on *happiness* because the forced-choice format provides few or no alternative labels for faces judged as pleasant. For the negative emotion labels, 50 or 60% "correct" responses are easily understood. Suppose that an "anger" expression is perceived as conveying extreme displeasure and moderately high arousal. This combination occurs in labels such as *anger, fear,* and *disgust. Anger* is closest and chosen by the greatest number, *disgust* is next closest and is chosen by the second greatest number, and so on. This hypothesis also provides an account for the "confusions" reported by Ekman (1972) and others. For instance, the Dani of New Guinea "confused" (labeled similarly) "anger" and "disgust" expressions, which are similar in pleasure and arousal. The Fore of New Guinea confused "surprise" and "fear" expressions, which are similar in arousal.

The relation of a dimensional to a categorical account can be thought of in various ways, but one way concerns the amount of information inferred from a facial expression. Thus, in comparing a dimensional account to the categorical account implicit in many statements of the universality thesis, the number of categories "recognized" and the precise recognition scores become telling issues. Very high agreement on a large number of specific labels favors the categorical account, whereas lower agreement on fewer labels favors the dimensional account (the exact numbers required varies of course with the details of the judgment procedure). I have argued that the available evidence does not prove the categorical account even in Western college students. But even if the impact of method is less than I have estimated, the recognition scores in studies of non-Western societies are not so high as to force a categorical interpretation. Dimensions may therefore provide an account of what is universal in the interpretation of facial expression, whereas categories might be culture specific. For instance, one possibility is that the "anger" expression is universally (or widely) interpreted as conveying displeasure and moderately high arousal. In Western cultures, that expression is further interpreted as conveying frustration, determination, and a threat of violence. Displeasure, high arousal, frustration, determination, and threat of violence together suggest anger.

4. The observer might initially interpret a facial expression as a response to a type of situation. For instance, the observer might take a smile to be a response to the arrival of a friend, a wrinkled nose to be a response to a foul odor, raised eyebrows and wide open eyes to be a response to something new or unexpected, and an open mouth (and yelling) to be a response to danger. Seeing the facial expression allows an observer to infer the situation. Arrival of friend, foul odor, something new, and danger are types of situation, not internal states. Some of the labels seen in free-label studies, despite instructions to produce an *emotion* label, support this alternative: *frustration, bad news,* and *sees something pleasant.*

On this alternative, the situational interpretation is initial, spontaneous, and fast. An emotion might then be inferred, but more slowly and with more effort, and perhaps only if asked or only in some cultures. Thus, the observer quickly guesses that the person with a wrinkled nose is smelling something foul. Asked what emotion that person is feeling, the observer must work out an answer. If the experimenter allows a completely free response, the observer might say, "She's smelling a rotten egg" (Frijda, 1958). If the experimenter asks for a freely chosen *emotion* label, then different observers might reason to somewhat different answers: the person facing the foul smell might feel nausea, upset, bewilderment, discomfort, or some other emotion, depending on the specific circumstance imagined. If the experimenter provides a fixed list of emotions, the majority of observers might reason that, of the options provided, disgust is the most appropriate answer, although a minority might reason otherwise.

5. The observer might initially interpret facial expression as part of an instrumental action. Indeed, there is a history of interpreting facial expressions in this way (Darwin, 1872/1965; Eibl-Eibesfeldt, 1973b; Frijda, 1986). On such an account, for instance, the observer might take a smile to be an action with the purpose of greeting someone in a friendly (especially nonaggressive) manner. Wrinkling the nose has the purpose of blocking off an odor. Raising the eyebrows and widening the eyes has the purpose of seeing better. Lowering the brow while widening the eyes has the purpose of threatening. Eibl-Eibesfeldt (1973a) suggested that such facial actions are innate social signals, such as greetings, refusals, and threats, and that these same facial actions are innately responded to as such.

On this alternative, interpretation of a facial expression as a greeting, a refusal, or a threat is spontaneous, quick, automatic, effortless. If asked, the subject in an experiment could, with effort, reason to a possible emotional state. Someone greeting a friend is more likely to be happy than sad, angry, or lonely, so the reasoning might go. But the connection is not a necessary one: someone can greet a friend with a smile and still be sad, lonely, and so on.

6. The observer might initially interpret not the whole facial expression, but its component actions. Scherer (1984), Smith (1989), and Ortony and Turner (1990) suggested that components of the facial expression occur separately and have separate meaning. For example, the hypothesized "facial expression of anger" consists of raised eyelids, wrinkled brow, compressed lips, and bared teeth. The raised eyelids are part of visual attention, the wrinkled brow a sign of frustration, the compression of lips a sign of resolve, and bared teeth part of an aggressive action. Interpretation of components would be quick, spontaneous, and effortless. Inference of an emotion would be based on interpretation of the components and would be slow, deliberate, and effortful—and perhaps culture specific. Ekman (1992b) and Izard (1992) have commented on this account, and Turner and Ortony (1992) have replied.

7. Some of the hypotheses above might be joined together into a fuller account. The dimensional account might be combined with expression-as-instrumental action. Thus an observer might simultaneously interpret

a particular face as conveying displeasure and high arousal as well as a threat of violence. Alternatively, the meaning of a facial expression might be both situation and instrumental action. Fridlund (1991a) argued that current biological theory favors just such an account.

It would be possible to combine alternatives 3, 5, and 6. According to one account along these lines (Fehr & Russell, 1984), each emotion word expresses a concept that is structured as a *script*. For instance, to attribute anger to someone is to see a resemblance between that person's current state and a generic script or prototypical case for anger. In the anger script, an offense occurs; the person responds with arousal and displeasure; an impulse to violence occurs and then results in action. Observing a facial movement, the observer automatically infers the situation, internal feelings, and the action. Then, with some additional effort, the observers use their cues to infer one or more scripts, which constitute emotion concepts. (For alternative uses of the notion of script, see Abelson, 1981, and Tomkins, 1984.)

8. The preceding hypotheses sometimes assume that the same hypothesis would apply to each of the "basic" facial expressions, to all cultures, and to all individuals within a culture. This assumption need not be correct. Regarding hypothesis 2, for instance, it is also possible that the categories into which emotion is divided vary to some extent with language and culture (Russell, 1991a). If so, then the exact message inferred from a facial expression might vary (within limits) with culture. What actually occurs might involve some complex mixture of the above alternatives, a mixture that varies from one culture, or even one individual, to another. In one culture, or for one individual, a smile might be interpreted as indicating happiness (an emotion), a wrinkled nose as indicating a foul odor (situation), and lowered brows with staring eyes as indicating a threat (action). In another culture, or for another individual, some other mixture might apply. Another possibility is that some cultures or individuals have no habitual way to interpret a specific facial expression, but must create an interpretation on the spot.

Conclusion   We Westerners might find some of these alternative explanations implausible, but to assume that all people in all cultures think as we do is to assume what the studies under review were designed to test. The available evidence is consistent with any of the preceding eight hypotheses—and undoubtedly more: these eight simply illustrate the existence of alternative explanations. The only alternative I mean to leave out is the null hypothesis of completely random association between a face and the emotion attributed to it. Some association is assumed, and the question is the nature of the association and the role of culture in it. The eight alternative explanations listed here, although obviously preliminary, may provide a beginning in answering that question. The eight are not necessarily mutually exclusive, and may all be part of the truth. Such a thought is comforting, but a more useful tactic in planning research is to view these as competing hypotheses. As a minimum, future research can include comparison levels that are more telling than random assortment. For example, I used pleasantness–unpleasantness as a comparison level in analyzing several studies in this review. Even moving from a one-dimensional (pleasant–unpleasant) to a two-dimensional baseline would be informative. More interesting comparison levels would be created by more complex accounts.

CONCLUSION

This chapter did not address the adequacies of different theories of emotion, the existence, discreteness, basicness, or universality of specific emotions, the origin of facial behavior, genetic and epigenetic influences on facial behavior, or other related topics. Nor is this chapter the final word on the topic it addressed. Articles in psychology exist in a social dialogue. My turn was aimed at raising questions about a small but influential set of studies. Relevant evidence might have escaped my selection criteria. In their turn, proponents of alternative views may cite evidence that answers the questions raised here. New researchers will bring forward new evidence and new methods.

This is a topic on which opinions can differ. The merits of alternative explanations cannot now be decided on the basis of the empirical evidence available, and are therefore decided on the basis of a subjective judgment of plausibility. With concepts such as *emotion, anger, fear,* and so on lacking a clear consensual definition and with the universality thesis a background assumption of our everyday thought, many readers of this literature might find the universality thesis the most plausible alternative available. On the other hand, those who wait until the evidence compels them to decide must seek further evidence.

I hope that this chapter provides an opportunity for a renewal of the basic questions that initiated this field of study. We have the advantage today of new techniques for the measurement of facial behavior (Cacioppo & Petty, 1983; Ekman & Friesen, 1982b; Izard, 1983). We have new ideas on the processes involved in the production of facial behavior (Fridlund, 1991a; Ortony & Turner, 1990; Scherer, 1984; Zajonc, Murphy, & Inglehart, 1989). And we have hypotheses to refine and test about the meaning that observers attribute to facial behavior, such as the eight hypotheses just listed.

How might future research best be approached? As a first step, we need to abandon any implicit assumption that we have only two alternatives: randomness and universality. This forced choice underestimates our options. Ambiguities in phrases such as "universality of facial expression" must then be reduced. More precise statements of the universality thesis, and indeed of all the alternatives listed above, would aid in the design of more useful studies. The assumptions and implications for each alternative must be spelled out. How much "recognition" does it predict? In what contexts does it apply? For each hypothesis, it is helpful to specify what it predicts will *not* happen, which alternatives it excludes. A version of the universality thesis compatible with all or most of the eight alternatives listed above is too vague to be scientifically useful. As long as a hypothesis remains vague or ambiguous, the results of empirical efforts will be difficult to assess.

In gathering new data, the issues of internal, convergent, and ecological validity must be raised earlier and more often. Doing so would encourage the development and use of new and multiple methods, rather than reliance on any one. In raising the issue of ecological validity, I am not advocating an abandonment of experimental techniques. Rather, the method chosen must suit the question asked, and I believe that ecological questions should be among those asked. Even when experimental techniques are used, ecologically oriented questions should be borne in mind: How often do the stimuli being used occur, in that strength, for that length of time, in natural settings? How reflective is the response measure of naturally occurring interpretations given to the facial expressions observed? Recall how little information is available on the spontaneous interpretations given to spontaneous facial actions, especially in unfamiliar cultures. We need basic descriptive information on the sorts of facial movements that occur in everyday settings, with what frequency and in what contexts. When facial movements occur, we need to know how observers naturally interpret them, with what frequency and in what contexts. A breakthrough in the study of facial expression in infants came from looking at the behavior of one infant in actual situations (Camras, 1992).

Facial movements include not just the 7 ± 2 "facial expressions of emotion," but laughs, pouts, yawns, winces, grimaces, and all manner of actions difficult to describe. In our culture, people use facial cues to infer sleepiness, relaxation, puzzlement, confusion, pain, boredom, interest, attention, and other states besides seven "basic" emotions. An understanding of "facial expressions" would be helped by integrating studies over the full range of facial movements and inferences from them.

Understanding facial expression requires more than just a change in method, but also changes in the assumptions underlying the choice of method. To illustrate, consider this question: why did the method I have called standard come to be used more than any other? I have argued so far that methodological rigor and ecological validity were not the reasons for choosing the standard method. The standard method evolved and survived. What was the mechanism of selection? Since initial research in the nineteenth century, various methods have been used, but most were abandoned. Spontaneous facial expressions were studied (Landis, 1924; Munn, 1940; Sherman, 1927; Vinacke, 1949), but posed expressions worked better. Subjects were allowed to describe their interpretation of the facial expression in their own words (Darwin, 1872/1965; Frijda, 1953), but forced choice worked better. "To work" is to produce plausible or meaningful results. As one colleague put it, the standard method produced "positive results." Plausible, meaningful, or positive results are those that make most sense to someone with our cultural background. In short, the mechanism underlying the evolution of the standard method was something that has existed since the time of Aristotle, the common sense appeal of the universality thesis.

Tellingly, even the standard method was abandoned when it stopped working. In the first studies of isolated cultures, Ekman et al. (1969) used the standard method, but it worked only moderately well. They then turned to other methods, principally the Dashiell technique in which a story was substituted for the emotion name. And this new method worked much better.

A similar process was also implicit in reviews of the relevant literature. Studies less supportive of universality, mainly carried out in the 1920s, are often forgotten. Studies reported in or after 1969 are more strongly emphasized the more their results agree with universality. Results within a study such as lower or nonsignificant agreement with prediction for particular facial expressions are forgotten. (Examine the conclusions in Table I.) Nonsupportive studies, anomolies in the data, methodological problems, and other qualifications gradually fade from sight. As the evidence makes its way into a review of the literature or a textbook, and then is cited in articles or chapters, that evidence tends to be gradually assimilated to the background assumption, the universality thesis.

The universality thesis is an idea we Western psychologists find plausible, especially given randomness as the alternative. We speakers of English find it plausible that our concepts of *anger, fear, contempt* and the like are universal categories, exposing nature at the joints. One way to overcome the influence of such implicit assumptions is to emphasize alternative conceptualizations. And, I believe, the most interesting means to this end is to take seriously the conceptualizations (ethnotheories, cultural models) found in other cultures. Rather than ask whether or not a given culture agrees with one preformulated hypothesis, we might more usefully ask how members of that culture conceptualize emotions and facial behavior. There may be no shortcut to obtaining the needed information. Although the task is great, what we know about the peoples of different cultures suggests that carrying it out will be fascinating. In studying the beliefs of other cultures, we cannot expect to know right away whether those beliefs are correct or not. Their theories are not to be believed any more than our own. I doubt whether even asking about their correctness is useful. We don't yet know whether Aristotle was right in his beliefs regarding physiognomy: whether soft hair reveals a coward or whether facial expressions reveal emotions. We might more usefully gather the beliefs of different cultures rather than evaluate them.

11

How Do We Account for Both Universal and Regional Variations in Facial Expressions of Emotion?

Russell's analysis in Chapter 10 shows little evidence for a universal set of prototype faces that corresponds to a set of fundamental emotions. Even with all the juggling of methods by advocates of the Emotions View, the extent of face-to-emotion term or face-to-situation matching was strongly dependent upon the test population, and seldom amounted to more than a positive–negative distinction. And it does seem that people across regions or cultures are able, by and large, to discern faces that connote "positive" situations or emotion terms from those that connote "negative" ones. Beyond these communalities, however, lie substantial differences.

This pattern of results implies nothing about genetic versus epigenetic influences upon either those faces that might be "universal" or those that are not. As I will show later in this chapter, there are many ways to explain the data from the "cross-cultural" studies, ranging from wholly genetic to entirely epigenetic models, or any combination in between.

Most advocates of the Emotions View assumed that any universal facial displays were due to a phyletic (genetic) contribution, whereas any regional differences were interpreted as "cultural" and thus reflected learning. This assumption was taken unabashedly and uncritically from Darwin:

> It seemed to me highly important to ascertain whether the same expressions and gestures prevail, as has often been asserted without much evidence, with all the races of mankind, especially with those who have associated but little with Europeans. Whenever the same movements of the features or body express the same emotions in several distinct races of man, we may infer with much probability, that such expressions are true ones—that is, are innate or instinctive. Conventional expressions or gestures, acquired by the individual during early life, would probably have differed in the different races, in the same manner as do their languages. (1872, p. 15)

Darwin's assumption was reasonable, but in actuality there would be many ways to account for both "universal" faces and variations among the test populations in the cross-cultural studies. Moreover, as I mentioned in Chapter 9, the assumption was self-confirming. Testing people in diverse geographic regions and then ascribing any facial variations to "culture" discounts the possibility that the regional variations were genotypic, conceivably as genotypic as the "universals."[1]

Darwin's view nonetheless became the most common interpretation

[1] For this reason I use the word "cultural" advisedly in describing these studies, and substitute or append the more neutral word *regional* when appropriate. Attributing regional variations in facial displays to enculturation is only permissible if genetic differences among the test populations are excluded. Note that Darwin suggested comparisons of races, not "cultures."

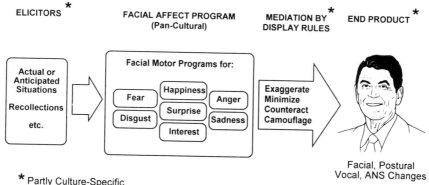

FIGURE 11.1.   Ekman's neurocultural model for explaining communalities and variations in human facial displays. Communalities in facial displays were attributed to the operation of genetic "facial affect programs." Variations in subject populations were considered "cultural" and attributed to the learning of "display rules," or social conventions about facial expression.

of the cross-cultural studies. It was translated into mechanistic terms by Ekman in his "neurocultural" model of facial display (e.g., Ekman, 1972, 1973, 1977). The model is still current in Ekman's writings, and his terminology became common currency in the 1970s and 1980s research on faces and emotion. In Chapter 8 I already discussed Ekman's model in the context of deception and "emotional" facial movements; here I focus upon its predications about facial "universals" and cultural variants.

EKMAN'S NEUROCULTURAL MODEL

I have provided a depiction of Ekman's neurocultural model (Ekman, 1972) in Figure 11.1.

Although Ekman's model derived ultimately from Darwin, its roots are two more immediate sources. First was the corpus of writings by Silvan Tomkins (1962, 1963), who postulated an innate system of categorical "differential emotions" discriminable from facial movements. The second was Lorenz's mechanistic ethology (e.g., Lorenz, 1967). Lorenz proposed the existence of "Innate Releasing Mechanisms," actuated by specific releasing stimuli, which triggered the emission of sequences of motor behavior that included "expressive" displays. The sequences were innate, but their components could be amplified or attenuated by social conventions (Lorenz, 1967).

Tenets of the Model

At the heart of Ekman's model was a central "facial affect program," which "links each primary emotion to a distinctive patterned set of neural impulses to the facial muscles" (Ekman, 1972, p. 216).[2] This neural program, when activated, normally led to the contraction of a fixed, partly innate configuration of facial muscles, by a "mechanism which stores the patterns for these complex organized responses, and which when set off directs their occurrence" (Ekman, 1977, p. 57). The facial patterns corresponded categorically to each of the "primary emotions," which included happiness, anger, surprise, fear, disgust, interest, and sadness (Figure 11.1).

As Figure 11.1 also shows, the elicitors of the primary emotions and thus the facial affect program can be either exogenous or endogenous, with the latter including expectancies or reminiscences. Although Ekman emphasized the universality and innateness of the facial patterns that corresponded to each primary emotion, there were three ways in which the model allowed for departures from universality and prototypicality in facial expressions. These allowances were for: (1) cultural differences in emotion elicitors; (2) blended emotions; and (3) cultural display rules. I discuss these three and their implications for the testability of the model.

First, Ekman held that the elicitors of emotions, and thus of their facial expressions, were strongly influenced by culture:

> It is Tomkins' theory which led us to propose that most of the elicitors of facial expression are socially learned and may be expected to vary with culture and with social groupings within a culture; and, by late childhood, these socially learned elicitors will by sheer number overwhelm any possible unlearned elicitors. (Ekman, 1972, p. 215)

For example, Ekman believed that a universal event like a funeral might cause sadness in one culture and happiness in another (Ekman, 1972, p. 215).

A second way that the neurocultural model allowed for faces that departed from prototypicality was Ekman's proposal of "blended" emotions. Ekman acknowledged the existence of emotions other than the seven primaries in his neurocultural model, and thus the faces linked with these complex emotions would depart from the seven prototypes. He proposed that these emotions and their associated faces represented "secondary" or "blended" emotions. Blended emotions could occur, for example, when more than one emotion was evoked concurrently, as when "winning the sweepstakes might commonly elicit both surprise

---

[2] As I noted earlier, the straightforward derivation from Lorenz is self-evident; the acronym for "facial affect program" (*FAP*) is identical to that of another of Lorenz's mechanisms, the "fixed action pattern."

and happiness" (Ekman, 1972, p. 223); or when people experienced "feelings about feelings," as when one "immediately feels disgusted at himself for becoming angry" (Ekman, 1972, p. 224). But "blended faces" are only one possibility, because "feelings about feelings" can occasion even other kinds of faces:

> Let us assume, for example, that anger is aroused by a particular elicitor and, on the basis of habit, the person feels afraid of feeling anger in the particular social setting. There may be a display rule operable to neutralize the facial expression of anger, but no rule for the expression of fear. So he will *look* afraid, not angry. Of course all the other permutations are equally possible. (Ekman, 1972, p. 232)

The third way that the neurocultural model dealt with faces that varied from prototypicality was also the most important in the model. It lay in Ekman's belief that the facial affect program could be interrupted in its actions before it could produce "emotional" faces. In the neurocultural model, the facial configuration stipulated by the affect program erupted unimpeded unless interfered with by habits owing to culture-specific learning. For this reason, Ekman pointedly avoided stating that the facial affect program produced facial expressions directly. Instead, the instigation was indirect, and it was here that he introduced the final way that faces could depart from universality:

> We refer to "triggering a set of muscular movements," or a "patterned set of neural impulses to the facial muscles," rather than "movement of facial muscles," or "changes in facial appearance," because we will presently postulate that learned habits about controlling the appearance of the face . . . can and often do intervene between the triggering of the facial muscles by the facial affect program and a visible change in facial appearance. (Ekman, 1972, p. 216)

These habits were named "cultural display rules" (Ekman & Friesen, 1969*b*). Within a culture, display rules were held to govern what facial displays were observed, and to whom and in what context they were emitted. Display rules could exert their effects at nearly any point, ranging from the initial elicitation of an emotion, to the volley of neural activity to the facial muscles:

> Habits regarding the control of facial appearance . . . can interfere with the operation of the facial affect program, early or late in the sequence of internal events, in one of four ways: (a) they can prevent activation of the facial affect program with or without also preventing any other registration of emotion; or (b) if the facial affect program has been activated, they can prevent triggering of the facial muscles; or (c) if the facial muscles have been triggered, they can either interrupt the muscular contractions, making the appearance changes quite brief, or diminish the extent or scope of the muscular contractions, making the changes in appearance less pro-

nounced; or (d) whether or not the facial muscles have been triggered by the facial affect program, these habits can override and thus mask with a different set of muscular contractions those directed by the affect program. (Ekman, 1972, p. 217)

In other words, cultural display rules can block or attenuate a facial expression of emotion, or force a "masking" expression that obscures or even supplants an emotional face.

Overinclusiveness in the Model

The two-factor, neurocultural model was constructed explicitly to reconcile putative universalist data (i.e., the "cross-cultural" studies by Ekman and others, reviewed in Chapter 10) and cultural-relativist observations, mostly by anthropologists and linguists. It was successful in leading researchers to attend to both genetic and epigenetic features of facial display.

But even a cursory analysis reveals that the model was markedly *over*inclusive. Any facial display, in any circumstance, could be explained by one of the model's provisos. For example, if a facial display was observed to fit one of the proposed prototypes, then it *was* an expression of a primary emotion. If the face was not prototypic but had features of more than one prototype, then that face *was* a blend of the prototypes. If the face was in no sense prototypic, then it represented the action of a cultural display rule. If the face was prototypic but did not accord with expectations given the situational elicitors, then the single face might have emerged from an emotion about an emotion, with the face that would normally be linked to the primary emotion blocked by a display rule. These assignations would be no problem if there were independent criteria for determining when the facial affect program was activated, when a blend of emotions was being elicited, and when a cultural display rule was operative. Unfortunately, the neurocultural model provides no such criteria.

The Model's Ambiguity and Circularity in Face–Emotion Relations

Apart from its overinclusiveness, the model suffered in one other, crucial aspect. It left the relation of facial display to emotion ambiguous. Part of the difficulty lay in the model's circular argument. First, Ekman interpreted universal, prototype faces as indicating the elicitation of primary emotions:

What is universal in facial expressions of emotion is the particular set of facial muscular movements triggered when a given emotion is elicited. (Ekman, 1972, p. 216)

However, if certain faces are universal by virtue of their association with emotion, then what emotions are universal? As Ekman states:

> We have listed seven emotions within the facial affect program. This list . . . reflects both our theoretical orientation and our empirical results. The list is close to that of the emotion categories consistently found by all investigators within Western cultures who have, over a 30-year period, attempted to determine how many categories of emotion can be judged from the face . . . . (1972, p. 222)

Thus prototype faces arise from universal emotions, and the emotions are discerned from putative findings of universal faces. This circular definition might be tolerable if the model consistently identified emotions with faces; were this so, then universality in one would imply the universality of the other. But this cannot be the case if the concept of cultural display rules is maintained. Only if "emotions" are separable from faces can one maintain that display rules interfere with instigation of faces by emotions. Again, the neurocultural model does not provide criteria for discerning emotions apart from their associated faces.

The viability of the "cultural display rules" concept poses a special problem, and I will discuss both the ontological and empirical difficulties in a later portion of this chapter.

Contributions of the Neurocultural Model

Ekman's neurocultural theory was a "two-factor" theory which followed Darwin's beliefs in two kinds of facial expressions. First were the innate, hard-wired patterns of facial movements that occurred due to the activation of a "facial affect program" linked to the elicitation of primary emotions. Second were those faces that resulted from the internalization of social convention or from willful exertion. At any moment, the facial movements an individual exhibited might reflect either of the two or any admixture. I discuss the appeal of this two-factor conception later in this chapter.

What can be said about the impact of the neurocultural model? It was useful in the way it was intended, as a way of helping investigators reconcile relativistic accounts of facial behavior with putative findings of universality. In retrospect, its greater accomplishment may have been to extend the nature–nurture problem to facial displays *qua* everyday human behavior. This was no small feat for its time—the theory and initial "universality" findings began to emerge in the midst of behaviorism's stranglehold on psychology, when any discussion of evolutionary bases of behavior was heresy to many and heterodoxy to most. The neurocultural model and the findings it attempted to explain were instrumental in forcing psychologists to reconsider evolutionary thought in their accounts of behavior.

On the other hand, the model's inclusiveness was also its downfall. One might cynically remark that the neurocultural model was like psychoanalysis, with so many provisos and escape clauses that it was untestable from the start. A more reasoned sentiment would be that, in attempting with a simple model to explain both "universal" faces and nonconformist faces, it led to premature closure of questioning about the extent of facial universality versus diversity, and about the variety of genetic and epigenetic factors that might account for each.

There are, in fact, ready explanations for both the cultural commonality and difference findings that do not conform with the neurocultural model. I discuss these next.

ALTERNATIVE EXPLANATIONS OF COMMUNALITY FINDINGS

What can the cross-cultural studies establish? First, if different regions or cultures show similar displays, then there *may* be a phyletic basis for the displays. Several alternative hypotheses must be excluded. This section details these hypotheses.

Are Subjects Matching Faces to "Emotions"?

One of the first and most telling critiques of the cross-cultural matching experiments was provided by the ethologist W. John Smith (1985). Smith discerned that these studies leave untested the assumption that the iconlike faces used in the matching experiments are actually communicating information about emotion. As Smith stated:

> It is not sufficient to give subjects a list of emotions and a set of pictures of facial configurations to see if they can match any. They can match some, but the technique does not show how the configurations contribute to communication in real events. (p. 57)

There are several points here. First, do the faces convey information about emotion? Smith (1985) cited a study by Frijda (1969) that showed that subjects indeed could match emotion terms to still photographs of faces if asked.[3] However, if the subjects were responding freely to the

---

[3] That subjects can match emotion terms or scenarios to still photographs of faces does not imply that emotion terms are meaningful categories by which to describe them. This logical fallacy is made obvious by example. One could conceivably ask subjects to match personality descriptors (e.g., lethargic, competent, arrogant) to automobiles (e.g., Volkswagens, BMWs, Rolls-Royces), and subjects might indeed score better than chance. Above-chance matching does not imply that the automobiles possess the traits.

Nor do the still photo-matching studies allow assertions that the words/scenarios or faces elicit or signify emotions that are *fundamental*. An example serves here as well. One could, across cultures,

photographs, they tended to provide situations or intentions. For example, a smile produced the association, "she looks as if she is watching a small child play" (also see Frijda, Kuipers, & ter Schure, 1989).

The New Guinea preliterate-culture matching study by Ekman and Friesen (1971) is widely cited as supporting the view that faces portray emotion, but the face stimuli were elicited by scenarios, *not* by emotion terms (Ekman, 1984; Ekman et al., 1987). Examples of these situational elicitors were: "Your friend has come and you are happy"; "A man has learned that his child has just died"; "You see a dead pig that has been lying there for a long time"; and "You are angry and about to fight." Notable is the striking similarity of Ekman and Friesen's last elicitor to Andrew's (1963b) illustration of the intention-movement view of agonistic display (Chapter 7).

Frijda's (1969) data and, in this reanalysis, those of Ekman and Friesen (1971), support a social-motive, behavioral ecology account more than one based on emotions. In many cross-cultural studies, the subjects were in fact matching faces to situations and intentions. This was true whenever a translator could not provide ready translations for single emotion terms.

I believe that in the matching studies that did use emotion words, subjects in fact interpreted the still photographs as cues to situations and intentions, which they then further translated into emotion terms in order to make the match. Russell's review in Chapter 10 also suggests this as a possibility.

To extend this analysis, in nearly all cases in which "emotional expression" occurs, there is an intention or social motive, embedded in a given social context, to which the facial display can be better attributed. That we regard faces as expressing emotions rather than symbolizing motives and context may just be social shorthand. From an evolutionary standpoint, faces should be specific to motives and contexts rather than emotions, because there can be no ritualization unless displays portend social acts.

As I have reviewed, human experimental data that corroborate the social-motive account are provided not only by Frijda (1969) on face association and Ekman and Friesen (1971) on pancultural still photograph–emotion term matching, but also by Kraut and Johnston (1979) on public adult smiles, Jones et al. on infant smiles (Jones & Raag, 1989; Jones et al., 1991), Fridlund et al. (1990, 1992a) on social versus solitary imagery, the Bavelas et al. (1986, 1989) motor mimicry studies, and the audience-effect studies by Fridlund (1991a) and Chovil (1991).

---

distribute pieces of paper colored orange, pink, and blue-green, and then, as appropriate to each culture, supply the words "orange," "pink," and "blue-green." Successful paper–word matching by members of each culture would not imply that the colors or color words signified chromatic primaries (cf. Geldard, 1972).

Other than the Fridlund et al. studies, I know of only one experiment that allows parsing of the relative roles of social motive and context versus emotion in determining facial displays.

Ancoli (1980) conducted a widely cited study of solitary subjects exposed to three pleasant videotape segments: a monkey playing, an ocean scene, and a small dog playing with a flower. The three segments produced equivalent happiness ratings, but disparate degrees of smiling. Subjects smiled strongly to the monkey and dog scenes, but only a few subjects smiled during the ocean segment. Curiously, the face and self-report findings from the ocean condition did not appear in the published report of the study (Ekman et al., 1980), and the authors proceeded to endorse an emotions view of subjects' smiles based on correlations of *zygomatic major* contractions (i.e., normal smiling) with felt happiness in the conditions they reported.

Consideration of Ancoli's full data set (Ancoli, 1980) makes this emotions interpretation problematic, because the subjects' smiling in the three film conditions should have paralleled their equivalent happiness ratings. In contrast, the Behavioral Ecology View affords a ready interpretation. The monkey and dog scenes were social, and viewers—via dramatic suspension of disbelief—in effect became social interactants. Consequently, subjects' smiles signaled solicitation of or readiness for play, as elicited by the playful antics of the electronic, on-screen interactants. On the other hand, an ocean scene is prototypically asocial, and there is no motive to affiliate even though one is happy (notwithstanding examples such as memories of romantic interludes on a beach, and these instances may have accounted for the few subjects who *did* smile).

In order to retain an emotions account of the Ancoli ocean data, it might be objected that subjects experienced two different kinds of happiness in the ocean versus animal conditions, for example, "contentment" versus "amusement." This position is untenable within classical emotions theory, which stipulates that happiness is a *fundamental* emotion. Axiomatically, fundamentals are not subdivisible.

It is nonetheless reasonable to suggest that subjects are adopting a different stance toward the ocean than the animals. I have suggested elsewhere (Fridlund, 1986; also, Chapter 8) that many emotion terms do not depict hedonics so much as they are reified descriptions of actions, contexts, or intentions. These reifications often serve social etiquette (e.g., again using Andrew's example, "I feel angry" is more *palatable* than "I'm inclined to attack you"; Andrew, 1963b). In the happiness case, "amusement" and "contentment" reflect, respectively, "I want to solicit or sustain play," and "I want to maintain *status quo*." Stating one's "feelings" is refined; stating one's intentions is brazen and uncivil. That common emotion terms carry implicit social motives was corroborated by Frijda et al. (1989), who showed that individuals readily associated emotion categories with "action tendencies."

In an intention-movement view of the smile, instigation of smiling does not occur via an elemental state of "happiness." Rather, there are distinct social relations in which smiles are likely to be deployed, and the different experiences accompanying these diverse social relations are labeled "happiness" merely out of convenience. Amusement, sensual pleasure, serenity, delight, pride, awe, contentment, and so on, depict different social relations, are phenomenologically distinct, and all may engender smiles in the appropriate social context.

This analysis is also valuable in analyzing the "contempt" findings I summarized earlier. Ekman and Friesen (1986) concluded that a sneerlike face is prototypical for contempt. Izard and Haynes (1987) disagreed, positing instead a variety of contempt displays, including behaviors such as narrowed gaze and head tilts. In the Behavioral Ecology analysis, the error both commit is in assuming a reified, generalized state of "contempt," and related terms like derision, sardonicism, disdain, scorn, and moral outrage, probably denote separable motives, perhaps with separable associated intention movements.

My belief that many emotion terms should be "deconstructed" to social motives (or, ultimately, classes of behavior) is superficially close to the position taken by Ekman and Friesen (1987) in their reply to the contempt study rejoinder by Izard and Haynes. They inquire whether derision, scorn, and so on, should be regarded as distinct emotions with distinct displays, rather than conflated as "contempt."

I have already discussed (Chapters 7 and 8) the shell game played by emotion theorists who have evaded good definition in order to keep the "emotion" concept in the scientific lexicon. The question arises nonetheless whether a hermeneutical dissection of emotions and displays is equivalent to the tabulation of social motives/contexts and intention movements I advocate. Because many emotion terms may be reified social motives to begin with, I believe that dissecting them in order to segregate the associated displays is a dead end. I maintain this position for two reasons, one conceptual and the other utilitarian.

Conceptually, hermeneutical dissection of emotions will inevitably lead to the level of explanation by social motive. This is because emotion terms, when dissected sufficiently, usually become statements of motives and context. For example, "happiness," an emotion term without obvious motives and context, includes "amusement," "serenity," and "relief," to pick a few. Yet the definitions of each of the putative subtypes denote motives, roles, or context: "amusement" implies affiliation and play behavior with another, "serenity" implies repose and preference for solace, and "relief" implies termination of an aversive interaction.

On utilitarian grounds, the intentional analysis of displays will lead to a display taxonomy that predicts (and would be validated by) classes of observable behavior, rather than depending upon progressively finer distinctions among emotions, distinctions that tend to become more dubious phenomenologically.

Whether the communalities in photographic stills of faces across regions or cultures better depict social motives or "fundamental emotions" can be determined experimentally. Cross-cultural picture-matching studies are done using *two* conditions: (1) faces are to be matched with emotion terms (i.e., "pick the face closest to anger"), and (2) with social motives and context cues ("pick the face closest to that one would show a friend who steals a prized possession"). Matching should be superior across regions or cultures in the motive/context cue condition. The second condition was in fact closely approximated by the social scenarios used in the preliterate-culture studies. Unfortunately, it seems that only emotion words were provided to subjects among the literate regions or cultures.

Would even this two-condition matching experiment be informative about real-world faces? Successful matching in either condition would depend upon the stills of faces having some iconic, prototypic meaning apart from the social context of their issuance, a meaning that could sensibly be matched to either a word or a scenario. In the Behavioral Ecology View, faces display social motives that are understandable only in the context in which the motives arise. Matching experiments involving iconic stills of faces, then, should produce only guesses based upon base rates of social contexts in which the faces might occur.

Russell's review in Chapter 10 cited compelling evidence for the importance of context in judgments about faces, drawn from studies such as the one by Russell and Fehr (1987). Such findings challenge the view of faces as iconic representations of fundamental emotions. To summarize, Russell and Fehr found that a face that Ekman and Friesen (1975) regarded as prototypical of "surprise" was judged more exciting or fearful depending upon the face seen just before; similarly, the viewing context altered judgments of an ostensibly prototypical "anger" face from "anger" to "sadness." Russell also documented a similar context dependency for the "contempt" face used in the cross-cultural studies (Russell, 1991a,c, and see interchanges by Ekman, O'Sullivan, & Matsumoto, 1991a,b; and Russell, 1991b). A related development is the attempt to categorize interactional contexts parsimoniously and predict the faces made in them (Fernandez-Dols, 1990).

The codification of patterns of motives and social contexts is the task undertaken by researchers of the "social construction of emotions." In this view, emotions are redefined as "socially determined patterns of ritual action" (Armon-Jones, 1985, p. 1). Armon-Jones (1985), Averill

(1980, 1990), and Harré (1980, 1985) present the ramifications of the social-constructionist position. As I discussed earlier, redefining "emotion" in order to save the term is an endless pursuit of researchers of emotions and facial behavior, and any recasting of emotion so as to identify it with social motives will, I suspect, render it more applicable to facial behavior.

It is undeniable, however, that even if faces do not express "emotions" as the classical emotion theorist construes them, we commonly *attribute* those emotions to faces. It thus makes sense to question why they *seem* so related. I previously indicated that emotion language is more palatable than the language of social intent; this may account for our predilection to use emotion language to describe both our own faces and others' as well. There may be other reasons:

1. As I illustrated for smiles and threat faces, personal dispositions and cultural traditions often mandate how we should act toward others when we are emotional (e.g., happiness is to be shared vs. humbly acknowledged, anger demands retaliation vs. supplication and negotiation). In the Behavioral Ecology View, our faces signal our social inclinations. If we exhibit social inclinations and we are emotional, our faces signal the former and not the latter. We may be especially inclined to attribute emotion to *others'* faces because of our propensity to cast their actions in terms of internal states (Jones & Nisbett, 1972)

2. We seldom seek to disconfirm our beliefs that others' faces and social motives are accompanied by the expected emotions. When others approach us with smiles and cheery conversation, we expect that they are happy when they may in fact be lonely. When others make threat faces toward us, we expect that they are angry when they may actually be bluffing and enjoying the showdown. We seldom pause to ask smilers whether they are happy or aggressors whether they are angry.

Ecological Validity

Are the still photographs used in picture-matching studies ecologically valid? Although a few studies asked subjects to judge spontaneous faces connoting emotion, none was performed in regions or cultures unexposed to the mass media. Skepticism about the cross-cultural studies is justified, because it is not known how often the canonical faces used in the matching experiments are seen in real life. The canonical faces may just be intensified variants of spontaneous faces. Alternatively, they may be Roschian prototypes (Rosch, 1973), idealized amalgams of attributes of real-world faces. Russell and Bullock (1986) presented evidence that judgments of facial displays are graded rather than categorical, and that the emotions terms connoted by faces should be considered "fuzzy concepts" rather than prototypes. That the "prototype" faces used in matching studies must portray fundamental "prototype" emotions is a *platonic fallacy* (Fridlund, 1986).

Cultural Transmission

Cultural transmission must be considered before cross-cultural communalities are attributed to genetic control. The importance attributed to the study of preliterate cultures relies on the hidden and unsupportable assumption that whereas various languages are transmitted culturally, facial displays are not. Interpretations of the preliterate studies also tend to regard cultures like those populating regions of Papua New Guinea as though they arose *de novo*, rather than via general eastern migration. Migratory influences could be ruled out only by examining faces in geographically proximate cultures. In summary, studies of preliterate, isolated peoples control only for transmission via mass media; but they do not rule out transmission via migration or trade—or "cheating," as I suggest below. I do not know of any systematic research on the cultural transmission of displays among early civilizations.

The issue of horizontal cultural transmission, that is, cross-lineage borrowing, is of special concern in the recent studies (Ekman & Friesen, 1986; Ekman et al., 1987) that used college students as subjects. Most college students have ready access to books, magazines, movies, television, and fellow students from many cultures. These students would not only be expected to show "universality" on judgments of "emotional" faces—they would probably also show near-perfect recognition of movie or television celebrities. Given this situation, still photo word-matching studies done in literate cultures, and with college students in particular, must be regarded more as measures of media saturation than inherent universality.

There is one final type of cultural transmission to be excluded in examining the matching studies in the preliterate cultures—"cheating" by the members of the cultures who may have helped each other perform the matching tasks. Russell's review in Chapter 10 discussed Sorenson's (1975) belief that the most important of the preliterate studies, those from the Fore of Papua New Guinea, may have been contaminated, with subjects being coached by the translators. If Sorenson is correct, then the studies represent a lost and irretrievable opportunity.

Common Learning

Displays may be shaped anew in each region or culture from co-option of preadapted facial reflexes, as Ekman (1972) suggested. This process would be a kind of ontogenetic convergence, with the facial reflexes as the only common substrate. Excluding this hypothesis would require either that: (1) the displays in question exist without adaptive advantage in at least one region or culture; or (2) ontogenetic data show that the displays exist despite no current function (e.g., in the improbable but decisive circumstance of congenitally blind children reared by blind caretakers). On both counts, the available evidence is inconclusive, and definitive data may be impossible to obtain.

ALTERNATIVE EXPLANATIONS OF FINDINGS OF CULTURAL DIFFERENCES

How different are cultures in their facial displays connoting emotion? Fridlund, Ekman, and Oster (1987) concluded that little was known, with most accounts of extreme cultural variability coming from anecdotal observations by single observers (cf. observations by Birdwhistell, 1970; LaBarre, 1947; Leach, 1972; Mead, 1975; reviewed by Ekman, 1973, 1977). There are just a few quantitative studies. Heider (1974) showed that one West Irian culture, but not another, made "disgust" faces instead of the expected "angry" ones when asked to portray angry themes. Yearbook photographs and conversations (Seaford, 1976) suggested a facial display "dialect" in patterns of smiling among southeastern Americans. Finally, the Ekman et al. (1987) 10-culture college student study found that the samples (largely Asian vs. non-Asian) differed in their intensity ratings of "emotion" in still photographs held to express happiness, surprise, and fear.

What can be made of any cultural differences in facial displays connoting emotion? In contrast to Darwin's summary beliefs about faces and their extension in Ekman's neurocultural model, differences in facial displays from one population to the next do not necessarily imply epigenesis. If this model were general, then one would have to interpret skin color and hemoglobin type as "cultural" and therefore "learned." Clearly there are both genetic and epigenetic mechanisms that could explain regional variations in facial displays. Here I present two. The first is genetic. The second is epigenetic and should by now be familiar—the concept of "cultural display rules." As I mentioned earlier, the neurocultural model, and the thinking of most contemporary facial-expressions researchers, rely upon the display rules concept. Nonetheless as I hope to show, the concept may be unworkable and unsupportable.

Genetic Drift and Founder Effects

After Darwin visited the Galapagos Islands in 1835, he discovered just how much variation could occur in one kind of animal given just a little geographic isolation. As he traversed the Galapagos, he found trees, tortoises—and most notably, finches—that differed in ways peculiar to each island (Desmond & Moore, 1991; Sulloway, 1982, 1984).

That a species might show dramatic clusters of morphological variations within even a small geographical region is now one of the mundane facts in evolutionary biology. It is thus perplexing why differences in facial displays among various peoples are so automatically attributed to "culture."

There are two requirements for the emergence of such novel strains in a single species. First, the trait in question has to be polymorphous, that is, it has to appear in many forms (it is "uncanalized"). For example, having two eyes or four limbs are, for practical purposes, monomorphic traits, but our skin and eye color, blood type, and height are not. The second requirement is a little reproductive isolation between groups and the time for each group to interbreed. The Galapagos were an ideal population to observe this process, now called *genetic drift* (e.g., Wright, 1931). When the finches migrated to the islands, they largely mated with their island-mates, with the result that the traits of birds on each island eventually stabilized and subspecies emerged. That the consequence of genetic drift is an array of variants is a simple artifact of sampling: the smaller the sample on each island, the more each sample is likely to vary from the parent population.

The effects of reproductive isolation can go further. Within each small interbreeding group, even odd traits may predominate to the extent that they can overwhelm all but the strongest natural selection pressures (Wright, 1960). Thus comparatively isolated cultures often originate with just a few individuals—the "founders" of the new population—who may have quite atypical genotypes; these are *founder effects* (Dobzhansky et al., 1977). Founder effects and genetic drift are thought to explain local human racial variations (Grant, 1985), especially blood types (Cavalli-Sforza, 1973). These effects would be most apparent in regions of several nearby but reproductively isolated populations, such as the island groups of Polynesia and New Guinea—the latter being where Ekman and colleagues conducted cross-"cultural" facial expression research.

Displays can of course arise conventionally, but genetic drift and founder effects are important to consider when comparing the facial displays of peoples from diverse geographic regions. The reason, by now, should be obvious. Like morphological traits, relatively isolated groups of individuals may rapidly develop variations in their signal systems, even profound variations, due to genetic differences and *not* necessarily to enculturation.

In accounting for a cultural difference in a display, genetic drift and founder effects must both be excluded. Counterevidence for either would entail: (1) the existence of a display in individuals transported at birth, without caretakers from the culture, to a new culture lacking the display in question; (2) the emergence of a display in the culture's history at a rate faster than predicted from founder effect and/or genetic drift models; and (3) the failure to find corresponding display differences in cultures known to have differentiated through genetic drift.

Problems with the Concept of "Cultural Display Rules"

As I reviewed in this chapter and elsewhere, the classical Emotions View, as exemplified by Ekman's neurocultural model, presupposes the universality of "facial expressions of emotion," with any cultural differences in facial behavior necessarily due to cultural conventions about expression. The best developed formulation of this concept is Ekman's "cultural display rules" (Ekman & Friesen, 1969b, Ekman, 1972). These are "overlearned habits about who can show what emotion to whom and when they can show it," and they ostensibly circumvent issuance of "the biologically based, evolved, universal expressions of emotion" (Ekman, 1984, pp. 320–321). In accordance with training or tradition, display rules are said to interfere with the patterned muscular output of the "facial affect program" triggered by one's emotional state, in one of four ways: (1) attenuation; (2) histrionic intensification; (3) neutralization (i.e., making a "poker face"); and (4) masking or camouflage with another type of face (Ekman, 1972, p. 225).

In other words, given any emotional state, people may make different faces in public than in private, with the public faces being distortions of the emotional faces that would naturally (i.e., in private) erupt by virtue of emotion. Obviously the display rules concept is a priori problematic, because it relies upon the premise that one's emotional state in public *could* be equivalent to one's state in private. In my discussion of Ekman's neurocultural model, I noted the model's failure to specify criteria for discerning the occurrence of emotion independent of facial action. This point is crucial when we consider cultural display rules. Without independent criteria for emotion, how could one ever determine whether an individual's behavior indicated the operation of a cultural display rule? Within the classical Emotions View, any differences in facial movements might simply reflect differences in emotion.

An example will clarify this point. An adult male who has suffered a loss should typically not cry in public, even if he cries copiously in private. This norm is often cited as a cultural display rule (see Ekman, 1972, p. 226). But the individual who is suffering in private may merely feel sad; in public, he may alternatively feel: (1) afraid of ridicule for crying; (2) guilty about foisting his suffering upon others; (3) relieved that he is not suffering alone; (4) angry that he cannot "let out his tears"; (5) humiliated if the loss engendered a fall in social status, and so on.

Any of these other emotional states would be more likely to co-occur with one's sadness when one is in public. According to the classical Emotions View, any of these emotions would trigger its own facial expression; thus, the face made in public would represent not "managed sadness," but sadness in combination with the ancillary emotions engendered by others' presence. Conceivably, the man who cries in private but refrains in public may merely be managing his facial muscles (and diaphragm) out of habit. However, invoking this display rules account requires that his emotional state must not differ in public versus in private. This state of affairs would be most improbable.

(In the Behavioral Ecology View, one cries in public when one believes the other is a potential source of succor or sometime remediation. One cries in private when one *imagines* another who is a source of succor, or when we offer ourselves succor. We sometimes cry more frequently in private because we create an idealized succorer.)

What, then, constitutes the evidence for cultural display rules? Many studies purport to investigate display rules, but they either: (1) ask subjects to verbalize their beliefs about the appropriateness of certain faces in certain contexts, while assuming that these accounts have currency in explaining actual facial behavior; or (2) examine differences in facial behavior in various situations and then ascribe the difference ad hoc to display rules (see Cole, 1985, for review of studies).

Thus far, the paradigmatic "demonstration" of display rules has been the best known study of cultural differences in facial behavior, the study of Japanese versus United States (hereafter, "American") students reported by Ekman and Friesen (e.g., Ekman, 1972; Friesen, 1972). Like the cross-cultural studies reviewed by Russell, the Japanese–American study and its conclusion about cultural display rules have gained canonical status, appearing not only in texts on emotion and facial expression, but also many introductory psychology texts.

Unfortunately, the study and its findings were never described completely or accurately. Most sources depended on Ekman and Friesen's own description of the study and summary of the data. Here is the usual description of the Japanese–American study (Ekman & Friesen, 1975):

> Research conducted in our laboratory played a central role in settling the dispute over whether facial expressions are universal or specific to each culture. In one experiment, stress-inducing films were shown to college students in the United States and to college students in Japan. Part of the time, each person watched the film alone and part of the time the person watched while talking about the experience with a research assistant from the person's own culture. Measurements of the actual facial movements, captured on videotapes, showed that when they were alone, the Japanese and Americans had virtually identical facial expressions. When in the

presence of another person, however, where cultural rules about the management of facial appearance (display rules) would be applied, there was little correspondence between Japanese and American facial expressions. The Japanese masked their facial expressions of unpleasant feelings more than did the Americans. This study was particularly important in demonstrating what about facial expression is universal and what differs for each culture. The universal feature is the distinctive appearance of the face for each of the primary emotions. But people in various cultures differ in what they have been taught about managing or controlling their facial expressions of emotion. (p. 24)

In this description, repeated often by Ekman and tertiary sources, Japanese and Americans viewed a film in each of two conditions, alone and with a same-culture experimenter. The facial expressions for the two groups were identical when subjects were alone, but dissimilar when "in the presence of another person." As will be apparent, the description and interpretation are inaccurate. Apart from the issue of reportage, the study itself illustrates the difficulties with the display rules concept. To obtain a fuller description of the Japanese–American display rules study, I obtained the unpublished dissertation by W. V. Friesen (1972) from the Microfilm Archives of the University of California.

According to Friesen (1972), the Japanese–American study actually involved *three* experimental conditions, not two as reported subsequently. Here were the conditions (actually phases or episodes, since the same subjects participated in all three):

Phase 1

Twenty-five Japanese and 25 American undergraduate males, each in his own country, individually viewed a total of 4 movies lasting 20 minutes. The first clip was designed to be mildly pleasant, and showed two men taking a canoe trip. The three remaining clips were intended to be stressful; these included ritual circumcision, a suction-aided delivery, and nasal sinus surgery.

Friesen did not include this solitary viewing phase in his dissertation. Instead, he referred to it as one previously conducted by Ekman, Friesen, and Malmstrom (unpublished), and reported in the chapter by Ekman (1972). Ekman's chapter contains the sole published listing of any of the solitary viewing data, and this listing was only fragmentary.

Phase 2

Immediately following the solitary viewing, a graduate student of the subject's own culture entered the viewing room and engaged the subject in a 1-minute face-to-face interview about his experience while viewing. The data for this second phase consisted of the subject's facial behavior in response to, and for approximately 10–20 seconds after the graduate student began the interview with the question, "How are you feeling right now?" (Friesen, 1972, p. 75).

Phase 3

Following this initial interview, the graduate student was positioned facing the subject with his back to the viewing screen. The most unpleasant portions of the final stressful clip (the nasal sinus surgery) were replayed. As the replay began, the graduate student resumed his interview with the question, "Tell me how you feel right now as you look at the film" (Friesen, 1972, p. 75). The data for this third experimental condition consisted of about 20–30 seconds of the subject's facial behavior following this question.

For all phases, the subject's facial behavior was viewed and videotaped using a hidden camera. Facial behavior concurrent with speech was excluded. The facial behavior was then coded using the *Facial Affect Scoring Technique* (Ekman, Friesen, & Tomkins, 1971), a predecessor to Ekman and Friesen's *Facial Action Coding System* (Ekman & Friesen, 1978).

The first condition thus involved solitary viewing, and both the second and third conditions were conducted in the presence of an experimenter. This fact is crucial to the interpretation of the results for the three conditions; I have depicted the data for the stressful films in Figure 11.2. One interpretive problem is that the scoring method used for Phases 2 and 3 by Friesen (1972) differed from that reported for the solitary viewing by Ekman (1972). This prevents direct comparisons between solitary viewing and the two interview conditions (Friesen used part-face scoring; Ekman reported mostly whole-face scoring data and only fragmentary part-face data).

A further problem is that these data do not depict facial behavior. Instead, subjects were categorized according to whether they showed (1) any "positive-affect" faces (largely smiles), (2) any "negative-affect" faces, (3) no facial behavior, or (4) unclassifiable facial behavior.

Inspection of the data in Figure 11.2 leads to three main conclusions:

1. Subjects in the first, solitary viewing phase produced a preponderance of putative "negative-affect" faces, equivalent for the two cultures. Eleven of the 50 subjects made no faces at all despite viewing such gory films.

2. In the second phase, about two-thirds of the faces made during this interview consisted of smiles, with the remainder interpreted as "negative-affect" faces. Statistical analysis showed *no* differences between the two cultures (Friesen, 1972, pp. 51–53).

3. In this third and final phase, the Japanese did not change either in smiling or "negative-affect" faces compared to the preceding interview. In contrast, the Americans smiled less and made more "negative-affect" faces.

The standard interpretation of the findings is that the Americans' faces were more authentic, whereas the Japanese subjects masked their revulsion with a "false smile" (Ekman, 1985).[4] This interpretation reinforces unfortunate jingoistic stereotypes ("orientals are inscrutable"; cf. Ekman, 1972, p. 241). It is also unsupportable on five counts:

1. Without direct comparisons between social and solitary viewing, no statement about "masking" by the Japanese subjects is tenable. It may well have been that the Americans were histrionic.

2. About 20% of the subjects in the solitary viewing condition (6 Americans and 5 Japanese) displayed no observable facial activity whatsoever. Is it conceivable that the stressful films left all of these subjects entirely unaffected? Moreover, if the Japanese "masked their revulsion with a false smile," then why did the 5 Japanese students who made *no* observable facial movements during solitary viewing make smiles during the interview?

3. Cultural differences were found only in the interview-while-viewing condition, and there was no prior basis for believing that any display rules would operate in one interview condition but not in another.

4. Subjects' facial behavior in the solitary viewing condition was regarded as "authentic" and unfettered by display rules; hence the faces were "emotional." To repeat Ekman's subsequent summary interpretation of the study:

> In private, when no display rules to mask expression were operative, we saw the biologically based, evolved, universal facial expressions of emotion. In a social situation, we had shown how rules for the management of expression led to culturally different facial expressions. (Ekman, 1984)

As I indicated in my previous discussion of implicit sociality (Chapter 8), the absolutism about the solitary viewing condition is unwarranted.

---

[4] As I discussed in Chapter 6, Ekman and Friesen (1982a) drew from Duchenne's observations (Duchenne, 1867/1959) in asserting that some facial expressions were "felt" because they portrayed emotion (e.g., "happy" smiles), and others were "false" because they did not (e.g., the smiles in the Japanese–American study). This felt/false view makes sense only if smiles are assumed a priori to portray happiness. In the Behavioral Ecology View, the smile of appeasement or politesse may have different timing and topography than the smile of play or amusement, but it is no less authentic. The felt/false dichotomy is erroneous because it: (1) so closely relates faces to emotion; (2) discounts as "false" those faces that arise in the service of social motives like appeasement, placation, compliance, submission, and face-saving ("embarrassment"); and (3) ignores the probabilistic relation of display to behavior (Smith, 1985).

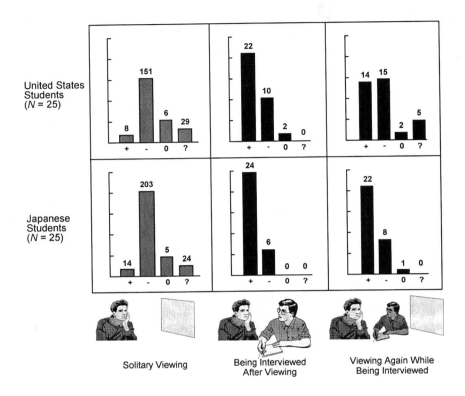

FIGURE 11.2.   Data from all three conditions of Ekman and Friesen's Japanese–American "display rules" study. The study was never reported completely or accurately. These data were taken from Ekman's summary, (Ekman, 1972), and from W. V. Friesen's unpublished dissertation (Friesen, 1972), as obtained from the Microfilm Archives of the University of California. Contrary to published interpretations of these data, the presence of an interviewer (middle panel) produced *no* statistical differences between the facial behavior of the Japanese and American subjects; only when being interviewed *while* watching the films did differences appear. Across the three phases of the experiment, abcissas denote visually scored facial behavior which the experimenters believed indicated: (+) positive emotion and (−) negative emotion. The (0) symbol indicates *no* facial behavior during that experimental phase (this is a tally of subjects, not facial scores), and (?) signifies the number of facial movements unclassifiable within the coding system. Instances of facial behavior classifiable as concurrent positive and negative emotion were tallied in both categories. Faces classified "surprise" were excluded. The absolute numbers listed for the solitary viewing condition (hatched bars in left panel) are not comparable to those for the two interview conditions (solid bars in middle and right panels) because of procedural differences in scoring methods.

The Japanese–American study is of course a study of audience effects, and just because the viewer is alone *physically* does not mean that he is alone *psychologically*. As I mentioned earlier, the experimenter is always an implicit audience, and his or her laboratory is always the stage for the directorial effort known as an "experiment." Thus the "alone" phase of the study was implicitly social, and the two interview phases were simply more explicitly social. Thus contrasting the facial behavior in the "alone" versus interview phases as authentic versus managed is overstatement at minimum.

It would also be presumptuous to regard subjects' facial activity as unrelated to speech. Even though facial behavior was selected so as to exclude concurrent speech, a facial movement that follows or precedes an utterance may be just as much a modifier of speech as one that occurs concurrently. In other words, much of the subjects' facial behavior was probably facial paralanguage (I discuss facial paralanguage in Chapter 12).

5. Most critically, attributing the Japanese–American differences to display rules would, as the definition of display rules stipulates, have required verification that both cultures had equivalent emotions in the condition in which their faces differed. Ekman (1972) stipulated this qualification himself when he discussed facial behavior at funerals:

> All too often a common emotional state is inferred simply because the same event was compared. For example, at funerals Culture Y might show down-turned, partially open or trembling lips, inner corners of the brows drawn together and up, and tightened lower lids (the sad face), while Culture X might show up-turned, partially opened lips, deep nasolabial folds, wrinkling in the corners of the eyes, and bagging of the lower eyelid (the broad smiling face). Before declaring that the facial expression of sadness varies across these two cultures, it would be necessary to verify that the stimulus *funeral* normatively elicits the same emotion in the two cultures rather than being an occasion for sadness in one culture and happiness in another. (p. 215)

By this reasoning, prerequisite to any comparisons of facial behavior in the Japanese–American study would be ensuring equivalence of emotion in the two groups of students. Above, I discussed the lack of independent criteria for emotion as a pitfall of the neurocultural model, and here the problem comes to roost. Ekman's discussion of the study admits this shortcoming (Ekman, 1972, p. 260), and suggests emotional self-report as possible validation. Curiously, these data were collected and available. After the conclusion of Phase 3, subjects completed questionnaires that inquired about their emotions during the viewing, as well as the entire California Psychological Inventory (Friesen, 1972, pp. 25–26). Surprisingly, these data were not reported or considered either by Ekman (1972) or Friesen (1972).

There is a simpler explanation than masking via display rules to account for the results Friesen reports. Simply stated, the Japanese subjects smiled out of politeness to the graduate student interviewer. Indeed, Japanese custom is to smile when being addressed, especially by an authority. When the film was being replayed, the positioning of the interviewer left subjects the choice to look at him or the film. Although the object of the film replay was to obtain reactions to the film with the interviewer present, it would be rude for the Japanese student to ignore the interviewer who was addressing him, and thus the Japanese students' faces were unaffected by the replay. It would be far less rude for the American student to view the film while being addressed. Thus the cultural difference may not have been in managing facial behavior, but in attending to the film. In the Behavioral Ecology View, the faces issued by the Japanese and Americans were equally authentic displays of social motives. The Americans were authentically moved to comment facially on the film, whereas the Japanese were authentically moved to show *politesse* to the experimenter.

In cross-cultural studies, social roles and the context of interaction are potential confounds in assessing display rules. Thus in any "display rules" study, not only must the emotion of the subject be controlled, but one's relation to those to whom one is displaying (i.e., in terms of power, status, obligation, etc.) must be controlled as well. These controls call for careful ethnographic or maturational comparison.[5]

These confounds also apply to studies claiming that at certain ages, children "learn display rules" (see review by Cole, 1985). In explaining changes in facial behavior in child development, two alternatives must always be excluded: (1) changes in the behavior may be programmed as part of maturation; or (2) the child may learn not about faces but about social roles and contexts, and the appropriate facial role behavior is issued as a consequence. Furthermore, studies of "display rules" that rely upon verbal accounts about facial manners (Saarni, 1978, 1982) must exclude the possibility that verbal accounts about facial manners may have little to do with actual facial behavior. When they do, they may result from observing one's own facial behavior, rather than being the cause of it.

To put it succinctly, demonstrating the operation of a display rule requires showing that what the individual is doing (and, as required by the neurocultural model, *learning* to do) is merely altering the predisposition to make a facial display by controlling the musculature—and

---

[5] Importantly, this position is consistent with either genetic or epigenetic accounts of the faces made by the two cultures. Even if all facial displays were under substantial genetic control, a display could occur in one culture but not another because the social roles and contexts that release the displays are present in one culture but not the other. Indeed, the role specificity itself could be genetically determined. It is possible that humans are "wired" to smile when addressed by certain kinds of authority, but only in Japanese culture did the graduate student interviewer possess the kind of authority requisite for the smiling.

TABLE I   Rousseauean *Leitmotif* Underlying Two-Factor Theories of Facial Expression

Emotional	Category of face	Social
	Creature domain	
Animal (savage)		Human (noble)
	Context of occurrence	
Natural (solitary)		Civil (public)
	Veridicality	
Authentic		Deceptive
	Type of issuance	
Released, reflexive		Rule governed, instrumental
	Governing mechanism	
Endogenous "facial affect programs"		Exogenous "cultural display rules"

nothing else. It is axiomatic that "emotion" and intention must be held constant in order to establish that the changes in facial expressions derive only from control of the *face*. Furthermore, attributing any facial behavior to "display rules" requires that individuals not alter their facial behavior by other strategies (i.e., distracting themselves, inhibiting themselves emotionally, or reframing or reinterpreting the situation).[6]

Thus, although individuals certainly do inhibit their own facial actions (i.e., holding back a belch), there is currently no acceptable evidence that display rules account for normal cultural or developmental differences in facial behavior.

WHY HAVE CLASSICAL EMOTIONS VIEWS OF FACES PERSISTED?

Given the weight of evidence favoring the Behavioral Ecology View of human faces, one must question why the two-factor, classical emotions theories of faces—and their most systematic presentation in the neuro-cultural model—have endured. My conjecture is that the appeal of these theories, and their contentions about "emotional" versus "social" faces, exploited a tacit but familiar Rousseauean romanticism: emotional faces signified authenticity, and rule-governed social faces denoted the inevitable loss of innocence forced by society. Table I depicts the romanticist *leitmotif* which I believe underlies two-factor theories of faces.

---

[6] Paul Rozin provided a useful analogy. If one looks impassive while urinating alone, but embarrassed in front of another, the embarrassed face can be due to a display rule (i.e., "look embarrassed while urinating") *only* if the individual does not in fact experience embarrassment. If an individual from another culture shows an impassive face in both conditions, it may be that the impassivity in the observed condition reflects not a masking face, but the culture's benign attitude toward public excretion. I also thank John Sabini for his helpful insights on this issue.

As Table I indicates, two-factor theories posit that "emotional" and "social" faces, respectively: (1) belong to the "animal" (primitive and impulsive) versus "human" (noble and rational) parts of our nature; (2) appear in natural (i.e., solitary) versus civil (public) contexts; (3) are due to emotion versus social convention; (4) are authentic (portraying "real" feeling) versus deceptive (representing Rousseau's "corrupted," dissembling social self); (5) are released reflexively versus performed instrumentally; and (6) are governed by endogenous "facial affect programs" versus exogenous "display rules." This romanticized view admits to worldly duplicity but appeals to our naive belief in an "authentic self," independent of social relations, manifest in heartfelt emotion erupting on the face.

This two-factor view depends upon several outmoded concepts discussed elsewhere in this volume. Specifically, it depends upon the:

1. outdated concept of displays as issuing from the context-free, reflexive mechanisms of Lorenzian ethology (Chapters 2 and 4, this volume), translated into the form of hermeutic emotion "circuits" (Chapter 8).
2. recapitulationist notion that phylogenetically "primitive" areas in our brain are held in check by other, more "advanced" parts (Chapters 3 and 6);
3. belief that we are innately innocent and egocentric, and must therefore *acquire* a social cognition (Chapter 7);
4. moralistic, dichotomous, propositional view of displays as "true" or false" (Chapter 7).

Plainly, the Behavioral Ecology View is less romantic. There is no fundamental innocence to lose. All parts of our brains are equally evolved, and act in coordinated fashion to promote our survival amid the social matrix into which we are born. Facial displays have meanings in the social context of their issuance, and they reflect not any "true" self or hermetic emotions but one's motives within a specific context of interaction. Adopting this view of faces and jettisoning two-factor emotion theories will obviously not be automatic or easy, because it will require our adopting new conceptions of ourselves.

12

FACIAL
PARALANGUAGE
AND GESTURE

Most facial displays do not even *connote* emotion; instead, they occur amid speech. Darwin (1872) remarked that "the movements of expression give vividness and energy to our spoken words" (p. 366). In the most fine-grained measurement of facial displays yet performed under naturalistic conditions, Ekman and Friesen (unpublished data; see Ekman, 1977; Ekman & Fridlund, 1987), viewed videotapes of psychiatric interviews of patients who were diagnosed as having largely affective disorders. Ekman and Friesen tabulated nearly 6000 facial displays, scored over 30 10-minute clinical interviews, and they—even in their "two-factor" terms—were able to classify fewer than one-third of the facial actions as "expressions of emotion." Ekman and Friesen believed that this proportion may overestimate what may occur in nonpatients, since when the patients were observed they were mostly "discussing their feelings"!

In noting this preponderance of "conversational signs" (Ekman, 1977), Fridlund and Gilbert (1985) asserted that the face's chief display role was not emotional but paralinguistic (i.e., accompanying and supplementing speech). Considering its importance, there is depressingly little formal research on human facial paralanguage. This is not to say that researchers have ignored facial paralinguistic movements; ironically, given their preponderance in normal facial behavior, they may in fact constitute the bulk of those facial actions studied under the rubric of "expressions of emotion." What is scant, though, is research on facial paralanguage as a category of facial actions distinct from, say, facial reflexes as well as those faces that communicate social intent.

How do we use our faces paralinguistically? I next describe two typologies of facial paralanguage. These will clarify just what constitutes these movements, and their apparent roles in human speech.

TYPES OF HUMAN FACIAL PARALANGUAGE

An early typology of facial paralanguage was the inductive scheme suggested by Ekman and Friesen (1969b). Their typology distinguished four main types of facial paralanguage.

1. Emblems Ekman and Friesen (1969b) borrowed Efron's (1941) term to refer to symbolic gestures we enact with our faces. We use them to replace words, modify, or remark upon ongoing speech, whether we are speakers or listeners.

I view emblems essentially as sentences imparted using the face. For example, the "tongue in cheek" display may say, "I'm skeptical" or "I'm worried about what you will say." A conversational smile may say, for example, "I agree with you" or "I recognize what you're talking about."

We frequently deploy facial emblems to circumvent speech taboos or speech accountability. When we are asked to comment on a boss, we may speak positively but make a grimace; a waiter may react likewise if asked whether an entree is worth ordering. Emblems can also signify the purpose of an utterance; the emblematic smile is crucial in humor, because it cues listeners that what is said, or will be said, must not be "taken seriously"—and the immediate reciprocation of the smile indicates that it will not.

Facial emblems are often just part of a larger emblematic display. For example, collusive winks ("I'm with you," or "You're in on this with me") often co-occur with a yaw of the head that points the wink to the conspirator. And the "facial shrug" (Ekman, 1985), which announces "I don't know" or "You've stumped me," is marked facially by a down-turned, horseshoe-shaped mouth but is usually accompanied by a momentary tilt of the head.

The omnipresence of emblematic faces, and their integral role in elaborating speech, became especially evident as computer bulletin board services (BBSs) and electronic mail (EMail) began to proliferate in the 1980s. Typewritten communications, especially humorous ones, were often misunderstood because they lacked the smiles and grins that would normally accompany them in face-to-face communication. Frequent BBS and EMail users filled the gap by inventing "smileys" (sometimes called "emoticons") that supplied the missing facial emblems. The types of "smileys" have proliferated (Sanderson, 1993); some common ones are shown in Figure 12.1.

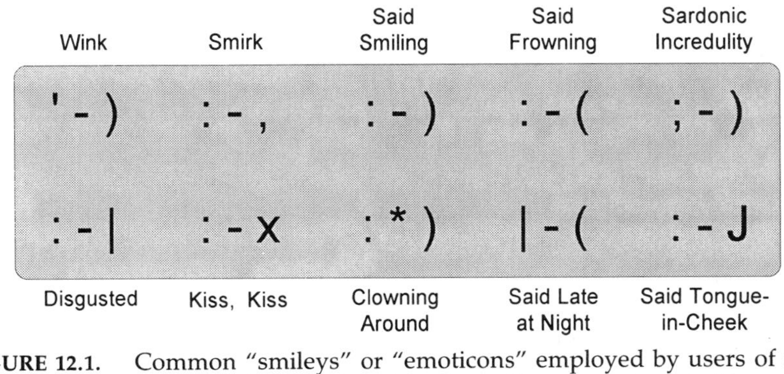

Wink	Smirk	Said Smiling	Said Frowning	Sardonic Incredulity
'-)	:-,	:-)	:-(	;-)
:-|	:-X	:*)	|-(	:-J
Disgusted	Kiss, Kiss	Clowning Around	Said Late at Night	Said Tongue-in-Cheek

FIGURE 12.1.   Common "smileys" or "emoticons" employed by users of electronic mail and computer bulletin board services. They were invented to replace the facial paralanguage missing from informal written communications (see Sanderson, 1993). "Smileys" are created from standard typed characters and are meant to be viewed with one's head tilted 90 degrees to the left.

2. [Self-]manipulators   Ekman and Friesen (1969b) termed these *adaptors*. We often rub, scratch, or pick at ourselves during interaction, but most of these self-manipulative acts involve the limbs rather than the face. These include actions like crossing and swinging our legs, biting our nails, scratching our necks, or running our hands through our hair. Self-manipulative facial actions are probably rarer because the facial muscles offer fewer opportunities. But they do occur; examples include biting our lips, wiping our lips, running our tongues in the crevices between our teeth and cheeks, clamping and then widening our eyelids, working our jaws, and brushing our teeth.

3. Illustrators   Illustrative facial movements are those that, as Darwin put it, "give vividness and energy to our spoken words." In Ekman and Friesen's typology, there are three major ways that illustrators vivify and energize speech. First, they can place accents on words as they are uttered, as when we raise our brows when we say beseechingly, "What do you *want*?" Second, they can be used indexically, as substitutes for finger-pointing, as when we tilt our heads and raise our brows when we say, "That's my friend over *there*." Third, they can indicate spatial relationships, as when we raise and lower our brows to indicate "above" and "below."

4. Regulators   Conversation requires regulation, and who takes the floor and who yields it are governed by a subtle stream of paralanguage that prevents either awkward speech gaps or collisions of run-on utterances. To negotiate access to the floor, we nod our heads to indicate that we have gotten the point, or we exaggerate the mouth movements preparatory to speech to show that we wish to squeeze in a word or two. And if we've yielded the floor, we try to regulate the speaker's content and pacing. We do this with brow raises if we like what others are saying and want them to continue, with frowns and head shakes if we don't like it and want them to stop, with yawns if we find it tiresome, and with forward head jerks if we want them to say it faster. Finally, mutual smiles among conversation partners serve to endorse the tone of the conversation and affirm the relationships of the partners (see Rosenfeld, 1987).

Ekman and Friesen's typology and terminology made sense and caught on. They were not derived from formal experiment; rather, they were inductions from informal observations of both natural and contrived (laboratory) conversations. Because of this fact, they describe more how the face *can* act in conversation than how it *does* act. More precise, quantitative evidence would be required to determine how often each kind of facial paralanguage occurs, and for that matter, whether Ekman and Friesen's scheme is exhaustive.

This task was undertaken by Chovil (1989), whose research on facial behavior and implicit sociality (Chovil, 1991) was described in part in Chapter 7. Chovil arranged for 12 dyads (4 male–male, 4 female–female, and 4 male–female) to have nominal 5-minute conversations about each of three topics designed to elicit frequent facial displays. The three topics were: (1) planning a nutritional meal consisting entirely of foods the subjects disliked; (2) describing a minor conflict that had occurred with another person; and (3) telling of a "close call" or "near miss" incident that they had either experienced or heard about.

Chovil videotaped the conversations and facial movements were coded from the videotape records. Excluding smiles because of their ubiquity, Chovil coded each movement in terms of: (1) the specific topography of the facial movement; (2) when in the conversation the movement occurred (e.g., during silences, ongoing speech, or moments of turn-taking); and (3) the gist of the conversation during the movement's occurrence. Chovil aimed to develop a typology of facial paralanguage based upon whether a facial movement: (1) was issued by speakers or listeners, or (2) conveyed syntactic, semantic, or nonlinguistic information.

Across the 12 dyads and 3 conversations Chovil and her independent judge scored 1184 facial movements. From this dataset Chovil arrived at a parsimonious hierarchical scheme that accounted for 99% of these movements. Her hierarchy is shown in Table I. Overall, the frequencies of facial movements listed in Table I did not change with either the conversation topic or the sex composition of the dyad.

Chovil listed five primary types of facial paralanguage, with subtypes for most. Chovil's emphasis was on the links between faces and language, so her descriptions are more functionalist than Ekman and Friesen's. Here are descriptions of the primary types and the four most frequent subtypes of each (all from Chovil, 1989; underlines indicate occurrences of the paralanguage):

1. We make *syntactic displays* that are usually connected with our speech intonation or its syntactical features, and are redundant with what we are saying. They consist largely of eyebrow raising and lowering, with tightening or widening of the eyes. Our most frequent syntactic displays are (a) *emphasizers*, which place stress on words ("He's <u>really</u> bad."); (b) *underliners*, which act similarly, but to phrases ("He's <u>too much for words</u>"); (c) *question markers*, which indicate that the utterance should be taken as a question; and (d) *story continuations*, which we usually issue with words or phrases to indicate that we want to continue talking ("And <u>that's not all</u> . . .", or "So <u>anyway</u> . . .").

TABLE I   Chovil's Topology of Facial Paralanguage and Observed Frequencies of Each Type

Type of facial movement		N	%
Linguistic movements			
Syntactic		315	27
Emphasizer	156		
Underliner	57		
Question marker	45		
Story continuation	18		
Other subtypes	39		
Speaker illustrator		243	21
Personal reaction	87		
Portrayal	83		
Thinking/Remembering	20		
Facial shrug	17		
Other subtypes	36		
Speaker comment		162	14
Personal reaction	73		
Thinking/Remembering	43		
Facial shrug	31		
Interactive	7		
Other subtypes	8		
Listener comment		160	14
Backchannel	84		
Personal reaction	48		
Motor mimicry	21		
Understanding	3		
Other subtypes	4		
Nonlinguistic movements (adaptors)		301	25
Unclassified		3	<1
Total		1184	100

Notes: From Chovil (1989). See text for descriptions of facial paralanguage types. N's are subtype and type totals.

2. We make *speaker illustrators* to depict or represent what we are saying. These include (a) *personal reactions*, which depict our sentiments about what we are saying (e.g., our making a "yuch" face when we say, "Rap music is <u>vile</u>"); (b) *portrayals*, or reenactments of our own previous reactions or those of others ("Well, I was absolutely <u>aghast</u> . . ."); (c) *thinking/remembering* displays, which echo our statements that we are thinking or reminiscing ("And so I <u>thought to myself</u> . . ."); (d) facial shrugs ("<u>You've got me</u>," and see discussion above).

3. We make *speaker comments* that convey information that is *non*redundant with what we are saying. These comments include (a) *personal reactions*, which add our sentiments to our otherwise neutral ut-

terances ("Well, they served Salisbury steak on the plane"); (b) *think-ing/remembering* displays, which signify themselves that we are think-ing or reminiscing ("Let's see, 34 times 86 is . . ."); (c) *facial shrugs*, which we issue as above, but with nonequivalent words ("It's possible that what you say is true"); (d) *interactive* displays, which recruit or enhance another's attention or reaction ("Do you know what I mean?").

4. And when we have yielded the floor, we make facial *listener comments* whose connotations are typically distinct from what the other is say-ing. The most common listener comments are (a) *backchannel* displays, which we make to indicate that we are listening and tracking what the speaker is saying. We often produce listener comments along with utterances like "Uh-huh" or "Yeah"; (b) *personal reactions*, which indi-cate our immediate reactions to the speaker's utterances. We might make such a facial comment if a speaker exclaims his or her enthusi-asm for a political view we detest; (c) *motor mimicry* displays, which echo the speaker's sentiments, as when we wince at hearing of the speaker's pain; (d) *understanding* displays, which signify that we have comprehended the substance of the speaker's utterance. We make such a display when we nod our heads as if to say, "I know what you mean."

5. Finally, whether as speakers or listeners, we issue *adaptors* that seem to have no systematic relationship to the ongoing speech. As I men-tioned above, examples include biting the lips or wiping them with the tongue.

In the examples I provided for each of Chovil's facial paralanguage categories, it is obvious that I have excluded the precise facial muscular patterns that characterize each. This is deliberate. Except for the brow movements that comprise most syntactic displays, Chovil observed *no* facial movements that were peculiar to any paralinguistic category. Rath-er, the facial movements were interpretable only in the context of the ongoing conversation. This is, of course, the same claim I make for the displays of social intent which the classical emotions theorist considers to be context-independent "facial expressions of emotion."

Chovil's study provides another relevant datum. Her tallies indicate that only 18% of her subjects' facial movements could be classified as personal reaction displays, arguably the closest match to "emotional faces." The data confirm that Ekman and Friesen's estimate that "emo-tional faces" constituted one-third of facial behavior was, as they specu-lated, an overestimate. And Chovil's "personal reaction" displays in-cluded responses that are only loosely definable as "emotional"; for example, they included indications of agreement and disagreement, difficulty in performing the task, and distastes for the foods in the "nutritional meal." Thus, the massive effort dedicated to understanding "facial expressions of emotion" appears to have been sunk on only a small portion of the displays we make in our everyday lives.

How did these paralinguistic actions arise? The sheer variety in the kinds of paralanguage implied by Ekman and Friesen (1969b) and observed by Chovil (1989) makes plausible a variety of origins. I present these next.

PROBABLE ORIGINS OF PARALANGUAGE

Although propositional language is thought to be a relatively recent development in human evolution, nonlinguistic vocalization was probably present among all protohumans, and with it, paravocal facial movements. As Richard Andrew stated, "vocalization and facial expression are inextricably associated in their evolution in the Primates" (1964, p. 284). And just as vocalizations emerged as ritualized social signals, it is not fanciful to suppose that the facial movements required to make those vocalizations might become emancipated and ritualized as signals themselves. Consequently, it cannot be assumed that those faces that signal social motives—the "expressions of emotion" of the classical emotions theorist—antedated the paralinguistic use of the face. Thus Darwin's casual implication that facial displays highlight speech may, in evolutionary terms, be slightly off the mark. The evolutionary trend was probably more complex. It is likely that speech arose from the vocalizations accompanying facial reflexes, others oriented to the face to detect the speech, and thus in the human, facial behavior became especially formalized. As human language evolved, so did the associated facial paralanguage. This may help explain infants' fascination with faces; it may promote greater attention to the nuances of caretaker sounds and result in faster language acquisition (Locke, 1992).

How might we determine the phylogenetic contributions to human facial paralanguage? One way might be to compare species, but such comparisons must confront the obvious obstacle that formal, propositional language is probably uniquely human (Premack, 1985). As a consequence, any nonhuman homologies with human paralanguage will be nonobvious (see Birdwhistell, 1970). If they exist, they will be discovered by comparing human facial paralanguage with nonhuman para*vocal* facial movements. Research on these movements is in its infancy, and I will discuss some early findings. Neural localization data might be informative, but I know of none that bear directly on facial paralanguage. Localization studies of amimias and aphasias are plentiful, but they not enlightening about origins because they are based on individuals who have acquired language and then lost aspects of it. Nor do I know of any relevant selective breeding or ontogenetic (e.g., adoption or twin) studies. All the available evidence derives from the comparative approach, and then almost totally in primates. I therefore give only brief and selective reviews, first of cross-species comparisons, followed by cross-cultural human comparisons.

Respiration and Vocalization

The upshot of this section is that facial paralanguage arose from respiration, because respiratory modulation is the basis of vocalization. Understanding facial paralanguage thus requires understanding vocalization. This is a complex story, and I will only sketch the outlines.

Darwin made the link between respiration and vocalization in *Expression*:

> With many kinds of animals, man included, the vocal organs are efficient in the highest degree as the means of expression. We have seen . . . that when the sensorium is strongly excited, the muscles of the body are generally thrown into violent action; and as a consequence, loud sounds are uttered, however silent the animal may generally be, and although the sounds may be of no use. . . .
>
> Involuntary and purposeless contractions of the muscles of the chest and glottis, excited in the above manner, may have first given rise to the emission of vocal sounds. (1872, pp. 83–84)

Wind (1970, 1976) endorsed the importance of respiration when he compared vocalizations among land-dwellers and the determinants of their extent and variety. Wind argues persuasively that the larynx evolved not as a "voice-box" but as a sphincter that protected the lungs and regulated airway patency. Any influence that speeded respiratory rate would naturally increase airflow through the larynx and make more probable the emission of accidental sounds. The respiratory pattern and airway structure that produced these sounds would then serve as preadaptations for auditory signaling. As I outlined in Chapter 4, natural selection would favor both creatures who could emit such sounds strategically, and the coevolution of auditory and discriminative mechanisms attuned to them and what they portend in the context of their emission.

Amphibians, reptiles, and mammals all make auditory displays using their larynxes.[1] Amphibians and reptiles, however, vocalize only infrequently, and their sounds are limited to comparatively stereotyped displays like the hissing of snakes, the croaking of frogs, and the roar of crocodiles. Several factors limit the vocal proclivities of amphibians and reptiles. First is their ectothermy ("cold-bloodedness"), which implies a lower metabolism and respiratory rate, and less use of the airway as a

---

[1] Insects make auditory displays, too, but they are not vocalizations. Usually they result from the chafing of body parts (e.g., cricket calls).

consequence. Second is the relative inflexibility of airway structures up to and including the rigid oral cavity and mouth. Birds and mammals, in contrast, are the chatterboxes of the animal kingdom, and they took airway-mediated auditory displays to the greatest degree of specialization.[2] Perhaps surprisingly, the vocal sophistication of mammals is accidental, and as Wind (1976) clarifies, the explanation may extend to facial paralanguage as well:

> Two other characteristics of mammals are related to vocalization; i.e., homeothermy and the very activity for which this Class is named: sucking. Apart from the consequences for the respiratory functions mentioned, a raised metabolism associated with *endothermy* must have implied (1) a more frequent taking in of food and a faster digestion of it, selecting for oropharyngeal adaptations; these include tooth specialization, greater tongue mobility, the development of facial and cheek muscles, and a rostrally located larynx enabling the animal to continue breathing and smelling while eating, and (2) a better insulation which must have been of selective value especially for the small-sized early mammals (because of the allometrical relationship between body size and body surface); this was achieved by skin adaptations like hairs that worked more efficiently when they could be erected. From these superficial muscles evolved those ensuring the subtle mobility of the whiskers (or vibrissae) and later the facial muscles so important for communication in the primates.
>
> The adaptations associated with *sucking* are partly the same as for endothermy; i.e., oropharyngeal specializations enabling the buildup of a negative pressure and the possibility of simultaneously drinking and breathing, and the development of facial and cheek musculature. (p. 623)

Thus mammalian endothermy and the necessity of suckling entailed a complex of changes that include a heightened respiratory rate with potentially greater sound production, and a hypermobile orofacial apparatus capable of nearly complete modulation of respiration or sound emission (recall the neurological consequences; Chapter 5). This hypermobility may be greatest in humans, and Lieberman (1984) has argued that the idiosyncratic morphology of the human supralaryngeal tract, which may permit greater lip and tongue mobility, evolved primarily for speech.

It only remains to speculate how particular mammalian, and then primate, facial movements arose as modulations of respiration or sound production. Richard Andrew has provided accounts for several kinds of mammalian and primate facial movements (see Andrew, 1963a,b, 1964, 1972). I mention three: the grin, the lip thrust, and the lip-smack.

---

[2] I will be skipping birds in this comparison for two reasons. First, modern birds are an offshoot of the endothermic reptiles known as theropods, and thus they represent neither modern reptiles nor mammals (Desmond, 1976). Second, birdsong is generated by a distinct nonlaryngeal mechanism, and the articulatory features it shares with mammalian vocalization seem to be the result of convergence and not homology (Wind, 1976).

Grins in Appeasement and Play

Andrew (1964) noted that in startle, many mammals, including nearly all primates, show mouth-corner retraction (i.e., a grin) along with glottal closures and exhalations likely to produce vocalizations. Indeed, the grin occurs with shrill vocalizations in many species: the meow of the cat, the clicks and crackles of lemurs, the whinny of the horse, screeches of monkeys, and screams of baboons and humans. In most primates, the grin is associated with scalp retraction, which Andrew and I argue is homologous with human brow raises. Reflex grins and vocalization would naturally occur when threatened. Consequently, the perioral actions and the shriek would be preadapted for general threat displays.

Andrew suggests as well that this reflexive grin-and-shriek pattern may explain the most common of all human facial movements, the human smile, both "emotional" (i.e., an intention movement of affiliation, appeasement, or play) and emblematic (signifying agreement or compliance). Andrew speculates that since one would likely produce the grin-shriek when threatened, the display became one that indicated, "I do not intend to attack." The smile's omnipresence, it follows, is due to the many motives it would serve, such as appeasement, submission, and affiliation. In these terms, the conversational smile used in agreement denotes "I will not oppose you" (or your point). The smile used in turn-taking denotes "I won't oppose your taking the floor" (i.e., the turf). Smiles would also serve well as signals for the mock attacks and predations that define primate play, because play approaches would be accompanied by an "I won't attack" display that, in context, says "Don't take me seriously."

That the ubiquitous smile derived from a basic grin-and-shriek pattern was called into question by Ekman's anecdotal observation (reported by Redican, 1982) that the muscles that comprise the human smile may be different than those for the grimace. Ekman's observation suggests either that: (1) the grimace and human smile indeed have different origins; *or* (2) they have common muscular origins, but the rapid neotenous trends in human craniofacial structure resulted in morphological changes in the muscles that produce the display. Van Hooff (1969) clearly distinguished the primate "staring bared-teeth scream face," an agonistic display, from the "silent bared-teeth face" associated with assurance and affiliation, and the "relaxed open-mouth face" associated with play. It is likely that the separate primate faces are ramifications of the original protective response accompanying vocalization. Like their modern primate counterparts, the human smile and grimace are now nonvocal, although vocal concomitants do occur, that is, laughs and titters, or shrieks and screams, respectively.

In drawing on Andrew's (1964) observations, I believe that the smile's origin was for its vocal and not its visual properties. I would argue that smiling changes vocal tract morphology to optimize transmission of the high-pitched vocalizations seen in submissive threat and in juvenile play. Both neotenously extended to human adults. (For speculations on different origins of smiling and laughter, see Lockard et al., 1977.)

Lip Thrusts in Dominance Displays

Another commonplace paravocal action Andrew noted is the outward lip thrust, often accompanied by rounding of the lips. This lip thrust occurs in the howl of the dog, the roar of the lion, the low of a deer, and in dominant threat in many primates (including humans, but not often in the chimp). Andrew speculated that the lip thrust served the expulsion of air during loud vocalizations. Notably, the Behavioral Ecology View that threat displays oftentimes convey RHP (Resource Holding Potential) explains why dominant threat displays so often include low-pitched vocalizations, whereas submissive threats are largely high-pitched squeals. Although data on the relation are sparse, a low-pitched call would most likely emanate from an individual with a high body weight, that is, one who *would* win a skirmish if provoked.

Lip Smacks in Babbling

Van Hooff (1969) and Andrew (1972) both noted a third paravocal display which Van Hooff called the "lip-smacking face." This display, especially prominent in the baboon, consists of lip smacking and rhythmic tongue protrusion that together modulate a stream of grunts. Reportedly these grunts often sound like human vowels. This display is usually associated with grooming and affiliation, often by a mother to young, and is regarded by many as homologous to some human speech, especially the endearing infant kind known as *babbling*.

Articulatory Movements in Auditory Calls

Other than these anecdotal observations, paravocal facial behavior in nonhumans is virtually *terra incognita*. Hauser and colleagues have provided preliminary evidence, however, that reliable facial movements do accompany discrete calls. Hauser, Evans, and Marler (1993) found that one group of rhesus monkeys reliably showed modifications of lip protrusion, lip separation, teeth separation, and mandibular position, that were selective to different call types. Hauser and Ybarra (1994) confirmed the importance of lip protrusion for one rhesus call, the affiliative "coo." Monkeys received injections of the dental nerve block, Xylocaine, that prevented lip protrusion; the injection should have produced shortening of the vocal tract and higher call pitches as a result. Following the injection, the coo calls had different harmonic structures, indicating the effects of the Xylocaine, but the fundamental frequencies of the calls were unchanged. This suggests both that rhesus monkeys rely on lip protrusion to make calls, and if lip protrusion is impossible, that they approximate their intended call by some compensatory vocal tract maneuver (probably, changing laryngeal position).

Vervet monkeys may also show complex articulations of calls using facial movements. Hauser et al. (1993) refer to a suggestive study by Owren and Bernacki (1988), who found that vervet calls contained formants (harmonics) whose amplitudes were independent of the fundamental frequencies of the calls; this finding implies that vervets articulate their calls using oropharyngeal modifications.

Finally, Hauser and Fowler (1992) document that vervet monkey calls reliably show a decline in frequency throughout the call, with a rapid drop at the end (rhesus monkey calls tended to show only the gradual decline). Technically, this gradual drop and the rapid, terminal one are termed the "fundamental frequency declination" and the "final fall." This pattern is nearly identical to the one humans use in conversation: the average frequency of speech declines throughout an utterance, and we drop the frequency when we've reached the "period" at the end of our final sentence. Hauser and Fowler (1992) did not measure any facial behavior associated with their subjects' pitch changes, but it would be unexpected if reliable facial movements did not accompany these call frequency declinations. One last finding from this study is particularly dramatic. Typically, our own final fall indicates the opportunity for a listener to take the floor. And like our own conversational turn-taking, final falls in vervet calls tended to precede interruptions by other vervets. This may be the first finding of conversational turn-taking in nonhumans.

Together, these studies demonstrate that, at least for some nonhuman primates, orofacial articulatory maneuvers accompany vocalization. Furthermore, data by Hauser and Fowler (1992) suggest that, at least for one species of monkey, vocal prosody assumes the frequency contours that characterize human conversation and turn-taking. We must now ask whether, in accord with the above mechanisms, the facial movements that nonhumans use in the course of vocalization have themselves become formalized as signals. This question is not yet answerable, but it is a crucial one, as I explain at the end of this chapter.

Formalization of Facial Paralanguage

Thus far I have discussed the links between specific facial displays and vocalizations, and reviewed hypotheses that many have vocal origins. But we are still a long way from understanding the range of facial paralanguage captured by Ekman and Friesen's early typology, and especially by Chovil's interaction data. How, for example, do facial movements become syntactic markers? We might as well ask how humans evolved syntax. We know neither, and so a comprehensive theory of human facial paralanguage awaits a comprehensive theory of *language*. Nonetheless, one can formulate reasonable explanations of some cases of facial paralanguage.

One case comprises those kinds of paralanguage that Ekman and Friesen termed manipulators or adaptors, of which biting the lower lip is probably the most common. Manipulators seem simply to be instances of the redirected behavior seen during conflict episodes in many species (see Alcock, 1984). For example, a bird at a territorial boundary may want *both* to attack and to remain on safe ground. Instead, it either preens or pecks at the grass near the boundary (a redirected attack; see Figure 12.2).

We bite our lower lips in a variety of conflict situations (e.g., when we try to solve a difficult problem, when we exert ourselves, or when we are in physical pain or mental anguish). It is used in conversation when there are words that we both *want* to say and *don't*, and our listeners/observers usually draw this conclusion. Of course, examples of redirected behavior emitted by humans in conflict are not confined to the face. Others suggest the preening of Figure 12.2, including nail-biting, running the hand through one's hair, adjusting one's collar, or compulsions like hand-wringing or trichotillomania (hair-pulling; see Kishnan, Davidson, & Guajardo, 1985). Redirected behavior, of course, can be used by "mind-readers" (i.e., observers) to discern that the displayer is in conflict, as Chovil (1989) observed in her listeners.

Other cases of facial paralanguage may be the endpoints of a formalization of facial movements that originate in reflexes but become nonverbal symbols. For example, we raise our brows momentarily to novelty, a reflex probably derived from auditory orientation. We also raise them in conversation to convey that the speaker's point commanded our attention (orientation), or when, as speakers, we wish our listeners to attend specially to *our* point. Similarly, we protrude our tongues reflexively when we expel noxious substances from our mouths (a reflex), and we may come to use the same protrusion symbolically. It may become an illustrator ("your argument disgusts me") or even an emblem (i.e., a "razz" or "Bronx cheer").[3] Smith et al. (1974) provided a compendium of the uses of tongue-showing.

How much of the formalization of paralanguage is ritualization? No doubt some, even much, facial paralanguage is entirely conventionalized, arising within one generation. Cross-cultural data on facial

---

[3] The endpoint of formalization of paravocal display may be onomatopoeia, wherein a word (e.g., "screech") both elicits and refers to the facial-vocal display.

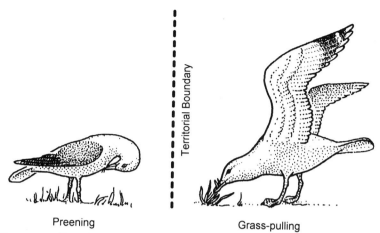

Preening   Grass-pulling

FIGURE 12.2.   Two herring gull males at a territorial boundary, torn between fending off the potential interloper and staying on one's own turf, redirect their conflict to neutral behavior like preening (*left*) or grass-pulling (*right*). Such redirection may explain the common variety of human paralanguage known as *manipulators* or *adaptors*, such as biting the lower lip. Like the avian case, such human movements usually indicate that one is in conflict. Illustration from Alcock (1984), reprinted with permission.

paralanguage are scant and decidedly mixed. I discuss these data and what they imply about phylogenesis.

POPULATION SIMILARITIES AND DIFFERENCES IN HUMAN PARALANGUAGE

The most systematic observations of facial gesture and paralanguage in varying geographic regions were performed by Eibl-Eibesfeldt (1972). In order to minimize self-consciousness in his subjects, he gathered data using movie cameras with "angle" lenses (i.e., the camera records a scene oblique to the position it is pointed). Regrettably much of his evidence is anecdotal. True to his naturalistic emphasis and Lorenzian training, he did not code the facial movements anatomically, nor were the elicitors standardized. His observations are still instructive.

Eibl-Eibesfeldt reported a number of cross-cultural communalities. He observed that during greeting, many cultures show a brief (about 1/6 second) raise of the eyebrows. He calls this movement a "brow flash." It is often accompanied by a vertical head nod and a smile. During flirtation or embarrassment, individuals across many cultures engage in "cutoff" movements such as averting gaze, hiding the face, or hiding the mouth behind the hand.

Eibl-Eibesfeldt also reported considerable cultural variation in facial gestures. For example, indignation and arrogance are signified in only some cultures by prolonged brow raises with backward head movements. Girls in one culture (Waika Indians) flirt with males using tongue protrusions.

Perhaps the facial displays that vary most widely across cultures are emblems for negation and affirmation. Darwin's own correspondents reported that the head shakes associated with affirmation and negation in Anglo-Saxon cultures varied greatly worldwide (Darwin, 1872).

Darwin questioned whether the lateral head-shake negation display derives from an infantile response associated with oral rejection (i.e., turning away from the breast with satiation). Van Hooff (1969) observed a lateral head-shake in many primates, but interpreted it as ritualized looking-away. Eibl-Eibesfeldt (1972) believed that the head-shake negation may derive from a general mammalian "shaking-off" movement. He reported this gesture's wide use across cultures for signaling an emphatic "no!," and observed the display in thalidomide children born deaf and blind. However, he believed that weaker displays of rejection were more variable (e.g., the Greek "no" signaled by head retraction and a brow raise).

Signals of affirmation may be more variable. For example, Eibl-Eibesfeldt reported that Samoans use the brow flash to signal "yes," whereas one use of "yes" (as a display of compliance) in Ceylonese is signaled using slow sideways head-swaying. Many anthropologists (e.g., LaBarre, 1947) have remarked upon the smile's widely different uses across cultures. For example, it appears to signal affiliation, play, or appeasement in Western cultures, but in African cultures it is also deployed during embarrassment or shame.

There are precious few other data on facial paralanguage, except for wholly anecdotal accounts, and except for Chovil's (1989) observations of English-speaking Canadians, I know of no detailed, anatomically based observations of facial paralanguage. I next discuss how the existing data can be interpreted.

INTERPRETATION OF EVIDENCE FROM DIVERSE HUMAN POPULATIONS

It is tempting to try to understand the origins of the instances of paralanguage reported above, and to determine how much is conventional. Others have. Investigators like Birdwhistell and LaBarre used cultural differences in facial paralanguage to assert a cultural relativism and to mitigate a phyletic contribution. I consider this dispositiveness premature. As I have tried to make clear for nonparalinguistic facial displays, regional differences in facial paralanguage do not imply that it is conventional (i.e., epigenetic). Determination of what is "nature" and what is "nurture" in facial paralanguage is just as labyrinthine, and any attempt must consider the following:

1. Genetic drift or founder effects may have produced variations in facial paralanguage among diverse cultures. As I indicated in Chapter 11, these are strictly genetic mechanisms, but they can produce quite pronounced variations in local populations that masquerade as "cultural."

2. Population comparisons of facial paralanguage that find regional variation must still control for *language*. Some paralanguage may be universally, innately coupled to certain aspects of language, but its manifestation would depend entirely upon the existence or nonexistence of those aspects of the language in the given population. This point can be clarified with an example. Conceivably, humans might be "prewired" to display a head tilt with eyebrow raise whenever they use the subjunctive mood; the action might occur as an illustrator during speech, or as an emblematic conversational response (symbolizing the sentence, "It could be true."). What if we found wide variations in usage of this display across geographic regions or cultures? It would be presumptuous to consider this a variation in *display*, because it might as well represent a difference in language. Populations that did not show the display might, for example, lack the subjunctive mood for demarcating counterfactuals (e.g., putatively the Chinese; see Au, 1983; Bloom, 1981). Conversely, a population may lack the language for counterfactuals and depend upon paralanguage to denote them. And we simply do not know what constitutes the innate, "deep structure" of facial paralanguage. It may be coupled with phonological, syntactic, and/or semantic features of language, and it may be "released" with the emphatic or prosodic features of particular dialects.

3. Even if facial actions like emblems appear wholly symbolic, it cannot be assumed that they are simply conventions. As I illustrated in the case of the hypothetical subjunctive-illustrator, and in my earlier discussion of display rules, rapid cultural evolution does not exclude phyletic contribution. To take a sample emblem, Elvis Presley's cinematic sneer while speaking to female costars became a teenage American male flirtation display nearly instantaneously in the 1960s, although its use in contempt (and derision, scorn, etc.) was an excellent preadaptation. Are we to conclude that this emblem was entirely conventional (i.e., a learned token)? This position is defensible *only* if it is demonstrated that attitudes females found attractive in males did not change. Instead, the sneer may be entirely canalized in displaying contempt, derision, and so on, and Elvis Presley induced males to

take this *attitude* toward females. Ultimately, had the sneer persisted culturally, males genetically predisposed to sneering should have greater reproductive advantage. Furthermore, morphological change (a lip structure conducive to sneers) might become weakly selected for, but detecting such selection would take many generations.

4. The above three dicta urge against the disqualification of a genetic basis for facial paralanguage even amid population variations in it. Conversely, communalities in facial paralanguage among human populations—or resemblances among human paralinguistic and non-human paravocal actions—do not guarantee a phyletic contribution. This is so for the same arguments cited in my discussion of "facial expressions of emotion." As before, it is necessary to exclude cultural transmission, convergent evolution, and common learning. As in those cases, both nonhuman and human ontogenetic data are crucial, even though the ideal human experiments (i.e., blind children reared and taught to speak solely by blind caretakers) are wildly improbable and perhaps ill advised.

These are just cautions. It is too early to determine just which elements of facial paralanguage are under genetic control and which are conventional. We know far too little about human facial paralanguage in even one population, much less across humanity *in toto*. And as I indicated with respect to putative "display rules," ethnographic and linguistic perspectives must come to bear before the existence or nonexistence of any facial paralanguage is taken to implicate genetic versus epigenetic contributions.

WHAT ISN'T PARALANGUAGE ABOUT THE FACE?

Although we know little about human facial paralanguage, a few conclusions are obvious. The first is forced by Chovil's (1989) data and earlier observations by Ekman and Friesen (cited above), and it is the overwhelming predominance of the paralinguistic role of the face. Given this predominance, debates about "facial expressions of emotion" have received too much attention. This is especially true if nonhuman facial movements are increasingly found to relate to articulated calls and even conversational turn-taking, because it would invalidate using homologies in nonhumans to infer which human faces are *non*paralinguistic.

The second is the likelihood that so much facial behavior, paralinguistic or otherwise, and even the facial muscles themselves, had their roots in vocalization. Assuming these origins, then, perhaps even facial displays of intent—the "facial expressions of emotion" of the classical emotions theorists—are paralanguage. Like the verbal interjections we insert in our ongoing speech, they may be nonverbal interjections, once derived from vocalization but now emancipated from it, making them appear autonomous and wholly apart from the stream of our facial paralanguage. If so, then like our verbal interjections, those faces that have preoccupied generations of researchers, and which form the focus of this volume, may be seen simply as "parts of speech" in a future facial grammar.

13

EPILOGUE: THE STUDY OF FACIAL DISPLAYS— WHERE DO WE GO FROM HERE?

What we know about our faces has advanced remarkably since our physiognomist predecessors began their studies. The morphology of our face and the workings of its muscles are now well understood. We are much smarter about how our facial reflexes govern or facilitate many mundane but altogether vital orofacial actions: eating, drinking, breathing, yawning, sneezing, and gagging, to name just a few. And we have proceeded to complete our maps of the connections between the face and the brain; the outlook here is especially sanguine, given that neural imaging technology is just catching up with our questions (Posner & Raichle, 1994). Perhaps most important, we have just begun to glimpse the intimate relations between the face and language, and the intimacy lies both in their revolutionary origins and in the crucial participation of the face in modern spoken language.

What of those facial displays that were historically considered "facial expressions of emotion," and which form the bulk of facial-expression research? Here we know less. Despite over a century of inquiry regarding universality and innateness of facial displays, the key questions remain unanswered. I believe that the role of natural selection can be discerned only when facial displays, like morphological features, are subjected to the full armamentarium of modern behavior-genetic and population-genetic methods. I have tried in this paper to elaborate the questions to be answered and the means to answer them.

Does genetic evolution play the major role in accounting for cultural similarities and differences in, and the meaning of, facial displays? The within-species (i.e., cross-cultural) comparative data are inconclusive. This state of affairs reflects the difficulty of acquiring such data, and the inherent limitations of the comparative method with respect to behavior. Moreover, the early cross-cultural studies on displays connoting emotion did not have the Behavioral Ecology View I present as an alternative account. Given wide cultural migration and trade, and the omnipresence of mass media, cross-cultural studies are now of dubious value. With increased awareness (wholly welcome) of social and political rights of the handicapped, ontogenetic data on children reared in isolation, or with minimal caretaking, are now exceedingly hard to obtain.

Consequently, it may be too late to answer the questions of innateness and universality using cross-cultural comparative methods, and more difficult to answer them ontogenetically.

One major shortcoming of past research has been solved. Anecdotal or inductive reportage of human facial displays has been supplanted by anatomically based facial scoring (Ekman & Friesen's Facial Action Coding System; Ekman & Friesen, 1978; and its gestaltist counterpart, the Maximally Discriminative Facial Movement Coding System; Izard, 1983). Such anatomical coding could profitably be extended to each species of social primate, and beyond the primates. Although manual facial scoring is now tedious and expensive, computer pattern recognition technology will enable the determination of analogies and homologies in facial displays more precisely within and across species.

The precision already achieved in facial scoring must now be achieved in specifying elicitors of displays and the correlates of display. Past research was handicapped considerably by its preoccupation with linking displays to ineffable and undefinable emotions, as Kendon (1975) presciently noted. Hinde (1985b) voiced similar sentiments. As I have outlined, contemporary ethologists no longer view most vertebrate displays as reflexive or drive instigated, but rather as referential and strategic. It is thus ironic that the predominant, classical view of human displays retains a quasi releaser conception that many faces are eruptile expressions of "fundamental emotions" (A. K. Jaffey, personal communication, May, 1988). Our obsession with linking faces with emotion has led us to neglect the face's role in paravocal display among nonhumans and paralinguistic display among humans.

In line with a Behavioral Ecology View of facial displays, I believe that a "Facial Elicitor Coding System" is overdue. FECS would consist not of emotions but of social interactions that are specified, and ethnographically equated, according to social roles, motives, and interaction contexts. In the case of paralanguage, facial displays would be compared while controlling for semantic, syntactic, and prosodic features of speech. These efforts constitute a formidable challenge, psychologically and anthropologically, but they are necessary for our knowledge to advance.

I also anticipate a more sophisticated treatment of facial displays as complex traits determined both genetically and epigenetically. Twin and adoption research on facial displays will produce additional knowledge of how much of which facial behavior is heritable, as will interactive theories of genetic and cultural selection (Barkow, Cosmides, & Tooby, 1992; Boyd & Richerson, 1985).

Finally, we are close to mapping the human genome, and developing rapid individual whole-genotype testing (National Research Council, 1988). New protein assays may allow independent determination of the extent of ongoing genetic evolution (Grant, 1985; Kimura, 1983). These developments, together with precision facial coding, may provide a way to answer definitively the question of phyletic contributions to human and nonhuman facial displays. It may indeed be possible to reconstruct from extant species the evolutionary origins of facial signal systems, and to chart the emergence of human facial display.

Abelson, R. P. (1981). Psychological status of the script concept. *American Psychologist, 36,* 715–729.

Abelson, R. P., & Sermat, V. (1962). Multidimensional scaling of facial expressions. *Journal of Experimental Psychology, 63,* 546–554.

Adams, E. S., & Caldwell, R. L. (1990). Deceptive communication in asymmetric fights of the stomatopod crustacean *Gonodactylus bredini. Animal Behaviour, 39,* 706–716.

Alberch, P., Gould, S. J., Oster, G. F., & Wake, D. B. (1979). Size and shape in ontogeny and phylogeny. *Paleobiology, 5,* 296–317.

Alcock, J. (1984). *Animal behavior: An evolutionary approach* (3rd. ed.). Sunderland, MA: Sinauer.

Alexander, R. D., Hoogland, J. L., Howard, R. D., Noonan, K. M., & Sherman, P. W. (1979). Sexual dimorphisms and breeding systems in pinnipeds, ungulates, primates, and humans. In N. A. Chagnon & W. Irons (Eds.), *Evolutionary biology and human social behavior* (pp. 402–435). North Scituate, MA: Duxbury.

Alford, R. D. (1983). Sex differences in lateral facial facility: The effects of habitual emotional concealment. *Neuropsychologia, 21,* 567–570.

Alford, R. D., & Alford, K. F. (1981). Sex differences in asymmetry in the facial expression of emotion. *Neuropsychologia, 19,* 605–608.

Allport, F. M. (1924). *Social psychology.* Boston: Houghton-Mifflin.

Allport, G. (1937). *Personality: A psychological interpretation.* New York: Holt.

Altmann, L. (1987). *Who's next! The history of self-experimentation in medicine.* New York: Random House.

American Psychiatric Association (1987). *Diagnostic and statistical manual for mental disorders* (3rd ed., revised) (DSM-III-R). Washington, DC: Author.

Ancoli, S. (1980). Physiological response patterns of emotion. Unpublished doctoral dissertation, University of California, San Francisco. San Francisco: University of California Microfilm Archives.

Andersson, M. (1982). Female choice selects for extreme tail length in a widowbird. *Nature, 299,* 818–820.

Andrew, R. J. (1963a). Evolution of facial expression. *Science, 141,* 1034–1041.

Andrew, R. J. (1963b). The origin and evolution of the calls and facial expressions of the primates. *Behaviour, 20,* 1–109.

Andrew, R. J. (1964). The displays of the primates. In J. Buettner-Janusch (Ed.), *Evolutionary and genetic biology of primates* (Vol. II, pp. 227–309). New York: Academic Press.

Andrew, R. J. (1972). The information potentially available in displays. In R. A. Hinde (Ed.), *Nonverbal communication.* New York: Cambridge University Press.

Angell, J. R. (1904). *Psychology: An introductory study of the structure and function of human consciousness.* New York: Holt.

Archibald, H. C., & Tuddenham, R. D. (1965). Persistent stress reaction after combat. *Archives of General Psychiatry, 12,* 475–481.

Argyle, M. (1972). Non-verbal communication in human social interaction. In R. A. Hinde (Ed.), *Nonverbal communication* (pp. 243–269). New York: Cambridge University Press.

Aristotle. (1913). *Physiognomonica.* In W. D. Ross (Ed.) & T. Loveday & E. S. Forster (Trans.), *The works of Aristotle* (pp. 805–813). Oxford, England: Clarendon.

Armon-Jones, C. (1985). Prescription, explication, and the social construction of emotions. *Journal for the Theory of Social Behavior, 15,* 1–22.

Arnold, M. B. (1945). Physiological differentiation of emotional states. *Psychological Review, 52,* 34–48.

Arnold, M. B. (1960). *Emotion and personality* (Vol. 1). New York: Columbia University Press.

Arnold, S. (1983). Sexual selection: The interface of theory and empiricism. In P. Bateson (Ed.), *Mate choice.* Cambridge: Cambridge University Press.

Aronfreed, J. A. (1968). *Conduct and conscience: The socialization of internalized control over behavior.* New York: Academic Press.

Ashton, E. H., & Zuckerman, S. (1951). Some cranial indices of *Plesianthropus* and other primates. *American Journal of Physical Anthropology, 9,* 283–296.

Au, T. K. (1983). Chinese and English counterfactuals: The Sapir-Whorf hypothesis revisited. *Cognition, 15,* 155–187.

Averill, J. R. (1969). Autonomic response patterns during sadness and mirth. *Psychophysiology, 5,* 399–414.

Averill, J. R. (1980). A constructivist view of emotions. In R. Plutchik & H. Kellerman (Eds.), *Emotion: Theory, research, and experience.* New York: Academic Press.

Averill, J. R. (1990). Emotion in relation to systems of behavior. In N. L. Stein, B. Leventhal, & T. Trabasso (Eds.), *Psychological and biological approaches to emotion* (pp. 385–404). Hillsdale, NJ: Erlbaum.

Ax, A. F. (1953). The physiological differentiation between fear and anger in humans. *Psychosomatic Medicine, 5,* 433–442.

Axelrod, R. (1984). *The evolution of cooperation.* New York: Basic Books.

Bain, A. (1855). *The senses and the intellect.* London: Parker.

Bain, A. (1859). *The emotions and the will.* London: Parker.

Bainum, C. K., Lounsbury, K. R., & Pollio, H. R. (1984). The development of laughing and smiling in nursery school children. *Child Development, 55,* 1946–1957.

Bakhtin, M. M. (1981). *The dialogical imagination* (M. Holquist, Ed.). Austin, TX: University of Texas Press.

Baldwin, J. M. (1895). *Mental development in the child and the race: Methods and processes.* New York: Macmillan.

Baldwin, J. M. (1896). A new factor in evolution. *American Naturalist, 30,* 441–451, 536–553.

Barkow, J. H., Cosmides, L., & Tooby, J. (Eds.). (1992). *The adapted mind.* New York: Oxford University Press.

Barlow, G. (1977). Modal action patterns. In T. A. Sebeok (Ed.), *How animals communicate.* Bloomington, IN: Indiana University Press.

Barrett, P. H., Gautrey, P. J., Herbert, S., Kohn, D., & Smith, S. (Eds.). (1987). *Charles*

Darwin's notebooks: Geology, transmutation of species, metaphysical enquiries. Ithaca, NY: Cornell University Press.

Basmajian, J. V., & DeLuca, C. J. (1985). *Muscles alive: Their functions as revealed by electromyography* (5th ed.). Baltimore: Williams & Wilkins.

Bavelas, J. B. (1989). Treating deception as discourse. Paper presented at the 19th Annual Meeting of the International Communication Association, San Francisco.

Bavelas, J. B., Black, A., Lemery, C. R., & Mullett, J. (1986). "I *show* how you feel": Motor mimicry as a communicative act. *Journal of Personality and Social Psychology, 50,* 322–329.

Bavelas, J. B., Black, A., Chovil, N., Lemery, C. R., & Mullett, J. (1988). Form and function in motor mimicry. Topographic evidence that the primary function is communicative. *Human Communication Resesarch, 14,* 275–299.

Bavelas, J. B., Black, A., Chovil, N., & Mullett, J. (1990). Truths, lies, and equivocations: The effects of conflicting goals on discourse. *Journal of Language and Social Psychology, 9,* 135–161.

Bekoff, M., & Allen, C. (1992). Intentional icons: Towards an evolutionary cognitive ethology. *Ethology, 91,* 1–16.

Bell, C. (1806). *Essays on the anatomy of expression in painting.* London: Longman.

Bell, C. (1833). *The hand, its mechanism and vital endowments as evincing design.* Bridgewater Treatises on the Power, Wisdom, and Goodness of God, as manifested in the Creation. Treatise IV. London: W. Pickering.

Bell, C. (1844). *Anatomy and philosophy of expression as connected with the fine arts* (3rd ed.). London: Murray.

Bergson, H. (1911). *Creative evolution* (trans.). New York: Holt.

Berlin, B., & Kay, P. (1969). *Basic color terms: Their universality and evolution.* Berkeley & Los Angeles: University of California Press.

Berlyne, D. E. (1969). Laughter, humor, and play. In G. Lindzey & E. Aronson (Eds.), *The handbook of social psychology* (Vol. 3). Reading, MA: Addison-Wesley.

Birdwhistell, R. L. (1963). The kinesic level in the investigation of the emotions. In P. H. Knapp (Ed.), *Expression of the emotions in man* (pp. 123–139). New York: International Universities Press.

Birdwhistell, R. L. (1970). *Kinesics and context.* Philadelphia: University of Pennsylvania Press.

Bloom, A. H. (1981). *The linguistic shaping of thought: A study in the impact of language on thinking in China and the West.* Hillsdale, NJ: Erlbaum.

Bock, W. J. (1959). Preadaptation and multiple evolutionary pathways. *Evolution, 13,* 194–211.

Bolles, R. C. (1979). *Learning theory* (2nd ed.). New York: Holt, Rinehart, & Winston.

Borod, J. C., & Koff, E. (1984). Asymmetries in affective facial expression: Behavior and anatomy. In N. Fox & R. J. Davidson (Eds.), *The psychobiology of affective development.* Hillsdale, NJ: Erlbaum.

Boucher, J. D. (1973). Facial behavior and the perception of emotion: Studies of Malays and Temuan Orang Asli. Paper presented at the Conference on Psychology Related Disciplines, Kuala Lumpur.

Boucher, J. D., & Carlson, G. E. (1980). Recognition of facial expression in three cultures. *Journal of Cross-Cultural Psychology, 11,* 263–280.

Bowlby, J. (1990). *Charles Darwin.* London: Hutchinson.

Boyd, R., & Richerson, P. J. (1985). *Culture and the evolutionary process.* Chicago: University of Chicago Press.

Bratzlavsky, M. (1979). Feedback control of human lip muscle. *Experimental Neurology, 65,* 209–217.

Bratzlavsky, M., & vander Eecken, H. (1977). Altered synaptic organization in facial nucleus following facial nerve regeneration: An electrophysiological study in man. *Annals of Neurology, 2,* 71–73.

Braun, J., & Linder, D. E. (1979). *Psychology today* (4th ed.). New York: Random House.

Brightman, V. J., Segal, A. L., Werther, P., & Steiner, J. (1975). Ethologic study of facial expressions in response to taste stimuli. *Journal of Dental Research, 54,* L141 (Abstract).

Brightman, V. J., Segal, A. L., Werther, P., & Steiner, J. (1977). Facial expression and hedonic response to taste stimuli. *Journal of Dental Research, 56,* B161 (Abstract).

Brodal, A. (1981). *Neurological anatomy: In relation to clinical medicine.* New York: Oxford University Press.

Brothers, L. (1989). A biological perspective on empathy. *American Journal of Psychiatry, 146,* 10–19.

Brothers, L. (1990). The social brain: A project for integrating primate behavior and neurophysiology in a new domain. *Concepts in Neuroscience, 1,* 27–51.

Brothers, L. (1992). Perception of social acts in primates: cognition and neurobiology. *Seminars in the Neurosciences, 4,* 409–414.

Brothers, L., & Ring, B. (1992). A neuroethological framework for the representation of minds. *Journal of Cognitive Neuroscience, 4,* 107–118.

Brown, D. E. (1991). *Human universals.* New York: McGraw-Hill.

Brown, J. D. (1972). *Aphasia, apraxia, and agnosia.* Springfield, IL: Charles Thomas.

Brown, R. (1986). *Social psychology* (2nd ed). New York: The Free Press.

Browne, J. (1985). Darwin and the expression of the emotions. In D. Kohn (Ed.), *The Darwinian heritage* (pp. 307–326). Princeton: Princeton University Press.

Bruce, C., Desimone, R., & Gross, C. G. (1981). Visual properties of neurons in a polysensory area in superior temporal sulcus of the macaque. *Journal of Neurophysiology, 46,* 381–384.

Bruner, J. (1973). Organization of early skilled action. *Child Development, 44,* 1–11.

Bruner, J. S., & Tagiuri, R. (1954). The perception of people. In G. Lindzey (Ed.), *Handbook of social psychology* (Vol. 2). Cambridge: Addison-Wesley.

Buck, R. (1977). Nonverbal communication of affect in preschool children: Relationships with personality and skin conductance. *Journal of Personality and Social Psychology, 35,* 225–236.

Buck, R. (1979). Measuring individual differences in the nonverbal communication of affect: the slide-viewing paradigm. *Human Communication Research, 6,* 47–57.

Buck, R. (1980). Nonverbal behavior and the theory of emotion: The facial feedback hypothesis. *Journal of Personality and Social Psychology, 38,* 811–824.

Buck, R. (1984). *The communication of emotion.* New York: Guilford.

Buck, R. (1985). Prime theory: An integrated view of motivation and emotion. *Psychological Review, 92,* 389–413.

Buck, R. (1988). *Human motivation and emotion* (2nd ed.). New York: Wiley.

Buck, R., Savin, V. J., Miller, R. E., & Caul, W. F. (1972). Communication of affect through facial expressions in humans. *Journal of Personality and Social Psychology, 23,* 362–371.

Buck, R., Miller, R. E., & Caul, W. F. (1974). Sex, personality, and physiological variables in the communication of affect via facial expression. *Journal of Personality and Social Psychology, 30,* 587–596.

Bullock, M., & Russell, J. A. (1986). Concepts of emotion in developmental psychology. In C. E. Izard & P. B. Read (Eds.), *Measuring emotions in infants and children, Vol. II.* Cambridge: Cambridge University Press.

Burkhardt, R. W. (1985). Darwin on animal behavior and evolution. In D. Kohn (Ed.), *The Darwinian heritage* (pp. 327–365). Princeton: Princeton University Press.

Buss, D. (1992). Is there a universal human nature? *Contemporary Psychology, 37,* 1262–1263.

Buzby, D. E. (1924). The interpretation of facial expression. *American Journal of Psychology, 35,* 602–604.

Cacioppo, J. T., & Petty, R. E. (1983). *Social psychophysiology: A sourcebook.* New York: Guilford Press.

Cacioppo, J. T., & Tassinary, L. G. (1987). The relationship between EMG response and overt facial actions. *Face Value, 1,* 2–3.

Cade, W. (1981). Alternative male strategies: Genetic differences in crickets. *Science, 212,* 563–564.

Campbell, R. (1982). Asymmetries in moving faces. *British Journal of Psychology, 73,* 95–103.

Campbell, B. (1985). *Human evolution.* Hawthorne, NY: Aldine.

Camras, L. A. (1988, April). Darwin revisited: An infant's first emotional facial expressions. In H. Oster (Chair), Emotional expressions in infants: New perspectives on an old controversy. Symposium conducted at the meeting of the International Conference on Infant Studies, Washington, DC.

Camras, L. A. (1992). A dynamic systems perspective on expressive development. In K. Strongman (Ed.), *International review of studies on emotion* (pp. 16–28). New York: Wiley.

Camras, L. A., Malatesta, C., & Izard, C. E. (1991). The development of facial expression in infancy. In R. Feldman & B. Rime (Eds.), *Fundamentals of nonverbal behavior.* New York: Cambridge University Press.

Cannon, W. B. (1929). *Bodily changes in pain, hunger, fear and rage* (2nd ed.). New York: Appleton.

Carlson, J. G., & Hatfield, E. (1992). *Psychology of emotion.* New York: Holt, Rinehart, & Winston.

Carpenter, M. B., & Sutin, J. (1983). *Human neuroanatomy* (8th ed.). Baltimore: Williams & Wilkins.

Carr, H. A. (1925). *Psychology: A study of mental activity.* New York: Longmans, Green.

Carroll, J. B. (1956). *Language, thought, and reality: Selected writings of Benjamin Lee Whorf.* Boston: Technology Press of MIT.

Caryl, P. G. (1979). Communication by agonistic displays: What can games theory contribute to ethology? *Behaviour, 68,* 136–169.

Cavalli-Sforza, L. L. (1973). Some current problems of human genetics. *American Journal of Human Genetics, 25,* 82–104.

Chan, D. W. (1985). Perception and judgment of facial expressions among the Chinese. *International Journal of Psychology, 20,* 681–692.

Chapman, C. A., Chapman, L. J., & Lefebvre, L. (1990). Spider monkey alarm calls: Honest advertisement or warning kin? *Animal Behaviour, 39,* 197–198.

Charlesworth, W. R., & Kreutzer, M. A. (1973). Facial expression of infants and children. In P. Ekman (Ed.), *Darwin and facial expression* (pp. 91–168). New York: Academic Press.

Cheney, D. L., & Seyfarth, R. M. (1980). Vocal recognition in free-ranging vervet monkeys. *Animal Behaviour, 28,* 362–367.

Cheney, D. L., & Seyfarth, R. M. (1982). Recognition of individuals within and between groups of free-ranging vervet monkeys. *Animal Behaviour, 30,* 739–751.

Cheney, D. L., & Seyfarth, R. M. (1985). The social and nonsocial world of non-human primates. In R. A. Hinde, A. Perret-Clermont, & J. Stevenson-Hinde (Eds.), *Social relationships and cognitive development* (pp. 33–44). Oxford: Oxford University Press.

Cheney, D. L., & Seyfarth, R. M. (1988). Assessment of meaning and the detection of unreliable signals by vervet monkeys. *Animal Behaviour, 36,* 477–486.

Cheney, D. L., & Seyfarth, R. M. (1990). *How monkeys see the world.* Chicago: University of Chicago Press.

Cheney, D. L., Seyfarth, R. M., & Smuts, B. (1986). Social relationships and social cognition in nonhuman primates. *Science, 234,* 1361–1366.

Chernoff, H. (1973). Using faces to represent points in *k*-dimensional space graphically. *Journal of the American Statistical Association, 68,* 361–368.

Chevalier-Skolnikoff, S. (1973). Facial expression of emotion in nonhuman primates. In P. Ekman (Ed.), *Darwin and facial expression*. New York: Academic Press.

Chovil, N. (1988). Are facial expression and emotion synonymous? Unpublished manuscript, University of Victoria.

Chovil, N. (1989). Communicative functions of facial displays in conversation. Unpublished dissertation, University of Victoria.

Chovil, N. (1991). Communicative functions of facial displays. *Journal of Nonverbal Behavior*, 15, 141–154.

Chovil, N., & Fridlund, A. J. (1991). Why emotionality cannot equal sociality: Reply to Buck. *Journal of Nonverbal Behavior*, 15, 163–167.

Chusid, J. G. (1976). *Correlative neuroanatomy and functional neurology* (16th ed.). Los Altos, CA: Lance.

Clark, H. H., & Brennan, S. E. (1991). Grounding in communication. In L. B. Resnick, J. M. Levine, & S. D. Teasley (Eds.), *Perspectives on socially shared cognition* (pp. 127–149). Washington, D.C.: American Psychological Association.

Cohen, A. A. (1977). The communicative functions of hand illustrators. *Journal of Communication*, 27, 54–63.

Cohen, A. A., & Harrison, R. P. (1973). Intentionality in the use of hand illustrators in face-to-face communication situations. *Journal of Personality and Social Psychology*, 28, 276–279.

Cole, P. M. (1985). Display rules and socialization. In G. Zivin (Ed.), *The development of expressive behavior* (pp. 27–50). Orlando, FL: Academic Press.

Colgan, P. W. (1978). *Quantitative ethology*. New York: Wiley-Interscience.

Cosmides, L., & Tooby, J. (in press). Origins of domain-specificity: The evolution of functional organization. In L. Hirshfield & S. Gelman (Eds.), *Domain-specificity in cognition and culture*. New York: Cambridge University Press.

Courville, J. (1966). The nucleus of the facial nerve: the relation between cellular groups and peripheral branches of the nerve. *Brain Research*, 1, 338–354.

Craig, W. (1921–1922). A note on Darwin's work on the expression of the emotions in man and animals. *Journal of Abnormal and Social Psychology*, 16, 356–366.

Cüceloglu, D. M. (1970). Perception of facial expressions in three cultures. *Ergonomics*, 13, 93–100.

Cullen, J. K., Fargo, N., Chase, R. A., & Baker, P. (1968). The development of auditory feedback monitoring: I. Delayed auditory feedback studies on infant cry. *Journal of Speech and Hearing Research*, 11, 85–93.

Daanje, A. (1950). On the locomotory movements of birds and the intention movements derived from them. *Behaviour*, 3, 49–98.

Daly, E. M., Lancee, W., & Polivy, J. (1983). A conical model for the taxonomy of emotional experience. *Journal of Personality and Social Psychology*, 45, 443–457.

Damasio, A. R., Damasio, H., & Van Hoesen, G. W. (1982). Prosopagnosia: Anatomical basis and behavioral mechanisms. *Neurology*, 32, 331–341.

Darwin, C. R. (1859). *On the origin of species, or the preservation of favoured races in the struggle for life*. London: Murray.

Darwin, C. R. (1868). *The variation of animals and plants under domestication* (2 vols.). London: Murray.

Darwin, C. R. (1871). *The descent of man, and selection in relation to sex*. London: Murray.

Darwin, C. R. (1872). *Expression of the emotions in man and animals*. London: Albemarle.

Darwin, C. R. (1877). A biographical sketch of an infant. *Mind*, 2, 285–294.

Darwin, E. (1794). *Zoonomia; or the laws of organic life* (Vol. 1). London: Johnson.

Darwin, F. (Ed.). (1887). *The life and letters of Charles Darwin, including an autobiographical chapter* (Vol. 1 & 2). London: Murray.

Davis, P. R., & Napier, J. (1963). A reconstruction of the skull of *Proconsul africanus* (R. S. 51). *Folia Primatologia*, 1, 20–28.

De Beer, G. R. (1963). *Charles Darwin: Evolution by natural selection*. London: Nelson.

De Jong, R. N. (1979). *The neurologic examination*. Hagerstown, MD: Harper & Row.

Dennett, D. C. (1987). Evolution, error, and intentionality. In *The intentional stance*. Cambridge, MA: Bradford Books/MIT Press.

Denny-Brown, D. (1939). *Selected writings of Sir Charles Sherrington*. New York: Harper & Brothers.

DePaulo, B. M. (1992). Nonverbal behavior and self-presentation. *Psychological Bulletin*, *111*, 203–243.

Desmond, A. J. (1976). *The hot-blooded dinosaurs: A revolution in paleontology*. New York: Dial Press.

Desmond, A., & Moore, J. (1991). *Darwin*. New York: Warner.

DeVries, J. I., Visser, G. H. A., & Prechtl, H. F. R. (1982). The emergence of fetal behavior. I. Qualitative aspects. *Early Human Development*, *7*, 301–322.

de Waal, F. (1982). *Chimpanzee politics*. New York: Harper & Row.

de Waal, F. (1989). *Peacemaking among primates*. Cambridge, MA: Harvard University Press.

Dewey, J. (1894). The theory of emotion. I. Emotional attitudes. *Psychological Review*, *1*, 553–569.

Dobzhansky, T. (1937). *Genetics and the origins of species*. New York: Columbia University Press.

Dobzhansky, T. (1951). *Genetics and the origins of species* (3rd ed.). New York: Columbia University Press.

Dobzhansky, T., Ayala, F. J., Stebbins, G. L., & Valentine, J. W. (1977). *Evolution*. San Francisco: Freeman.

Dolgin, K. M., & Sabini, J. (1982). Experimental manipulation of a human non-verbal display: The tongue show affects an observer's willingness to interact. *Animal Behaviour*, *30*, 935–936.

Down, J. L. H. (1886). Observations on an ethnic classification of idiots. *London Hospital Reports*, 259–262.

Ducci, L., Arcuri, L., W/Georgis, T., & Sineshaw, T. (1982). Emotion recognition in Ethiopia. *Journal of Cross-Cultural Psychology*, *13*, 340–351.

Duchenne, G. B. A. (1959). *Physiologie des mouvements*. E. B. Kaplan (Trans.). Philadelphia: Saunders. (Original published 1867.)

Duchenne, G. B. A. (1990). *The mechanism of human facial expression*. R. A. Cuthbertson (Ed. and Trans). Cambridge: Cambridge University Press. (Original published 1859.)

Duclos, S. E., Laird, J. D., Schneider, E., Sexter, M., Stern, L, & Van Lighten, O. (1989). *Journal of Personality and Social Psychology*, *57*, 100–108.

Dudai, Y., & Quinn, W. G. (1980). Genes and learning in *Drosophila*. *Trends in Neurosciences*, *3*, 28–30.

Dzubow, L. M. (1986). The fasciae of the face: An anatomic and histologic analysis. *Journal of the American Academy of Dermatology*, *14*, 502–507.

Ectors, L., Brookens, N. L., & Gerard, R. W. (1938). Autonomic and motor localization in the hypothalamus. *Archives of Neurology and Psychiatry*, *39*, 789.

Efron, D. (1941). *Gesture and environment*. New York: King's Crown Press.

Ehrlichman, H., & Bastone, L. (1992). Olfaction and emotion. In M. J. Serby & K. L. Chobor (Eds.), *Science of olfaction* (pp. 410–438). New York: Springer-Verlag.

Eibl-Eibesfeldt, I. (1970). *Ethology: The biology of behavior*. New York: Holt, Rinehart & Winston.

Eibl-Eibesfeldt, I. (1972). Similarities and differences between cultures in expressive movements. In R. A. Hinde (Ed.), *Nonverbal communication* (pp. 297–312). Cambridge: Cambridge University Press.

Eibl-Eibesfeldt, I. (1973a). The expressive behavior of the deaf-and-blind-born. In M. von Cranach & I. Vine (Eds.), *Social communciation and movement* (pp. 163–194). San Diego, CA: Academic Press.

Eibl-Eibesfeldt, I. (1973b). *The preprogrammed man.* New York: Viking Press.

Eibl-Eibesfeldt, I. (1979). Ritual and ritualization from a biological perspective. In J. Aschoff, M. von Cranach, K. Foppa, W. Lepenies, & D. Ploog (Eds.), *Human ethology.* Cambridge: Cambridge University Press.

Ekman, P. (1972). Universals and cultural differences in facial expressions of emotion. In J. Cole (Ed.), *Nebraska Symposium on Motivation, 1971* (Vol. 19, pp. 207–283). Lincoln, NE: University of Nebraska Press.

Ekman, P. (1973). *Darwin and facial expression: A century of research in review.* New York: Academic Press.

Ekman, P. (1977). Biological and cultural contributions to body and facial movement. In J. Blacking (Ed.), *The anthropology of the body.* London: Academic Press.

Ekman, P. (1979). About brows: Emotional and conversational signals. In J. Aschoff, M. von Cranach, K. Foppa, W. Lepenies, & D. Ploog (Eds.), *Human ethology.* Cambridge: Cambridge University Press.

Ekman, P. (1980). *The face of man: Expressions of universal emotions in a New Guinea village.* New York: Garland STPM Press.

Ekman, P. (1981). Mistakes when deceiving. *Annals of the New York Academy of Sciences, 364,* 269–278.

Ekman, P. (Ed.). (1982). *Emotion in the human face* (2nd ed.). Cambridge: Cambridge University Press.

Ekman, P. (1984). Expression and the nature of emotion. In P. Ekman & K. Scherer (Eds.), *Approaches to emotion* (pp. 319–343). Hillsdale, NJ: Erlbaum.

Ekman, P. (1985). *Telling lies.* New York: Norton.

Ekman, P. (1989). The argument and evidence about universals in facial expressions of emotion. In H. Wagner & A. Manstead (Eds.), *Handbook of social psychophysiology.* New York: Wiley.

Ekman, P. (1992a). An argument for basic emotions. *Cognition and Emotion, 6,* 169–200.

Ekman, P. (1992b). Are there basic emotions? *Psychological Review, 99,* 550–553.

Ekman, P. (1993). Facial expression and emotion. *American Psychologist, 48,* 384–392.

Ekman, P., & Fridlund, A. J. (1987). Assessment of facial behavior in affective disorders. In J. D. Maser (Ed.), *Depression and expressive behavior.* Hillsdale, NJ: Erlbaum.

Ekman, P., & Friesen, W. V. (1969a). Nonverbal leakage and clues to deception. *Psychiatry, 1,* 88–105.

Ekman, P., & Friesen, W. V. (1969b). The repertoire of nonverbal behavior: categories, origins, usage, and coding. *Semiotica, 1,* 49–98.

Ekman, P., & Friesen, W. V. (1971). Constants across cultures in the face and emotion. *Journal of Personality and Social Psychology, 17,* 124–129.

Ekman, P., & Friesen, W. V. (1975). *Unmasking the face.* Englewood Cliffs, NJ: Prentice-Hall.

Ekman, P., & Friesen, W. V. (1976). *Pictures of facial affect.* Palo Alto, CA: Consulting Psychologists Press.

Ekman, P., & Friesen, W. V. (1978). *The Facial Action Coding System.* Palo Alto, CA: Consulting Psychologists Press.

Ekman, P., & Friesen, W. V. (1982a). Felt, false, and miserable smiles. *Journal of Nonverbal Behavior, 6,* 238–252.

Ekman, P., & Friesen, W. V. (1982b). Measuring facial movement with the Facial Action Coding System. In P. Ekman (Ed.), *Emotion in the human face* (2nd ed). Cambridge: Cambridge University Press.

Ekman, P., & Friesen, W. V. (1986). A new pan-cultural expression of emotion. *Motivation and Emotion, 10,* 159–168.

Ekman, P., & Friesen, W. V. (1988). Who knows what about contempt: A reply to Izard and Haynes. *Motivation and Emotion, 12,* 17–22.

Ekman, P., & Heider, K. G. (1988). The universality of a contempt expression: A replication. *Motivation and emotion, 12,* 303–308.

Ekman, P., & Oster, H. (1979). Facial expressions of emotion. *Annual Review of Psychology*, *30*, 527–554.

Ekman, P., Sorenson, E. R., & Friesen, W. V. (1969). Pan-cultural elements in facial displays of emotions. *Science*, *164*, 86–88.

Ekman, P., Friesen, W. V., & Tomkins, S. S. (1971). Facial affect scoring technique (FAST): A first validity study. *Semiotica*, *3*, 37–58.

Ekman, P., Friesen, W. V., & Ellsworth, P. (1972). *Emotion in the human face*. New York: Pergamon.

Ekman, P., Friesen, W. V., & Ancoli, S. (1980). Facial signs of emotional experience. *Journal of Personality and Social Psychology*, *39*, 1125.

Ekman, P., Friesen, W. V., & Ellsworth, P. (1982). Conceptual ambiguities. In P. Ekman (Ed.), *Emotion in the human face* (2nd ed.) (pp. 98–110). Cambridge: Cambridge University Press.

Ekman, P., Levenson, R. W., & Friesen, W. V. (1983). Autonomic nervous system activity distinguishes among emotions. *Science*, *221*, 1208–1210.

Ekman, P., Friesen, W. V., & Simons, R. C. (1985). Is the startle reaction an emotion? *Journal of Personality and Social Psychology*, *49*, 1416–1426.

Ekman, P., Friesen, W. V., O'Sullivan, M., Diacoyanni-Tarlatzis, I., Krause, R., Pitcairn, T., Scherer, K., Chan, A., Heider, K., LeCompte, W. A., Ricci-Bitti, P. E., Tomita, M., & Tzavaras, A. (1987). Universals and cultural differences in the judgments of facial expressions of emotion. *Journal of Personality and Social Psychology*, *53*, 712–717.

Ekman, P., Davidson, R. J., & Friesen, W. V. (1990). The Duchenne smile: Emotional expression and brain physiology II. *Journal of Personality and Social Psychology*, *58*, 342–353.

Ekman, P., O'Sullivan, M., & Matsumoto, D. (1991a). Confusions about context in the judgment of facial expression: A reply to "Contempt and the relativity thesis." *Motivation and Emotion*, *15*, 169–176.

Ekman, P., O'Sullivan, M., & Matsumoto, D. (1991b). Contradictions in the study of contempt: What's it all about? Reply to Russell. *Motivation and Emotion*, *15*, 293–296.

Emlen, S., & Oring, L. W. (1977). Ecology, sexual selection, and the evolution of mating systems. *Science*, *197*, 215–223.

Enquist, M., & Leimar, O. (1990). The evolution of fatal fighting. *Animal Behaviour*, *39*, 1–9.

Evans, C. S., & Marler, P. (1991). On the use of video images as social stimuli in birds: Audience effects on alarm calling. *Animal Behaviour*, *41*, 17–26.

Evans, C. S., & Marler, P. (in press). Food calling by male chickens [*Gallus gallus*] and its relation to food availability, courtship and motivational state. *Animal Behaviour*.

Evans, C. S., Evans, L., & Marler, P. (1993). On the meaning of alarm calls: Functional reference in an avian vocal system. *Animal Behaviour*, *46*, 23–38.

Evans, E. C. (1969). Physiognomics in the ancient world. *Transactions of the American Philosophical Society*, *59*(5), 1–101.

Faigin, G. (1990). *The artist's complete guide to facial expression*. New York: Watson-Guptill.

Fehr, B., & Russell, J. A. (1984). Concept of emotion viewed from a prototype perspective. *Journal of Experimental Psychology: General*, *113*, 464–486.

Feinman, S., & Lewis, M. (1983). Social referencing at 10 months: A second order effect on infants' responses to strangers. *Child Development*, *54*, 878–887.

Feleky, A. M. (1914). The expression of the emotions. *Psychological Review*, *21*, 33–41.

Feleky, A. M. (1922). *Feelings and emotions*. New York: Pioneer Press.

Fernandez-Dols, J.-M. (1990, June). Facial expression and context: Toward an ecology of emotional expression recognition. Paper presented at the Nag's Head Conference on Motivation and Emotion, Nag's Head, North Carolina.

Fernandez-Dols, J.-M. (1991). Il ruolo del contesto nell'attribuzione del contenuto emozionale alle espressioni facciali. [The role of the context in the attribution of emotional content to facial expressions.] In G. Bellelli (Ed.), *Sapere e sentire [Knowing and feeling]*. Napoli, Italy: Liguori.

Fernandez-Dols, J.-M., Wallbott, H., & Sanchez, F. (1991). Emotion category accessibility and the decoding of emotion from facial expression and context. *Journal of Nonverbal Behavior, 15,* 107–123.

Fernandez-Dols, J.-M., Sierra, B., & Ruiz-Belda, M. A. (1993). On the clarity of expressive and contextual information in the recognition of emotions: A methodological critique. *European Journal of Social Psychology, 23,* 195–202.

Fernberger, S. W. (1928). False suggestion and the Piderit model. *American Journal of Psychology, 40,* 562–568.

Fink, L. S., & Brower, L. P. (1981). Birds can overcome the cardenolide defence of monarch butterflies in Mexico. *Nature (London), 291,* 67–70.

Fisher, R. A. (1930). *The genetical theory of natural selection.* Oxford: Clarendon Press.

Flynn, J. P. (1967). The neural basis of aggression in cats. In D. C. Glass (Ed.), *Neurophysiology and emotion.* New York: Rockefeller University Press.

Foulke, E., & Sticht, T. G. (1969). Review of research on the intelligibility and compression of accelerated speech. *Psychological Bulletin, 72,* 50–62.

Fraiberg, S. (1974). Blind infants and their mothers: An examination of the sign system. In M. Lewis & L. A. Rosenblum (Eds.), *The effect of the infant on its caregiver.* New York: Wiley.

Frank, M. G., Ekman, P., & Friesen, W. V. (1993). Behavioral markers and recognizability of the smile of enjoyment. *Journal of Personality and Social Psychology, 1,* 83–93.

Freeman, D. (1983). *Margaret Mead and Samoa: The making and unmaking of an anthropological myth.* Cambridge: Harvard University Press.

Freeman, G. L. (1948). *The energetics of human behavior.* Ithaca, NY: Cornell University Press.

Freud, S. (1938). Wit and its relation to the unconscious. In A. A. Brill (Ed. & Trans.), *The basic writings of Sigmund Freud.* New York: Random House.

Freud, S. (1946). Instincts and their vicissitudes. In *Collected papers* (Vol. 4). London: Hogarth Press. (Original work published 1921.)

Fridlund, A. J. (1986, October). Emotion—how we have strayed from Darwin and lost our way. Paper presented at the Historical Symposium on Emotion, 26th Annual Meeting of the Society for Psychophysiological Research, Montreal.

Fridlund, A. J. (1988). What can asymmetry and laterality in facial EMG tell us about the face and brain? *International Journal of Neuroscience, 39,* 53–69.

Fridlund, A. J. (1991a). Evolution and facial action in reflex, social motive, and paralanguage. *Biological Psychology, 32,* 3–100.

Fridlund, A. J. (1991b). Sociality of solitary smiling: potentiation by an implicit audience. *Journal of Personality and Social Psychology, 60,* 229–240.

Fridlund, A. J. (1992a). Darwin's anti-Darwinism in *The Expression of the Emotions in Man and Animals*. In K. Strongman (Ed.), *International review of emotion* (Vol. 2) (pp. 117–137). Chichester, UK: Wiley.

Fridlund, A. J. (1992b). The behavioral ecology and sociality of human faces. In M. S. Clark (Ed.), *Review of personality and social psychology* (Vol. 13, pp. 90–121). Newbury Park, CA: Sage.

Fridlund, A. J., & Cacioppo, J. T. (1986). Guidelines for human electromyographic research. *Psychophysiology, 23,* 567–589.

Fridlund, A. J., & Fowler, S. C. (1978). An eight-channel computer-controlled scanning electromyograph. *Behavior Research Methods & Instrumentation, 10,* 652–662.

Fridlund, A. J., & Gilbert, A. N. (1985). Emotions and facial expressions. *Science, 230,* 607–608.

Fridlund, A. J., & Izard, C. E. (1983). Electromyographic studies of facial expressions of emotions and patterns of emotions. In J. T. Cacioppo & R. E. Petty (Eds.), *Social psychophysiology: A sourcebook* (pp. 243–286). New York: Guilford Press.

Fridlund, A. J., & Loftis, J. M. (1990). Relations between tickling and humorous laughter: Preliminary support for the Darwin-Hecker hypothesis. *Biological Psychology, 30,* 141–150.

Fridlund, A. J., Schwartz, G. E., & Fowler, S. C. (1984). Pattern-recognition of self-reported emotional state from multiple-site facial EMG activity during affective imagery. *Psychophysiology, 21,* 622–637.

Fridlund, A. J., Ekman, P., & Oster, H. (1987). Facial expressions of emotion. In A. Siegman & S. Feldstein (Eds.), *Nonverbal behavior and communications* (2nd ed.) (pp.143–224). Hillsdale, NJ: Erlbaum.

Fridlund, A. J., Sabini, J. P., Hedlund, L. E., Schaut, J. A., Shenker, J. I., & Knauer, M. J. (1990). Social determinants of facial expressions during affective imagery: Displaying to the people in your head. *Journal of Nonverbal Behavior, 14,* 113–137.

Fridlund, A. J., Kenworthy, K. G., & Jaffey, A. K. (1992a). Audience effects in affective imagery: Replication and extension to affective imagery. *Journal of Nonverbal Behavior, 16,* 191–212.

Fridlund, A. J., MacDonald, M., & Laverty, B. (1992b). Approaches to Goldie: A field study of human response to canine juvenescence. Submitted for publication.

Fried, I., Mateer, C., Ojemann, G., Wohns, R., & Fedio, P. (1982). Organization of visuospatial functions in human cortex. *Brain, 105,* 349–371.

Friesen, W. V. (1972). Cultural differences in facial expressions in a social situation: An experimental test of the concept of display rules. Unpublished doctoral dissertation, University of California, San Francisco. San Francisco: University of California Microfilm Archives.

Frijda, N. H. (1953). The understanding of facial expression of emotion. *Acta Psychologica, 9,* 294–362.

Frijda, N. H. (1958). Facial expression and situational cues. *Journal of Abnormal and Social Psychology, 57,* 149–154.

Frijda, N. H. (1969). Recognition of emotion. In L. Berkowitz (Ed.), *Advances in experimental social psychology IV.* New York: Academic Press.

Frijda, N. H. (1986). *The emotions.* New York: Cambridge University Press.

Frijda, N. H., & Philipszoon, E. (1963). Dimensions of recognition of expression. *Journal of Abnormal and Social Psychology, 66,* 45–51.

Frijda, N. H., Kuipers, P., & ter Schure, E. (1989). Relationships among emotions, appraisals, and emotion action readiness. *Journal of Personality and Social Psychology, 57,* 212–278.

Funkenstein, D. H. (1955). The physiology of fear and anger. *Scientific American, 192,* 74–80.

Gallistel, C. R. (1980). *The organization of action: A new synthesis.* Hillsdale, NJ: Erlbaum.

Geen, R. G., & Gange, J. J. (1977). Drive theory of social facilitation: Twelve years of theory and research. *Psychological Bulletin, 84,* 1267–1288.

Geldard, F. A. (1972). *The human senses.* New York: Wiley.

Gesell, A. (1928). *The mental growth of the pre-school child.* New York: Macmillan.

Ghiselin, M. T. (1969). *The triumph of the Darwinian method.* Berkeley, CA: University of California Press.

Gilbert, A. N., Fridlund, A. J., & Sabini, J. (1987). Hedonic and social determinants of facial displays to odors. *Chemical Senses, 12,* 355–363.

Gilman, S. L. (Ed.). (1977). *The face of madness: Origin of psychiatric photography.* Secaucus, NJ: Citadel.

Ginsburg, G. P., & Harrington, M. (1993, May). Emotions as features of situated lines of action. Paper presented at the Nag's Head Conference on The Experience and Expression of Emotion, Boca Raton, Florida.

Gleitman, H. (1985, August). Some reflections on drama and the dramatic experience. Presidential address presented at the meeting of Division 10 of the American Psychological Association, Los Angeles.

Gleitman, H. (1991). *Psychology* (3rd ed.). New York: Norton.

Goldberg, H. D. (1951). The role of "cutting" in the perception of the motion picture. *Journal of Applied Psychology, 35,* 70–71.

Goldenthal, P., Johnston, R. E., & Kraut, R. E. (1981). Smiling, appeasement, and the silent bared-teeth display. *Ethology and Sociobiology, 2,* 127–133.

Goldstein, M. L. (1968). Physiological theories of emotion: A critical historical review from the standpoint of behavior theory. *Psychological Bulletin, 69,* 23–40.

Goodenough, F. L. (1931). The expression of the emotions in infancy. *Child Development, 2,* 96–101.

Goodenough, F. L. (1932). The expression of the emotions in a blind-deaf child. *Journal of Abnormal Psychology, 27,* 328–333.

Goodenough, F. L., & Tinker, M. A. (1931). The relative potency of facial expression and verbal description of stimulus in the judgment of emotion. *Journal of Comparative Psychology, 12,* 365–370.

Goodman, M., & Lasker, G. W. (1975). Molecular evidence as to man's place in nature. In R. Tuttle (Ed.), *Primate functional morphology and evolution* (pp. 71–101). Paris: Mouton.

Gorney, M., & Harries, T. (1974). The preoperative and postoperative consideration of natural facial asymmetry. *Plastic and reconstructive surgery, 54,* 187–191.

Gottesman, I. I., & Shields, J. (1982). *Schizophrenia: The epigenetic puzzle.* Cambridge: Cambridge University Press.

Gould, J. L., & Marler, P. (1987). Learning by instinct. *Scientific American, 256,* 74–85.

Gould, S. J. (1977). *Ontogeny and phylogeny.* Cambridge, MA: Belknap Press of Harvard University Press.

Gould, S. J. (1980). *The panda's thumb.* New York: Norton.

Gould, S. J. (1981). *The mismeasure of man.* New York: Norton.

Gould, S. J., & Vrba, E. S. (1982). Exaptation—a missing term in the science of form. *Paleobiology, 8,* 14–15.

Grant, V. (1985). *The evolutionary process: A critical review of evolutionary theory.* New York: Columbia University Press.

Gratiolet, P. (1865). *De la physionomie et des mouvements d'expression.* Paris: J. Hetzel.

Green, J. A., Jones, L. E., & Gustafson, G. E. (1987). Perception of cries by parents and nonparents: Relation to cry acoustics. *Developmental Psychology, 23,* 370–382.

Gross, C. G., Rocha-Miranda, C. E., & Bender, D. B. (1972). Visual properties of neurons in inferotemporal cortex of the macaque. *Journal of Neurophysiology, 35,* 96–111.

Gruber, H. E., with Barnett, H. P. (1974). *Darwin on man: A psychological study of scientific creativity.* New York: Dutton.

Gudykunst, W. B., & Ting-Toomey, S. (1988). *Culture and interpersonal communciation.* Beverley Hills, CA: Sage.

Guilford, J. P. (1929). An experiment in learning to read facial expression. *Journal of Comparative Psychology, 24,* 191–202.

Guilford, T., & Dawkins, M. S. (1991). Receiver psychology and the evolution of animal signals. *Animal Behaviour, 42,* 1–14.

Guthrie, E. R., & Horton, G. P. (1946). *Cats in a puzzle box.* New York: Holt, Rinehart, & Winston.

Gyger, M., & Marler, P. (1988). Food calling in the domestic fowl, *Gallus gallus*: the role of external referents and deception. *Animal Behaviour, 36,* 358–365.

Haeckel, E. (1874). *The evolution of man: A popular exposition of the principal points of human ontogeny and phylogeny* (2 vols.). International Science Library. New York: A. L. Fowle.

Hager, J. C., & Ekman, P. (1985). The asymmetry of facial actions is inconsistent with models of hemispheric specialization. *Psychophysiology, 22*, 307–318.

Haldane, J. B. S. (1932). *The causes of evolution.* London: Longmans, Green.

Hall, G. S. (1914). A synthetic genetic study of fear. *American Journal of Psychology, 25*, 149–200, 321–392.

Harré, R. (1980). *Social being.* Totowa, NJ: Littlefield, Adams.

Harré, R. (Ed.). (1985). *The social construction of emotions.* Oxford: Blackwell.

Hasselmo, M. E., Rolls, E. T., & Baylis, G. C. (1986). Selectivity between facial expressions in the responses of a population of neurons in the superior temporal sulcus of the monkey. *Neuroscience Letters, 26*, S571.

Hauri, P. (1977). *The sleep disorders.* Kalamazoo, MI: Upjohn Pharmaceuticals.

Hauser, M. D. (1989). Ontogenetic changes in the comprehension and production of vervet monkey (*Cercopithecus aethiops*) vocalizations. *Journal of Comparative Psychology, 2*, 149–158.

Hauser, M. D., & Fowler, C. A. (1992). Fundamental frequency declination is not unique to human speech: Evidence from nonhuman primates. *Journal of the Acoustic Society of America, 91*, 363–369.

Hauser, M. D., & Nelson, D. A. (1991). 'Intentional' signaling in animal communication. *Trends in Ecology and Evolution, 6*, 186–189.

Hauser, M. D., & Ybarra, M. S. (1994). The role of lip configuration in monkey vocalizations? Experiments using xylocaine as a nerve block. *Brain & Language.*

Hauser, M. D., Evans, C. S., & Marler, P. (1993). The role of articulation in the production of rhesus monkey (*Macaca mulatta*) vocalizations. *Animal Behaviour, 45*, 423–433.

Head, H. (1926). *Aphasia and kindred disorders of speech.* Cambridge: Cambridge University Press.

Hecker, E. (1873). *Die Physiologie und Psychologie des Lachen und des Komischen.* Berlin: F. Dümmler.

Heider, K. (1974). Affect display rules in the Dani. Paper presented at the Annual Meeting of the American Anthropological Association, New Orleans.

Heilman, K. M., & Valenstein, E. (1979). *Clinical neuropsychology.* New York: Oxford University Press.

Heinroth, O. (1911). Beitrage zur Biologie namentlich Ethologie und Psychologie dee Anatiden. *Verhalte 5 International Ornithologishe Kongress* Berlin, 333–342.

Heit, G., Smith, M. E., & Halgren, E. (1988). Neural encoding of individual words and faces by the human hippocampus and amygdala. *Nature (London), 333*, 773–775.

Held, R., & Hein, A. (1963). Movement-produced stimulation in the development of visually guided behavior. *Journal of Comparative and Physiological Psychology, 56*, 872–876.

Helson, H. (1964). *Adaptation-level theory.* New York: Harper & Row.

Heron, W. T. (1935). The inheritance of maze learning ability in rats. *Journal of Comparative Psychology, 19*, 77–89.

Hess, W. R. (1954). *Diencephalon: Autonomic and extrapyramidal functions.* New York: Grune & Stratton.

Hiatt, J. L., & Gartner, L. P. (1982). *Textbook of head and neck anatomy.* New York: Appleton-Century-Crofts.

Hiatt, S., Campos, J. J., & Emde, R. N. (1979). Facial patterning and infant emotional expression: Happiness, surprise, and fear. *Child Development, 50*, 1020–1035.

Hillman, J. (1962). *Emotion.* Evanston, IL: Northwestern University Press.

Hinde, R. A. (1966). Ritualization and social communication in Rhesus monkeys. *Philosophical Transactions of the Royal Society of Biology, 251*, 285–294.

Hinde, R. A. (1985a). Expression and negotiation. In G. Zivin (Ed.), *The development of expressive behavior* (pp. 103–116). Orlando, FL: Academic Press.

Hinde, R. A. (1985b). Was 'The Expression of the Emotions' a misleading phrase? *Animal Behaviour, 33,* 985–992.

Hohmann, G. W. (1966). Some effects of spinal cord lesions on experienced emotional feelings. *Psychophysiology, 3,* 143–156.

Hoikkala, A., & Lumme, J. (1987). The genetic basis of evolution of the male courtship sounds in the *Drosophila virilis* group. *Evolution, 41,* 827–845.

Holder, D. S. (1987). Feasibility of developing a method of imaging neuronal activity in the human brain: A theoretical review. *Medical and Biological Engineering and Computing, 25,* 2–11.

Honkavaara, S. (1961). The psychology of expression. *British Journal of Psychology* (Monograph Supplement 32).

Hooten, E. A. (1939a). *Crime and the man.* Cambridge, MA: Harvard University Press.

Hooten, E. A. (1939b). *The American criminal: An anthropological study.* Cambridge, MA: Harvard University Press.

Howell, R. J., & Jorgenson, E. (1970). Accuracy of judging emotional behavior in a natural setting: A replication. *Journal of Social Psychology, 81,* 269–270.

Hubel, D. H., & Wiesel, T. N. (1962). Receptive fields, binocular interaction, and functional architecture in the cat's visual cortex. *Journal of Physiology, 160,* 106–154.

Huber, E. (1930). Evolution of facial musculature and cutaneous field of trigeminus. *The Quarterly Review of Biology 5, 2,* 133–437.

Huber, E. (1931). Evolution of facial musculature and facial expression. Baltimore: Johns Hopkins University Press.

Huxley, J. (1914). The courtship habits of the great crested grebe (*Podiceps cristatus*); with an addition to the theory of natural selection. *Proceedings of the Zoological Society of London, 35,* 491–562.

Huxley, J. (1923). Courtship activities in the red-throated diver (*Colymbus stellatus*); together with a discussion of the evolution of courtship in birds. *Journal of the Linnean Society of London, Zoology, 53,* 253–292.

Huxley, J. (1966). A discussion on ritualization of behaviour in animals and man. Introduction. *Philosophical Transactions of the Royal Society of Britain, 251,* 249–271.

Izard, C. E. (1971). *The face of emotion.* New York: Appleton-Century-Crofts.

Izard, C. E. (1972). *Patterns of emotion: A new analysis of anxiety and depression.* New York: Academic Press.

Izard, C. E. (1977). *Human emotions.* New York: Plenum.

Izard, C. E. (1978). On the ontogenesis of emotions and emotion–cognition relationships in infancy. In M. Lewis & L. Rosenblum (Eds.), *The development of affect* (pp. 389–413). New York: Plenum.

Izard, C. E. (1980). Cross-cultural perspectives on emotion and emotion communication. In H. Triandis & W. Lonner (Eds.), *Handbook of cross-cultural psychology: Basic processes* (Vol. 3). Boston: Allyn & Bacon.

Izard, C. E. (1983). *The maximally discriminative facial movement coding system* (Rev. ed.). Newark, DE: Instructional Resources Center, University of Delaware.

Izard, C. E. (1990). Facial expressions and the regulation of emotions. *Journal of Personality and Social Psychology, 58,* 487–498.

Izard, C. E. (1991). *The psychology of emotions.* New York: Plenum.

Izard, C. E. (1992). Basic emotions, relations among emotions, and emotion–cognition relations. *Psychological Review, 99,* 561–565.

Izard, C. E., & Haynes, O. M. (1987). On the form and universality of the contempt expression: A correction for Ekman and Friesen's claim of discovery. *Motivation and Emotion, 12,* 1–16.

Izard, C. E., & Haynes, O. M. (1988). On the form and universality of the contempt expression: A correction for Ekman and Friesen's claim of discovery. *Motivation and Emotion, 12,* 1–16.

Izard, C. E., & Malatesta, C. Z. (1987). Perspectives on emotional development I: Differential emotions theory of early emotional development. In J. Osofsky (Ed.), *Handbook of infant development* (rev. ed.). New York: Wiley-Interscience.

Izard, C. E., & Saxton, P. M. (1988). Emotions. In R. C. Atkinson, R. J. Herrnstein, G. Lindzey, & R. D. Luce (Eds.), *Stevens' handbook of experimental psychology* (2nd ed.). (Vol. 1, pp. 627–676). New York: Wiley.

Jackson, J. H. (1958a). Evolution and dissolution of the nervous system. In J. Taylor (Ed.), *Selected writings of John Hughlings Jackson* (Vol. 2). New York: Basic Books. (Original work published 1875.)

Jackson, J. H. (1958b). On the anatomical and physiological localization of movements in the brain. In J. Taylor (Ed.), *Selected writings of John Hughlings Jackson* (Vol. 2). New York: Basic Books. (Original work published 1875.)

James, W. (1884). What is an emotion. *Mind, 9,* 188–204.

James, W. (1890). *The principles of psychology.* New York: Holt.

Jenny, A. B., & Saper, C. B. (1987). Organization of the facial nucleus and corticofacial projection in the monkey—A reconsideration of the upper motor neuron facial palsy. *Neurology, 37,* 930–939.

Johnson-Laird, P. N., & Oatley, K. (1989). The language of emotions: An analysis of a semantic field. *Cognition and Emotion, 3,* 81–123.

Jones, E. E., & Nisbett, R. E. (1972). The actor and the observer: Divergent perceptions of the causes of behavior. In E. E. Jones, D. E. Karouse, H. H. Kelley, R. E. Nisbett, S. Valins, & B. Weiner (Eds.), *Attribution: Perceiving the causes of behavior.* Morristown, NJ: General Learning Press.

Jones, H. E. (1935). The galvanic skin reflex as related to overt emotional expression. *American Journal of Psychology, 47,* 241–251.

Jones, S. S., & Raag, T. (1989). Smile production in older infants: The importance of a social recipient for the facial signal. *Child Development, 60,* 811–818.

Jones, S. S., Collins, K., & Hong, H.-W. (1991). An audience effect on smile production in 10-month-old infants. *Psychological Science, 2,* 45–49.

Kagan, J., & Havemann, E. (1976). *Psychology: An introduction.* New York: Harcourt Brace.

Kappeler, P. M., & van Schaik, C. P. (1992). Methodological and evolutionary aspects of reconciliation among primates. *Ethology, 92,* 51–69.

Karakashian, S. J., Gyger, M., & Marler, P. (1988). Audience effects on alarm calling in chickens (*Gallus gallus*). *Journal of Comparative Psychology, 102,* 129–135.

Keating, C. F., & Keating, E. G. (1982). Visual scan patterns of rhesus monkeys viewing faces. *Perception, 11,* 211–219.

Keddy Hector, A. C., Seyfarth, R. M., & Raleigh, M. R. (1989). Male parental care, female choice, and the effect of an audience in vervet monkeys. *Animal Behaviour, 38,* 262–271.

Kendon, A. (1975). Some functions of the face in a kissing round. *Semiotica, 15,* 299–334.

Kendon, A. (1981). Introduction: Current issues in the study of "nonverbal communication." In A. Kendon (Ed.), *Nonverbal communication, interaction, and gesture* (pp. 1–53). Paris: Mouton.

Kendon, A. (1983). Gesture and speech: How they interact. In J. M. Wiemann & R. P. Harrison (Eds.), *Nonverbal interaction.* Beverly Hills, CA: Sage.

Kendrick, K. M., & Baldwin, B. A. (1987). Cells in temporal cortex of conscious sheep can respond preferentially to the sight of faces. *Science, 236,* 448–450.

Kilbride, J. E., & Yarczower, M. (1976). Recognition of happy and sad facial expressions among Baganda and U.S. children. *Journal of Cross-Cultural Psychology, 7,* 181–194.

Kilbride, J. E., & Yarczower, M. (1980). Recognition and imitation of facial expressions: A cross-cultural comparison between Zambia and the United States. *Journal of Cross-Cultural Psychology*, *11*, 281–296.

Kilbride, J. E., & Yarczower, M. (1983). Ethnic bias in the recognition of facial expression. *Journal of Nonverbal Behavior*, *8*, 27–41.

Kimura, M. (1982). Evolutionary rate at the molecular level. *Nature (London)*, *217*, 624–626.

Kimura, M. (1983). *The neutral theory of molecular evolution.* Cambridge: Cambridge University Press.

Kinsbourne, M. (1978a). The biological determinants of functional bisymmetry and asymmetry. In M. Kinsbourne (Ed.), *Asymmetrical function of the brain* (pp. 3–13). New York: Cambridge University Press.

Kinsbourne, M. (1978b). The evolution of language in relation to lateral action. In M. Kinsbourne (Ed.), *Asymmetrical function of the brain* (pp. 553–565). New York: Cambridge University Press.

Kirkevold, B. C., Lockard, J. S., & Heestand, J. E. (1982). Developmental comparisons of grimace and play mouth in infant pigtail macaques (*Macaca nemestrina*). *American Journal of Primatology*, *3*, 277–283.

Kishnan, K. R. R., Davidson, J. R. T., & Guajardo, C. (1985). Trichotillomania: A review. *Comprehensive Psychiatry*, *26*, 123–128.

Kleck, R. E., Vaughan, R. C., Cartwright-Smith, J., Vaughan, K. B., Colby, C. Z., & Lanzetta, J. T. (1976). Effects of being observed on expressive, subjective, and physiological responses to painful stimuli. *Journal of Personality and Social Psychology*, *34*, 1211–1218.

Klineberg, O. (1938). Emotional expression in Chinese literature. *Journal of Abnormal and Social Psychology*, *33*, 517–520.

Klineberg, O. (1940). *Social psychology.* New York: Holt.

Klinnert, M. D., Campos, J. J., Sorce, J., Emde, R. N., & Svejda, M. J. (1983). Social referencing: An important appraisal process in human infancy. In R. Plutchik & H. Kellerman (Eds.), *The emotions* (Vol. 2). New York: Academic Press.

Klopfer, P. H., & Klopfer, L. (1982). On 'human ethology.' *Semiotica*, *39*, 175–185.

Knudsen, H. R., & Muzekari, L. H. (1983). The effects of verbal statements of context on facial expressions of emotion. *Journal of Nonverbal Behavior*, *7*, 202–212.

Koff, E., Borod, J., & White, B. (1981). Asymmetries for hemiface size and mobility. *Neuropsychologia*, *19*, 505–514.

Kohne, D. E., Chiscon, J. A., & Hoyer, B. H. (1972). Evolution of primate DNA sequences. *Journal of Human Evolution*, *1*, 627–644.

Kolb, B., & Milner, B. (1981). Observations on spontaneous facial expression after focal cerebral excisions and after carotid injection of sodium amytal. *Neuropsychologia*, *19*, 505–514.

Kolb, B., & Whishaw, I. Q. (1990). *Fundamentals of human neuropsychology.* New York: W. H. Freeman

Kosslyn, S. M., Pinker, S., Smith, G. E., & Schwartz, S. P. (1979). On the demystification of mental imagery. *Behavioral and Brain Sciences*, *2*, 535–581.

Kraus, B. (1964). *The basis of human evolution.* New York: Harper & Row.

Kraut, R. E. (1982). Social presence, facial f eedback, and emotion. *Journal of Personality and Social Psychology*, *42*, 853–863.

Kraut, R. E., & Johnston, R. E. (1979). Social and emotional messages of smiling: An ethological approach. *Journal of Personality and Social Psychology*, *37*, 1539–1553.

Krebs, J. R., & Davies, N. B. (1987). *An introduction to behavioral ecology* (2nd ed.). Sunderland, MA: Sinauer.

Krebs, J. R., & Dawkins, R. (1984). Animal signals: Mind-reading and manipulation. In

J. R. Krebs & N. B. Davies (Eds.), *Behavioural ecology* (2nd ed.) (pp. 380–402). Oxford: Blackwell.

Kretschmer, E. (1925). *Physique and character* (2nd ed.). (W. J. H. Sprott, Trans.). New York: Harcourt, Brace.

La Barre, W. (1947). The cultural basis of emotions and gestures. *Journal of Personality, 16,* 49–68.

Laird, J. D. (1974). Self-attribution of emotion: The effects of expressive behavior on the quality of emotional experience. *Journal of Personality and Social Psychology, 24,* 475–486.

Laird, J. D. (1984). The real role of facial response in the experience of emotion: A reply to Tourangeau and Ellsworth, and others. *Journal of Personality and Social Psychology, 47,* 909–917.

Lamarck, J.-B. (1809). *Philosophie zoologique* (2 vols.). (H. Elliot, Trans). London: Macmillan.

Landau, B., & Gleitman, L. R. (1985). *Language and experience: Evidence from the blind child.* Cambridge, MA: Harvard University PRess.

Landau, T. (1989). *About faces.* New York: Doubleday Anchor Books.

Lande, R. (1981). Models of speciation by sexual selection of polygenic traits. *Proceedings of the National Academy of Sciences U.S.A., 78,* 3271–3275.

Landis, C. (1924). Studies of emotional reactions: II. General behavior and facial expression. *Journal of Comparative Psychology, 4,* 447–509.

Landis, C., & Hunt, W. A. (1939). *The startle pattern.* New York: Farrar, Straus, & Giroux.

Lang, P. J., Bradley, M. M., & Cuthbert, B. N. (1990). Emotion, attention, and the startle reflex. *Psychological Review, 97,* 377–395.

Langfeld, H. S. (1918a). The judgment of emotions from facial expressions. *Journal of Abnormal and Social Psychology, 13,* 172–184.

Langfeld, H. S. (1918b). Judgments of facial expression and suggestion. *Psychological Review, 25,* 488–494.

Lanzetta, J. T., & Kleck, R. E. (1970). Encoding and decoding of nonverbal affect in humans. *Journal of Personality and Social Psychology, 16,* 12–19.

Lanzetta, J. T., & McHugo, G. J. (1986, October). The history and current status of the facial feedback hypothesis. Paper presented at the Historical Symposium on Emotion, 26th Annual Meeting of the Society for Psychophysiological Research, Montreal.

Lanzetta, J. T., Cartwright-Smith, J., & Kleck, R. (1976). Effects of nonverbal dissimulation on emotional experience and autonomic arousal. *Journal of Personality and Social Psychology, 33,* 354–370.

Larsen, B., Skinhoj, E., & Lassen, N. (1978). Variations in regional blood flow in the right and left hemispheres during automatic speech. *Brain, 101,* 193–209.

Latané, B. (1981). The psychology of social impact. *American Psychologist, 36,* 343–356.

La Vergata, A. (1985). Images of Darwin: A historiographic overview. In D. Kohn (Ed.), *The Darwinian heritage.* Princeton: Princeton University Press.

Leach, E. (1972). The influence of cultural context on nonverbal communication in man. In R. A. Hinde (Ed.), *Nonverbal communication.* Cambridge: Cambridge University Press.

Leary, M. R., Britt, T. W., Cutlip, W. D., & Templeton, J. L. (1992). Social blushing. *Psychological Bulletin, 112,* 446–460.

Le Brun, C. (1982). *Methode pour apprendre dessiner les passions, propose dans une conference sur l'expression generale et particuliere.* [*Method for learning to draw the emotions, proposed in a lecture on particular expressions and expression in general*]. Hildesheim: Verlag. (Original published 1702.)

Le Gros Clark, W. E. (1950). New paleontological evidence bearing on the evolution of the Hominoidea. *Quarterly Journal of the Geological Society of London, 105,* 225–264.

Leonard, C. M., Voeller, K. K. S., & Kuldau, J. M. (1991). When's a smile a smile? Or how to detect a message by digitizing the signal. *Psychological Science, 2,* 166–172.

Leventhal, H., & Scherer, K. (1987). The relationship of emotion to cognition: A functional approach to a semantic controversy. *Cognition and Emotion, 1*, 3–28.

Lewis, M., & Michalson, L. (1982). The socialization of emotions. In T. Field & A. Fogel (Eds.), *Emotion and early interaction*. Hillsdale, NJ: Erlbaum.

Lewis, M., & Michalson, L. (1985). Faces as signs and symbols. In G. Zivin (Ed.), *The development of expressive behavior* (pp. 183–219). Orlando, FL: Academic Press.

Lewontin, R. C. (1976). Race and intelligence. In N. J. Bolck & G. Dworkin (Eds.), *The IQ controversy* (pp. 78–92). New York: Pantheon.

Lieberman, P. (1984). *The biology and evolution of language*. Cambridge, MA: Harvard University Press.

Lindsay, W. (1991). *The great dinosaur atlas*. Illustrations by G. Fornari. London: Dorling-Kindersley.

Lloyd, J. E. (1975). Aggressive mimicry in *Photuris* fireflies: Signal repertoires by femmes fatales. *Science, 149*, 653–654.

Lockard, J. S., Fahrenbruch, C. E., Smith, J. L., & Morgan, C. J. (1977). Smiling and laughter: Different phyletic origins? *Bulletin of the Psychonomic Society, 10*, 183–186.

Locke, J. L. (1990). Structure and simulation in the ontogeny of spoken language. *Developmental Psychobiology, 23*, 621–643.

Locke, J. L. (1992). Neural specializations for language: A developmental perspective. *The Neurosciences, 4*, 425–431.

Lombroso, C. (1968). *Crime: Its causes and remedies*. Montclair, NJ: Patterson Smith. (Originally published 1899.)

London, P. (1978). *Beginning psychology* (rev. ed). Homewood, IL: Dorsey.

Lorenz, K. Z. (1952). *King Solomon's ring*. New York: Crowell.

Lorenz, K. (1965). *Evolution and modification of behavior*. Chicago: Univeristy of Chicago Press.

Lorenz, K. Z. (1966). *On aggression*. New York: Harcourt Brace Jovanovich.

Lorenz, K. Z. (1967). The biology of expression and impression. *Psychologische Forschung, 37*.

Lorenz, K. Z. (1970). *Studies on animal and human behavior* (Vol. 1 & 2). Cambridge, MA: Harvard University Press.

Loveday, T., & Forster, E. S. (Trans.). (1913). Physiognomonica. In W. D. Ross (Ed.), *The works of Aristotle*. Oxford, England: Clarendon.

Lovtrup, S. (1978). On von Baerian and Haeckelian recapitulation. *Systematic Zoology, 27*, 348–352.

McAndrew, F. T. (1986). A cross-cultural study of recognition thresholds for facial expression of emotion. *Journal of Cross-Cultural Psychology, 17*, 211–224.

McClintock, M. K. (1971). Menstrual synchrony and suppression. *Nature (London), 229*, 244–245.

McDougall, W. (1908). *An introduction to social psychology*. London: Methuen.

McGuigan, F. J. (1978). *Cognitive psychophysiology—Principles of covert behavior*. Englewood Cliffs, NJ: Prentice-Hall.

MacLean, P. D. (1967). The brain in relation to empathy and medical education. *Journal of Nervous and Mental Disorders, 144*, 374–382.

MacLean, P. D. (1968). Alternative neural pathways to violence. In L. Ng (Ed.), *Alternatives to violence* (pp. 24–34). New York: Time-Life Books.

MacLean, P. D. (1970). The triune brain, emotion, and scientific bias. In F. O. Schmitt (Ed.), *The neurosciences*. New York: Rockefeller University Press.

MacLean, P. D. (1982). On the origin and progressive evolution of the triune brain. In E. Armstrong & D. Falk (Eds.), *Primate brain evolution*. New York: Plenum.

MacLean, P. D. (1990). *The triune brain in evolution*. New York: Plenum.

MacLean, P. D., & Rosenfeld, A.H. (1976). *The archaeology of affect*. Rockville, MD: National Institutes of Mental Health.

Malatesta, C. Z. (1985). Human infant: Emotion expression development. In G. Zivin (Ed.), *The development of expressive behavior* (pp. 183–219). Orlando, FL: Academic Press.

Malatesta, C. Z., Fiore, M. J., & Messina, J. J. (1987). Affect, personality, and facial expressive characteristics of older people. *Psychology and Aging, 2,* 64–69.

Malinowski, B. (1961). *Sex and repression in savage society.* Cleveland: World. (Original published 1927.)

Malotki, E. (1983). *Hopi time: A linguistic analysis if the temporal concepts of the Hopi language.* Berlin: Mouton.

Mandler, G. (1975). *Mind and emotion.* New York: Wiley.

Mandler, G. (1984). *Mind and body.* New York: Norton.

Manis, M. (1967). Context effects in communication. *Journal of Personality and Social Psychology, 5,* 326–334.

Manis, M. (1971). Context effects in communication. In M. H. Appley (Ed.), *Adaptation level theory* (pp. 237–255). New York: Academic Press.

Marler, P. R. (1970). A comparative approach to vocal learning: song development in white-crowned sparrows. *Journal of Comparative and Physiological Psychology Monographs, 71,* Monograph 2, 1–25.

Marler, P. R. (1982). Avian and primate communication: The problem of natural categories. *Neuroscience & Biobehavioral Reviews, 6,* 87–94.

Marler, P. (1991). The instinct to learn. In S. Carey & R. Gelman (Eds.), *The epigenesis of mind* (pp. 37–66). Hillsdale, NJ: Erlbaum.

Marler, P. & Evans, C. S. (1993, May). The dynamics of vocal communication in animals. Paper presented at the Nag's Head Conference on Emotion, West Palm Beach.

Marler, P. R., & Mitani, J. (1988). Vocal communication in primates and birds: Parallels and contrasts. In D. Todt, P. Goedeking, & D. Symmes (Eds.), *Primate vocal communication* (pp. 3–14). Berlin: Springer-Verlag.

Marler, P. R., & Peters, S. (1977). Selective vocal learning in a sparrow. *Science, 198,* 519–521.

Marler, P. R., & Peters, S. (1981). Birdsong and speech: Evidence for special processing. In P. Eimas & J. Miller (Eds.), *Perspectives on the study of speech* (pp. 75–112). Hillsdale, NJ: Erlbaum.

Marler, P. R., Duffy, A., & Pickert, R. (1986a). Vocal communication in the domestic chicken: I. Does a sender communicate information about the quality of a food referent to a receiver? *Animal Behaviour, 34,* 188–193.

Marler, P. R., Duffy, A., & Pickert, R. (1986b). Vocal communication in the domestic chicken: II. Is a sender sensitive to the presence and nature of a receiver? *Animal Behaviour, 34,* 194–198.

Marriott, B. M., & Salzen, E. A. (1978). Facial expressions in captive squirrel monkeys (*Saimiri sciureus*). *Folia Primatologica, 29,* 1–18.

Martin, A. D. (1988). The assessment of verbal expression. In F. C. Rose, R. Whurr, & M. A. Wyke (Eds.), *Aphasia.* London: Whurr.

Martin, G. B., & Clark, R. D. (1982). Distress crying in neonates: Species and peer specificity. *Developmental Psychology, 18,* 3–9.

Martin, R. D. (1990). *Primate origins and evolution: A phylogenetic reconstruction.* London: Chapman and Hall.

Matsumoto, D. (1987). The role of facial response in the experience of emotion: More methodological problems and a meta-analysis. *Journal of Personality and Social Psychology, 52,* 769–774.

Matsumoto, D. (1990). Cultural similarities and differences in display rules. *Motivation and Emotion, 14,* 195–214.

Matsumoto, D. (1992a). American-Japanese cultural differences in the recognition of universal facial expressions. *Journal of Cross-Cultural Psychology, 23,* 72–84.

Matsumoto, D. (1992*b*). More evidence for the universality of a contempt expression. *Motivation and Emotion, 16,* 363–368.

Matsumoto, D., & Ekman, P. (1988). Japanese and Caucasian facial expressions of emotion (JACFEE). Slide set and brochure available from first author, San Francisco State University.

Matsumoto, D., & Ekman, P. (1989). American-Japanese cultural differences in intensity ratings of facial expressions of emotion. *Motivation and Emotion, 13,* 143–157.

Maurer, D., & Salapatek, P. (1976). Developmental changes in the scanning of faces by young infants. *Child Development, 47,* 523–527.

Maynard Smith, J. (1974). The theory of games and the evolution of animal conflict. *Journal of Theoretical Biology, 57,* 239–242.

Maynard Smith, J. (1982). *Evolution and the theory of games.* Cambridge: Cambridge University Press.

Maynard Smith, J., & Price, G. R. (1973). The logic of animal conflict. *Nature (London), 246,* 15–18.

Mayr, E. (1960). The emergence of evolutionary novelties. In S. Tax (Ed.), *The evolution of life.* Chicago: University of Chicago Press.

Mayr, E. (1982). *The growth of biological thought.* Cambridge, MA: Belknap Press of Harvard University Press.

Mead, G. H. (1934). *Mind, self, and society from the standpoint of a social behaviorist.* Chicago: University of Chicago Press.

Mead, M. (1928). *Coming of age in Samoa.* New York: Morrow.

Mead, M. (1935). *Sex and temperament in three primitive societies.* New York: Morrow.

Mead, M. (1975). Review of *Darwin and Facial Expression* (P. Ekman, Ed.). *Journal of Communication, 25,* 209–213.

Meehl, P. E. (1978). Theoretical risks and tabular asterisks: Sir Karl, Sir Ronald, and the slow progress of soft psychology. *Journal of Consulting and Clinical Psychology, 46,* 806–834.

Meltzoff, A. N., & Moore, M. K. (1977). Imitation of facial and manual gestures by neonates. *Science, 198,* 75–78.

Mesquita, B., & Frijda, N. H. (1992). Cultural variations in emotions: A review. *Psychological Bulletin, 112,* 179–204.

Meyer, M. F. (1933). That whale among the fishes—the theory of emotions. *Psychological Review, 40,* 292–300.

Miller, E. H. (1975). A comparative study of facial expressions of two species of pinnipeds. *Behaviour, 53,* 268–284.

Miller, G. A., Galanter, E., & Pribram, K. H. (1960). *Plans and the structure of behavior.* New York: Holt.

Mitchell, R. W., & Thompson, N. S. (1991). Projects, routines, and enticements in dog-human play. In P. P. G. Bateson & P. H. Klopfer (Eds.), *Perspectives in ethology.* Vol. 9. *Human understanding and animal awareness* (pp. 189–216). New York: Plenum.

Moldaver, J. (1980). Anatomical and functional characteristics of the muscles supplied by the facial nerve. In J. Moldaver & J. Conley (Eds.), *The facial palsies* (pp. 16–19). Springfield, IL: Thomas.

Monrad-Krohn, G. H. (1924). On the dissociation of voluntary and involuntary innervation in facial paresis of central origin. *Brain, 47,* 22–35.

Montgomery, W. (1985). Charles Darwin's thought on expressive mechanisms in evolution. In G. Zivin (Ed.), *The development of expressive behavior* (pp. 27–50). Orlando, FL: Academic Press.

Moore, B. R., & Stuttard, S. (1979). Dr. Guthrie and *Felix domesticus* or: Tripping over the cat. *Science, 205,* 1031–1033.

Mora, F., Rolls, E. T., & Burton, M. J. (1976). Modulation during learning of the responses of neurones in the lateral hypothalamus to the sight of food. *Experimental Neurology*, 53, 508–519.

Morris, D. (1988). *Catwatching*. New York: Crown.

Motley, M. T., & Camden, C. T. (1988). Facial expression of emotion: A comparison of posed expressions versus spontaneous expressions in an interpersonal communication setting. *Western Journal of Speech Communication*, 52, 1–22.

Mourant, A. E., Kopec, A. C., & Domainiewska-Sobczak, K. (1976). *The distribution of the human blood groups and other polymorphisms* (2nd ed.). London: Oxford University Press.

Movshon, J. A., & van Sluyters, R. C. (1981). Visual neural development. *Annual Review of Psychology*, 32, 477–522.

Mowrer, O. H. (1960). *Learning theory and behavior*. New York: Wiley.

Moynihan, M. (1970). The control, suppression, decay, disappearance and replacement of displays. *Journal of Theoretical Biology*, 29, 85–112.

Mueller, J. (1983). Neuroanatomical correlates of emotion. In C. Van Dyke, L. Temoshok, & L. S. Zegans (Eds.), *Emotions in health and illness*. Orlando, FL: Academic Press.

Muller, E., Hallien, H., & Murry, T. (1974). Perceptual responses to infant crying: Identification of cry types. *Journal of Child Language*, 1, 89–95.

Müller, J. (1833–1834). *Handbuch der Physiologie des Menschens für Vorlesungen*. Koblenz, Germany: Hölscher.

Munn, N. L. (1940). The effect of knowledge of the situation upon judgment of emotion from facial expressions. *Journal of Abnormal and Social Psychology*, 35, 324–338.

Nakamura, M., Buck, R., & Kenny, D. A. (1990). Relative contribution of expressive behavior and contextual information to the judgment of the emotional state of another. *Journal of Personality and Social Psychology*, 59, 1032–1039.

National Research Council (1988). *Mapping and sequencing the human genome*. Washington, DC: National Academy Press.

Naylor, B. G. (1982). Vestigial organs are evidence of evolution. *Evolutionary Theory*, 6, 91–96.

Nelson, C. A. (1987). The recognition of facial expressions in the first two years of life: Mechanisms of development. *Child Development*, 58, 889–909.

Niit, T., & Valsiner, J. (1977). Recognition of facial expressions: An experimental investigation of Ekman's model. *Acta et Commentationes Universitatis Tarvensis*, 429, 85–107.

Noback, C. R., & Demarest, R. J. (1977). *The nervous system*. New York: McGraw-Hill.

Nolte, J. (1988). *The human brain* (2nd ed.). St. Louis: Mosby.

Notarius, C. I., & Levenson, R. W. (1979). Expressive tendencies and the response to stress. *Journal of Personality and Social Psychology*, 37, 1204–1210.

Nottebohm, F. (1980). Brain pathways for vocal learning in birds: A review of the first 10 years. In J. M. Sprague & A. N. Epstein (Eds.), *Progress in psychobiology and physiological psychology* (Vol. 9). New York: Academic Press.

Nurnberger, J. I., & Gershon, E. S. (1984). Genetics of affective disorders. In R. M. Post & J. C. Ballenger (Eds.), *Neurobiology of mood disorders* (pp. 76–101). Baltimore: Williams & Wilkins.

Oatley, K. (1992). *Best laid schemes: The psychology of emotions*. Cambridge: Cambridge University Press.

Oatley, K., & Jenkins, J. M. (1992). Human emotions: Function and dysfunction. *Annual Review of Psychology*, 43, 55–85.

Obrist, P. A. (1976). The cardiovascular-behavioral interaction—as it appears today. *Psychophysiology*, 13, 95–107.

Oken, L. (1847). *Elements of physiophilosophy*. (A. Tulk, Trans.). London: Ray Society.

Olds, J., Allan, W. S., & Briese, E. (1971). Differentiation of hypothalamic drive and reward centers. *American Journal of Physiology*, 221, 672–674.

Ortony, A., & Turner, T. J. (1990). What's so basic about basic emotions? *Psychological Review, 97*, 315–331.

Osgood, C. E. (1966). Dimensionality of the semantic space for communication via facial expressions. *Scandinavian Journal of Psychology, 7*, 1–30.

Oster, H. (1992). The development of emotional expressions: A question of differentiation? Manuscript submitted for publication.

Oster, H., & Ekman, P. (1978). Facial behavior in child development. *Minnesota Symposia on Child Psychology, 11*, 231–276.

Oster, H., Daily, L., & Goldenthal, P. (1989). Processing facial affect. In A. W. Young & H. D. Ellis (Eds.), *Handbook of research on face processing*. Amsterdam: Elsevier.

Oster, H., Hegley, D., & Nagel, L. (1992). Adult judgments and fine-grained analysis of infant facial expressions: Testing the validity of *a priori* coding formulas. *Developmental Psychology, 28*, 1115–1131.

O'Sullivan, M., Matsumoto, D., & Ekman, P. (1991). Context or research design? Unpublished manuscipt, San Francisco State University.

Owren, M. J., & Bernacki, R. (1988). The acoustic features of vervet monkey (*Cercopithecus aethiops*) alarm calls. *Journal of the Acoustic Society of America, 83*, 1927–1935.

Paley, W. (1816). *Natural theology; or evidences of the existence and attributes of the Deity, collected from the appearances of nature*. London: Baynes.

Parducci, A. (1965). Category judgment: A range-frequency model. *Psychological Review, 72*, 407–418.

Parisi, S. E. A. (1977). Five-, seven-, and nine- month-old infants' facial responses to 20 stimulus situations. Unpublished Master's thesis, Vanderbilt University, Nashville, Tennessee.

Parker, G. A. (1974). Assessment strategy and the evolution of animal conflicts. *Journal of Theoretical Biology, 47*, 223–243.

Peck, S. R. (1987). *Atlas of facial expression*. New York: Oxford University Press.

Peiper, A. (1963). *Cerebral function in infancy and childhood*. New York: Consultants Bureau.

Pernkopf, E. (1963). *Atlas of topographical and applied human anatomy*. Philadelphia: Saunders.

Perrett, D. I., Rolls, E. T., & Caan, W. (1982). Visual neurones responsive to faces in the monkey temporal cortex. *Experimental Brain Research, 47*, 329–342.

Perrett, D. I., Smith, P. A. J., Potter, D. D., Mistlin, A. J., Head, A. S., Milner, A. D., & Jeeves, M. A. (1984). Neurones responsive to faces in the temporal cortex: studies of functional organization, sensitivity to identity and relation to perception. *Human Neurobiology, 3*, 197–208.

Perrett, D. I., Smith, P. A. J., Mistlin, A. J., Chitty, A. J., Head, A. S., Potter, D. D., Broennimann, R., Milner, A. D., & Jeeves, M. A. (1985a). Visual analysis of body movements by neurones in the temporal cortex of the macaque monkey: A preliminary report. *Behavioral Brain Research, 16*, 153–170.

Perrett, D. I., Smith, P. A. J., Potter, D. D., Mistlin, A. J., Head, A. S., Milner, A. D., & Jeeves, M. A. (1985b). Visual cells in the temporal cortex sensitive to face view and gaze direction. *Proceedings of the Royal Society of London (Biology), 223*, 293–317.

Perrett, D. I., Mistlin, A. J., & Chitty, A. J. (1987). Visual neurones responsive to faces. *Trends in Neurosciences, 10*, 358–364.

Phelps, M., & Mazziotta, J. (1985). Positron emission tomography: Human brain function and biochemistry. *Science, 228*, 799–809.

Piderit, T. (1858). *Grundzüge der Mimik und physiognomik*. Brunswick, Germany: F. Vieweg und Sohn.

Piderit, T. (1867). *Wissenschaftliches system der mimik und physiognomik*. [*Scientific system of mimicry and physiognomy*]. Detmold: Kingenberg.

Piderit, T. (1886). *Mimik und physiognomik*. Detmold, Germany: Meyer.

Plutchik, R. (1962). *The emotions: Facts, theories, and a new model.* New York: Random House.

Plutchik, R. (1980). *Emotion: A psychoevolutionary synthesis.* New York: Harper & Row.

Popper, K. R. (1962). *Conjectures and refutations.* New York: Basic Books.

Posner, M. I., & Raichle, M. E. (1994). *Images of mind.* New York: Freeman.

Potegal, M., Blau, A., & Miller, S. (1980). Preliminary observations with technique for measuring current spread in the rat brain. *Physiology & Behavior, 25,* 769–773.

Premack, D. (1985). "Gavagai!" or the future of the animal language controversy. *Cognition, 19,* 207–296.

Provine, R. R. (1986). Yawning as a stereotyped action pattern and releasing stimulus. *Ethology, 72,* 109–122.

Provine, R. R. (1989a). Contagious yawning and infant imitation. *Bulletin of the Psychonomic Society, 27,* 125–126.

Provine, R. R. (1989b). Faces as releasers of contagious yawning: An approach to face detection using normal human subjects. *Bulletin of the Psychonomic Society, 27,* 211–214.

Provine, R. R., & Fischer, K. R. (1989). Laughing, smiling and talking: Relation to sleeping and social context in humans. *Ethology, 83,* 295–305.

Provine, R. R., & Hamernik, H. B. (1986). Yawning: Effects of stimulus interest. *Bulletin of the Psychonomic Society, 24,* 437–438.

Provine, R. R., Hamernik, H. B. & Curchack, B. C. (1987a). Yawning: Relation to sleeping and stretching in humans. *Ethology, 76,* 152–160.

Provine, R. R., & Yong, Y. L. (1991). Laughter: A stereotyped human vocalization. *Ethology, 89,* 115–124.

Provine, R. R., Hamernik, H. B., & Curchack, B. C. (1987). Yawning: Relation to sleeping and stretching in humans. *Ethology, 76,* 152–160.

Provine, R. R., Tate, B. C., & Geldmacher, L. L. (1987b). Yawning: No effect of 3–5% CO_2, 100% O_2, and exercise. *Behavioral and Neural Biology, 48,* 382–393.

Redican, W. K. (1982). An evolutionary perspective on human facial displays. In P. Ekman (Ed.), *Emotion in the human face* (2nd ed.) (pp. 212–280). Elmsford, NY: Pergamon.

Reuter-Lorenz, P., & Davidson, R. J. (1981). Differential contributions of the two cerebral hemispheres to the perception of happy and sad faces. *Neuropsychologia, 19,* 609–613.

Ribot, T. (1897). *The psychology of the emotions.* London: Walter Scott.

Ricci Bitti, P. E., Brighetti, G., Garotti, P. L., & Boggi-Cavallo, P. (1989). Is contempt expressed by pancultural facial movements? In *Recent advances in social psychology: An international perspective* (pp. 329–339).

Ricklefs, R. E. (1979). *Ecology* (2nd ed.). New York: Chiron Press.

Rinn, W. E. (1984). The neuropsychology of facial expression: a review of the neurological and psychological mechanisms for producing facial expressions. *Psychological Bulletin, 95,* 52–77.

Robarchek, C. (1977). Frustration, aggression, and the nonviolent Semai. *American Ethnologist, 4,* 762–779.

Robertson, J. G. (1939). *Lessing's dramatic theory.* London: Cambridge University Press.

Rodman, H. R., Skelly, J. P., & Gross, C. G. (1991). Stimulus selectivity and state dependence of activity in inferior temporal cortex of infant monkeys. *Proceedings of the National Academy of Sciences, U.S.A., 88,* 7572–7575.

Rolls, B. J., Wood, R. J., & Rolls, E. T. (1980). Thirst: The initiation, maintenance, and termination of drinking. In J. M. Sprague & A. N. Epstein (Eds.), *Progress in psychobiology and physiological psychology* (Vol. 9). New York: Academic Press.

Rolls, E. T. (1978). Neurophysiology of feeding. *Trends in Neuroscience, 1,* 1–13.

Romanes, G. J. (1883). *Mental evolution in animals. With a posthumous essay on instinct by Charles Darwin.* London: Kegan Paul, Trench & Company.

Romanes, G. J. (1888). *Mental evolution in man: Origin of human faculty.* London: Kegan Paul, Trench & Company.

Rosch, E. H. (1973). Natural categories. *Cognitive Psychology, 4*, 328–350.

Rosenfeld, H. M. (1987). The experimental analysis of interpersonal influence processes. *Journal of Communication, 22*, 424–442.

Rosenfeld, S. A., & Van Hoesen, G. W. (1979). Face recognition in the rhesus monkey. *Neuropsychologia, 17*, 503–509.

Rosenstein, D., & Oster, H. (1988). Differential facial responses to four basic tastes in newborns. *Child Development, 59*, 1555–1568.

Rosensweig, M. R., & Leiman, A. L. (1982). *Physiological psychology.* Lexington, MA: D. C. Heath.

Rozin, P., & Fallon, A. (1987). A perspective on disgust. *Psychological Review, 94*, 23–41.

Rozin, P., & Schull, J. (1988). The adaptive-evolutionary point of view in experimental psychology. In R. C. Atkinson, R. J. Herrnstein, G. Lindzey, & R. D. Luce (Eds.), *Stevens' handbook of experimental psychology (Vol. 1). Perception and motivation.* New York: Wiley-Interscience.

Rozin, P., Haidt, J., & McCauley, C. R. (1993). Disgust. In M. Lewis & J. M. Haviland (Eds.), *Handbook of emotions* (pp. 575–594). New York: Guilford.

Ruckmick, C. A. (1921). A preliminary study of the emotions. *Psychological Monographs, 30*(3) (Whole No. 136), 30–35.

Russell, J. A. (1980). A circumplex model of affect. *Journal of Personality and Social Psychology, 39*, 1161–1178.

Russell, J. A. (1989a). Culture, scripts, and children's understanding of emotion. In C. Saarni & P. L. Harris (Eds.), *Children's understanding of emotion* (pp. 293–318). Cambridge: Cambridge University Press.

Russell, J. A. (1989b). Measures of emotion. In R. Plutchik & H. Kellerman (Ed.), *Emotion: theory, research, and experience* (Vol. 4, pp. 83–112). San Diego, CA: Academic.

Russell, J. A. (1991a). Negative results on a reported facial expression of contempt. *Motivation and Emotion, 15*, 281–291.

Russell, J. A. (1991a). Negative results on a reported facial expression of contempt. *Motivation and Emotion, 15*, 281–291.

Russell, James A. (1991b). Confusions about context in the judgment of facial expression: A reply to "The contempt expression and the relativity thesis." *Motivation & Emotion, 15*, 177–184.

Russell, J. A. (1991c). The contempt expression and the relativity thesis. *Motivation and Emotion, 15*, 149–168.

Russell, J. A. (1994). Is there universal recognition of emotion from facial expression? *Psychological Bulletin, 115*, 102–141.

Russell, J. A. (in press). Forced-choice response format in the study of facial expression. *Motivation and Emotion.*

Russell, J. A., & Bullock, M. (1986). Fuzzy concepts and the perception of emotion in facial expressions. *Social Cognition, 4*, 309–341.

Russell, J. A., & Fehr, B. (1987). Relativity in the perception of emotion in facial expressions. *Journal of Experimental Social Psychology: General, 116*, 223–237.

Russell, J. A., & Lanius, U. F. (1984). Adaptation level and the affective appraisal of environments. *Journal of Environmental Psychology, 4*, 119–135.

Russell, J. A., Lewicka, M., & Niit, T. (1989). A cross-cultural study of a circumplex model of affect. *Journal of Personality and Social Psychology, 57*, 848–856.

Russell, J. A., Suzuki, N., & Ishida, N. (1993). Freely produced labels for facial expressions of emotion. *Motivation and Emotion, 17*, 337–351.

Ryle, G. (1949). *The concept of mind.* London: Hutchinson.

Saarni, C. (1978). Cognitive and communicative features of emotional experience, or do you show what you think you feel? In M. Lewis & L. Rosenblum (Eds.), *The development of affect.* New York: Plenum.

Saarni, C. (1982). Social and affective functions of nonverbal behavior. In R. S. Feldman (Ed.), *Development of nonverbal behavior in children*. New York: Springer-Verlag.

Sabini, J. (1992). *Social psychology*. New York: W. W. Norton.

Sackeim, H. A., & Gur, R. C. (1982). Facial asymmetry and the communication of emotion. In J. T. Cacioppo & R. E. Petty (Eds.), *Social psychophysiology: A sourcebook* (pp. 307–352). New York: Guilford Press.

Sackett, G. (1966). Monkeys reared in isolation with pictures as visual input: Evidence for an innate releasing mechanism. *Science, 154*, 1468–1473.

Saha, G. B. (1973). Judgment of facial expression of emotion—a cross-cultural study. *Journal of Psychological Research, 17*, 59–63.

Salapatek, P. (1975). Pattern perception in early infancy. In L. B. Cohen & P. Salapatek (Eds.), *Infant Perception: From Sensation to Cognition. Vol. 1. Basic Visual Processes*. New York: Academic Press.

Sanderson, D. W. (1993). *Smileys*. Sebastopol, CA: O'Reilly.

Santibanez, G., Espinoza, B., Astorga, L., & Strozzi, L. (1974). Macro-electrodic activity of the facial nucleus of the cat. *Acta Neurobiologiae Experimentalis, 34*, 265–276.

Sapir, E. (1929). The status of linguistics as a science. *Language, 5*, 207–214.

Satinoff, E. (1978). Neural organization and evolution of thermoregulation in mammals. *Science, 201*, 16–22.

Satoda, T., Takahashi, O., Tashiro, T., Matsushima, R., Uemura-Sumi, M., & Mizuno, N. (1987). Representation of the main branches of the facial nerve within the facial nucleus of the Japanese monkey (*Macaca fuscata*). *Neuroscience Letters, 78*, 283–287.

Schachter, J. (1957). Pain, fear, and anger in hypertensives and normotensives: a psychophysiological study. *Psychosomatic Medicine, 19*, 17–29.

Scherer, K. (1984). On the nature and function of emotion: a component process approach. In K. Scherer & P. Ekman, *Approaches to emotion*. Hillsdale, NJ: Erlbaum.

Scherer, K. (1992). What does a facial expression express? In K. Strongman (Ed.), *International review of studies on emotion*. New York: Wiley.

Schlosberg, H. S. (1941). A scale for the judgment of facial expressions. *Journal of Experimental Psychology, 44*, 229–237.

Schlosberg, H. (1952). The description of facial expressions in terms of two dimensions. *Journal of Experimental Psychology, 44*, 229–237.

Schlosberg, H. S. (1954). Three dimensions of emotion. *Psychological Review, 61*, 81–88.

Schneirla, T. C. (1959). An evolutionary and developmental theory of biphasic processes underlying approach and withdrawal. In M. R. Jones (Ed.), *Nebraska Symposium on Motivation, 7*, 1–42.

Schulze, R. (1912). *Experimental psychology and pedagogy*. New York: Macmillan.

Schwartz, G. E., Weinberger, D. A., & Singer, J. A. (1981). Cardiovascular differentiation of happiness, sadness, anger, and fear following imagery and exercise. *Psychosomatic Medicine, 43*, 343–364.

Schwartz, G. M., Izard, C. E., & Ansul, S. A. (1985, April). Heart rate and facial response to novelty in 7- and 13-month-old infants. Unpublished manuscript based on paper presented at the International Conference on Infant Studies, Austin, Texas.

Seaford, H. W. (1976). Maximizing replicability in describing facial behavior. Paper presented at the Annual Meeting of the American Anthropological Association, Washington, DC.

Seiler, R. (1973). On the function of facial muscles in different behavioral situations. A study based on muscle morphology and electromyography. *American Journal of Physical Anthropology, 38*, 567–572.

Seligman, M. E. P. (1970). On the generality of the laws of learning. *Psychological Review, 77*, 406–418.

Seyfarth, R. M., & Cheney, D. L. (1986). Vocal development in vervet monkeys. *Animal Behaviour, 34,* 1640–1658.

Seyfarth, R. M., Cheney, D. L., & Marler, P. (1980a). Vervet monkey alarm calls: semantic communication in a free-ranging primate. *Animal Behaviour, 28,* 1070–1094.

Seyfarth, R. M., Cheney, D. L., & Marler, P. (1980b). Monkey responses to three different alarm calls: evidence of predator classification and semantic communication. *Science, 210,* 801–803.

Sheldon, W. H. (with S. S. Stevens & W. B. Tucker). (1940). *The varieties of human physique.* New York: Harper.

Sheldon, W. H. (with S. S. Stevens). (1942). *The varieties of temperament.* New York: Harper.

Sherman, M. (1927). The differentiaton of emotional responses in infants: II. The ability of observers to judge the emotional characteristics of the crying of infants and of the voice of an adult. *Journal of Comparative Psychology, 7,* 335–351.

Sherman, P. W. (1977). Nepotism and the evolution of alarm calls. *Science, 197,* 1246–1253.

Shimoda, K., Argyle, M., & Ricci Bitti, P. (1978). The intercultural recognition of emotional expressions by three national racial groups: English, Italian and Japanese. *European Journal of Social Psychology, 8,* 169–179.

Simpson, G. G. (1953). The Baldwin effect. *Evolution, 7,* 110–117.

Skinner, M., & Mullen, B. (1991). Facial asymmetry in emotional expression: A meta-analysis of research. *British Journal of Social Psychology, 30,* 113–124.

Slatkin, M. (1978). On the equilibrium of fitnesses by natural selection. *American Naturalist, 110,* 31–55.

Slavkin, H. C. (1979). *Developmental craniofacial biology.* Philadelphia: Lea & Fibiger.

Smith, C. A. (1989). Dimensions of appraisal and physiological response in emotion. *Journal of Personality and Social Psychology, 56,* 339–353.

Smith, W. J. (1969). Messages of vertebrate communication. *Science, 165,* 145–150.

Smith, W. J. (1977). *The behavior of communicating.* Cambridge, MA: Harvard University Press.

Smith, W. J. (1985). Consistency and change in communication. In G. Zivin (Ed.), *The development of expressive behavior* (pp. 51–75). Orlando, FL: Academic Press.

Smith, W. J. (1986). An "informational" perspective on manipulation. In R. W. Mitchell & N. S. Thompson (Ed.), *Perspectives on human and nonhuman deceit* (pp. 71–87). Albany, NY: State University of New York Press.

Smith, W. J., Chase, J., & Lieblich, A. K. (1974). Tongue showing: A facial display of humans and other primate species. *Semiotica, 11,* 201–246.

Smythe, N. (1970). On the existence of "pursuit invitation" signals in mammals. *American Naturalist, 104,* 491–494.

Sorenson, E. R. (1975). Culture and the expression of emotion. In T. R. Williams (Ed.), *Psychological anthropology* (pp. 364–372). The Hague: Mouton.

Sorenson, E. R. (1976). The edge of the forest: Land, childhood and change in a New Guinea protoagricultural society. Washington, DC: Smithsonian Institution Press.

Spencer, H. (1855). *Principles of psychology.* London: Longman, Brown, Green, & Longmans.

Spencer, H. (1860). The physiology of laughter. *Macmillan's magazine, 1,* 396. (Reprinted in *Essays* (Vol. II, pp. 452–466). New York: Appleton.)

Spencer, H. (1863). *Essays* (Vol. II). London: Appleton.

Spignesi, A., & Shor, R. (1982). The judgment of emotion from facial expressions, contexts and their combination. *Journal of General Psychology, 104,* 41–58.

Spiro, M. (1982). *Oedipus in the Trobriands.* Chicago: University of Chicago Press.

Sroufe, L. A., & Waters, E. (1976). The ontogenesis of smiling and laughter: A perspective on the organization of development in infancy. *Psychological Review, 83,* 173–189.

Stanislavski, K. S. (1936). *An actor prepares* (E. R. Hapgood, Trans.). New York: Theatre Arts.

Stanislavski, K. S. (1965). *Creating a role* (H. I. Popper, Ed., & E. R. Hapgood, Trans.). New York: Theatre Arts.

Steiner, J. E. (1974). Discussion paper: innate discriminative human facial expressions to taste and smell stimulation. *Annals of the New York Academy of Sciences, 237,* 229–233.

Steiner, J. E. (1976). Further observations on sensory motor coordinations induced by gustatory and olfactory stimuli. *Israeli Journal of Medical Science, 12,* 1231.

Steiner, J. E. (1977). Facial expressions of the neonate infant indicating the hedonics of food-related chemical stimuli. In. J. W. Weiffernback (Ed.), *Taste and development: The genesis of sweet preferences* (pp. 173–189). (DHEW Publication No. NIH 77-1068). Washington, DC: U.S. Government Printing Office.

Stenberg, C., & Campos, J. J. (1990). The development of anger expressions in infancy. In N. Stein, H. Leventhal, & T. Trabasso (Eds.), *Psychological and biological approaches to emotion.* Hillsdale, NJ: Erlbaum.

Stenberg, C., Campos, J. J., & Emde, R. N. (1983). The facial expression of anger in seven-month-old infants. *Child Development, 54,* 178–184.

Sternberg, R. (1977). *Intelligence, information processing, and analogical reasoning: The componential analysis of human abilities.* Hillsdale, NJ: Erlbaum.

Stevens, S. S. (1956). The direct estimation of sensory magnitude—loudness. *American Journal of Psychology, 69,* 1–25.

Stevens, S. S. (1975). *Psychophysics: Introduction to its perceptual, neural, and social prospects.* New York: Wiley.

Stoddart, D. M. (1980). *The ecology of vertebrate olfaction.* London & New York: Chapman and Hall.

Strack, F., Martin, L. L., & Stepper, S. (1988). Inhibiting and facilitating conditions of facial expressions: A non-obtrusive test of the facial feedback hypothesis. *Journal of Personality and Social Psychology, 54,* 768–777.

Stratton, G. M. (1921). The control of another person by obscure signs. *Psychological Review, 28,* 301–314.

Sulloway, F. J. (1979). *Freud: Biologist of the mind.* New York: Basic Books.

Sulloway, F. J. (1982). Darwin and his finches: The evolution of a legend. *Journal of the History of Biology, 15,* 1–53.

Sulloway, F. J. (1989). Darwin and the Galapagos. *Biological Journal of the Linnean Society, 21,* 29–59.

Systat, Inc. (1992). *Systat for Windows: Graphics* (Version 5 Ed.). Evanston, IL: Author.

Tanaka, T., & Asahara, T. (1981). Synaptic actions of vagal afferents on facial motoneurons in the cat. *Brain Research, 212,* 188–193.

Tanaka-Matsumi, J., Nelson, S., Attivissimo, D., & D'Urso, T. (1993). *Positive and negative context effects on the judgment of basic emotions in the face.* Manuscript submitted for publication.

Tassinary, L. G. (1985). *Odor hedonics: Psychophysical, respiratory, and facial measures.* Unpublished doctoral dissertation, Dartmouth College, Hanover, NH.

Taylor, L. (1979). Psychological assessment of neurosurgical patients. In T. Rasmussen & R. Marino (Eds.), *Functional neurosurgery.* New York: Raven Press.

Teilhard de Chardin, P. (1959). *The phenomenon of man* (trans.). New York: Harper & Row.

Tellegen, A., Lykken, D. T., Bouchard, T. J., Wilcox, K. J., Segal, N. L., & Rich, S. (1988). *Journal of Personality and Social Psychology, 54,* 1031–1039.

Teuber, H. L. (1955). Physiological psychology. *Annual Review of Psychology, 6,* 267–294.

Thayer, S. (1980a). The effect of facial expression sequence upon judgments of emotion. *Journal of Nonverbal Psychology, 5,* 71–79.

Thayer, S. (1980b). The effect of facial expression sequence upon judgments of emotion. *Journal of Social Psychology, 111,* 305–306.

Thompson, J. (1941). Development of facial expression of emotion in blind and seeing children. *Archives of Psychology, 37,* 1–47.

Tinbergen, N. (1939). On the analysis of social organization among vertebrates, with special reference to birds. *American Midland Naturalist, 21,* 210–234.

Tinbergen, N. (1952). "Derived" activities: their causation, biological significance, origin and emancipation during evolution. *Quarterly Review of Biology, 27,* 1–32.

Tinbergen, N. (1953). *Social behaviour in animals.* London: Chapman and Hall.

Tomkins, S. S. (1962). *Affect, imagery, consciousness. Vol. 1, The positive affects.* New York: Springer.

Tomkins, S. S. (1963). *Affect, imagery, consciousness. Vol. 2, The negative affects.* New York: Springer.

Tomkins, S. S. (1980). Affect as amplification: Some modifications in theory. In R. Plutchik & H. Kellerman (Eds.), *Emotion: Theory research, and experience* (Vol. 1, pp. 141–187). New York: Academic Press.

Tomkins, S. S. (1984). Affect theory. In K. R. Scherer & P. Ekman (Eds.), *Approaches to emotion* (pp. 163–195). Hillsdale, NJ: Erlbaum.

Tomkins, S. S., & McCarter, R. (1964). What and where are the primary affects? Some evidence for a theory. *Perceptual and Motor Skills, 18,* 119–158.

Tooby, J., & Cosmides, L. (1990). On the universality of human nature and the uniqueness of the individual: the role of genetics and adaptation. *Journal of Personality, 58,* 17–67.

Tourangeau, R., & Ellsworth, P. C. (1979). The role of facial response in the experience of emotion. *Journal of Personality and Social Psychology, 37,* 1519–1531.

Triandis, H. C., & Lambert, W. W. (1958). A restatement and test of Schlosberg's Theory of Emotion with two kinds of subjects from Greece. *Journal of Abnormal and Social Psychology, 56,* 321–328.

Trivers, R. L. (1972). Parental investment and sexual selection. In B. Campbell (Ed.), *Sexual selection and the descent of man* (pp. 52–97). Chicago: Aldine.

Tryon, R. C. (1942). Individual differences. In F. A. Moss (Ed.), *Comparative psychology* (rev. ed.). Englewood Cliffs, NJ: Prentice-Hall.

Tschiassny, K. (1953). Eight syndromes of facial paralysis and their significance in locating the lesion. *Annals of otology, rhinology, and laryngology, 62,* 677–691.

Turner, T. J., & Ortony, A. (1992). Basic emotions: Can conflicting criteria converge? *Psychological Review, 99,* 566–571.

Tytler, G. (1982). *Physiognomy in the European novel: Faces and fortunes.* Princeton: Princeton University Press.

Valenstein, E. S., Cox, V. C., & Kakolewski, J. W. (1970). Reexamination of the role of the hypothalamus in motivation. *Psychological Review, 77,* 16–31.

Van Hooff, J. A. R. A. M. (1969). The facial displays of the Catarrhine monkeys and apes. In D. Morris (Ed.), *Primate ethology* (pp. 9–88). Garden City, NY: Anchor.

Van Hooff, J. A. R. A. M. (1972). A comparative approach to the phylogeny of laughter and smiling. In R. A. Hinde (Ed.), *Nonverbal communication* (pp. 209–238). Cambridge: Cambridge University Press.

Van Hooff, J. A. R. A. M. (1976). The comparison of facial expression in man and higher primates. In M. von Cranach (Ed.), *Methods of inference from animal to human behaviour* (pp. 165–196). Chicago: Aldine.

Van Lawick-Goodall, J. (1971). *In the shadow of man.* Boston: Houghton-Mifflin.

Vaughan, B. E., & Sroufe, L. A. (1976). The face of surprise in infants. Paper presented at the Annual Meeting of the Animal Behavior Society, Boulder, CO.

Vaughan, K. B., & Lanzetta, J. T. (1980). Vicarious instigation and conditioning of facial expressive and autonomic responses to a model's expressive display of pain. *Journal of Personality and Social Psychology, 38,* 909–923.

Vinacke, W. E. (1949). The judgment of facial expressions by three national-racial groups in Hawaii: I. Caucasian faces. *Journal of Personality, 17,* 407–429.

von Baer, K. E. (1828). *Entwicklungsgeschichte der Thiere: Beobachtung und Reflexion*. Königsberg, Germany: Bornträger.

Vraa-Jensen, G. (1942). *The motor nucleus of the facial nerve. With a Survey of the Efferent Innervation of the Facial Muscles*. Copenhagen: Munksgaard.

Vygotsky, L. S. (1962). *Thought and language*. Cambridge, MA: MIT Press.

Waddington, C. H. (1957). *The strategy of the genes*. London: Allen and Unwin.

Wagner, H. L. (1993). On measuring performance in category judgment studies of nonverbal behavior. *Journal of Nonverbal Behavior, 17*, 1–28.

Wagner, H. L., & Smith, J. (1991). Facial expression in the presence of friends and strangers. *Journal of Nonverbal Behavior, 15*, 201–214.

Wagner, H. L., MacDonald, C. J., & Manstead, A. S. R. (1986). Communication of individual emotions by spontaneous facial expression. *Journal of Personality and Social Psychology, 50*, 737–743.

Walker, P., & Murray, P. (1975). An assessment of masticatory efficiency in a series of anthropoid primates with special reference to the *colobinae* and *cercopithecinae*. In R. Tuttle (Ed.), *Primate functional morphology and evolution* (pp. 135–150). Paris: Mouton (Chicago: Aldine).

Wall, P. D., & Pribram, K. H. (1950). Trigeminal neurotomy and blood pressure responses from stimulation of lateral cerebral cortex in *Macaca mulatta*. *Journal of Neurophysiology, 13*, 409–412.

Wallbott, H. G. (1988). In and out of context: Influences of facial expresion and context information on emotion attributions. *British Journal of Social Psychology, 27*, 357–369.

Watson, D., & Tellegen, A. (1985). Toward a consensual structure of mood. *Psychological Bulletin, 98*, 219–235.

Watson, S. G. (1972). Judgment of emotion from facial and contextual cue combinations. *Journal of Personality and Social Psychology, 24*, 334–342.

Weigel, R. M. (1979). The facial expressions of the brown capuchin monkey. *Behaviour, 68*, 250–276.

Weinstein, E. A., & Bender, M. B. (1943). Integrated facial patterns elicited by stimulation of the brain stem. *Archives of Neurology and Psychiatry, 50*, 34–42.

Wells, S. R. (1871). *New physiognomy*. New York: American Book Company.

Wertsch, J. V. (1985). *Vygotsky and the social formation of mind*. Cambridge, MA: Harvard University Press.

Wiepkema, P. R. (1961). An ethological analysis of the reproductive behavior of the bitterling (*Rhodeus amarus* Bloch). *Archives Neerl. Zoology, 14*, 103–109.

Wierzbicka, A. (1992). *Semantics, culture and cognition*. New York: Oxford.

Wikan, U. (1990). *Managing turbulent hearts: A Balinese formula for living*. Chicago: University of Chicago Press.

Wilkinson, L. (1982). An experimental evaluation of multivariate graphical point representations. In *Human factors in computer systems: Proceedings* (pp. 202–209). Gaithersburg, MD.

Wilson, J. Q., & Herrnstein, R. J. (1985). *Crime and human nature*. New York: Simon & Schuster.

Wilson, S. A. K. (1924). Some problems in neurology. II. Pathological laughing and crying. *Journal of Neurology and Psychopathology, 16*, 299–333.

Wind, J. (1970). *On the phylogeny and the ontogeny of the human larynx*. Groningen: Wolters-Noordhoff.

Wind, J. (1976). Phylogeny of the human vocal tract. *Annals of the New York Academy of Sciences, 280*, 612–630.

Winkelmayer, R., Exline, R. V., Gottheil, E., & Paredes, A. (1978). The relative accuracy of U.S., British, and Mexican raters in judging the emotional displays of schizophrenic and normal U.S. women. *Journal of Clinical Psychology, 34*, 600–608.

Winton, W. M. (1986). The role of facial response in self-reports of emotion: A critique of Laird. *Journal of Personality and Social Psychology, 50*, 808–812.

Wise, R. A. (1974). Lateral hypothalamic electrical stimulation: Does it make animals 'hungry'? *Brain Research, 67*, 187–209.

Wolff, P. H. (1966). The causes, controls, and organization of behavior in the neonate. *Psychological Issues, 5* (Monograph 17).

Wolff, P. H. (1969). The natural history of crying and other vocalizations in early infancy. In B. M. Foss (Ed.), *Determinants of infant behavior* (Vol. 4). London: Methuen.

Wolfgang, A., & Cohen, M. (1988). Sensitivity of Canadians, Latin Americans, Ethiopians, and Israelis to interracial facial expressions of emotions. *International Journal of Intercultural Relations, 12*, 139–151.

Wolpoff, M. H. (1980). *Paleoanthropology.* New York: Knopf.

Woodworth, R. S. (1938). *Experimental psychology.* New York: Henry Holt and Company.

Woodworth, R. S., & Schlosberg, H. (1954). *Experimental psychology.* New York: Holt, Rinehart, & Winston.

Wright, S. (1931). Evolution in Mendelian populations. *Genetics, 16*, 97–159.

Wright, S. (1960). Evolution and the genetics of populations. In S. Tax (Ed.), *Evolution after Darwin.* Chicago: University of Chicago Press.

Wundt, W. (1896). *Outline of psychology* (C. H. Judd, Trans.). New York: Stechert.

Wyer, R. S., Jr., & Srull, T. K. (1981). Category accessibility: Some theoretical and empirical issues concerning the processing of social stimulus information. In E. T. Higgins, C. P. Herman, & M. P. Zanna (Eds.), *Social cognition: The Ontario symposium* (Vol. 1, pp. 161–197). Hillsdale, NJ: Erlbaum.

Yoon, M. (1979). Specificity and plasticity of retinotectal connections. *Neuroscience Research Program Bulletin, 17*, 255–359.

Young, A. W., & Dcarie, T. G. (1977). An ethology-based catalogue of facial/vocal behaviour in infancy. *Animal Behaviour, 25*, 95–107.

Zahavi, A. (1975). Mate selection—a selection for a handicap. *Journal of Theoretical Biology, 53*, 205–214.

Zahavi, A. (1977). The cost of honesty (further remarks on the handicap principle). *Journal of Theoretical Biology, 67*, 603–605.

Zajonc, R. B. (1965). Social facilitation. *Science, 149*, 269–274.

Zajonc, R. B., & McIntosh, D. N. (1992). Emotions research: Some promising questions and some questionable promises. *Psychological Science, 3*, 70–74.

Zajonc, R. B., Murphy, S. T., & Inglehart, M. (1989). Feeling and facial efference: Implications of the vascular theory of emotion. *Psychological Review, 96*, 396–416.

Zillman, D. (1983). Transfer of excitation in emotional behavior. In J. T. Cacioppo & R. E. Petty (Eds.), *Social psychophysiology: A sourcebook* (pp. 215–240). New York: Guilford Press.

Zivin, G. (1985). *The development of expressive behavior.* San Diego, CA: Academic Press.

Zoloth, S. R., Petersen, M. R., Beecher, M. D., Green, S., Marler, P., Moody, D. B., & Stebbins, W. (1979). Species-specific perceptual processing of vocal sounds by monkeys. *Science, 204*, 870–873.

Zuckerman, M., & Driver, R. E. (1985). Telling lies: Verbal and nonverbal correlates of deception. In A. W. Siegman & S. Feldstein (Eds.), *Multichannel interpretations of nonverbal behavior.* Hillsdale, NJ: Erlbaum.

Zuckerman, M., DePaulo, B. M., & Rosenthal, R. (1981a). Verbal and nonverbal communications of deception. In L. Berkowitz (Ed.), *Advances in experimental social psychology* (Vol. 14). New York: Academic Press.

Zuckerman, M., Klorman, R., Larrance, D. T., & Spiegel, N. H. (1981b). Facial, autonomic, and subjective components of emotion: The facial feedback hypothesis versus the externalizer–internalizer distinction. *Journal of Personality and Social Psychology, 41,* 929–944.

Zuckerman, M., DePaulo, B. M., & Rosenthal, R. (1986). Humans as deceivers and lie detectors. In P. Blanck, R. Buck, & R. Rosenthal (Eds.), *Nonverbal communication in the clinical context.* University Park, PA: Pennsylvania State University Press.

Author Index

A

Abelson, R. P. 261, 264
Adams, E. S. 143
Alberch, P. 42
Alcock, J. 125, 138, 147, 308–309
Alexander, R. D. 133
Alford, K. F. 93
Alford, R. D. 93
Allan, W. S. 103
Allen, C. 61
Allport, F. M. 15, 111–112, 120, 175, 195
Allport, G. 80
Altmann, L. 178
American Psychiatric Association, 119
Ancoli, S. 117, 202, 220, 278
Andersson, M. 58
Andrew, R. J. 41, 42, 44, 61–62, 64, 107,
    129–130, 277, 278, 302, 304–306
Angell, J. R. 26
Apfelbaum, B. 167
Archibald, H. C. 119
Arcuri, L. 204–205, 207, 210–211, 251
Argyle, M. 132, 252
Aristotle 2, 3, 4, 9, 192, 194, 251, 267–268
Armon-Jones, C. 280
Arnold, M. B. 15, 141–142, 169
Arnold, S. 83
Aronfreed, J. A. 120
Asahara, T. 101
Ashton, E. H. 33
Astorga, L. 102
Attivissimo, D. 211, 213

Au, T. K. 311
Averill, J. R. 169, 280
Ax, A. F. 169, 171
Axelrod, R. 76, 139
Ayala, F. J. 35, 41, 284

B

Bain, A. 21, 22, 194
Bainum, C. K. 154
Baker, P. 161
Bakhtin, M. M. 160
Baldwin, B. A. 65
Baldwin, J. M. 14, 53
Barkow, J. H. 316
Barlow, G. 30
Barrett, P. H. 16, 20
Basmajian, J. V. 10
Bastone, L. 156
Bavelas, J. B. 137–138, 144, 157, 170, 277
Baylis, G. C. 65
Beecher, M. D. 71
Bekoff, M. 61
Bell, C. 10, 14, 16, 18–21, 25, 93, 176–177,
    194
Bender, D. B. 65
Bender, M. B. 102
Bergson, H. 46, 185
Berlin, B. 188
Berlyne, D. E. 115
Bernacki, R. 307
Birdwhistell, R. L. 188, 196, 283, 302, 310

Black, A. 138, 144, 157
Blau, A. 103
Bleuler, E. 167
Bloom, A. H. 311
Bock, W. J. 76
Boggi-Cavallo, P. 203
Bolles, R. C. 147
Borod, J. C. 83, 93
Bouchard, T. J. 32, 39
Boucher, J. D. 204, 207, 210, 225, 227–228, 231–232, 236, 239, 247–251, 255
Bowlby, J. 16
Boyd, R. 45, 139, 316
Bradley, M. M. 119
Bratzlavsky, M. 102, 108
Braun, J. 198, 211
Brennan, S. E. 130
Breuer, J. 100–101
Briese, E. 103
Brighetti, G. 203
Brightman, V. J. 155, 158
Britt, T. W. 105
Broca, P. 39
Brodal, A. 97
Brookens, N. L. 102
Brothers, L. 26, 65, 67–68
Brower, L. P. 74
Brown, D. E. 188, 192–193
Brown, J. D. 97
Brown, R. 238
Browne, J. 9, 17, 104, 115, 168
Browne, W. A. 16
Bruce, C. 65
Bruner, J. 108, 197–198, 200
Buck, R. 15, 125, 127–128, 158, 160, 7–5, 8–35, 175–176, 193, 216, 238
Bullock, M. 208, 234, 236, 261, 281
Burgess, T. 104–105
Burkhardt, R. W. 25–26
Burton, M. J. 68
Buss, D. 192
Buzby, D. E. 195

C

Caan, W. 65
Cacioppo, J. T. 158, 172, 8–53, 265
Cade, W. 39
Caldwell, R. L. 143
Camden, C. T. 217–219, 238, 255
Campbell, B. 34–35, 42, 49
Campbell, R. 93

Campos, J. J. 145
Camras, L. A. 126, 202, 252, 266
Cannon, W. B. 169, 171
Carlson, G. E. 204, 207, 210, 225, 227–228, 231–232, 236, 239, 247–248, 250, 254–255
Carlson, J. G. 184, 193, 199
Carpenter, M. B. 89
Carr, H. A. 26
Carroll, J. B. 188
Cartwright-Smith, J. 175, 180
Caryl, P. G. 78, 136–137
Caul, W. F. 175, 216
Cavalli-Sforza, L. L. 284
Chan, A. 233, 282–283
Chan, D. W. 205
Chapman, C. A. 147
Chapman, L. J. 147
Charlesworth, W. R. 112
Chase, J. 45, 166, 306
Chase, R. A. 161
Cheney, D. L. 71–72, 74–75, 138, 141, 146–149
Chernoff, H. 66
Chevalier-Skolnikoff, S. 15, 62, 64, 143
Chitty, A. J. 65
Chovil, N. 138, 144, 157–158, 162–163, 165, 277, 299–302, 307–308
Chusid, J. G. 97, 100
Clark, W. E. Le Gros 33
Clark, H. 130
Clark, R. D. 160
Cohen, A. A. 205, 210
Colby, C. Z. 175
Cole, P. M. 286, 292
Colgan, P. W. 29–30
Collins, K. 166
Confucius, 2
Cosmides, L. 26, 315
Courville, J. 44, 66
Cox, V. C. 103
Craig, W. 15
Cüceloglu, D. M. 205
Cullen, J. K. 161
Curchack, B. C. 106
Cuthbert, B. N. 119
Cutlip, W. D. 105

D

D'Urso, T. 211, 213
Daanje, A. 61, 64

Daily, L. 193, 201–202, 220, 229
Daly, E. M. 261
Damasio, A. R. 67
Damasio, H. 67
Darwin, C. R. 2, 5, 10–12, 14–27, 29–30, 32, 40, 56–58, 60–61, 63–64, 75, 104–105, 107–108, 112–118, 124–125, 128, 141, 154, 168, 174–175, 189, 193–197, 210, 225, 238, 263, 267, 270–271, 275, 283, 296, 298, 302–303, 310
Darwin, E. 21
Darwin, F. 15–18, 21
Darwin, W. 16
Dashiell, J. F. 239, 241, 243, 246–247, 249, 255, 267
Davidson, R. J., 117, 158, 216
Davidson, J. R. T. 308
Davies, N. B. 57–58, 124
Davis, P. R. 33
Dawkins, R. 65, 75, 77, 124, 138
De Beer, G. R. 15
De Jong, R. N. 96
DeLuca, C. J. 10
Demarest, R. J. 92, 96
Dennett, D. C. 61, 134, 146
Denny-Brown, D. 102–103
DePaulo, B. M. 75, 137, 192
Descartes, R. 9, 101, 117
Desimone, R. 65
Desmond, A. J. 284, 304
DeVries, J. I. 106
Dewey, J. 141
Diacoyanni-Tarlatzis, I. 233, 282–283
Dobzhansky, T. 31, 35, 39, 41, 284
Dolgin, K. M. 166
Domainiewska-Sobczak, K. 36
Down, J. L. H. 6
Driver, R. E. 137
Du Bois-Reymond, E. 10
Ducci, L. 204–205, 207, 210–211, 251
Duchenne, G. B. A. 10, 115–118, 129, 194, 195, 289
Duclos, S. E. 181
Dudai, Y. 53
Duffy, A. 149
Dzubow, L. M. 33

E

Ectors, L. 102
Efron, D. 296

Ehrlichman, H. 156
Eibl-Eibesfeldt, I. 53, 61, 68, 113, 189, 196, 202, 263, 309–310
Ekman, P. 15, 29, 41, 93, 107, 115–119, 121, 125–126, 128, 131–132, 137, 143, 145, 156, 158, 169, 171, 175, 179, 189–190, 192–194, 196–200, 202–207, 210–217, 219, 221–224, 228–235, 237–242, 245–249, 252–255, 260, 262–263, 265, 267, 271–275, 277–280, 282–283, 285–291, 296–299, 301–302, 305, 307–308, 312, 315
Eliot, T. S. 8–23
Ellsworth, P. 175–176, 189, 198, 237–238
Emde, R. N. 145
Emlen, S. 141
Enquist, M. 76
Espinoza, B. 102
Evans, C. S. 71, 150, 306, 307
Evans, E. C. 192, 195
Evans, L. 71
Exline, R. V. 203, 207, 212, 215, 219

F

Fahrenbruch, C. E. 40, 306
Faigin, G. 210
Fallon, A. 45, 120
Fargo, N. 161
Fedio, P. 65
Fehr, B. 211, 221, 224, 264, 280
Feinman, S. 145
Feleky, A. M. 195–197
Fernandez-Dols, J.-M. 238, 246, 280
Fernberger, S. W. 195
Fink, L. S. 74
Fiore, M. J. 215
Fischer, K. R. 154
Fisher, R. A. 31, 58
Fliess, W. 185
Flynn, J. P. 102
Forster, E. S. 192
Foulke, E. 70
Fowler, S. C. 169, 172
Fowler, C. A. 307
Fraiberg, S. 112
Frank, M. 117
Freeman, D. 189
Freeman, G. L. 107, 171
Freud, S. 14, 115, 130, 133, 137, 145, 175, 185

Fridlund, A. J. 17, 22, 26, 29, 36, 38–39, 64, 75, 80, 93, 107, 114–115, 157–158, 161–165, 169–170, 172–173, 181, 190, 193, 202, 264, 265, 277–278, 282–283, 296
Fried, I. 65
Friesen, W. V. 115–119, 121, 127–128, 137, 156, 158, 169, 171, 175, 179, 189, 198–200, 202–207, 210–213, 215, 219, 223, 233, 237–242, 247–248, 252–255, 260, 265, 267, 273, 277–280, 282–283, 285–292, 296–299, 301–302, 307–308, 312, 315
Frijda, N. H. 193, 225, 238, 263, 267, 276–277, 279
Funkenstein, D. H. 169

G

Galanter, E. 30
Galen, 2
Gall, F. J. 5, 11
Gallistel, C. R. 30
Galvani, L. 10
Gange, J. J. 145
Gantry, Elmer (S. Lewis), 4
Garotti, P. L. 203
Gartner, L. P. 37, 44, 81–82, 86, 88
Gautrey, P. J. 16, 20
Geen, R. G. 145
Geldard, F. A. 277
Geldmacher, L. L. 106
Gerard, R. W. 102
Gershon, E. S. 39
Gesell, A. 106
Ghiselin, M. T. 15, 20–22, 48
Gilbert, A. N. 157–158, 173, 296
Gilman, S. L. 8
Ginsburg, G. P. 130
Gleitman, H. 46, 173
Gleitman, L. R. 52
Goethe, J. W. von 5
Goldberg, H. D. 238
Goldenthal, P. 64, 193, 201–202, 220, 229
Goldstein, M. L. 169
Goodenough, F. L.197, 202, 238
Goodman, M. 35
Gorney, M. 83
Gottesman, I. I. 39
Gottheil, E. 203, 207, 212, 215, 219
Gould, S. J. 7, 19, 42–43, 48, 108, 141
Grant, V. 31–32, 36, 46, 108, 284, 316
Gratiolet, P. 167

Green, J. A. 134
Green, S. 71
Gross, C. G. 65, 66
Gruber, H. E. 15–17, 19, 21, 23, 168
Guajardo, C. 308
Gudykunst, W. B. 193
Guilford, J. P. 195
Guilford, T. 65
Gur, R. C. 83
Gustafson, G. E. 134
Guthrie, E. R. 147, 148
Gyger, M. 150

H

Haeckel, E. 81, 108
Hager, J. C. 93
Haidt, J. 120
Haldane, J. B. S. 31
Halgren, E. 65
Hall, G. S. 14
Hallien, H. 134
Hamernik, H. B. 106
Harré, R. 281
Harries, T. 83
Harrington, M. 130
Hasselmo, M. E. 65
Hatfield, E. 184, 193, 199
Hauri, P. 177
Hauser, M. D. 39, 61, 71, 149, 306–307
Havemann, E. 198, 211
Haynes, O. M. 203, 279
Head, H. 97
Hecker, E. 114, 117
Hedlund, L. E. 64, 164–165, 173
Heestand, J. E. 62
Hegley, D. 202, 252
Heider, E. R. 239
Heider, K. G. 203, 233, 239, 254, 282–283
Heilman, K. M. 97
Hein, A. 4–12
Heinroth, O. 27, 60–61, 64
Heit, G. 65
Held, R. 4–12
Helmholtz, H. von 10, 20, 29, 63
Helson, H. 211
Herbert, S. 16, 20
Hering, E. 100–101
Heron, W. T. 53
Herrnstein, R. J. 2, 9
Hess, W. R. 102
Hiatt, J. L. 37, 44, 81–82, 86, 88
Hillman, J. 185

Hinde, R. A. 64, 78, 136, 315
Hippocrates, 2, 3
Hobbes, T. 76, 145
Hohmann, G. W. 176
Hoikkala, A. 39
Holder, D. S. 38
Hong, H.-W. 166
Honkavaara, S. 15
Hoogland, J. L. 133
Hooten, E. A. 9
Horton, G. P. 147–148
Howard, R. D. 133
Howell, R. J. 216
Hoyer, B. H. 35
Hubel, D. H. 68
Huber, E. 42, 44
Hume, D. 22
Hunt, W. A. 118
Huschke, 10–11
Huxley, J. 27, 60–61

I

Inglehart, M. 265
Ishida, N. 225, 229, 231, 258
Izard, C. E. 15, 119, 121, 124–126, 133,
    135, 145, 169, 172, 175, 184, 189–190,
    192–194, 197–200, 202–207, 210–211,
    213, 215, 219, 223, 225–227, 229,
    231–232, 252–253, 256, 258, 260, 263,
    265, 279, 315

J

Jackson, J. H. 97, 108–109, 133
Jaffey, A. K. 164, 315
James, W. 14, 22, 60, 169, 174–176, 185
Jenkins, J. M. 192, 194
Jenny, A. B. 44
Johnson-Laird, P. N. 224
Johnston, R. E. 64, 152–154, 166, 277
Jones, H. E. 175
Jones, L. E. 134
Jones, N. 281
Jones, S. S. 166, 277
Jorgenson, E. 216
Juliet (W. Shakespeare), 111

K

Kagan, J. 198, 211
Kakolewski, J. W. 103
Kappeler, P. M. 77

Karakashian, S. J. 150
Kay, P. 188
Keating, C. F. 66
Keating, E. G. 66
Keddy Hector, A. C. 149
Kendon, A. 132, 315
Kendrick, K. M. 65
Kenny, D. A. 216, 238
Kenworthy, K. G. 164
Kilbride, J. E. 205
Kimura, M. 32, 35, 316
Kinsbourne, M. 124
Kirkevold, B. C. 62
Kishnan, K. R. R. 308
Kleck, R. E. 175, 180
Klineberg, O. 196–198, 200
Klinnert, M. D. 145
Klopfer, L. 40
Klopfer, P. H. 40
Klorman, R. 175
Knauer, M. J. 64, 164–165, 173
Knudsen, H. R. 238, 255
Koff, E. 83, 93
Kohn, D. 16, 20
Kohne, D. E. 35
Kolb, B. 38, 67, 94
Kopec, A. C. 36
Kosslyn, S. M. 161, 181
Kraus, B. 24
Krause, R. 233, 282–283
Kraut, R. E. 64, 152–154, 156, 166, 277
Krebs, J. R. 75, 77, 57–58, 124, 138
Kretchmer, E. 9
Kreutzer, M. A. 112
Kuipers, P. 277, 279
Kuldau, J. M. 73–74, 117

L

La Vergata, A. 15
La Barre, W. 188, 196, 283, 310
Laird, J. D. 176, 178, 181
Lamarck, J.-B. 23–27, 46, 59–60, 63, 168
Lambert, W. W. 196–197
Lancee, W. 261
Landau, T. 2–3
Landau, B. 52
Lande, R. 58
Landis, C. 118, 195, 200, 219, 267
Lang, P. J. 119
Langfeld, H. S. 195, 197
Lanzetta, J. T. 128, 175–176, 180
Larrance, D. T. 175

Larsen, B. 38
Lasker, G. W. 35
Lassen, N. 38
Latané, B. 160
Lavater, J. C. 4–5, 11, 14
Laverty, B. 17
Leach, E. 196, 283
Leary, M. R. 105
Le Brun, C. 9, 195
Le Comte, W. A. 233, 282–283
Lefebvre, L. 147
Leibniz, G. W. von, 9
Leiman, A. L. 103
Leimar, O. 76
Lemery, C. R. 157
Leonard, C. M. 73–74, 117
Lessing, 173, 179
Levenson, R. W. 169, 175, 179
Leventhal, H. 124
Lewicka, M. 261
Lewis, M. 134, 145
Lewontin, R. C. 45–46
Lieberman, P. 304
Lieblich, A. K. 45, 166, 306
Linder, D. E. 198, 211
Lindsay, W. 142
Lloyd Morgan, 22
Lloyd, J. E. 143
Lockard, J. S. 40, 62, 306
Locke, J. 17, 22
Locke, J. L. 66, 161, 302
Loftis, J. M. 114–115
Lombroso, C. 7
London, P. 198, 211
Lorenz, K. Z. 27, 29, 61–63, 68–69, 115,
    133, 152, 196, 271–272, 294, 309
Lounsbury, K. R. 154
Loveday, T. 192
Lovtrup, S. 108
Lumme, J. 39
Lykken, D. T. 32, 39

M

McAndrew, F. T. 204, 207, 209–210
McCarter, R. 198, 229, 260
McCauley, C. R. 120
McClintock, M. K. 62
McDougall, W. 124
McGuigan, F. J. 173
McHugo, G. J. 176
MacDonald, C. J. 217–219, 261

MacDonald, M. 2–16
MacLean, P. D. 108–110, 145
Magendie, F. 16
Malatesta, C. Z. 124, 126, 133, 135, 145,
    202, 215, 252
Malinowski, B. 188–189
Malmstrom, E. 287
Malotki, E. 188
Mandal, M. K. 205
Mandler, G. 169, 185
Manis, M. 211
Manstead, A. S. R. 217–219, 261
Marler, P. R. 50, 52–53, 69–71, 75, 146,
    149–152, 306–307
Marriott, B. M. 62
Martin, A. D. 97
Martin, G. B. 160
Martin, L. L. 180
Martin, R. D. 33
Mateer, C. 65
Matsumoto, D. 176, 192, 200, 203,
    205–206, 212, 214, 221–222, 224,
    228–229, 230–235, 256, 280
Matsushima, R. 44
Maurer, D. 66
Maynard Smith, J. 136, 139
Mayr, E. 40, 76
Mazziotta, J. 38
Mead, G. H. 160, 167
Mead, M. 188–189, 196, 283
Meehl, P. E. 178
Meltzoff, A. N. 51, 133
Mendel, G. 23, 24, 26, 27, 31
Mesquita, B. 193
Messina, J. J. 215
Meyer, M. F. 185
Michalson, L. 134
Miller, E. H. 62
Miller, G. A. 30
Miller, R. E. 175, 216
Miller, S. 103
Milner, 38
Mistlin, A. J. 65
Mitani, J. 146
Mitchell, R. W. 17
Mizuno, N. 44
Moldaver, J. 33
Monrad-Krohn, G. H. 97
Montgomery, W. 21, 195
Moody, D. 71
Moore, B. R. 147–148
Moore, J. 284

Moore, M. K. 51, 133
Mora, F. 68
Morgan, C. J. 40, 306
Morris, D.
Motley, M. T. 217–219, 238, 255
Mourant, A. E. 36
Movshon, J. A. 66
Mowrer, O. H. 127–128
Moynihan, M. 128
Mullen, B. 216
Muller, E. 134
Mullett, J. 138, 144, 157
Munn, N. L. 197, 200, 219, 238, 267
Murphy, S. T. 265
Murray, P. 33
Murry, T. 134
Muzekari, L. H. 238, 255
Müller, J. 10, 20

N

Nagel, L. 202, 252
Nakamura, M. 216, 238
Napier, J. 33
National Research Council, 316
Naylor, B. G. 48
Nelson, C. A. 202
Nelson, D. A. 61
Nelson, S. 211, 213
Niit, T. 204, 261
Nisbett, R. E. 281
Noback, C. R. 92, 96
Nolte, J. 119
Noonan, K. M. 133
Notarius, C. I. 175
Nottebohm, F. 4–16

O

O'Sullivan, M. 200, 203, 212, 233, 256,
    280, 282–283
Oatley, K. 192, 224
Obrist, P. A. 107
Ojemann, G. 65
Oken, L. 10–11, 19
Olds, J. 103
Oring, L. W. 141
Ortony, A. 128, 168, 192, 263, 265
Osgood, C. E. 196–197
Oster, G. F. 42
Oster, H. 29, 107, 190, 193, 201–202, 220,
    229, 252, 11–16
Owren, M. J. 307

P

Paley, W. 19
Parducci, A. 211, 257
Paredes, A. 203, 207, 212, 215, 219
Parker, G. A. 136
Pavlov, I. P. 120, 127
Peck, S. R. 210
Pernkopf, E. 81
Perrett, D. I. 65
Peters, S. 70
Petersen, M. R. 71
Petty, R. E. 265
Phelps, M. 38
Pickert, R. 149
Piderit, T. 3, 5, 9, 10–11, 22, 111, 167, 168,
    179, 194
Pinker, S. 161, 181
Pitcairn, T. 233, 282–283
Plato 3
Plutchik, R. 15, 29, 125
Polivy, J. 261
Pollio, H. R. 154
Popper, K. R. 178
Porta, G. della, 3–4
Posner, M. I. 315
Potegal, M. 103
Potter, D. D. 65
Prechtl, H. F. R. 106
Premack, D. 14, 50, 302
Prescott, J. 178
Presley, E. 311
Pribram, K. H. 30, 107, 170
Price, G. R. 139
Provine, R. R. 38, 105–106, 115, 154
Pythagoras, 2

Q

Quinn, W. G. 53

R

Raag, T. 166, 277
Raichle, M. E. 315
Raleigh, M. R. 149
Rand, A. S. 144
Redfield, J. W. 7
Redican, W. K. 41, 44, 62, 64, 305
Reuter-Lorenz, P. 216
Ribot, T. 167
Ricci-Bitti, P. E. 203, 233, 252, 282, 283

Rich, S. 32, 39
Richerson, P. J. 45, 139, 316
Ricklefs, R. E. 137
Ring, B. 68
Rinn, W. E. 44, 89, 216
Robarchek, C. 229
Robertson, J. G. 173
Rocha-Miranda, C. E. 65
Rodman, H. R. 66
Rolls, B. J. 36
Rolls, E. T. 36, 65, 68
Romanes, G. J. 14, 26
Romeo (W. Shakespeare), 111
Rosch, E. H. 281
Rosenfeld, A. H. 108
Rosenfeld, H. M. 298
Rosenfeld, S. A. 65
Rosensweig, M. R. 103
Rosenthal, R. 75, 137
Rousseau, J.-J. 97, 133–134, 293–294,
    11–28, 11–32
Rozin, P. 26, 45, 63, 120, 120, 293
Ruckmick, C. A. 197
Ruiz-Belda, M. A. 238
Russell, J. A. 29, 127, 190, 203, 208,
    211–214, 221, 224–225, 228–229, 231,
    232, 234, 236, 246, 258, 261, 264, 270,
    277, 280–282, 286
Ryle, G. 186

S

Saarni, C. 134, 292
Sabini, J. P. 64, 157, 158, 164, 165, 166,
    173, 180, 293
Sackeim, H. A. 83
Sackett, G. 50–51, 113
Salapatek, P. 66–67
Salzen, E. A. 62
Sanchez, F. 238
Sanderson, D. W. 297
Santibanez, G. 102
Saper, C. B. 44
Sapir, E. 188
Satinoff, E. 175
Satoda, T. 44
Savin, V. J. 175, 216
Saxton, P. M. 193
Schachter, J. 169
Schaut, J. A. 64, 164–165, 173
Scherer, K. 124, 233, 263, 265, 282–283

Schlosberg, H. S. 29, 196–200, 208, 215,
    232, 261
Schneider, E. 181
Schneirla, T. C. 124
Schull, J. 26, 63
Schulze, R. 197
Schure, ter E. 277, 279
Schwartz, G. E. 164, 169–170
Schwartz, S. P. 161, 181
Seaford, H. W. 283
Segal, A. L. 155, 159
Segal, M. L. 32, 39
Seiler, R. 44
Seligman, M. E. P. 53
Sermat, V. 261
Sexter, M. 181
Seyfarth, R. M. 71, 72, 74–75, 138, 141,
    146, 147–149
Shakespeare, W. 111
Sheldon, W. H. 9
Shenker, J. I. 64, 164–165, 173
Sherman, M. 195, 200, 219, 267
Sherman, P. W. 133, 147
Sherrington, C. S. 30
Shields, J. 39
Shimoda, K. 252
Shor, R. 238
Sierra, B. 238
Simons, R. C. 118
Simpson, G. G. 53
Sineshaw, T. 204–205, 207, 210–211, 251
Singer, J. A. 169–170
Skelly, J. P. 66
Skinhoj, E. 38
Skinner, M. 216
Slatkin, M. 139
Slavkin, H. C. 82–83, 90
Smith, C. A. 263
Smith, G. E. 161, 181
Smith, J. 164
Smith, J. L. 40, 306
Smith, M. E. 65
Smith, P. A. 65
Smith, S. 16, 20
Smith, W. J. 30, 45, 53, 56, 63–64, 74, 120,
    128–129, 138–139, 144, 166, 276, 289,
    308
Smuts, B. 141
Smythe, N. 77
Socrates 2, 9
Sorce, J. 145

Sorenson, E. R. 198, 202, 204, 207, 2–6, 239–244, 246, 248, 250, 258, 267, 282, 11–16
Spencer, H. 20–21, 41, 45–46, 59–61, 63, 75, 115, 125, 174–175, 194
Spiegel, N. H. 175
Spignesi, A. 238
Spiro, M. 188
Spurzheim, J. G. 11
Sroufe, L. A. 118, 166
Srull, T. K. 220
Stanislavski, K. S. 171, 178, 180–181
Stebbins, G. L. 35, 41
Stebbins, W. 71
Steiner, J. 155–156, 158
Stepper, S. 180
Stern, L. 181
Sternberg, R. 111
Stevens, S. S. 9
Sticht, T. G. 70
Stoddart, D. M. 62
Strack, F. 180
Stratton, G. M. 197
Strozzi, L. 102
Stuttard, S. 147–148
Sulloway, F. J. 14, 26, 284
Sutin, J. 89
Suzuki, N. 225, 229, 231, 258
Svejda, M. J. 145

T

Tagiuiri, R. 197–198, 200
Takahashi, O. 44
Tanaka, T. 101
Tanaka-Matsumi, J. 211, 213
Tashiro, T. 44
Tassinary, L. G. 156–158
Tate, B. C. 106
Taylor, L. 96
Teilhard de Chardin, P. 46
Tellegen, A. 29, 32, 39, 261
Templeton, J. L. 105
Teuber, H. L. 96
Thayer, S. 211
Thompson, J. 202
Thompson, N. S. 17
Thorndike, E. L. 148
Tinbergen, N. 27, 29, 57, 59, 61–63, 74, 76, 78, 125, 132, 136, 152
Ting-Toomey, S. 193

Tinker, M. A. 238
Tomita, M. 233, 282–283
Tomkins, S. S. 29, 118, 125, 126, 176, 181, 198, 229, 253, 260, 264, 271–272, 288
Tooby, J. 26, 315
Tourangeau, R. 175–176
Triandis, H. C. 196–197
Trivers, R. L. 141
Tryon, R. C. 53
Tschiassny, K. 97
Tuddenham, R. D. 119
Turner, T. J. 128, 168, 192, 263, 265
Tytler, G. 2, 4, 5
Tzavaras, A., 233, 282–283

U

Uemura-Sumi, M. 44

V

Valenstein, E. S. 97, 103
Valentine, J. W. 35, 41, 284
Valsiner, J. 204, 207
Van Boxtel, A. 44
Van Hoesen, G. W. 65, 67
Van Hooff, J. A. R. A. M. 62, 107, 305–306, 310
Van Lawick-Goodall, J. 62
Van Lighten, O. 181
Van Schaik, C. P. 77
Van Sluyters, R. C. 66
Vander Eecken, H. 102
Vaughan, B. E. 118
Vaughan, K. B. 128, 175
Vaughan, R. C. 175
Vinacke, W. E. 238, 267
Visser, G. H. A. 106
Voeller, K. K. S. 73–74, 117
von Baer, K. E. 108, 135
Vraa-Jensen, G. 44
Vygotsky, L. S. 160

W

Waal, F. de 76, 138, 143
Waddington, C. H. 32
Wagner, H. L. 164, 217–219, 259, 261
Wake, D. B. 42
Wall, P. D. 107, 170
Wallace, A. R. 14, 17

Wallbott, H. 238
Waters, E. 166
Watson, S. G. 238
Watson, D. 29, 261
Weigel, R. M. 62
Weinberger, D. A. 169–170
Weinstein, E. A. 102
Wells, S. R. 7
Werther, P. 155, 158
Wertsch, J. V. 160
W/Georgis, T. 204–205, 207, 210–211, 251
Whishaw, I. Q. 67, 94
White, B. 83
Whorf, B. 188
Wiepkema, P. R. 30
Wierzbicka, A. 261
Wiesel, T. N. 68
Wikan, U. 261
Wilcox, K. J. 32, 39
Wilkinson, L. 66
Wilson, J. Q. 2, 9
Wilson, S. A. K. 96
Wind, J. 303–304
Winkelmayer, R. 203, 207, 211–212, 215, 219
Winton, W. M. 176
Wise, R. A. 103

Wohns, R. 65
Wolff, P. H. 118, 134
Wolfgang, 205, 210
Wolpoff, M. H. 33
Woodworth, R. S. 29, 196–200, 208, 227, 232, 261
Wright, S. 31, 284
Wundt, W. 29, 111, 167, 173
Wyer, R. S. Jr. 220

Y

Yakovlev, P. E. 94
Yarczower, M. 205
Ybarra, M. S. 306
Yong, Y. L. 115
Yoon, M. 66

Z

Zahavi, A. 58
Zajonc, R. B. 145, 265
Zillman, D. 174
Zoloth, S. R. 71
Zuckerman, S. 33
Zuckerman, M. 75, 137, 175

Subject Index

Note: Page references followed by an *n* indicate location of entry in a footnote.

A

Adaptationism, 15, 41*n*, 44
Adaptors, 298, 301
Adoption studies, in ascertaining genetic
    control of facial displays, 39, 73
Adult faces
  as analogies, 111–112
  as dissimulated variations of infant
    faces, 133–135
  as products of pedagogy, 109–110
  as products of reflex cooption,
    108–109
Affective space, representing
    dimensionality of emotion, 29
Affirmation
  head shakes associated with, 310
  smiles of, 155
Allometries, in morphological change, 42
Altruism, reciprocal, 147*n*
Amimia (mimetic palsy), 38, 96
Amyotrophic lateral sclerosis, 97*n*
Analogy
  distinguished from homology, 40–41,
    49–50
  ontogenetic, and mimetic theory,
    111–112
  phylogenetic, distinguishing from
    homology, 40–41
*Anatomy and physiology of expression as
    connected with the fine arts* (Bell), 16,
    105

Anger and "anger" faces, 22, 62, 113, 125,
    127–129, 132, 136, 157, 168–170, 175,
    179
  depicted, 126
  reinterpreted, 129
  threat and, 136–137
  "universality" of, *see* Classical emotions
    view of facial expressions
Anhedonia, 38
Animal signaling, *see also specific displays*
  affect versus referential views, 150–152
  conflict views of, 77–78
  as coevolved with and complementary
    to vigilance, 65, 75–78
  as formalized intention movements, 64
  as hypertrophied behavior, 56–64
  associationist accounts of, 59–60
  audience effects in, 146–152
  Darwinian reflexology and, 20–27
  early ethology and, 29–30
  emancipation of, 61
  facial reflexes and, 107, 302–307
  intentionality of, 146
  "mind reading" and "manipulation" in,
    138–139
  modalities of, 61–62
  negotiation in, 76–78
  numbers of displays, in diverse species,
    128
  perception by conspecifics
    selectivity, cognitive templates and,
      68–73

Animal signaling (*cont.*)
  sensitivity, 65–68
    skepticism and "calibration" in, 73–75
  phylogeny of, and species comparisons,
    45–54
  ritualization of, 23, 61, 100
  selectionist accounts of, 60–64
  selective breeding of, 39
  sexual selection and, 56–58
  vocal, *see* Vocalization
Animism, faces and, 166
Antithesis, Principle of (Darwin), 22
Appeasement, smiles, 64, 78, 305–306
  "false" smiles reinterpreted, 129
Apraxia
  defined, 38
  ideomotor, 97–98
  speech, 97
Argument from design (Paley)
  Darwin's *Expression* as attack on, 18–20
  forms of, 19
Articulatory movements, in auditory calls,
    306–307
"Artificial selection", 39
Associationist accounts, of facial displays,
    59–60
Association of analogous feelings,
  principle of (Wundt), 111
Atavisms, manifest in criminality, and
  mental illness and retardation, 5–6
Audience effects
  definition of, 145–46
  human
    faces to odors and taste, 155–157
    motor mimicry, 157
    smiling, 152–155
  solitary faces, 157–168
  intentionality, 146
  Japanese–American study, 29
  nonhuman,
    referential versus emotional views of,
      150–152
    research, 146–150
  yawning and, 106
Auditory calls
  articulatory movements, 306–307
  birdsong, 50, 70–71, 304*n*
  monkey, 71–74
Auditory displays, *see* Vocalization
Autocatalysis, *see* Facial feedback
  hypothesis

Automatic expression, neglect of cost in
  classical emotions view, 131–132
Automatic speech, 97, 98
Autonomic nervous system, and relations
  with facial displays
  emotional inductions, 169–171
  facial feedback hypothesis and, 175,
    178, 184
  facial nerve and, 101–102
  general relations, 107
  in Darwinian reflexology, 21
  respiration
    laughing and, 115
    yawning and, 106

B

Babbling
  congenitally deaf infants, 161
  lip smacks, baboon, as homologues, 306
Backchannel displays, 301
Baldwin effect, 53*n*
Basic emotions, *see* Classical emotions
  view
Behavioral ecology view, of facial display
  anti-romanticism, 293–294
  communalities in ("universals"),
    explanation, 276–283
  complementarity of display and
    vigilance in, 75–78
  context-dependency of display in,
    128–129
  cultural differences in, explanation,
    283–293
  deception, 143
  emotions versus, state of the evidence,
    141–186
  "Facial Elicitor Coding System", 316
  "felt" vs. "false" displays in, 130
  interpretation of "cultural display
    rules", 286
  neglect of cost of automatic expression,
    131–132
  recipient's coevolutionary role, 132
  reinterpretations of "facial expressions
    of emotion", 129
  relationship between emotions and
    facial displays, 135–137
  social motives, 280, 281
  social tools, displays as, 129–130
  threat displays, 306

transition from Darwinian reflexology, 26–27
view of deception, 137–139
Bell-Magendie Law, 16n
Bell's palsy, 93, 176–177
Biogenetic law, *see* Recapitulation
Bipedalism, 41
Birdsong, 304n
  acquisition, 50
  cognitive templates for, 70–71
Blended emotions, *see* Classical emotions view
Blindness, congenital, displays in, 112–113, 121
Blink reflex of Descartes, 101–102, 115
Blushing, 104–105
Branchial arches, 81
Breeding, selective, 39
Broca's area, 39
Brow
  flash, 309
  homology with pinna (earflap) actions, 42–45, 102
  knitting, 41, 44–45, 49–50, 107
  raising, 42, 44, 107
  ridges, 42
Buccal branch, of facial nerve, 87–88
Buccinator, 85

C

Calibration, of display perception, 74–75
Canalization, 32
Cartesian system of emotion, 9
Central facial paralysis, 95
Central nervous system control, of face
  facial nerve nuclei, 89–91
  facial reflexes, 101–103
  laterality of control of upper versus lower face, 91–94
  subcortical versus cortical influences, 94–98
Central pattern generators (CPG's), 38
Cerebral hemispheric specialization, 93n
Cervical branch, of facial nerve, 88
Character, portrayed in faces, *see* Physiognomy
Cheating, 282
Chernoff faces, 66
Cladistics, 35n

Classical emotions view, of facial expression
  as two-factor theory, 175, 275, 293
  basic emotions
    Cartesian, 9
    LeBrun and, 9
  crypto-moralistic view of deception in, 137–139
  neurocultural model (Ekman), 29, 285, *see also* Cultural display rules
    ambiguity and circularity in face-emotion relations, 274–275
    as two-factor theory, 127
    contributions, 275–276
    overinclusiveness of, 274
    summarized, 271–274
  reasons for persistence, 293–294
  romanticism of, 293–294
  universality and, 192–268
  universality thesis, 194–199
    alternative interpretations
    history, 194–198
      common learning, 282–283
      cultural display rules, 285–293
      cultural transmission, 282
      ecological validity, 281–282
      emotion or social motives, 276–281
      founder effects, 283–285
      genetic drift, 283–285
  judgment studies
    cological relevance, 200
    facial stimuli, 215–220
    isolated cultures, 238–251
    lack of contextual information, 237–238
    literate cultures, 203–208
    presentation of stimuli, 211–215
    response format, 220–237
    results, 208–209
    specificity, 199–200
    subjects, 210–211
    substance, 200–202
    validity, 251
      convergent, 254–256
      ecological, 251–254
      internal, 256–259
Cleft lip, 83
Cleft palate, 83
Cognitive templates, for display detection, 68–73

Comparative approach
  general strategy, 40–47
  usefulness, 48–54
Competition, sibling, facial display
  variation with, 144
Contempt and "contempt" faces, 22,
  120–121, 126, 129
  analogies, 120–121
  reinterpreted, 129
  "universality" of, see Classical emotions
    view
Conventionalized signals, 63–64
Conversational signs, in facial displays,
  296
Coronoid process, of mandible, 87
Corrugator supercilii, 85, 93, 100
Corticalization, 126
Corticobulbar fibers, 92
Corticobulbar palsy, 95–96
Cranial nerves, see also Facial nerve,
    Glossopharyngeal nerve, Trigeminal
    nerve
  depicted, 90
Craniofacial embryology and maturation,
  80–83
Criminal anthropology, faces in, 7
Criminals, facial study, 5–9
Cross-cultural studies, facial expressions,
  see Classical emotions view
Cross-lineage borrowing, 40, 282
Crying, see Sadness and "sad" faces
Cultural display rules
  infancy, authenticity of, 134
  Japanese–American study,
    reinterpreted, 286–293
  neurocultural model, 271–276
  problems with concept, 283–286
  solitary faces and, 158
  two-factor emotion theory and, 127–128
Cultural relativism, and "universal faces,"
  188

D

Darwinian reflexology, transition to
    behavioral ecology, 26–27
Dashiell method, 243–246
Deception
  crypto-moralism in classical emotions
    view, 137–139
  phylogeny of, 143–144
  skepticism and, 73, 75

Decoupled reflexes, emotions as, 124–125
De humana physiognomica (Della Porta), 3
Depressor anguli oris, 85
Depressor labii inferioris, 85
Descent of Man (Darwin), 17, 20, 22, 24–26,
  40, 56–57
Differential emotions theory, see Classical
  emotions view
Differentiation, von Baer's Law, 135
Direct Action of the Nervous System,
    Principle of (Darwin), 21
Directed evolution, as form of argument
    from design, 19
Disgust and "disgust" faces, 119–121, 125,
  169, 177
  analogy and, 120–121
  reinterpreted, 120
  tongue protrusion, 45
  "universality" of, see Classical emotions
    view
Displacement behavior
  blocked drives and, 27
  deception, 137
  conflict and redirection, 308–309
Display rule, see Cultural display rules
Displays, see specific types
Dive reflex (Hering-Breuer reflex), 100
Divergent evolution, 41–42, 50
DNA-hybridization taxonomies, 33–34
Dogs, in Darwin's Expression and Descent,
  17
Dominance displays
  lip thrusts in, 306
  negotiation and, 75, 77, 142
Dorsomedial group, see Facial nerve
Down's syndrome, 6–7
Dramaturgical analysis, of facial feedback
    studies, 177n, 179
"Duchenne" smiles, 115–118
Dyads, displays observed in, 145

E

Earflap (pinna) actions, 42–45, see also
  Brow
Ecological relevance of universality thesis,
  200
Ecological validity, judgment studies,
  251–254
Electroencephalography, 38
Electromyography, facial, 171–173
Emancipation, 61

Embarrassment, blushing in, 105
Emblems, 296–297
Embryology, facial, and maturation, 80–83
Emoticons, 297
Emotions, *see also* Classical emotions view
  blended, 272–273
  cerebral hemispheric specialization for, 93
  decoupled reflexes and, 124–125
  hermeneutical dissection and social motives, 279
  inadequacy of action as criterion, 182–183
  inadequacy of physiology as criterion, 184
  inadequacy of self-report as criterion, 183
  nonexistent consensus on what constitutes, 184–186
  putative relations of physiological patterns to, 169–182
    facial electromyography, 171–173
    facial feedback and emotional experience, 173–182
  relationship between facial displays and, 135–137
  social construction, 280
Empathy, 65
Emphasizers, 299
Endothermy, link to vocalization, 304
Essays on the anatomy of expression in painting (Bell), 10, 16
Ethogrammatic methods, 29–30
Ethology
  contemporary, 30, 63–64, 75, 136–137
  early, 27, 30, 53*n*, 60–63, 125, 271, 294
Evolution
  convergent, and analogy, 40–41
  directed, 19
  divergent, 41–42, 50
  orthogenesis, 46*n*
  progressivism, 46*n*
  via natural selection
    Darwin and, 17, 19–20
    defined, 31–33
    displays and, 75–78
  synthetic theory, 31
Expression and physiognomy (Piderit), 11
Expression of the emotions in man and animals (Darwin), 10–12, 14–27, 29, 40, 104, 105, 115, 303
Evolutionary stable strategy (ESS), 139

"Expression" as problematic term, 15
Extrapyramidal motor system, 38, 95–96

F

Face cells, and perception of faces, 65–68
"Face-reading," 2
Facial Action Coding System (*FACS*), 156, 288, 315
Facial affect program, 29, 272, 273, 275
Facial Affect Scoring Technique (*FAST*), 288
Facial analogies, mimetic theory and production, 111–112
Facial canal, of cranium, 87
Facial displays, *see also* Behavioral-ecology view, Classical emotions view
  associationist accounts, 59–60
  cognitive templates for detection, 69
  genetic control, 36–37
  heritability, 39
  homology, 40–41
  hypertrophy of behavior, 65
  hypertrophy of vigilance, 65
  niche factors in differentiation, in evolutionary line, 142
  nonprimate, 61–62
  protective reflexes as phyletic preadaptations, 107
  ramification in phylogeny, 141–142
  reflexes as constituent actions in ontogenesis, 108–112
  relationship between emotions and, 135–137
  selectionist accounts, 60–64
  social versus solitary species, 144
  variation with sibling competition, 144
  viability of emotions account, 182
Facial electromyography, 161, 162, 165, 169, 170, 171–173
"Facial Elicitor Coding System" (FECS), hypothetical, 316
Facial expressions, *see* Facial displays
Facial expressivity, as specific trait, 31
Facial feedback hypothesis, 173–182
Facial musculature
  as metamorphosed limb musculature, 10
  as social mask, 81
  depicted, 34, 37, 44, 81, 86, 88
  deep (masticatory), 33–34, 85, 87
  superficial, 83–85
    listed, 84

Facial nerve
  afferent pathways, 89
  branches, 87–88
  insertions in upper- versus lower-face
    muscles, 92–94
  laterality of facial muscle control, 91–94
  nuclei, 89–91
  relations with audition, and pinna
    (earflap) movements, 44
Facial paralanguage
  emblems, 296–297
  formalization of, 307–309
  illustrators, 298
  interpretation of cross-"cultural"
    evidence, 310–311
  language acquisition and, 66
  population similarities and differences
    in human, 309–310
  regulators, 298–302
  respiration and vocalization, origins in,
    50, 107, 303–307
  self-manipulators, 298
  typologies, 296–302
Facial reflexes, see also Reflexes
  blushing, 104–105
  cranial nerve nuclei and, 91
  constituent actions in the ontogenesis of
    displays, 108
  coordination of, in complex actions, 102
  conventionalization of reflex actions,
    109–110
  gagging, 119
  general relations with autonomic
    nervous system, 107
  imitation and social shaping, 110
  listed, 101
  mimetic theory and production of facial
    analogies, 111–112
  pathological, 100–101
  protective, as phyletic preadaptations
    for displays, 107
  reflex cooption during maturation,
    108–109
  yawning, 105–106
Facial shrugs, 301
Facial structure, see also Craniofacial
    embryology and maturation, Facial
    musculature, Facial nerve,
    Glossopharyngeal nerve, Trigeminal
    nerve
Faciogustatory reflexes, 38
Faciorespiratory reflexes, 38

Fear and "fear" faces, 51, 60, 62, 125, 135,
    151, 157, 169–170, 177, 178
  depicted, 126
  reinterpreted, 129
  threat and, 136–137
  "universality" of, see Classical emotions
    view
Fixed action patterns, 29, 30, 61, 62–63
Flank-rubbing, feline, 147
Foramen, cranial
  stylomastoid foramen, 87
  foramen ovale, 88
Fossil evidence, in constructing species
    taxonomies, 33–34
Founder effects, 283–285, 311
*Fragments of physiognomy for the increase of
    knowledge and love of mankind*
    (Lavater), 4
Frontalis, 85, 93
Frontonasal prominence, 80–81

G

Gagging
  as reflex, 119
  disgust displays and, 120–121
Galea aponeurotica, 85
Galvanism, of facial muscles, 9, 10, 115,
    117
Genetic control
  of displays, defined, 31–33
  determination
    morphological comparison, 33–36
    neural localization, 36–39
    selective breeding, 40
  homology and, 40
  learning and, 52–54
  not implied by display communalities,
    45
  of smile, 36–38
Genetic drift, alternative explanation for
    regional display differences, 283–285,
    311
Genetics and the origins of species
    (Dobzhansky), 31
Genome mapping, 39
Glabella reflex, 100
Glossopharyngeal nerve, 102
Goosebumps, see Piloerection
Grimacing, 48–50, 62, 102
Grins, see also Smiles
  appeasement and play, 305–306

monkey, submissive, 40
  skepticism and, 73
Guilt, 125
  blushing in, 104–105

H

Habits, see Specific habits
Hair-pulling, see Trichotillomania
"Happiness" and "happy" faces, see also
    Smiles
  as differentiated approach, 125
  depicted, 126
  inferred from smiles, 73, 117
  physiology and, 169–171
  reinterpreted, 129
  "universality" of, see Classical emotions
    view
Harvard step test, 170
Head, as metamorphosed torso, 10
Head retraction reflex, 100
Hedonic/reflexive view, in displays to
    tastes and odors, 155
Helmholtzian physicalism, in early
    ethology, 29
Hering-Breuer (dive) reflex, 100
Hermeneutics, dissection of emotions to
    social motives, 279
Hippocratic typology of temperament, 3–4
Hissing
  from intracranial stimulation, 102
  respiration and, 303
Historia animalium (Aristotle), 2
Homology
  distinguishing from analogy, 40–41, 47,
    49–50
  inferring, 40–45
Horizontal (cultural) transmission, 40, 47,
    282
Human pedigree studies, 39
Humor, 115–118
Hyoid arches, 81, 83
Hypertrophied behavior, displays as,
    56–64
Hypothalamus, 36, 103

I

Ideomotor apraxia, 97–98
Imagery, faces in
  Darwin and, 168

restitutional interaction, 166–168
  social versus solitary, 161, 163–164, 277
Imitation and social shaping, of facial
    displays, 110
Implicit sociality, see Sociality
Infant faces, adult faces as dissimulated
    variation, 133–135
Inheritance
  Lamarckian, 23–24, 26, 30–31, 59–60
    depicted, 24
  Mendelian, 27, 31–33, 39
Innate releasing mechanisms (Lorenz), 69,
    271
Input specificity, cognitive templates, 151
"Instincts to learn," 53n
Intentionality, displays and, 146n
Intention movements
  conflict, 78
  definition, 61n
  displays as, 75–76
  formalization, 64–75
  smiles as, 279
Interactive displays, 301
Intermediate group, see Facial nerve
Internal capsule, 102
Internalizer-externalizer trait, 175n
Internal validity, judgment studies,
    256–259
Interpersonal sensitivity, 65
Intraorganismic signals, 124
Isolated cultures, judgment studies,
    238–251

J

Japanese-American "display rules" study,
    286–293
Judgment studies, see Classical emotions
    view
Juvenescence, human response to, 69–70

L

Lamarckian inheritance, see Inheritance
Larynx, links to respiration and
    vocalization, 303–304
Lateral frontalis, 85, 177
Lateral group, see Facial nerve
Lateral pterygoid, 87
Laterality, of neural control of face, 91–93
Laughter, 22, 102
  pathological, 97

Laughter (*cont.*)
  tickling, humor and, 115–118
  vocalization, appeasement and play,
    305–306
Law of differentiation (von Baer), 135
Learnability, genetic control, 52–54
Levator labii superioris, 85
Levator palpebrae superioris, 85
Levator palpebrae superioris, 88*n*
Lip-biting, 137
Lip retraction, 64, 305–306
Lip smacks, in babbling, 306
Lip thrusts, in dominance displays, 306
Listener comments displays, 301
Lou Gehrig's disease, *see* Amyotropic
    lateral sclerosis
Lower motor neurons, 92

M

M notebook (Darwin), 17, 20–21
Magnetic resonance imaging (MRI)
    scanning, 38
Magnetoencephalographic (MEG)
    recording, 38
Mandibular arch, 81, 83
Mandibular branch, of facial nerve, 87, 88
Mandibular process, of mandibular arch,
    83
"Manipulation," by displayers, *see* Animal
    signaling
Manipulators, *see* Adaptors
Masseter, 87
Masticatory compartment, 87
Maxillary division
  of facial nerve, 88
  of trigeminal nerve, 89
Maxillary portion, of mandibular arch, 83
Maximally Discriminative Facial
    Movement Coding System (MAX), 315
Medial frontalis, 85
Medial pterygoid, 87
Mentalis, 85
Migratory influences, in explaining
    regional differences in faces, 34–35,
    282
Mimetic palsy, *see* Amimia
Mimetic theory (Piderit-Wundt), and
    production of facial analogies,
    111–112
Mimicry, motor, *see* Motor mimicry

"Mind-reading," of displays, *see* Animal
    signaling
Modal action patterns, 30, *see also* Fixed
    action patterns
Modiolus, 85
Molecular evolutionary techniques, 33–36
Mongolism, *see* Down's syndrome
Morality, blushing and, 104–105
Morphology, comparison, 33–36
Motor mimicry displays, 157, 301
Motor neurons, *see* Lower-motor neurons;
    Upper-motor neurons
Muscles, *see* Facial musculature
Myotatic reflexes, 100

N

Nasal placodes, 80–81
Natural selection, 17, 19–20, 31–32, 77,
    315
  evolution via, defined, 31–33
  relation to sexual selection, 17
Neoteny, 42–45
Nerves, *see* Specific nerves
Neural insult, pathological reflexes in,
    100–101, 108
Neural localization, establishing genetic
    control via, 36–39
Neurocranium, neotenous enlargement
    and brow actions, 42
Neurocultural model, *see* Classical
    emotions view
Neurological influences, on facial
    displays, 94–98
Neurons, *see* Lower-motor neurons;
    Reflex-mediated neurons; Upper-
    motor neurons
Neutralism, evolutionary, 32
New Guinea preliterate culture matching
    study, 277
Niche factors, in differentiation of display,
    142
"Non-Duchenne" smiles, 117
Nonprimate displays, *see* Animal signals

O

Oculomotor nerve, 88*n*
Odors, faces to, 155–157
Olfacto-facial reflexes, 155–157
Onomatopoeia, 308

Ontogenetic hypotheses, 114
  disgust display, 120–121
  gagging, 119–121
  research strategy for evaluating,
    112–114
  startle displays, 118–119
  surprise displays, 118–119
  tickling, humor, and Duchenne smiles,
    114–118
Ophthalmic division, of trigeminal nerve,
  89
Orbicularis oculi, 85, 93, 115, 119
Orbicularis oris, 10, 85, 119
Origin of species (Darwin), 15, 17, 20, 23,
  40
Orthogenesis, 46*n*
Orthognathia, and human neoteny, 42, 94

P

Paedomorphosis, 42–43
Palpebral portion, *orbicularis oculi*, 85
Palsy
  Bell's, 93, 176–177
  corticobulbar, 95–96
  pseudobulbar, 97*n*
Parkinson's disease, 96
Passions, reading into facial actions, 9–12
Patella tendon reflex, 30
Pathological reflexes, 100
Persona, and facial "mask," 80
Personal reactions displays, 300, 301
Phenomenoscope, 176
Phenotypic trait, 31–32
Photic sneeze reflex, 100
Photo-matching studies, *see also* Classical
  emotions view; Judgment studies,
  276–277*n*
Phrenology, 5–6, 11
Phylogenesis, 40, 45–47, 48, 100
  early scale conception, 45
  modern tree conception, 46–47
Phylogeny, 32
  deception, 143–144
  ramifying of displays in, 14, 142
Physiognomonica (Aristotle), 2
Physiognomy
  history, 2–9
  mimetic theory (Piderit), 11
Physiological patterns, putative relations
  to emotions, 169–182

Physiology, inadequacy as criterion in
  viability of classical emotions view,
  184
Piloerection, 25, 56, 61, 115
Pinna (earflap) retraction, 42–45, 102
Play, grins, 62, 305–306
Pleitropy, and genetic origins of signaling,
  76
Pons, 89, 91
Portrayals displays, 300
Positron emission tomography, 38
Posterior auricular branches, of facial
  nerve, 88
Preadaptation, 91, 107?
Primary emotions, *see* Classical emotions
  view
Primates, contemporary, depicted, 49
Procerus, 85
Propositional speech, 50
Prosopagnosia, 67
Protective reflexes, 4, *see* Facial reflexes
Pseudobulbar palsy, 97*n*
Psychiatric photography, 8
Pterygoid muscles, 87

Q

Question marker displays, 299

R

Recapitulation
  ontogenetic, in infant reflexes, 108
  phylogenetic, biogenetic law, 108
  triune brain, implicit, 108–110
Receiver psychology, 65
Receptive/perceptual attunement, displays
  and, 65–68
Reciprocal altruism, 147*n*
Redirected behavior, paralanguage,
  308–309
Reflexes, *see also* Facial reflexes
  Darwinian grasp, 118*n*
  decoupled, 124–125
  deep, 100
  faciogustatory, 38
  faciorespiratory, 38
  gag, 119–121
  glabella, 100
  head retraction, 100
  Hering-Breuer (dive), 100

Reflexes (*cont.*)
  Moro, 118*n*
  myotatic, 100
  "olfacto-facial", 156–157
  pathological, 100
  photic-sneeze, 100
  rooting, 100, 109
  snout, 101
  startle, 109, 118–119
  superficial, 100
  tongue thrust, 101
  visceral, 100
Regional variations, accounting for, in
    facial expressions, 270–294
Releaser theory, 29
Resource Holding Potential (RHP), 136
Respiration, link between vocalization
    and, 303–307
Restitutional interaction, 167
Reverse facial paralysis, 96
Reversions, *see* Atavisms
Risorius, 85
Ritualization, 27, 63*n*, 100
Romeo and Juliet (Shakespeare), 111
Rooting reflex, 100
Rousseauean romanticism, in two-factor
    theories of facial expression, 293

S

Sadness and "sad" faces, 115, 181–183
  as solicitation of attention or succor,
      135–136
  crying
    infant, 112, 121, 133–134, 160–161
    ocular irritation, 22
    pain, 104
    pathological, 97
    tickling, 115, 117
  redefined, 129
  "universality" of, *see* Classical emotions
      view
  when emitted, 137
Scan patterns, visual, in perceiving faces,
    65–67
Selective breeding, 39
Selectivity, cognitive templates for display
    detection, 68–73
Self-manipulators, 298
Self-report, in adequacy as criterion in
    viability of classical emotions view,
    183

Sensitivity, in display detection, 65–68
Serviceable associated habits, principle of
    (Darwin), 21, 22, 26
Servomechanisms, as models of biological
    organization, 30
Sexual selection
  displays resulting from, 56–58
  relation to natural selection, 17
  sexual behavior, evolution of, 31
Shaking-off movement, negation and, 310
Sherringtonian concept, of nervous
    system, 30
Sibling competition, facial display
    variation with, 144
Signaling, *see* Animal signaling; Facial
    displays; Vocalization
"Silent bared-teeth face," 62
Skepticism, in display perception, 73–75
Sleep paralysis, as counter to facial
    feedback hypothesis, 178
Smiles, *see also* Grins; Happiness and
    "happy" faces
  audience effects on, 152–155
  cognitive templates for, 73–74
  "Duchenne," 115–118
  genetic control, determining, 36–37
  happiness, independence from, 135–137
  intention movement view, 279
"Smileys", 297
Snout reflex, 101
Social construction, of emotions, 280–281
Social facilitation, 145
Social instrumental habits, as origins of
    displays, 64
Sociality, *see also* Audience effects
  "emotion" manipulations as changes in,
      158–160
  fallacy of solitude as excluding, 160–166
  of solitary faces, 157–166
Social referencing, 145
Social shaping, and facial displays, 110
Social species, facial displays in, 144
Solitary faces, sociality of, 157–166
"Somatic feedback hypothesis," as
    revision to facial feedback hypothesis,
    181
Somatotype theory, as neo-physiognomy,
    9
Speaker comments, 300
Speaker illustrators, 300
Special creation, as form of argument
    from design, 19

Specific Nerve Energies, Law of (Müller),
    10
Speech, propositional, 50
Spread of effect, in electrical brain
    stimulation, as problem in neural
    localization, 103
Stapedius branch, of facial nerve, 88
Startle reflex, 22, 109, 118–119
Stereotypy, 63
Stomadeum, 80
Story continuations displays, 299
Striate muscle, contractility, as trait, effect
    on facial displays, 31
Stylomastoid foramen, of cranium, 87
"Surprise" display face, 62, 118–119
Syntactic displays, 299
Synthetic theory, of evolution, 31

T

Tactile modeling, in shaping displays, 113
Taste, faces in, 155–157
Taxonomy
    cladistics and, 35
    DNA-hybridization, 34
    molecular techniques, 33–36
Teeth baring, 60, 64
Temporal branch, of facial nerve, 87
Temporalis, 87
Temporomandibular joint syndrome, 87
"Tense-mouth display," 62
Theatrische bibliothek (Lessing), 173
The hand, its mechanism and vital
    endowments as evincing design (Bell), 18
Thermopods, 304n
Thermoregulation, 175n
"Thinking/remembering" displays, 300,
    301
Threat displays, 51, 136–137
Tickling, 22, 114–115
Tongue protrusion, 45, 308
Tongue thrust reflex, 101
Traits, genetic control, 31–32
Trichotillomania, 308
Trigeminal nerve, 88, 89, 102
Trisomy-21 syndrome, see Down's
    syndrome
Triune brain (MacLean), 108–109
Two-factor conception of facial expression,
    127–128, see also Classical emotions
    view
Two-factor learning theory, 127, 275

U

Underliners, 299
"Understanding" displays, 301
Universality thesis, 198–199
    ecological relevance, 200
    specificity, 199–200
    substance, 200–202
    studies pertaining to, 203–268
"Universality" of facial expressions, see
    Classical emotions view
Upper motor neurons, 92, 94
Use-inheritance, see Inheritance

V

Variation of plants and animals under
    domestication (Darwin), 17
Ventromedial group, see Facial nerve
Vervet monkeys, see also Animal signaling
    calls, 71, 307
    intent and context, 147–149
Vestiges, 23, 32, 48
Vigilance, coevolution with display
    behavior, 65
Visceroautonomic changes, see Autonomic
    nervous system
Vocalization, link between respiration
    and, 303–307

W

Wincing, 22, 115, 117–118

Y

Yawning
    contagion, 106
    described, 105–106
    neurology, 90–91
    selectionist theory, 105–107

Z

Zoonomia (E. Darwin), 21
Zygomatic arch, 87
Zygomatic branch, of facial nerve, 87–88
Zygomatic major, 37, 73, 85, 161, 164, 180,
    278
Zygomatic minor, 85